POLITICS AMONG NATIONS

The Struggle for Power and Peace

POLITICS AMONG NATIONS

The Struggle for Power and Peace

Brief Edition

Hans J. Morgenthau

*Late Albert A. Michelson
Distinguished Service Professor
of Political Science and Modern History
at the University of Chicago and
Late Director of the Center for the
Study of American Foreign Policy
at the University of Chicago*

Revised by

Kenneth W. Thompson

*Director, Miller Center of Public Affairs
J. Wilson Newman Professor of Governance
University of Virginia*

Boston, Massachusetts   Burr Ridge, Illinois   Dubuque, Iowa
Madison, Wisconsin   New York, New York   San Francisco, California   St. Louis, Missouri

McGraw-Hill

A Division of The McGraw·Hill Companies

POLITICS AMONG NATIONS
The Struggle for Power and Peace

18 19 20 QSR/QSR 0 9 8 7 6

ISBN-13: 978-0-07-043306-9
ISBN-10: 0-07-043306-2

This book was set in Caledonia by ComCom, Inc.
The editors were Peter Labella and John M. Morriss;
the production supervisor was Richard A. Ausburn.
R. R. Donnelley & Sons Company was printer and binder.

Library of Congress Cataloging-in-Publication Data

Morgenthau, Hans Joachim, (date).
    Politics among nations: the struggle for power and peace / Hans
J. Morgenthau: revised by Kenneth W. Thompson.—Brief ed.
        p.   cm.
    Includes bibliographical references and index.
    ISBN 0-07-043306-2
    1. International relations.   I. Thompson, Kenneth W., (date).
II. Title.
JX1391.M6   1993
327—dc20   92-3398

This book is printed on acid-free paper.

http://www.mhhe.com

About the Authors

Hans J. Morgenthau was born in Germany in 1904. Educated at the Universities of Berlin, Frankfort, and Munich, he taught and practiced law in Frankfort, where he was acting President of the Labor Law Court. A year before Hitler came to power, Professor Morgenthau went to teach at the University of Geneva; he taught in Madrid before going to the United States in 1937. He taught at Brooklyn College and the University of Kansas City before his appointment in 1943 to the University of Chicago. He was also University Professor of Political Science at The New School for Social Research, Albert A. Michelson Distinguished Service Professor of Political Science and Modern History at the University of Chicago, and Leonard Davis Distinguished Professor of Political Science at City College of the City University of New York. He was also Visiting Professor at Columbia, Harvard, Northwestern, Yale, and the University of California. Professor Morgenthau served as a consultant to the Departments of State and Defense and was Director of the Center for the Study of American Foreign Policy at the University of Chicago, a member of the Institute for Advanced Study at Princeton, Associate of the Washington Center for Foreign Policy Research, and a Senior Research Fellow of the Council on Foreign Relations. Among his many publications are *In Defense of the National Interest* (1951), *The Purpose of American Politics* (1960), *Politics in the Twentieth Century* (1962), *A New Foreign Policy for the United States* (1969), and *Science: Servant or Master?* (1972). Professor Morgenthau died in New York City on July 19, 1980.

Kenneth W. Thompson was born in Des Moines, Iowa, in 1921. He was educated at the University of Chicago, Augustana College, and St. Olaf College and taught at Northwestern University and the University of Chicago. He served as an infantry officer and military intelligence/counter intelligence officer in World War II. From 1955 to 1973, he held positions in the Rockefeller Foundation beginning as assistant director of the social sciences and concluding as vice president from 1961–1973. He directed a twelve donor agencies review of higher education and development in Africa, Asia, and Latin America from 1973–1976. In 1975, he was appointed Commonwealth Professor of Government and Foreign Affairs at the University of Virginia. In 1979, he became Director of the White Burkett Miller Center of Public Affairs at the University of Virginia and White Burkett Miller Professor of Government and Foreign Affairs. He has held major lectureships such as the Riverside Memorial, Lilly, Stokes, Rockwell, Cecil, and Stuber Lectures. He was named Virginia Laureate in 1981 and received the Virginia Phi Beta Kappa Prize and the College Stores Prize for his Churchill book in 1984. Among his many publications are *Political Realism and the Crisis of World Politics* (1960), *American Diplomacy and Emergent Patterns* (1962), *The Moral Issue in Statecraft* (1966), *Foreign Assistance* (1972), *Understanding World Politics* (1975), *Ethics, Functionalism and Power* (1979), *Morality and Foreign Policy* (1980), *Masters of International Thought* (1980), *The President and the Public Philosophy* (1981), *Cold War Theories* (1981), and *Winston S. Churchill's World View* (1983). One of his most recent efforts was to edit and bring to publication posthumously Hans J. Morgenthau's *Essays on Lincoln's Faith and Politics* (1983).

Contents

Preface to the Brief Edition

For over four decades, *Politics Among Nations* has been considered by many the premiere text in international politics. Now in its sixth edition its main themes, including national interest and power, are commonplace among practitioners of foreign policy. At the same time its value for a wider public is beginning to be felt.

The publication of *Politics* in paperback is inspired by at least four considerations. First, its use in the 1990s has been rendered more difficult by the mounting costs of higher education. While books constitute a relatively small part of educational expenses, the tripling of prices for hardback texts sometimes pushes student budgets to oppressive limits. Second, today's students have grown accustomed to paperbacks in every field from agronomy to zoology. It seems appropriate, therefore, that *Politics* in paperback should be available to citizens and students alike. Third, discussion of Professor Morgenthau's work has, if anything, intensified in the past twenty years. Derivative schools of thought such as neorealism have made their appearance. Making his *magnum opus* accessible to a broad spectrum of the American public has unquestioned merit. In this way, critics and sympathizers will be able to read his work first-hand, not as filtered through other minds. Fourth, faculties at respected institutions who have large and diverse classes in international relations have called for an edited edition available in an inexpensive format. The past twenty years have witnessed publication programs through which the majority of popular texts in the social sciences have become available in paperback form.

I have followed three working principles in preparing this edition. First, I have preserved intact the first ten chapters of the sixth edition. Professor Morgenthau considered these chapters as containing many of the basic principles of his philosophy of international relations: a realist theory, politics as a struggle for power, foreign policies, nationalism, and national power. Second,

I have included substantial segments of those chapters that make application of the aforementioned principles. These chapters include the balance of power, morality, and international law. Taken together, they provide a discussion, rich in historical examples, of the limitations of national power. From this section and those that follow I have eliminated some of the more technical and complex material whenever it was discussed later in the text or was dealt with in a manner more appropriate for advanced graduate and professional seminars. Third, I have made selections from those chapters that are concentrated on contemporary problems and the three fundamental approaches to peace: limitation of national power as with disarmament, collective security, and international government; transformation with the world state and world community; and accommodation through diplomacy. With the majority of chapters in this section, I have felt justified in eliminating historical details not essential to the analysis and deleting chapters, such as judicial settlement, considered in earlier sections on international law. I would urge students willing and able to examine these issues in depth to have recourse to the full sixth edition.

For most students of international relations, *Politics* requires no introduction. It has become a staple intellectual diet for faculty and graduate students and for thousands of undergraduate students. The present edition should serve to broaden its audience even further. In a word, we would expect that *Politics* in paperback would reach new readers. The new format is designed to serve the needs of a new era in higher education and public affairs.

Two explanatory notes are indicated. Throughout the manuscript the male pronoun predominates, as was customary at the time the book was first published. As is true on such matters throughout the text, we have chosen not to change the original. We would hope that we might be understood as referring to men and women wherever appropriate in our use of the male pronoun. Second, we have actively undertaken to correct temporal usage as with such references as "fifty years ago," referring to the turn of the century. If we should overlook such items at any point in the text, we ask the reader to remember that the author was writing at the midpoint of the twentieth century.

Kenneth W. Thompson

Preface to the Sixth Edition

As a graduate student at the University of Chicago following World War II, I had the privilege of serving as Professor Morgenthau's research assistant. Later we joined in the preparation of a book of text and readings entitled *Principles and Problems of International Politics*. He was primarily responsible for my returning to the university in the early 1950s as a member of the Department of Political Science. When it was agreed I should edit a *festschrift* in his honor, we worked together in identifying former students, colleagues, and friends especially familiar with his writings. In later years when our professional responsibilities brought us together in New York, we had frequent contacts and long discussions. As a member of several advisory committees, he contributed significantly to the programs of the Rockefeller Foundation for which I worked. A few weeks before he died he presented a paper on the presidency and foreign policy at a Miller Center conference at the University of Virginia. On a personal as well as a professional level, our friendship and intellectual collaboration continued until his last days.

Our close association has made the preparation of a sixth edition of his classic work, *Politics Among Nations,* both simpler and more difficult. On the one hand, I have kept myself reasonably familiar with the evolution of his thought from the publication of *Scientific Man vs. Power Politics* to the review after his death of certain unpublished essays. When Bertrand W. Lummus, Senior Editor of the College Department of Random House, invited me to prepare a new edition of *Politics*, I felt confident that I possessed the necessary knowledge for the task. On the other hand, upon undertaking the revision and reviewing Professor Morgenthau's last writings, I discovered important new developments in the final stages of his work of which I had not known. It would have been surprising if this had not been true, for he took as his guiding principle not the defense of an intellectual position but "the quest for truth."

In keeping with my discovery of the continuous unfolding of his thought, I have attempted in this edition to let Morgenthau speak for himself whenever possible. Thanks to the cooperation of his children, Susanna and Matthew, my assistant and I have had access to his papers on deposit at Alderman Library at the University of Virginia. Mr. Peter Gellman has been tireless in joining me in the search for further writings, whether published or unpublished, that touched on the most urgent problems confronting mankind in the late 1970s and 1980s. In his preface to the fifth edition, revised, Morgenthau wrote of that edition's continuing "in an organic and almost inevitable fashion the work of the preceding editions." Ever mindful of the fact that his great work has had an integrity throughout successive editions, I have undertaken to preserve it in ways that would have been impossible without the use of his own writings. I have also consulted his draft manuscripts, letters to editors, and professional correspondence.

At the same time, the fifth edition has had to be updated and revised to reflect changes that have occurred since Professor Morgenthau's death. Mr. Gellman and I have sought to substitute factual information and data wherever required while recognizing that even as we worked, the tides of history were making obsolete some of our evidence on topics like population, industrial production, decisions of the International Court of Justice, and actions by the United Nations. On subjects such as human rights, détente, and the nuclear problem, I have made substantial revisions—introducing wherever possible fragments of Morgenthau's own writings. Because his mind was so creative and subtle, no would-be literary executor can declare with certainty that Morgenthau would have formulated his views and presented them in precisely the context in which they are put forward here. I can only affirm that I have tried to be faithful to his philosophy and to his views on problems and policies as I understood them.

Kenneth W. Thompson

POLITICS AMONG NATIONS

The Struggle for Power and Peace

PART ONE

Theory and Practice of International Politics

1

why abide to on?
something no one?
else abides by.
act on your own
self-interest

A Realist Theory of International Politics

This book purports to present a theory of international politics. The test by which such a theory must be judged is not *a priori* and abstract but empirical and pragmatic. The theory, in other words, must be judged not by some preconceived abstract principle or concept unrelated to reality, but by its purpose: to bring order and meaning to a mass of phenomena which without it would remain disconnected and unintelligible. It must meet a dual test, an empirical and a logical one: Do the facts as they actually are lend themselves to the interpretation the theory has put upon them, and do the conclusions at which the theory arrives follow with logical necessity from its premises? In short, is the theory consistent with the facts and within itself?

The issue this theory raises concerns the nature of all politics. The history of modern political thought is the story of a contest between two schools that differ fundamentally in their conceptions of the nature of man, society, and politics. One believes that a rational and moral political order, derived from universally valid abstract principles, can be achieved here and now. It assumes the essential goodness and infinite malleability of human nature, and blames the failure of the social order to measure up to the rational standards on lack of knowledge and understanding, obsolescent social institutions, or the depravity of certain isolated individuals or groups. It trusts in education, reform, and the sporadic use of force to remedy these defects.

The other school believes that the world, imperfect as it is from the rational point of view, is the result of forces inherent in human nature. To improve the world one must work with those forces, not against them. This being inherently a world of opposing interests and of conflict among them, moral principles can never be fully realized, but must at best be approximated through the ever temporary balancing of interests and the ever precarious settlement of conflicts. This school, then, sees in a system of checks and balances a universal principle for all pluralist societies. It appeals to historic precedent rather than to abstract

3

principles, and aims at the realization of the lesser evil rather than of the absolute good.

This theoretical concern with human nature as it actually is, and with the historic processes as they actually take place, has earned for the theory presented here the name of realism. What are the tenets of political realism? No systematic exposition of the philosophy of political realism can be attempted here; it will suffice to single out six fundamental principles, which have frequently been misunderstood.

SIX PRINCIPLES OF POLITICAL REALISM

1. Political realism believes that politics, like society in general, is governed by objective laws that have their roots in human nature. In order to improve society it is first necessary to understand the laws by which society lives. The operation of these laws being impervious to our preferences, men will challenge them only at the risk of failure.

Realism, believing as it does in the objectivity of the laws of politics, must also believe in the possibility of developing a rational theory that reflects, however imperfectly and one-sidedly, these objective laws. It believes also, then, in the possibility of distinguishing in politics between truth and opinion—between what is true objectively and rationally, supported by evidence and illuminated by reason, and what is only a subjective judgment, divorced from the facts as they are and informed by prejudice and wishful thinking.

Human nature, in which the laws of politics have their roots, has not changed since the classical philosophies of China, India, and Greece endeavored to discover these laws. Hence, novelty is not necessarily a virtue in political theory, nor is old age a defect. The fact that a theory of politics, if there be such a theory, has never been heard of before tends to create a presumption against, rather than in favor of, its soundness. Conversely, the fact that a theory of politics was developed hundreds or even thousands of years ago—as was the theory of the balance of power—does not create a presumption that it must be outmoded and obsolete. A theory of politics must be subjected to the dual test of reason and experience. To dismiss such a theory because it had its flowering in centuries past is to present not a rational argument but a modernistic prejudice that takes for granted the superiority of the present over the past. To dispose of the revival of such a theory as a "fashion" or "fad" is tantamount to assuming that in matters political we can have opinions but no truths.

For realism, theory consists in ascertaining facts and giving them meaning through reason. It assumes that the character of a foreign policy can be ascertained only through the examination of the political acts performed and of the foreseeable consequences of these acts. Thus we can find out what statesmen have actually done, and from the foreseeable consequences of their acts we can surmise what their objectives might have been.

Yet examination of the facts is not enough. To give meaning to the factual raw material of foreign policy, we must approach political reality with a kind of rational outline, a map that suggests to us the possible meanings of foreign policy. In other words, we put ourselves in the position of a statesman who must meet a certain problem of foreign policy under certain circumstances, and we ask ourselves what the rational alternatives are from which a statesman may choose who must meet this problem under these circumstances (presuming always that he acts in a rational manner), and which of these rational alternatives this particular statesman, acting under these circumstances, is likely to choose. It is the testing of this rational hypothesis against the actual facts and their consequences that gives theoretical meaning to the facts of international politics.

2. The main signpost that helps political realism to find its way through the landscape of international politics is the concept of interest defined in terms of power. This concept provides the link between reason trying to understand international politics and the facts to be understood. It sets politics as an autonomous sphere of action and understanding apart from other spheres, such as economics (understood in terms of interest defined as wealth), ethics, aesthetics, or religion. Without such a concept a theory of politics, international or domestic, would be altogether impossible, for without it we could not distinguish between political and nonpolitical facts, nor could we bring at least a measure of systemic order to the political sphere.

We assume that statesmen think and act in terms of interest defined as power, and the evidence of history bears that assumption out. That assumption allows us to retrace and anticipate, as it were, the steps a statesman—past, present, or future—has taken or will take on the political scene. We look over his shoulder when he writes his dispatches; we listen in on his conversation with other statesmen; we read and anticipate his very thoughts. Thinking in terms of interest defined as power, we think as he does, and as disinterested observers we understand his thoughts and actions perhaps better than he, the actor on the political scene, does himself.

The concept of interest defined as power imposes intellectual discipline upon the observer, infuses rational order into the subject matter of politics, and thus makes the theoretical understanding of politics possible. On the side of the actor, it provides for rational discipline in action and creates that astounding continuity in foreign policy which makes American, British, or Russian foreign policy appear as an intelligible, rational continuum, by and large consistent within itself, regardless of the different motives, preferences, and intellectual and moral qualities of successive statesmen. A realist theory of international politics, then, will guard against two popular fallacies: the concern with motives and the concern with ideological preferences.

To search for the clue to foreign policy exclusively in the motives of statesmen is both futile and deceptive. It is futile because motives are the most illusive of psychological data, distorted as they are, frequently beyond recognition, by the interests and emotions of actor and observer alike. Do we really know what our own motives are? And what do we know of the motives of others?

Yet even if we had access to the real motives of statesmen, that knowledge would help us little in understanding foreign policies, and might well lead us astray. It is true that the knowledge of the statesman's motives may give us one among many clues as to what the direction of his foreign policy might be. It cannot give us, however, the one clue by which to predict his foreign policies. History shows no exact and necessary correlation between the quality of motives and the quality of foreign policy. This is true in both moral and political terms.

We cannot conclude from the good intentions of a statesman that his foreign policies will be either morally praiseworthy or politically successful. Judging his motives, we can say that he will not intentionally pursue policies that are morally wrong, but we can say nothing about the probability of their success. If we want to know the moral and political qualities of his actions, we must know them, not his motives. How often have statesmen been motivated by the desire to improve the world, and ended by making it worse? And how often have they sought one goal, and ended by achieving something they neither expected nor desired?

Neville Chamberlain's politics of appeasement were, as far as we can judge, inspired by good motives; he was probably less motivated by considerations of personal power than were many other British prime ministers, and he sought to preserve peace and to assure the happiness of all concerned. Yet his policies helped to make the Second World War inevitable, and to bring untold miseries to millions of people. Sir Winston Churchill's motives, on the other hand, were much less universal in scope and much more narrowly directed toward personal and national power, yet the foreign policies that sprang from these inferior motives were certainly superior in moral and political quality to those pursued by his predecessor. Judged by his motives, Robespierre was one of the most virtuous men who ever lived. Yet it was the utopian radicalism of that very virtue that made him kill those less virtuous than himself, brought him to the scaffold, and destroyed the revolution of which he was a leader.

Good motives give assurance against deliberately bad policies; they do not guarantee the moral goodness and political success of the policies they inspire. What is important to know, if one wants to understand foreign policy, is not primarily the motives of a statesman, but his intellectual ability to comprehend the essentials of foreign policy, as well as his political ability to translate what he has comprehended into successful political action. It follows that while ethics in the abstract judges the moral qualities of motives, political theory must judge the political qualities of intellect, will, and action.

A realist theory of international politics will also avoid the other popular fallacy of equating the foreign policies of a statesman with his philosophic or political sympathies, and of deducing the former from the latter. Statesmen, especially under contemporary conditions, may well make a habit of presenting their foreign policies in terms of their philosophic and political sympathies in order to gain popular support for them. Yet they will distinguish with Lincoln between their "*official* duty," which is to think and act in terms of the national interest, and their "*personal* wish," which is to see their own moral values and

Lincoln

political principles realized throughout the world. Political realism does not require, nor does it condone, indifference to political ideals and moral principles, but it requires indeed a sharp distinction between the desirable and the possible—between what is desirable everywhere and at all times and what is possible under the concrete circumstances of time and place. *realist*

It stands to reason that not all foreign policies have always followed so rational, objective, and unemotional a course. The contingent elements of personality, prejudice, and subjective preference, and of all the weaknesses of intellect and will which flesh is heir to, are bound to deflect foreign policies from their rational course. Especially where foreign policy is conducted under the conditions of democratic control, the need to marshal popular emotions to the support of foreign policy cannot fail to impair the rationality of foreign policy itself. Yet a theory of foreign policy which aims at rationality must for the time being, as it were, abstract from these irrational elements and seek to paint a picture of foreign policy which presents the rational essence to be found in experience, without the contingent deviations from rationality which are also found in experience.

Deviations from rationality which are not the result of the personal whim or the personal psychopathology of the policy maker may appear contingent only from the vantage point of rationality, but may themselves be elements in a coherent system of irrationality. The possibility of constructing, as it were, a counter-theory of irrational politics is worth exploring.

When one reflects upon the development of American thinking on foreign policy, one is struck by the persistence of mistaken attitudes that have survived—under whatever guises—both intellectual argument and political experience. Once that wonder, in true Aristotelian fashion, has been transformed into the quest for rational understanding, the quest yields a conclusion both comforting and disturbing: we are here in the presence of intellectual defects shared by all of us in different ways and degrees. Together they provide the outline of a kind of pathology of international politics. When the human mind approaches reality with the purpose of taking action, of which the political encounter is one of the outstanding instances, it is often led astray by any of four common mental phenomena: residues of formerly adequate modes of thought and action now rendered obsolete by a new social reality; demonological interpretations of reality which substitute a fictitious reality—peopled by evil persons rather than seemingly intractable issues—for the actual one; refusal to come to terms with a threatening state of affairs by denying it through illusory verbalization; reliance upon the infinite malleability of a seemingly obstreperous reality.

Man responds to social situations with repetitive patterns. The same situation, recognized in its identity with previous situations, evokes the same response. The mind, as it were, holds in readiness a number of patterns appropriate for different situations; it then requires only the identification of a particular case to apply to it the preformed pattern appropriate to it. Thus the human mind follows the principle of economy of effort, obviating an examination *de novo* of each individual situation and the pattern of thought and action appropriate to it. Yet when matters are subject to dynamic change, traditional patterns are no longer appropriate: they must be replaced by new ones reflecting such change. Otherwise a gap will open between traditional patterns and new realities, and thought and action will be misguided.

On the international plane it is no exaggeration to say that the very structure of international relations—as reflected in political institutions, diplomatic procedures, and legal arrangements—has tended to become at variance with, and in large measure irrelevant to, the reality of international politics. While the former assumes the "sovereign equality" of all nations, the latter is dominated by an extreme inequality of nations, two of which are called superpowers because they hold in their hands the unprecedented power of total destruction, and many of which are called "ministates" because their power is minuscule even compared with that of the traditional nation states. It is this contrast and incompatibility between the reality of international politics and the concepts, institutions, and procedures designed to make intelligible and control the former, which has caused, at least below the great-power level, the unmanageability of international relations which borders on anarchy. International terrorism and the different government reactions to it, the involvement of foreign governments in the Lebanese civil war, the military operations of the United States in Southeast Asia, and the military intervention of the Soviet Union in Eastern Europe cannot be explained or justified by reference to traditional concepts, institutions, and procedures.

All these situations have one characteristic in common. The modern fact of interdependence requires a political order which takes that fact into account, while in reality the legal and institutional superstructure, harking back to the nineteenth century, assumes the existence of a multiplicity of self-sufficient, impenetrable, sovereign nation states. These residues of an obsolescent legal and institutional order not only stand in the way of a rational transformation of international relations in light of the inequality of power and the interdependence of interests, but they also render precarious, if not impossible, more rational policies within the defective framework of such a system.

It is a characteristic of primitive thinking to personalize social problems. That tendency is particularly strong when the problem appears not to be susceptible to rational understanding and successful manipulation. When a particular person or group of persons is identified with the recalcitrant difficulty, that may seem to render the problem both intellectually accessible and susceptible of solution. Thus belief in Satan as the source of evil makes us "understand" the nature of evil by focusing the search for its origin and control upon a particular person whose physical existence we assume. The complexity of political conflict precludes such simple solutions. Natural catastrophes will not be prevented by burning witches; the threat of a powerful Germany to establish hegemony over Europe will not be averted by getting rid of a succession of German leaders. But by identifying the issue with certain persons over whom we have—or hope to have—control we reduce the problem, both intellectually and pragmatically, to manageable proportions. Once we have identified certain individuals and groups of individuals as the source of evil, we appear to have understood the causal nexus that leads from the individuals to the social problem; that apparent understanding suggests the apparent solution: Eliminate the individuals "responsible" for it, and you have solved the problem.

Superstition still holds sway over our relations within society. The demonological pattern of thought and action has now been transferred to other fields of human action closed to the kind of rational enquiry and action that have driven superstition from our relations with nature. As William Graham Sumner put it, "The amount of superstition is not much changed, but it now attaches to politics, not to religion."[1] The numerous failures of the United States to recognize and respond to the polycentric nature of Communism is a prime example of this defect. The corollary of this indiscriminate opposition to Communism is the indiscriminate support of governments and movements that profess and practice anti-Communism. American policies in Asia and Latin America have derived from this simplistic position. The Vietnam War and our inability to come to terms with mainland China find here their rationale. So do the theory and practice of counterinsurgency, including large-scale assassinations under the Phoenix program in Vietnam and the actual or attempted assassinations of individual statesmen. Signs of a similar approach have been evident more recently in Central America.

The demonological approach to foreign policy strengthens another pathological tendency, which is the refusal to acknowledge and cope effectively with a threatening reality. The demonological approach has shifted our attention and concern towards the adherents of Communism—individuals at home and abroad, political movements, foreign governments—and away from the real threat: the power of states, Communist or not. McCarthyism not only provided the most pervasive American example of the demonological approach but was also one of the most extreme examples of this kind of misjudgment: it substituted the largely illusory threat of domestic subversion for the real threat of Russian power.

Finally, it is part of this approach to politics to believe that no problems—however hopeless they may appear—are really insoluble, given well-meaning, well-financed, and competent efforts. I have tried elsewhere to lay bare the intellectual and historical roots of this belief;[2] here I limit myself to pointing out its persistent strength despite much experience to the contrary, such as the Vietnam War and the general decline of American power. This preference for economic solutions to political and military problems is powerfully reinforced by the interests of potential recipients of economic support, who prefer the obviously profitable transfer of economic advantages to painful and risky diplomatic bargaining.

The difference between international politics as it actually is and a rational

---

[1]"Mores of the Present and Future," in *War and Other Essays* (New Haven: Yale University Press, 1911), p. 159.

[2]*Scientific Man versus Power Politics* (Chicago: University of Chicago Press, 1946).

theory derived from it is like the difference between a photograph and a painted portrait. The photograph shows everything that can be seen by the naked eye; the painted portrait does not show everything that can be seen by the naked eye, but it shows, or at least seeks to show, one thing that the naked eye cannot see· the human essence of the person portrayed.

Political realism contains not only a theoretical but also a normative element. It knows that political reality is replete with contingencies and systemic irrationalities and points to the typical influences they exert upon foreign policy. Yet it shares with all social theory the need, for the sake of theoretical understanding, to stress the rational elements of political reality; for it is these rational elements that make reality intelligible for theory. Political realism presents the theoretical construct of a rational foreign policy which experience can never completely achieve.

At the same time political realism considers a rational foreign policy to be good foreign policy; for only a rational foreign policy minimizes risks and maximizes benefits and, hence, complies both with the moral precept of prudence and the political requirement of success. Political realism wants the photographic picture of the political world to resemble as much as possible its painted portrait. Aware of the inevitable gap between good—that is, rational—foreign policy and foreign policy as it actually is, political realism maintains not only that theory must focus upon the rational elements of political reality, but also that foreign policy ought to be rational in view of its own moral and practical purposes.

Hence, it is no argument against the theory here presented that actual foreign policy does not or cannot live up to it. That argument misunderstands the intention of this book, which is to present not an indiscriminate description of political reality, but a rational theory of international politics. Far from being invalidated by the fact that, for instance, a perfect balance of power policy will scarcely be found in reality, it assumes that reality, being deficient in this respect, must be understood and evaluated as an approximation to an ideal system of balance of power.

3. Realism assumes that its key concept of interest defined as power is an objective category which is universally valid, but it does not endow that concept with a meaning that is fixed once and for all. The idea of interest is indeed of the essence of politics and is unaffected by the circumstances of time and place. Thucydides' statement, born of the experiences of ancient Greece, that "identity of interests is the surest of bonds whether between states or individuals" was taken up in the nineteenth century by Lord Salisbury's remark that "the only bond of union that endures" among nations is "the absence of all clashing interests." It was erected into a general principle of government by George Washington:

A small knowledge of human nature will convince us, that, with far the greatest part of mankind, interest is the governing principle; and that almost every man is more or less, under its influence. Motives of public virtue may for a time, or in particular instances, actuate men to the observance of a conduct purely disinterested; but they are not of themselves sufficient to produce persevering conformity to the refined dictates and obligations of social duty. Few men are capable of making a continual sacrifice of all views of private interest, or advantage, to the common good. It is vain to exclaim against the depravity of human nature on this account; the fact is so, the experience of every age and nation has proved it and we must in a great measure, change the constitution of man, before we can make it otherwise. No institution, not built on the presumptive truth of these maxims can succeed.[3]

It was echoed and enlarged upon in our century by Max Weber's observation:

Interests (material and ideal), not ideas, dominate directly the actions of men. Yet the "images of the world" created by these ideas have very often served as switches determining the tracks on which the dynamism of interests kept actions moving.[4]

Yet the kind of interest determining political action in a particular period of history depends upon the political and cultural context within which foreign policy is formulated. The goals that might be pursued by nations in their foreign policy can run the whole gamut of objectives any nation has ever pursued or might possibly pursue.

The same observations apply to the concept of power. Its content and the manner of its use are determined by the political and cultural environment. Power may comprise anything that establishes and maintains the control of man over man. Thus power covers all social relationships which serve that end, from physical violence to the most subtle psychological ties by which one mind controls another. Power covers the domination of man by man, both when it is disciplined by moral ends and controlled by constitutional safeguards, as in Western democracies, and when it is that untamed and barbaric force which finds its laws in nothing but its own strength and its sole justification in its aggrandizement.

Political realism does not assume that the contemporary conditions under which foreign policy operates, with their extreme instability and the ever present threat of large-scale violence, cannot be changed. The balance of power, for instance, is indeed a perennial element of all pluralistic societies, as the authors of *The Federalist* papers well knew; yet it is capable of operating, as it does in the United States, under the conditions of relative stability and peaceful conflict. If the factors that have given rise to these conditions can be duplicated on the international scene, similar conditions of stability and peace will then prevail there, as they have over long stretches of history among certain nations.

What is true of the general character of international relations is also true

---

[3]*The Writings of George Washington,* edited by John C. Fitzpatrick (Washington: United States Printing Office, 1931–44), Vol. X, p. 363.

[4]Marianne Weber, *Max Weber* (Tuebingen: J. C. B. Mohr, 1926), pp. 347–8. See also Max Weber, *Gesammelte Aufsätze zur Religionssoziologie* (Tuebingen: J. C. B. Mohr, 1920), p. 252.

of the nation state as the ultimate point of reference of contemporary foreign policy. While the realist indeed believes that interest is the perennial standard by which political action must be judged and directed, the contemporary connection between interest and the nation state is a product of history, and is therefore bound to disappear in the course of history. Nothing in the realist position militates against the assumption that the present division of the political world into nation states will be replaced by larger units of a quite different character, more in keeping with the technical potentialities and the moral requirements of the contemporary world.

The realist parts company with other schools of thought before the all-important question of how the contemporary world is to be transformed. The realist is persuaded that this transformation can be achieved only through the workmanlike manipulation of the perennial forces that have shaped the past as they will the future. The realist cannot be persuaded that we can bring about that transformation by confronting a political reality that has its own laws with an abstract ideal that refuses to take those laws into account.

4. Political realism is aware of the moral significance of political action. It is also aware of the ineluctable tension between the moral command and the requirements of successful political action. And it is unwilling to gloss over and obliterate that tension and thus to obfuscate both the moral and the political issue by making it appear as though the stark facts of politics were morally more satisfying than they actually are, and the moral law less exacting that it actually is.

Realism maintains that universal moral principles cannot be applied to the actions of states in their abstract universal formulation, but that they must be filtered through the concrete circumstances of time and place. The individual may say for himself: *"Fiat justitia, pereat mundus* (Let justice be done, even if the world perish),"* but the state has no right to say so in the name of those who are in its care. Both individual and state must judge political action by universal moral principles, such as that of liberty. Yet while the individual has a moral right to sacrifice himself in defense of such a moral principle, the state has no right to let its moral disapprobation of the infringement of liberty get in the way of successful political action, itself inspired by the moral principle of national survival. There can be no political morality without prudence; that is, without consideration of the political consequences of seemingly moral action. Realism, then, considers prudence—the weighing of the consequences of alternative political actions—to be the supreme virtue in politics. Ethics in the abstract judges action by its conformity with the moral law; political ethics judges action by its political consequences. Classical and medieval philosophy knew this, and so did Lincoln when he said:

> I do the very best I know how, the very best I can, and I mean to keep doing so until the end. If the end brings me out all right, what is said against me won't amount to anything. If the end brings me out wrong, ten angels swearing I was right would make no difference.

5. Political realism refuses to identify the moral aspirations of a particular nation with the moral laws that govern the universe. As it distinguishes between truth and opinion, so it distinguishes between truth and idolatry. All nations are tempted—and few have been able to resist the temptation for long—to clothe their own particular aspirations and actions in the moral purposes of the universe. To know that nations are subject to the moral law is one thing, while to pretend to know with certainty what is good and evil in the relations among nations is quite another. There is a world of difference between the belief that all nations stand under the judgment of God, inscrutable to the human mind, and the blasphemous conviction that God is always on one's side and that what one wills oneself cannot fail to be willed by God also.

The lighthearted equation between a particular nationalism and the counsels of Providence is morally indefensible, for it is that very sin of pride against which the Greek tragedians and the Biblical prophets have warned rulers and ruled. That equation is also politically pernicious, for it is liable to engender the distortion in judgment which, in the blindness of crusading frenzy, destroys nations and civilizations—in the name of moral principle, ideal, or God himself.

On the other hand, it is exactly the concept of interest defined in terms of power that saves us from both that moral excess and that political folly. For if we look at all nations, our own included, as political entities pursuing their respective interests defined in terms of power, we are able to do justice to all of them. And we are able to do justice to all of them in a dual sense: We are able to judge other nations as we judge our own and, having judged them in this fashion, we are then capable of pursuing policies that respect the interests of other nations, while protecting and promoting those of our own. Moderation in policy cannot fail to reflect the moderation of moral judgment.

6. The difference, then, between political realism and other schools of thought is real, and it is profound. However much of the theory of political realism may have been misunderstood and misinterpreted, there is no gainsaying its distinctive intellectual and moral attitude to matters political.

Intellectually, the political realist maintains the autonomy of the political sphere, as the economist, the lawyer, the moralist maintain theirs. He thinks in terms of interest defined as power, as the economist thinks in terms of interest defined as wealth; the lawyer, of the conformity of action with legal rules; the moralist, of the conformity of action with moral principles. The economist asks: "How does this policy affect the wealth of society, or a segment of it?" The lawyer asks: "Is this policy in accord with the rules of law?" The moralist asks: "Is this policy in accord with moral principles?" And the political realist asks: "How does this policy affect the power of the nation?" (Or of the federal government, of Congress, of the party, of agriculture, as the case may be.)

The political realist is not unaware of the existence and relevance of standards of thought other than political ones. As political realist, he cannot but subordinate these other standards to those of politics. And he parts company with other schools when they impose standards of thought appropriate to other spheres upon the political sphere. It is here that political realism takes issue with the "legalistic-moralistic approach" to international politics. That this issue is not, as has been contended, a mere figment of the imagination, but goes to the very core of the controversy, can be shown from many historical examples. Three will suffice to make the point.[5]

In 1939 the Soviet Union attacked Finland. This action confronted France and Great Britain with two issues, one legal, the other political. Did that action violate the Covenant of the League of Nations and, if it did, what countermeasures should France and Great Britain take? The legal question could easily be answered in the affirmative, for obviously the Soviet Union had done what was prohibited by the Covenant. The answer to the political question depends, first, upon the manner in which the Russian action affected the interests of France and Great Britain; second upon the existing distribution of power between France and Great Britain, on the one hand, and the Soviet Union and other potentially hostile nations, especially Germany, on the other; and, third, upon the influence that the countermeasures were likely to have upon the interests of France and Great Britain and the future distribution of power. France and Great Britain, as the leading members of the League of Nations, saw to it that the Soviet Union was expelled from the League, and they were prevented from joining Finland in the war against the Soviet Union only by Sweden's refusal to allow their troops to pass through Swedish territory on their way to Finland. If this refusal by Sweden had not saved them, France and Great Britain would shortly have found themselves at war with the Soviet Union and Germany at the same time.

The policy of France and Great Britain was a classic example of legalism in that they allowed the answer to the legal question, legitimate within its sphere, to determine their political actions. Instead of asking both questions, that of law and that of power, they asked only the question of law; and the answer they received could have no bearing on the issue that their very existence might have depended upon.

The second example illustrates the "moralistic approach" to international politics. It concerns the international status of the Communist government of China. The rise of that government confronted the Western world with two issues, one moral, the other political. Were the nature and policies of that government in accord with the moral principles of the Western world? Should the Western world deal with such a government? The answer to the first question could not fail to be in the negative. Yet it did not follow with necessity that the answer to the second question should also be in the negative. The standard of thought applied to the first—the moral—question was simply to test the nature and the policies of the Communist government of China by the principles of Western morality. On the other hand, the second—the political—question had to be subjected to the complicated test of the interests involved

---

[5]See the other examples discussed in Hans J. Morgenthau, "Another 'Great Debate': The National Interest of the United States," *The American Political Science Review*, Vol. XLVI (December 1952), pp. 979 ff. See also Hans J. Morgenthau, *Politics in the 20th Century*, Vol. 1, *The Decline of Democratic Politics* (Chicago: University of Chicago Press, 1962), pp. 79 ff; and abridged edition (Chicago: University of Chicago Press, 1971), pp. 204 ff.

and the power available on either side, and of the bearing of one or the other course of action upon these interests and power. The application of this test could well have led to the conclusion that it would be wiser not to deal with the Communist government of China. To arrive at this conclusion by neglecting this test altogether and answering the political question in terms of the moral issue was indeed a classic example of the "moralistic approach" to international politics.

The third case illustrates strikingly the contrast between realism and the legalistic-moralistic approach to foreign policy. Great Britain, as one of the guarantors of the neutrality of Belgium, went to war with Germany in August 1914 because Germany had violated the neutrality of Belgium. The British action could be justified either in realistic or legalistic-moralistic terms. That is to say, one could argue realistically that for centuries it had been axiomatic for British foreign policy to prevent the control of the Low Countries by a hostile power. It was then not so much the violation of Belgium's neutrality per se as the hostile intentions of the violator which provided the rationale for British intervention. If the violator had been another nation but Germany, Great Britain might well have refrained from intervening. This is the position taken by Sir Edward Grey, British Foreign Secretary during that period. Under Secretary for Foreign Affairs Hardinge remarked to him in 1908: "If France violated Belgian neutrality in a war against Germany, it is doubtful whether England or Russia would move a finger to maintain Belgian neutrality, while if the neutrality of Belgium was violated by Germany, it is probable that the converse would be the case." Whereupon Sir Edward Grey replied: "This is to the point." Yet one could also take the legalistic and moralistic position that the violation of Belgium's neutrality per se, because of its legal and moral defects and regardless of the interests at stake and of the identity of the violator, justified British and, for that matter, American intervention. This was the position which Theodore Roosevelt took in his letter to Sir Edward Grey of January 22, 1915:

> To me the crux of the situation has been Belgium. If England or France had acted toward Belgium as Germany has acted I should have opposed them, exactly as I now oppose Germany. I have emphatically approved your action as a model for what should be done by those who believe that treaties should be observed in good faith and that there is such a thing as international morality. I take this position as an American who is no more an Englishman than he is a German, who endeavors loyally to serve the interests of his own country, but who also endeavors to do what he can for justice and decency as regards mankind at large, and who therefore feels obliged to judge all other nations by their conduct on any given occasion.

This realist defense of the autonomy of the political sphere against its subversion by other modes of thought does not imply disregard for the existence and importance of these other modes of thought. It rather implies that each should be assigned its proper sphere and function. Political realism is based upon a pluralistic conception of human nature. Real man is a composite of "economic man," "political man," "moral man," "religious man," etc. A man who was nothing but "political man" would be a beast, for he would be completely lacking in moral restraints. A man who was nothing but "moral man" would be a fool, for he would be completely lacking in prudence. A man who was nothing but "religious man" would be a saint, for he would be completely lacking in worldly desires.

Recognizing that these different facets of human nature exist, political realism also recognizes that in order to understand one of them one has to deal with it on its own terms. That is to say, if I want to understand "religious man," I must for the time being abstract from the other aspects of human nature and deal with its religious aspect as if it were the only one. Furthermore, I must apply to the religious sphere the standards of thought appropriate to it, always remaining aware of the existence of other standards and their actual influence upon the religious qualities of man. What is true of this facet of human nature is true of all the others. No modern economist, for instance would conceive of his science and its relations to other sciences of man in any other way. It is exactly through such a process of emancipation from other standards of thought, and the development of one appropriate to its subject matter, that economics has developed as an autonomous theory of the economic activities of man. To contribute to a similar development in the field of politics is indeed the purpose of political realism.

It is in the nature of things that a theory of politics which is based upon such principles will not meet with unanimous approval—nor does, for that matter, such a foreign policy. For theory and policy alike run counter to two trends in our culture which are not able to reconcile themselves to the assumptions and results of a rational, objective theory of politics. One of these trends disparages the role of power in society on grounds that stem from the experience and philosophy of the nineteenth century; we shall address ourselves to this tendency later in greater detail.[6] The other trend, opposed to the realist theory and practice of politics, stems from the very relationship that exists, and must exist, between the human mind and the political sphere. For reasons that we shall discuss later[7] the human mind in its day-by-day operations cannot bear to look the truth of politics straight in the face. It must disguise, distort, belittle, and embellish the truth—the more so, the more the individual is actively involved in the processes of politics, and particularly in those of international politics. For only by deceiving himself about the nature of politics and the role he plays on the political scene is man able to live contentedly as a political animal with himself and his fellow men.

Thus it is inevitable that a theory which tries to understand international politics as it actually is and as it ought to be in view of its intrinsic nature, rather than as people would like to see it, must overcome a psychological resistance that most other branches of learning need not face. A book devoted to the theoretical understanding of international politics therefore requires a special explanation and justification.

---

[6]See pages 37 ff.
[7]See pages 101 ff.

2

The Science of International Politics

UNDERSTANDING INTERNATIONAL POLITICS

Different Approaches

This book has two purposes. The first is to detect and understand the forces that determine political relations among nations, and to comprehend the ways in which those forces act upon each other and upon international political relations and institutions. In most other branches of the social sciences this purpose would be taken for granted, because the natural aim of all scientific undertakings is to discover the forces underlying social phenomena and the mode of their operation. In approaching the study of international politics, one cannot take this purpose for granted; it therefore requires special emphasis. As Dr. Grayson Kirk has put it:

> Until recent times the study of international relations in the United States has been dominated largely by persons who have taken one of three approaches. First there have been the historians who have considered international relations merely as recent history, in which the student is handicapped by the absence of an adequate amount of available data. A second group, the international lawyers, have properly concerned themselves primarily with the legal aspects of inter-state relations, but they have seldom made a serious effort to inquire into the fundamental reasons for the continuing incompleteness and inadequacy of this legal nexus. Finally, there have been those who have been less concerned with international relations as they are than with the more perfect system which these idealists would like to build. Only recently—and belatedly—have students undertaken to examine the fundamental and persistent forces of world politics, and the institutions which embody them, not with a view to praise or to condemn, but merely in an effort to provide a better understanding of these basic

drives which determine the foreign policies of states. Thus the political scientist is moving into the international field at last.[1]

Professor Charles E. Martin has taken up Dr. Kirk's theme by pointing to

... the problem which faces the students and the teachers of international relations more than any other, namely, that dualism we have to face in moving in two different and opposite areas. I mean the area of institutions of peace which are related to the adjustment of disputes and the area of power politics and war. Yet, it must be so. There is no escape from it. . . . I think probably one of the greatest indictments of our attitude in teaching in the last twenty years has been to write off glibly the institution of war and to write off the books the influence of power politics. I think political scientists make a great mistake in doing so. We should be the very ones who are studying power politics and its implications and the situations growing out of it, and we should be the ones who study the institution of war.[2]

Defined in such terms, international politics as an academic discipline is distinct from recent history and current events, international law, and political reform.

International politics embraces more than recent history and current events. The observer is surrounded by the contemporary scene with its ever shifting emphasis and changing perspectives. He cannot find solid ground on which to stand, or objective standards of evaluation, without getting down to fundamentals that are revealed only by the correlation of recent events with the more distant past and the perennial qualities of human nature underlying both.

International politics cannot be reduced to legal rules and institutions. International politics operates within the framework of such rules and through the instrumentality of such institutions. But it is no more identical with them than American politics on the national level is identical with the American Constitution, the federal laws, and the agencies of the federal government.

Concerning attempts to reform international politics before making an effort to understand what international politics is about, we share William Graham Sumner's view:

The worst vice in political discussions is that dogmatism which takes its stand on great principles or assumptions, instead of standing on an exact examination of things as they are and human nature as it is. . . . An ideal is formed of some higher or better state of things than now exists, and almost unconsciously the ideal is assumed as already existing and made the basis of speculations which have no root. . . . The whole method of abstract speculation on political topics is vicious. It is popular because it is easy; it is easier to imagine a new world than to learn to know this one; it is easier to embark on speculations based on a few broad assumptions than it is to study the history of states and institutions; it is easier to catch up a popular dogma than it is to analyze it to see whether it is true or not. All this leads

---

[1]*American Journal of International Law*, Vol. 39 (1945), pp. 369–70.
[2]*Proceedings of the Eighth Conference of Teachers of International Law and Related Subjects* (Washington: Carnegie Endowment for International Peace, 1946), p. 66.

to confusion, to the admission of phrases and platitudes, to much disputing but little gain in the prosperity of nations.[3]

Limitations to Understanding

The most formidable difficulty facing a theoretical inquiry into the nature and ways of international politics is the ambiguity of the material with which the observer has to deal. The events he must try to understand are, on the one hand, unique occurrences. They happened in this way only once and never before or since. On the other hand, they are similar, for they are manifestations of social forces. Social forces are the product of human nature in action. Therefore, under similar conditions, they will manifest themselves in a similar manner. But where is the line to be drawn between the similar and the unique?

This ambiguity of the events to be understood by a theory of international politics—it may be pointed out in passing—is but a special instance of a general impediment to human understanding. "As no event and no shape," observes Montaigne, "is entirely like another, so also is there none entirely different from another: *an ingenious mixture on the part of Nature. If there were no similarity in our faces, we could not distinguish man from beast; if there were no dissimilarity, we could not distinguish one man from another.* All things hold together by some similarity; every example is halting, and the comparison that is derived from experience is always defective and imperfect. And yet one links up the comparisons at some corner. And so do laws become serviceable and adapt themselves to every one of our affairs by some wrested, forced, and biased interpretation."[4] It is against such "wrested, forced, and biased interpretation" of political events that a theory of international politics must be continuously on guard.

We learn what the principles of international politics are from comparisons between such events. A certain political situation evokes the formulation and execution of a certain foreign policy. Dealing with a different political situation, we ask ourselves: How does this situation differ from the preceding one, and how is it similar? Do the similarities reaffirm the policy developed previously? Or does the blending of similarities and differences allow the essence of that policy to be retained while, in some aspects, it is to be modified? Or do the differences vitiate the analogy altogether and make the previous policy inapplicable? If one wants to understand international politics, grasp the meaning of contemporary events, and foresee and influence the future, one must be able to perform the dual intellectual task implicit in these questions. One must be able to distinguish between the similarities and differences in two political situations. Furthermore, one must be able to assess the import of these similarities and differences for alternative foreign policies.

---

[3]"Democracy and Responsible Government," *The Challenge of Facts and Other Essays* (New Haven: Yale University Press, 1914), pp. 245–6.

[4]*The Essays of Michel de Montaigne*, edited and translated by Jacob Zeitlin (New York: Alfred A. Knopf, 1936), Vol. III, p. 270. Montaigne's italics.

Three series of events, taken at random, will illustrate the problem and its difficulties.

On September 17, 1796, George Washington made a speech in which he bade farewell to the nation, outlining the principles of American foreign policy in terms of abstention from European affairs. On December 2, 1823, President Monroe sent a message to Congress in which he formulated the principles of American foreign policy in similar terms. In 1917, the United States joined France and Great Britain against Germany, which threatened the independence of both. In 1941, the United States followed a similar course of action. On March 12, 1947, President Truman, in a message to Congress, reformulated the principles of American foreign policy in terms of the worldwide containment of Communism.

In 1512, Henry VIII of England made an alliance with the Hapsburgs against France. In 1515, he made an alliance with France against the Hapsburgs. In 1522 and 1542, he joined the Hapsburgs against France. In 1756, Great Britain allied itself with Prussia against the Hapsburgs and France. In 1793, Great Britain, Prussia, and the Hapsburgs were allied against Napoleon. In 1914, Great Britain joined with France and Russia against Austria and Germany, and in 1939 with France and Poland against Germany.

Napoleon, William II, and Hitler tried to conquer the continent of Europe and failed.

Are there within each of these three series of events similarities that allow us to formulate a principle of foreign policy for each series? Or is each event so different from the others in the series that each would require a different policy? The difficulty in making this decision is the measure of the difficulty in making correct judgments in foreign policy, in charting the future wisely, and in doing the right thing in the right way and at the right time.

Should the foreign policy in Washington's Farewell Address be considered a general principle of American foreign policy, or did it stem from temporary conditions and was its validity therefore limited to them? Are the foreign policies of Washington's and Monroe's messages compatible with the Truman Doctrine? To state the problem another way, is the Truman Doctrine a mere modification of a general principle underlying Washington's and Monroe's conception of foreign affairs, or does the Truman Doctrine constitute a radical departure from the traditions of American foreign policy? If its does, is it justified in the light of changed conditions? Generally speaking, do the differences in the international position of the United States in 1796, 1823, 1917, 1941, and 1947 justify the different foreign policies formulated and executed with regard to these different political situations? What are the similarities and differences in the situation with which Europe confronted the United States in 1917, 1941, and 1947, and to what extent do they require similar or different foreign policies on the part of the United States?

What is the meaning of those shifts in British foreign policy? Have they grown from the whim and perfidy of princes and statesmen? Or are they inspired by the accumulated wisdom of a people mindful of the permanent forces, transcending any particular alignment, that determine their relations to the continent of Europe?

Are the disasters that followed in the wake of the three attempts at continental conquest so many accidents due to disparate causes? Or does the similarity in results point to similarities in the over-all political situation, similarities that convey a lesson to be pondered by those who might want to try again? More particularly, were the policies the Soviet Union pursued in the aftermath of the Second World War similar to those of Napoleon, William II, and Hitler? If they were did they call for policies on the part of the United States similar to those pursued in 1917 and 1941?

Sometimes, as in the case of the changes in British foreign policy, the answer seems to be clear: that policy proceeded from wisdom rather than from whim. Most of the time, however, and especially when we deal with the present and the future, the answer is bound to be tentative and subject to qualifications. The facts from which the answer must derive are essentially ambiguous and subject to continuous change. To those men who would have it otherwise, history has taught nothing but false analogies. When such men have been responsible for the foreign policies of their countries, they have achieved only disaster. William II and Hitler learned nothing from Napolean's fate, for they thought it could teach them nothing. Those who have erected Washington's advice into a dogma to be followed slavishly have erred no less than those who would dismiss it altogether.

The Munich settlement of 1938 is another case in point. In retrospect, of course, we all know from practical experience that it was a failure, and from that experience we have developed the theoretical categories which demonstrate that it was bound to be a failure. But I remember very well the consensus with which the Munich settlement was approved at the time of its conclusion by theoreticians and practitioners of foreign policy and by the man in the street as well. The Munich settlement was then generally regarded as a great act of statesmanship, a concession made to a would-be conqueror for the sake of peace. E. H. Carr so regarded it then, and A. J. P. Taylor so regards it now. The flaw in that reasoning, which few people were—and perhaps could be—aware of at the time, was again the neglect of the contingencies inherent in political prediction. That which reveals itself as a simple truth in retrospect was either completely unknown in prospect or else could not be determined by anything but an uncertain hunch.

Take finally the contemporary issue of nuclear war. From time to time American policymakers speak openly about "prevailing" in a nuclear war. In this they mirror comments made by Russian military leaders—although not by Soviet political leaders such as Brezhnev, who more than once warned that a thermonuclear war would be suicidal for both superpowers. Particularly in the 1980s, as cold-war tensions mounted again, voices in both countries echoed the belief that victory in a nuclear war was not unthinkable, provided augmented strategic forces were formed through vastly increased defense expenditures. It is possible to develop a theory of nuclear war which assumes nuclear war to be just another kind of violence, greater in magnitude but not different in kind from the types of violence with which history has acquainted us. It follows from this assumption that nuclear war is going to be much more terrible than conventional war, but not necessarily intolerable, provided we take the measures which will enable at least some of us to survive it. In other words, once one starts with this theoretical assumption of the nature and the consequences of nuclear war, one can logically arrive at the conclusion that the foreign policy of the United States does not need to limit itself to trying to avoid nuclear war, but that the United States must also prepare to survive it. And then it becomes perfectly legitimate to raise the question, provided 100 million Americans were to be killed in a nuclear war and nine-tenths of the economic capacity of the United States were to be destroyed, of how we enable the surviving Americans to rebuild the United States with the remaining one-tenth of economic capacity.

The contingent element in this theory of nuclear war is its utter uncertainty, and this uncertainty is typical of all levels of theoretical analysis and prediction in the field of politics, domestic and international. Even if one were to accept all its estimates of deaths and material destruction and of the rate of material recovery, this theory would have to be uncertain about the human reactions to the kind of human and material devastation which nuclear war is likely to bring about. Obviously, if a highly complex human society could be visualized to operate like a primitive ant society, its recuperative ability could be taken for granted. If one-half of the ants of one ant hill have been destroyed together with nine-tenths of the material of the ant hill, it is safe to conclude that the remaining ants will start all over again, building up the ant hill and reproducing until the next catastrophe will force them to start all over again.

But a human society does not have this type of mechanical recuperative ability. Societies have a breaking point as do individuals, and there is a point beyond which human endurance does not carry human initiative in the face of such unprecedented massive devastation. Once that point is reached, civilization itself will collapse. The exact location of that point in the scale of human reactions is beyond theoretical understanding. What we are left with are hunches which may or may not be confirmed by experience.

The first lesson the student of international politics must learn and never forget is that the complexities of international affairs make simple solutions and trustworthy prophecies impossible. Here the scholar and the charlatan part company. Knowledge of the forces that determine politics among nations, and of the ways by which their political relations unfold, reveals the ambiguity of the facts of international politics. In every political situation contradictory tendencies are at play. One of these tendencies is more likely to prevail under certain conditions. But which tendency actually will prevail is anybody's guess. The best the scholar can do, then, is to trace the different tendencies that, as potentialities, are inherent in a certain international situation. He can point out the different conditions that make it more likely for one tendency to prevail than for another and, finally, assess the probabilities for the different conditions and tendencies to prevail in actuality.

Thus world affairs have surprises in store for whoever tries to read the future from his knowledge of the past and from the signs of the present. In 1776, Washington declared that "the Fate of our Country depends in all human probability, on the Exertion of a Few Weeks." Yet it was not until seven years later that the War of Independence came to an end. In February 1792, British Prime Minister Pitt justified the reduction of military expenditures (particularly a drastic decrease in the personnel of the British navy) and held out hope for more reductions to come by declaring: "Unquestionably there never was a time in the history of this country when from the situation of Europe we might more reasonably expect fifteen years of peace than at the present moment." Only two months later the continent of Europe was engulfed in war. Less than a year later Great Britain was involved. Thus was initiated a period of almost continuous warfare which lasted nearly a quarter of a century. When Lord Granville became British Foreign Secretary in 1870, he was informed by the Permanent Undersecretary that "he had never, during his long experience, known so great a lull in foreign affairs, and that he was not aware of any important question that he [Lord Granville] should have to deal with." On that same day Prince Leopold of Hohenzollern-Sigmaringen accepted the Crown of Spain, an event that three weeks later led to the outbreak of the Franco-Prussian War. Six weeks before the Russian Revolution of March 1917, Lenin told a group of young socialists in Zurich: "We old people will probably not live to see the decisive battles of the coming revolution." Less than a year later, the decisive battles of the Russian Revolution began under his leadership.

When the prophecies of great statesmen fare so ill, what can we expect from the predictions of lesser minds? In how many books written on international affairs before the First World War, when common opinion held great wars to be impossible or at least of short duration, was there even an inkling of what was to come? Was any book written in the period between the two world wars which could have helped one anticipate what international politics would be like in the ninth decade of the century? Who could have guessed at the beginning of the Second World War what the political world would be like at its end? Who could have known in 1945 what the world would be like in 1955, or in 1960 what it would be like in 1970 or 1980? What trust then shall we place in those who today would tell us what tomorrow and the day after will bring or what the year 2000 will be like?[5]

In 1979 the intelligence community, and more particularly the Central Intelligence Agency, were criticized for their failure to warn American policymakers of the upheavals that culminated in the Shah of Iran's ouster. President

---

[5]The fallibility of prophecies in international affairs is strikingly demonstrated by the fantastic errors committed by the experts who have tried to forecast the nature of the next war. The history of these forecasts, from Machiavelli to General J. F. C. Fuller, is the story of logical deductions, plausible in themselves, which had no connection with the contingencies of the actual historic development. General Fuller, for instance, foresaw in 1923 that the decisive weapon of the Second World War would be gas! See *The Reformation of War* (New York: E. P. Dutton and Company, 1923).

Carter himself took the unprecedented step of publicly reprimanding the highest authorities in the intelligence field for their lack of foresight.

What accounts for this failure of foresight on the part of otherwise intelligent and responsible people? The answer lies in the nature of the empirical material with which these individuals had to deal. The observer is confronted with a multitude of factors, the totality of which shape the future. In order to foresee the future, the observer would have to know all these factors, their dynamics, their mutual actions and reactions, and so forth. What he actually knows and can know is but a small fragment of the total. He must guess—and only the future will show who chose rightly among the many possible guesses.

Thus, with regard to Iran the intelligence community guessed wrong. Instead of blaming it indiscriminately, one ought to ask oneself two questions: Could one have pinpointed in time the outbreak of popular discontent? If the answer is in the affirmative, What could the United States have done about it? The answer to the second question is, at best: very little. This is probably why the intelligence community paid less attention to Iran than it might have done in the first place.

It is sobering to note that the science of economics, presumed to be the most precise of the social sciences because its central concept, wealth, is quantitative by definition, is similarly incapable of reliable prediction. An examination of a large number of forecasts of year-to-year changes in the American GNP for the years 1953–63 established an average error of about 40 per cent.[6] In October 1966, the Prudential Life Insurance Company predicted that in 1967 consumer expenditures would rise by 31 billion dollars and inventory investments would amount to 7.5 billion dollars. In October 1967, it scaled its estimate of consumer expenditures down to 27 billion dollars, an error of almost 15 per cent, assuming the correctness of the revised estimate; it reduced its estimate of inventory investments to 7 billion dollars. The Council of Economic Advisors overestimated the growth of the GNP for the same year by about 12 per cent.

UNDERSTANDING THE PROBLEM
OF INTERNATIONAL PEACE

These questions lead us to the secondary purpose of this book. No study of politics, and certainly no study of international politics in the final decades of the twentieth century, can be disinterested in the sense that it is able to divorce knowledge from action and to pursue knowledge for its own sake. International politics is no longer, as it was for the United States during most of its history, a series of incidents, costly or rewarding, but hardly calling into question the nation's very existence and destiny. The existence and destiny of the United

---

[6]Viktor Zarnowitz, *An Appraisal of Short-Term Economic Forecasts* (New York: National Bureau of Economic Research, 1967).

States were more deeply affected by the domestic events of the Civil War than by the international policies leading up to, and evolving from, the Mexican War, the Spanish-American War, and the Roosevelt corollary to the Monroe Doctrine.[7]

Two facts peculiar to our time have completely reversed the relative importance of domestic and international policies for the United States. First of all, the United States is at the moment of this writing one of the two most powerful nations on earth. Yet, in comparison with its actual and potential competitors, it is not so powerful that it can afford to ignore the effect of its policies upon its position among the nations. From the end of the Civil War to the beginning of the Second World War it mattered little what policies the United States pursued with regard to its Latin-American neighbors, China, or Spain. The self-sufficiency of its own strength, in conjunction with the operation of the balance of power, made the United States immune to the boundless ambition born of success and the fear and frustration which goes with failure. The United States could take success and failure in stride without being unduly tempted or afraid. Now it stands outside the enclosures of its continental citadel, taking on the whole of the political world as friend or foe. It has become dangerous and vulnerable, feared and afraid.

The risk of being very powerful, but not omnipotent, is aggravated by the second fact: a threefold revolution in the political structure of the world. First, the multiple-state system of the past, whose center was in Europe, has been replaced by a world-wide, bipolar system, whose centers lie outside Europe. Furthermore, the moral unity of the political world, which has distinguished Western civilization during most of its history, has been split into two incompatible systems of thought and action, competing everywhere for the allegiance of men. More recently, the revolutions of eastern and central Europe and within the Soviet Union have reinstated a multipolar world whose final outline is yet to be determined. Finally, modern technology has made possible total war resulting in universal destruction. The preponderance of these three new elements in contemporary international politics has not only made the preservation of world peace extremely difficult, but has also increased the risks inherent in war to the point where all-out nuclear war becomes a self-defeating absurdity. Since in this world situation the United States holds a position of predominant power, and hence of foremost responsibility, the understanding of the forces that mold international politics and of the factors that determine its course has become for the United States more than an interesting intellectual occupation. It has become a vital necessity.

To reflect on international politics from the vantage point of the contemporary United States, then, is to reflect upon the vital problems that confront

---

[7]This corollary is found in the message of Theodore Roosevelt to Congress on December 6, 1904. In that message he proclaimed the right of the United States to intervene in the domestic affairs of the Latin-American countries. For the text, see Ruhl J. Bartlett, editor, *The Record of American Diplomacy: Documents and Readings in the History of American Foreign Relations*, 4th ed. (New York: Alfred A. Knopf, 1964), p. 539.

American foreign policy in our time. While at all times the promotion of the national interests of the United States as a power among powers has been the main concern of American foreign policy, in an age that has seen two world wars and has learned how to wage total war with nuclear weapons the preservation of peace has become the prime concern of all nations.

It is for this reason that this book is planned around the two concepts of power and peace. These two concepts are central to a discussion of world politics in the final decade of the twentieth century, when an unprecedented accumulation of destructive power gives to the problem of peace an urgency it has never had before. In a world whose moving force is the aspiration of sovereign nations for power, peace can be maintained only by two devices. One is the self-regulatory mechanism of the social forces, which manifests itself in the struggle for power on the international scene, that is, the balance of power. The other consists of normative limitations upon that struggle, in the form of international law, international morality, and world public opinion. Since neither of these devices, as they operate today, is likely to keep the struggle for power indefinitely within peaceful bounds, three further questions must be asked and answered: What is the value of the main current proposals for the maintenance of international peace? More particularly, what is the value of the proposal for transforming the international society of sovereign nations into a supranational organization, such as a world state? And, finally, what must a program for action be like that is mindful of the lessons of the past and endeavors to adapt them to the problems of the present?

PART TWO

International Politics as a Struggle for Power

3

Political Power

WHAT IS POLITICAL POWER?[1]

As Means to the Nation's Ends

International politics, like all politics, is a struggle for power. Whatever the ultimate aims of international politics, power is always the immediate aim. Statesmen and peoples may ultimately seek freedom, security, prosperity, or power itself. They may define their goals in terms of a religious, philosophic, economic, or social ideal. They may hope that this ideal will materialize through its own inner force, through divine intervention, or through the natural development of human affairs. They may also try to further its realization through nonpolitical means, such as technical co-operation with other nations or international organizations. But whenever they strive to realize their goal by means of international politics, they do so by striving for power. The Crusaders wanted to free the holy places from domination by the Infidels; Woodrow Wilson wanted to make the world safe for democracy; the Nazis wanted to open Eastern Europe to German colonization, to dominate Europe, and to conquer the world. Since they all chose power to achieve these ends, they were actors on the scene of international politics.[2]

Two conclusions follow from this concept of international politics. First, not every action that a nation performs with respect to another nation is of a political nature. Many such activities are normally undertaken without any

---

[1] The concept of political power poses one of the most difficult and controversial problems of political science. The value of any concept used in political science is determined by its ability to explain a maximum of the phenomena that are conventionally considered to belong to a certain sphere of political activity. Thus the coverage of a concept of political power, to be useful for the understanding of international politics, must be broader than the coverage of one adopted to operate in the field of municipal politics. The political means employed in the latter are much more narrowly circumscribed than are those employed in international politics.

[2] For some significant remarks on power in relation to international politics, see Lionel Robbins, *The Economic Causes of War* (London: Jonathan Cape, 1939), pp. 63 ff.

consideration of power, nor do they normally affect the power of the nation undertaking them. Many legal, economic, humanitarian, and cultural activities are of this kind. Thus a nation is not normally engaged in international politics when it concludes an extradition treaty with another nation, when it exchanges goods and services with other nations, when it co-operates with other nations in providing relief from natural catastrophes, and when it promotes the distribution of cultural achievements throughout the world. In other words, the involvement of a nation in international politics is but one among many types of activities in which a nation can participate on the international scene.

Second, not all nations are at all times to the same extent involved in international politics. The degree of their involvement may run all the way from the maximum at present attained by the United States and the Soviet Union, through the minimum involvement of such countries as Switzerland, Luxembourg, or Venezuela, to the complete noninvolvement of Liechtenstein and Monaco. Similar extremes can be noticed in the history of particular countries. Spain in the sixteenth and seventeenth centuries was one of the main active participants in the struggle for power on the international scene, but plays today only a marginal role in it. The same is true of such countries as Austria, Sweden, and Switzerland. On the other hand, nations like the United States, the Soviet Union, and China are today much more deeply involved in international politics than they were fifty or even twenty years ago. In short, the relation of nations to international politics has a dynamic quality. It changes with the vicissitudes of power, which may push a nation into the forefront of the power struggle, or may deprive a nation of the ability to participate actively in it. It may also change under the impact of cultural transformations, which may make a nation prefer other pursuits, for instance commerce, to those of power. The tendency of countries to be involved to a greater or lesser extent in the struggle for power prompted Arnold Wolfers to observe that they occupied positions at opposite extremes of a spectrum extending from what he called the pole of power to the pole of indifference.

Its Nature: Four Distinctions

When we speak of power in the context of this book, we have in mind not man's power over nature, or over an artistic medium, such as language, speech, sound, or color, or over the means of production or consumption, or over himself in the sense of self-control. When we speak of power, we mean man's control over the minds and actions of other men. By political power we refer to the mutual relations of control among the holders of public authority and between the latter and the people at large.

Political power is a psychological relation between those who exercise it and those over whom it is exercised. It gives the former control over certain actions of the latter through the impact which the former exert on the latter's minds. That impact derives from three sources: the expectation of benefits, the fear of disadvantages, the respect or love for men or institutions. It may be exerted through orders, threats, the authority or charisma of a man or of an office, or a combination of any of these.

In view of this definition, four distinctions must be made: between power and influence, between power and force, between usable and unusable power, between legitimate and illegitimate power.

The Secretary of State who advises the President of the United States on the conduct of American foreign policy has influence if the President follows his advice. But he has no power over the President; for he has none of the means at his disposal with which to impose his will upon that of the President. He can persuade but he cannot compel. The President, on the other hand, has power over the Secretary of State; for he can impose his will upon the latter by virtue of the authority of his office, the promise of benefits, and the threat of disadvantages.

Political power must be distinguished from force in the sense of the actual exercise of physical violence. The threat of physical violence in the form of police action, imprisonment, capital punishment, or war is an intrinsic element of politics. When violence becomes an actuality, it signifies the abdication of political power in favor of military or pseudo-military power. In international politics in particular, armed strength as a threat or a potentiality is the most important material factor making for the political power of a nation. If it becomes an actuality in war, it signifies the substitution of military for political power. The actual exercise of physical violence substitutes for the psychological relation between two minds, which is of the essence of political power, the physical relation between two bodies, one of which is strong enough to dominate the other's movements. It is for this reason that in the exercise of physical violence the psychological element of the political relationship is lost, and that we must distinguish between military and political power.

The availability of nuclear weapons makes it necessary to distinguish between usable and unusable power. It is one of the paradoxes of the nuclear age that, in contrast to the experience of all of prenuclear history, an increase in military power is no longer necessarily conducive to an increase in political power. The threat of all-out nuclear violence implies the threat of total destruction. As such, it can still be a suitable instrument of foreign policy when addressed to a nation which cannot reply in kind. The nation armed with nuclear weapons can assert power over the other nation by saying: Either you do as I say, or I will destroy you. The situation is different if the nation so threatened can respond by saying: If you destroy me with nuclear weapons, you will be destroyed in turn. Here the mutual threats cancel each other out. Since the nuclear destruction of one nation would call forth the nuclear destruction of the other, both nations can afford to disregard the threat on the assumption that both will act rationally.

It is only on the assumption that the nations concerned might act irrationally by destroying each other in an all-out nuclear war that the threat of nuclear war is credible and has indeed been used by the United States and the Soviet Union against each other, for instance by the Soviet Union during the Suez

Crisis of 1956, by the United States during the Berlin Crisis of 1961, and by both during the Arab-Israeli War of 1973. Yet while here the threat of force can be used as a rational instrument of foreign policy, the actual use of that force remains irrational; for the threatened force would be used not for the political purpose of influencing the will of the other side but for the irrational purpose of destroying the other side with the attendant assurance of one's own destruction.

Thus the magnitude of its destructiveness, as compared with the limited character of the political purposes which are the proper object of foreign policy, renders nuclear force unusable as an instrument of foreign policy. It can be rational under certain conditions to threaten the other side with destruction through the use of nuclear force in order to change the other side's will; it would be irrational to actually destroy the other side, thereby inviting one's own destruction. In contrast, conventional force is usable as an instrument of foreign policy; for by inflicting limited damage with commensurate risks to oneself, one can use it indeed as a suitable instrument for changing the other side's will.

Finally, legitimate power, that is, power whose exercise is morally or legally justified, must be distinguished from illegitimate power. Power exercised with moral or legal authority must be distinguished from naked power. The power of the police officer who searches me by virtue of a search warrant is qualitatively different from the power of a robber who performs the same action by virtue of his holding a gun. The distinction is not only philosophically valid but also relevant for the conduct of foreign policy. Legitimate power, which can invoke a moral or legal justification for its exercise, is likely to be more effective than equivalent illegitimate power, which cannot be so justified. That is to say, legitimate power has a better chance to influence the will of its objects than equivalent illegitimate power. Power exercised in self-defense or in the name of the United Nations has a better chance to succeed than equivalent power exercised by an "aggressor" nation or in violation of international law. Political ideologies, as we shall see, serve the purpose of endowing foreign policies with the appearance of legitimacy.

While it is generally recognized that the interplay of the expectation of benefits, the fear of disadvantages, and the respect or love for men or institutions, in ever changing combinations, forms the basis of all domestic politics, the importance of these factors for international politics is less obvious, but no less real. There has been a tendency to reduce political power to the actual application of force or at least to equate it with successful threats of force and with persuasion, to the neglect of charisma. That neglect, as we shall see,[3] accounts in good measure for the neglect of prestige as an independent element in international politics. Yet without taking into account the charisma of a man, such as Napoleon or Hitler, or of an institution, such as the United States government or Constitution, evoking trust and love through which the wills of

---

[3]See Chapter 6.

men submit themselves to the will of such a man or institution, it is impossible to understand certain phenomena of international politics which have been particularly prominent in modern times.

The importance which charismatic leadership and the response to it as love of the subject for the leader has for international politics is clearly revealed in a letter which John Durie, Scotch Presbyterian and worker for Protestant unity, wrote in 1632 to the British Ambassador Thomas Roe, explaining the decline of the power of Gustavus Adolphus of Sweden, then fighting for the Protestant cause in Germany:

> The increase of his authority is the ground of his abode; and love is the ground of his authority; it must be through love; for it cannot be through power; for his power is not in his own subjects but in strangers; not in his money, but in theirs; not in their good will, but in mere necessity as things stand now betwixt him and them; therefore if the necessity be not so urgent as it is; or if any other means be shown by God (who is able to do as much by another man as by him) to avoid this necessity; the money and the power and the assistance which it yieldeth unto him will fall from him and so his authority is lost, and his abode will be no longer: for the Love which was at first is gone . . .[4]

The President of the United States exerts political power over the executive branch of the government so long as his orders are obeyed by the members of that branch. The leader of the party has political power so long as he is able to mold the actions of the members of the party according to his will. We refer to the political power of an industrialist, labor leader, or lobbyist in so far as his preferences influence the actions of public officials. The United States exerts political power over Puerto Rico so long as the laws of the United States are observed by the citizens of that island. When we speak of the political power of the United States in Central America, we have in mind the conformity of the actions of Central American governments with the wishes of the government of the United States.[5] Thus the statement that A has or wants political power over B signifies always that A is able, or wants to be able, to control certain actions of B through influencing B's mind.

Whatever the material objectives of a foreign policy, such as the acquisition of sources of raw materials, the control of sea lanes, or territorial changes, they always entail control of the actions of others through influence over their minds. The Rhine frontier as a century-old objective of French foreign policy points to the political objective to destroy the desire of Germany to attack France by making it physically difficult or impossible for Germany to do so. Great Britain owed its predominant position in world politics throughout the

---

[4]Gunnar Westin, *Negotiations About Church Unity, 1628–1634* (Upsala: Almquist and Wiksells, 1932), p. 208. The spelling has been modernized.

[5]The examples in the text illustrate also the distinction between political power as mere social fact, as in the case of the lobbyist, and political power in the sense of legitimate authority, i.e., of the President of the United States. Both the President of the United States and the lobbyist exercise political power, however different its source and nature may be.

nineteenth century to the calculated policy of making it either too dangerous (because Great Britain was too strong) or unnecessary (because its strength was used with moderation) for other nations to oppose it.

The political objective of military preparations of any kind is to deter other nations from using military force by making it too risky for them to do so. The political aim of military preparations is, in other words, to make the actual application of military force unnecessary by inducing the prospective enemy to desist from the use of military force. The political objective of war itself is not per se the conquest of territory and the annihilation of enemy armies, but a change in the mind of the enemy which will make him yield to the will of the victor.

Therefore, whenever economic, financial, territorial, or military policies are under discussion in international affairs, it is necessary to distinguish between, say, economic policies that are undertaken for their own sake and economic policies that are the instruments of a political policy—a policy, that is, whose economic purpose is but the means to the end of controlling the policies of another nation. The export policy of Switzerland with regard to the United States falls into the first category. The economic policies of the Soviet Union with regard to the nations of Eastern Europe fall into the latter category. So do many economic policies of the United States in Latin America, Asia, and Europe. The distinction is of great practical importance, and the failure to make it has led to much confusion in policy and public opinion.

An economic, financial, territorial, or military policy undertaken for its own sake is subject to evaluation in its own terms. Is it economically or financially advantageous? What effects has acquisition of territory upon the population and economy of the nation acquiring it? What are the consequences of a change in a military policy for education, population, and the domestic political system? The decisions with respect to these policies are made exclusively in terms of such intrinsic considerations.

When, however, the objectives of these policies serve to increase the power of the nation pursuing them with regard to other nations, these policies and their objectives must be judged primarily from the point of view of their contribution to national power. An economic policy that cannot be justified in purely economic terms might nevertheless be undertaken in view of the political policy pursued. The insecure and unprofitable character of a loan to a foreign nation may be a valid argument against it on purely financial grounds. But the argument is irrelevant if the loan, however unwise it may be from a banker's point of view, serves the political policies of the nation. It may of course be that the economic or financial losses involved in such policies will weaken the nation in its international position to such an extent as to outweigh the political advantages to be expected. On these grounds such policies might be rejected. In such a case, what decides the issue is not purely economic and financial considerations but a comparison of the political chances and risks involved; that is, the probable effect of these policies upon the power of the nation.

Example

When the United States has provided loans or assistance to countries such as Poland which lay in the shadow of the Red Army, the purpose was not primarily economic or financial. It was rather to enable such countries to move towards a degree of independence of the influence and power of the Soviet Union. If the repayment of loans to American agencies or financial institutions was postponed with U.S. government approval, this was not for humanitarian or charitable reasons alone. Rather, it has been American policy to keep open certain options for the government of Poland, options which prevent its total dependence on the Soviet Union. Such actions in the economic sphere are based on political objectives which in the long run would assure the survival of Poland as a sovereign state—however much its geographic and political position forced it to accept the position of a satellite within the sphere of the Soviet Union at least for the short run. In a word, the aim of American economic policy toward Poland was to limit Soviet influence and power in Central and Eastern Europe while increasing the leverage of the United States in the area.

THE DEPRECIATION OF POLITICAL POWER

The aspiration for power being the distinguishing element of international politics, as of all politics, international politics is of necessity power politics. While this fact is generally recognized in the practice of international affairs, it is frequently denied in the pronouncements of scholars, publicists, and even statesmen. Since the end of the Napoleonic Wars, ever larger groups in the Western world have been persuaded that the struggle for power on the international scene is a temporary phenomenon, a historical accident that is bound to disappear once the peculiar historic conditions that have given rise to it have been eliminated. Thus Jeremy Bentham believed that the competition for colonies was at the root of all international conflicts. "Emancipate your colonies!" was his advice to the governments, and international conflict and war would of necessity disappear.[6] Adherents of free trade, such as Cobden[7] and Proudhon[8], were convinced that the removal of trade barriers was the only condition for the establishment of permanent harmony among nations, and might even lead to the disappearance of international politics altogether. "At some future election," said Cobden, "we may probably see the test 'no foreign

---

[6]*Emancipate Your Colonies* (London: Robert Heward, 1830).

[7]"Free Trade! What is it? Why, breaking down the barriers that separate nations; those barriers, behind which nestle the feelings of pride, revenge, hatred, and jealousy, which every now and then burst their bounds, and deluge whole countries with blood." "Free trade is the international law of the Almighty," and free trade and peace seem to be "one and the same cause." See *Speeches by Richard Cobden* (London: Macmillan & Company, 1870), Vol. I, p. 79; *Political Writings* (New York: D. Appleton and Company, 1867), Vol. II, p. 110; letter of April 12, 1842, to Henry Ashworth, quoted in John Morley, *Life of Richard Cobden* (Boston: Roberts Brothers, 1881), p. 154.

[8]"Let us suppress the tariffs, and the alliance of the peoples will thus be declared, their solidarity recognized, their equality proclaimed." *Oeuvres complètes* (Paris, 1867), Vol. I, p. 248.

politics' applied to those who offer to become the representatives of free constituencies."[9] For Marx and his followers, capitalism is at the root of international discord and war. They maintain that international socialism will do away with the struggle for power on the international scene and will bring about permanent peace. During the nineteenth century, liberals everywhere shared the conviction that power politics and war were residues of an obsolete system of government, and that the victory of democracy and constitutional government over absolutism and autocracy would assure the victory of international harmony and permanent peace over power politics and war. Of this liberal school of thought, Woodrow Wilson was the most eloquent and most influential spokesman.

In recent times, the conviction that the struggle for power can be eliminated from the international scene has been connected with the great attempts at organizing the world, such as the League of Nations and the United Nations. Thus Cordell Hull, then U.S. Secretary of State, declared in 1943 on his return from the Moscow Conference, which laid the groundwork for the United Nations, that the new international organization would mean the end of power politics and usher in a new era of international collaboration.[10] Mr. Philip Noel-Baker, then British Minister of State, declared in 1946 in the House of Commons that the British government was "determined to use the institutions of the United Nations to kill power politics, in order that, by the methods of democracy, the will of the people shall prevail."[11]

While we shall have more to say later about these theories and the expectations derived from them,[12] it is sufficient to state that the struggle for power is universal in time and space and is an undeniable fact of experience. It cannot be denied that throughout historic time, regardless of social, economic, and political conditions, states have met each other in contests for power. Even though anthropologists have shown that certain primitive peoples seem to be free from the desire for power, nobody has yet shown how their state of mind and the conditions under which they live can be recreated on a worldwide scale so as to eliminate the struggle for power from the international scene.[13] It would be useless and even self-destructive to free one or the other of the peoples of the earth from the desire for power while leaving it extant in others. If the desire for power cannot be abolished everywhere in the world, those who might be cured would simply fall victims to the power of others.

The position taken here might be criticized on the ground that conclusions drawn from the past are unconvincing, and that to draw such conclusions has always been the main stock in trade of the enemies of progress and reform. Though it is true that certain social arrangements and institutions have always

---

[9]Quoted in A. C. F. Beales, *A Short History of English Liberalism*, p. 195.

[10]*New York Times*, November 19, 1943, p. 1.

[11]*House of Commons Debates* (Fifth Series, 1946), Vol. 419, p. 1262.

[12]See Part Eight.

[13]For an illuminating discussion of this problem, see Malcolm Sharp, "Aggression: A Study of Values and Law," *Ethics*, Vol. 57, No. 4, Part II (July 1947).

existed in the past, it does not necessarily follow that they must always exist in the future. The situation is, however, different when we deal not with social arrangements and institutions created by man, but with those elemental bio-psychological drives by which in turn society is created. The drives to live, to propagate, and to dominate are common to all men.[14] Their relative strength is dependent upon social conditions that may favor one drive and tend to repress another, or that may withhold social approval from certain manifestations of these drives while they encourage others. Thus, to take examples only from the sphere of power, most societies condemn killing as a means of attaining power within society, but all societies encourage the killing of enemies in that struggle for power which is called war. Dictators look askance at the aspirations for political power among their fellow citizens, but democracies consider active participation in the competition for political power a civic duty. Where a monopolistic organization of economic activities exists, competition for economic power is absent, and in competitive economic systems certain manifestations of the struggle for economic power are outlawed, while others are encouraged. Ostrogorsky, invoking the authority of Tocqueville, states that "the passions of the American people are not of a political, but of a commercial, nature. In that world awaiting cultivation, the love of power aims less at men than at things."[15]

Regardless of particular social conditions, the decisive argument against the opinion that the struggle for power on the international scene is a mere historic accident must be derived from the nature of domestic politics. The essence of international politics is identical with its domestic counterpart. Both domestic and international politics are a struggle for power, modified only by the different conditions under which this struggle takes place in the domestic and in the international spheres.

The tendency to dominate, in particular, is an element of all human associations, from the family through fraternal and professional associations and local political organizations, to the state. On the family level, the typical conflict between the mother-in-law and her child's spouse is in its essence a struggle for power, the defense of an established power position against the attempt to establish a new one. As such it foreshadows the conflict on the international scene between the policies of the status quo and the policies of imperialism. Social clubs, fraternities, faculties, and business organizations are scenes of continuous struggles for power between groups that either want to keep what power they already have or seek to attain greater power. Competitive contests between business enterprises as well as labor disputes between

---

[14]Zoologists have tried to show that the drive to dominate is found even in animals, such as chickens and monkeys, who create social hierarchies on the basis of will and the ability to dominate. See e.g., Warder Allee, *Animal Life and Social Growth* (Baltimore: The Williams and Wilkens Company, 1932), and *The Social Life of Animals* (New York: W. W. Norton and Company, Inc., 1938). Cf. also the theories of Konrad Lorenz and the controversies concerning them.

[15]M. Ostrogorsky, *Democracy and the Organization of Political Parties* (New York: The Macmillan Company, 1902), Vol. II, p. 592.

employers and employees are frequently fought not only, and sometimes not even primarily, for economic advantages, but for control over each other and over others; that is, for power. Finally, the whole political life of a nation, particularly of a democratic nation, from the local to the national level, is a continuous struggle for power. In periodic elections, in voting in legislative assemblies, in lawsuits before courts, in administrative decisions and executive measures—in all these activities men try to maintain or to establish their power over other men. The processes by which legislative, judicial, executive, and administrative decisions are reached are subject to pressures and counterpressures by "pressure groups" trying to defend and expand their positions of power. As one of the Dead Sea scrolls puts it:

> What nation likes to be oppressed by a stronger power? Or who wants his property plundered unjustly? Yet, is there a single nation that has not oppressed its neighbour? Or where in the world will you find a people that has not plundered the property of another? Where indeed?

"Of the gods we know," to quote Thucydides, "and of men we believe, that it is a necessary law of their nature that they rule wherever they can."[16] Or, as Tolstoy put it: ". . . the very process of dominating another's will was in itself a pleasure, a habit, and a necessity to Dólokhov."[17]

And in the words of John of Salisbury:

> Though it is not given to all men to seize princely or royal power, yet the man who is wholly untainted by tyranny is rare or nonexistent. In common speech the tyrant is one who oppresses a whole people by a rulership based on force; and yet it is not over a people as a whole that a man can play the tyrant, but he can do so if he will even in the meanest station. For if not over the whole body of the people, still each man will lord it as far as his power extends.[18]

In view of this ubiquity of the struggle for power in all social relations and on all levels of social organization, is it surprising that international politics is of necessity power politics? And would it not be rather surprising if the struggle for power were but an accidental and ephemeral attribute of international politics when it is a permanent and necessary element of all branches of domestic politics?

TWO ROOTS OF THE DEPRECIATION OF POLITICAL POWER

The depreciation of the role power plays on the international scene grows from two roots. One is the philosophy of international relations which dominated the

---

[16]Thucydides, Book V, § 105.

[17]Leo Tolstoy, *War and Peace*, Book Eight, Chapter XI.

[18]John of Salisbury, *Policraticus*, translated by John Dickinson (New York: Alfred A. Knopf, 1927), Vol. VII, p. 17.

better part of the nineteenth century and still holds sway over much of our thinking on international affairs. The other is the particular political and intellectual circumstances that have determined the relations of the United States of America to the rest of the world.

Nineteenth-Century Philosophy

The nineteenth century was led to its depreciation of power politics by its domestic experience. The distinctive characteristic of this experience was the domination of the middle classes by the aristocracy. By identifying this domination with political domination of any kind, the political philosophy of the nineteenth century came to identify the opposition to aristocratic politics with hostility to any kind of politics. After the defeat of aristocratic government, the middle classes developed a system of indirect domination. They replaced the traditional division into the governing and governed classes, and the military method of open violence, characteristic of aristocratic rule, with the invisible chains of economic dependence. This economic system operated through a network of seemingly egalitarian legal rules which concealed the very existence of power relations. The nineteenth century was unable to see the political nature of these legalized relations. They seemed to be essentially different from what had gone, so far, under the name of politics. Therefore, politics in its aristocratic—that is, open and violent—form was identified with politics as such. The struggle, then, for political power—in domestic as well as in international affairs—appeared to be only a historic accident, coincident with autocratic government and bound to disappear with the disappearance of autocratic government.

The American Experience

This identification of power politics with aristocratic government found support in the American experience. It can be traced to three elements in that experience: the uniqueness of the American experiment, the actual isolation of the American continent from centers of the world conflict during the nineteenth century, and the humanitarian pacifism and anti-imperialism of American political ideology.

That the severance of constitutional ties with the British Crown was meant to signify the initiation of an American foreign policy distinct from what went under the name of foreign policy in Europe is clearly stated in Washington's Farewell Address. "Europe has a set of primary interests, which to us have none, or a very remote relation. Hence she must be engaged in frequent controversies, the causes of which are essentially foreign to our concerns. Hence, therefore, it must be unwise in us to implicate ourselves, by artificial ties, in the ordinary vicissitudes of her politics, or the ordinary combinations and collisions of her friendships or enmities." In 1796, European politics and power politics were identical; there was no other power politics but the one engaged in by the princes of Europe. "The toils of European ambition, rival-ship, interest, humor or caprice" were the only manifestations of the interna-tional struggle for power before the eyes of America. The retreat from Euro-pean politics, as proclaimed by Washington, could, therefore, be taken to mean retreat from power politics as such.

Yet American aloofness from the European tradition of power politics was more than a political program. Certain sporadic exceptions notwithstanding, it was an established political fact until the end of the nineteenth century. This fact was a result of deliberate choice as well as of the objective conditions of geography. Popular writers might see in the uniqueness of America's geo-graphic position the hand of God which had unalterably prescribed the course of American expansion as well as isolation. But more responsible observers, from Washington on, have been careful to emphasize the conjunction of geo-graphic conditions and a foreign policy choosing its ends in the light of geogra-phy, using geographic conditions to attain those ends. Washington referred to "our detached and distant situation" and asked: "Why forego the advantages of so peculiar a situation?" When this period of American foreign policy drew to a close, John Bright wrote to Alfred Love: "On your continent we may hope your growing millions may henceforth know nothing of war. None can assail you; and you are anxious to abstain from mingling with the quarrels of other nations."[19]

From the shores of the North American continent, the citizens of the new world watched the strange spectacle of the international struggle for power unfolding on the distant shores of Europe, Africa, and Asia. Since for the better part of the nineteenth century their foreign policy enabled them to retain the role of spectators, what was actually the result of a passing historic constellation appeared to Americans as a permanent condition, self-chosen as well as natu-rally ordained. At worst they would continue to watch the game of power politics played by others. At best the time was close at hand when, with democracy established everywhere, the final curtain would fall and the game of power politics would no longer be played.

To aid in the achievement of this goal was conceived to be part of Amer-ica's mission. Throughout the nation's history, the national destiny of the United States has been understood in antimilitaristic, libertarian terms. Where that national mission finds a nonaggressive, abstentionist formulation, as in the political philosophy of John C. Calhoun, it is conceived as the promotion of domestic liberty. Thus we may "do more to extend liberty by our example over this continent and the world generally, than would be done by a thousand victories." When the United States, in the wake of the Spanish-American War, seemed to desert this anti-imperialist and democratic ideal, William Graham Sumner restated its essence: "Expansion and imperialism are a grand onslaught on democracy . . . expansion and imperialism are at war with the best traditions,

---

[19]Quoted in Merle Curti, *Peace and War: The American Struggle 1636–1936* (New York: W. W. Norton and Company, 1936), p. 122.

principles, and interests of the American people."[20] Comparing the tendencies of European power politics with the ideals of the American tradition, Sumner thought with George Washington that they were incompatible. Yet, as a prophet of things to come, he saw that the settlement of the Spanish-American War irrevocably committed America to the same course that was engulfing Europe in revolution and war.

Thus the general conception the nineteenth century had formed of the nature of foreign affairs combined with specific elements in the American experience to create the belief that involvement in power politics is not inevitable, but only a historic accident, and that nations have a choice between power politics and other kinds of foreign policy not tainted by the desire for power.

THE SCIENCE OF PEACE:
CONTEMPORARY UTOPIANISM

A word should be said about a school of thought—still influential in political and intellectual circles today—which proffers a "scientific" alternative to the "perennial wisdom" of a rationalist approach to international politics. This school of thought we may call "scientific utopianism" for lack of a better term; like the sources of self-deception as to the persistence of political power discussed above, the scientific interpretation has strong roots in nineteenth-century experience, both in Europe and in America. In this case, however, neither the relations of class domination nor geographical accident gave rise to utopian hopes for a "science of peace." Instead, the fantastic progress of the natural sciences led various thinkers to assume that the same kinds of methods, applied to individual and collective human behavior, could yield progress toward what Herbert Marcuse and others have called "the pacification of human existence."

The modern science of peace starts from the assumption that the world is thoroughly accessible to science and reason and that it contains in itself all the elements necessary for the harmonious co-operation of all mankind. It is for science to detect those elements, variously defined as harmony of interests, laws of economics, free trade, and modern communications; it is for law to apply them where they do not prevail spontaneously; and it is for negotiation and compromise to discover them under the surface of apparent conflict.

For such rationalism, it is the atavism of power politics that conceals and distorts the harmony of interests which is the true nature of international relations. Adam Smith, a founding father of classical liberalism as well as of classical economics, discovered such a fundamental harmony of interests lying beneath the surface manifestations of self-regarding, competitive economic behavior. Selfish pursuits led to greater wealth for all through the workings of an "invisible hand." Governed by an inner logic, the free market operates to

---

[20]"The Conquest of the United States by Spain," *Essays of William Graham Sumner* (New Haven: Yale University Press, 1940), Vol. II, p. 295.

dispose all for the best. Nineteenth-century liberalism had no use for even such residual traces of the miraculous in its search for a means to establish harmonious relations among states. Only strictly rational principles would do: all international conflicts were considered capable of satisfactory solutions, either through compromise or arbitration. Since all men partake of reason, they must sooner or later meet on that common ground, discovering that their conflicts are apparent rather than real and can all be solved by a rational formula acceptable to all. Were all nations at all times fully aware of their real interests, they would realize that apparently opposing interests are actually identical, that what is good for one country is of necessity good for all other countries, and that conflict is merely the product of ignorance and error.

Conflicts among nations are due, then, to maladjustments arising from lack of understanding and to the influence of political passions. Except for ignorance and emotion, reason would solve international conflicts as easily and as rationally as it has solved so many problems in the natural sciences. Proudhon was among the first to glorify the blessings of science in the international field.

> Truth is everywhere identical with itself: science represents the unity of mankind. If therefore science, instead of religion or authority, is taken in each country as social norm, the sovereign arbiter of interests, with the government amounting to nothing, all the laws of the universe will be in harmony. Nationality or fatherland will no longer exist in the political meaning of the term; there will only be birthplaces. Man, of whatever race or colour he may be, will actually be a native of the Universe; the right of citizenship he will acquire everywhere. In the same way in which in a certain district of the national territory the municipality represents the nation and exercises its authority, each nation of the globe will represent humanity and in its natural boundaries act for it. Harmony will reign among the nations, without diplomacy nor council; nothing shall from now on disturb it.[21]

"The duty of the pacifist," according to C.E.M. Joad, "is above all things to be reasonable. He should, that is to say, rely on the use of his own reason in making his appeal and he should assume that other men may be brought to use theirs. . . . Truth, in fact, will win out, if people are only given a sufficient chance to find it."[22] It was with the same confidence in the power of reason that Clarence Streit asserted in 1941 that "the really big men in the United States Senate and British Parliament will champion the Union [of the two countries], once they understand it."[23]

Political history, then, becomes a succession of scientific problems capable of scientific solution—but most unreasonably handled by an ignorant and impassioned humanity. Even for so realistic an observer as Homer Lea, the problem of international affairs resolved itself into a problem of knowledge; if

---

[21]"Idée générale de la révolution au dix-neuvième siècle," *Oeuvres complètes*, IX (1868), p. 300; see also Proudhon, *La Guerre et la paix* (Paris: E. Dentu, 1861).

[22]"Pacifism: Its Personal and Social Implications," in G. P. Gooch, *In Pursuit of Peace* (London: Methuen & Company, Ltd., 1933), pp. 61, 63.

[23]*Union Now With Britain* (New York: Harper & Brothers, 1941), p. 197.

the "valour of ignorance" is replaced by the knowledge of the pertinent facts, man will be able to act successfully on the international scene. "The time can and will come," wrote the famous pacifist Bertha von Suttner, "when the science of politics will have replaced present day statecraft, when only those will have legislative and political power . . . who sincerely seek only the truth and through the truth strive to attain only the good—the universal good comprehending all civilized nations."

The time Suttner spoke of has already arrived as far as the mere possession of knowledge is concerned, according to Robert S. Lynd. "The diagnosis," he wrote,

> is already fairly complete, thanks to a long list of competent studies of nationalism, imperialism, international finance and trade, and other factors within our culture that encourage war. The problem of war, more than most others, has engaged the attention of scientists from several disciplines, and the dissection has proceeded to the point where fairly unequivocal knowledge exists. The causes of war are known and accepted by a wide group of thoughtful students. But the statement of what is to be done languishes because social science shrinks from resolving the austere findings of scholarly monographs into a bold programme for action. . . . In the case of an issue like this, where the problem does not arise from lack of knowledge, what social science appears to need is the will to mass its findings so that the truth they hold will not continue to trickle away as disparate bits of scholarship. We know enough about war and its causes to present these findings, point their meanings, and propose action in a way that will hold this damaging evidence steadily and authoritatively before the eyes of the humblest citizen.[24]

It was for this age of reason to replace the old methods of power politics, secret diplomacy and war by a new, scientific approach. Territorial claims, sovereignty over national minorities, the distribution of raw materials, the struggle for markets, disarmament, the relation between the "haves" and the "have-nots," peaceful change, and the peaceful organization of the world in general—these are not "political" problems, to be solved temporarily and always precariously according to the distribution of power among quarrelling nations and its possible balance. They are "technical" problems for which reason will find the one correct solution in each case.

Thus the nineteenth century developed a "science of peace" as a separate branch of scientific knowledge. Scores of books were published bearing this title. One even received first prize in a scholarly competition.[25] The concept of a "natural frontier"—which had had a strategical and political, but not a scientific, connotation in the sixteenth and seventeenth centuries—was construed by the French revolutionaries and Napoleon in the sense of a geographically "correct" frontier. In the seventies and eighties of the nineteenth century, public opinion in Great Britain discussed seriously the problem of the "scientific frontier," that is, a frontier which corresponds to reason, and which,

---

[24]*Knowledge for What?* (Princeton: Princeton University Press, 1939), p. 241.
[25]Louis Bara, *La Science de la paix* (1872).

consequently, makes all other frontiers in this geographical region scientifically incorrect. In his speech at Mansion House on November 9, 1878, Disraeli justified the Second Afghan War by saying that the frontier of India was "a haphazard and not a scientific one."

The search for such a "scientific" frontier started in the second half of the eighteenth century when, on the occasion of partitions and annexations of territory, the relative value of the pieces of territory to be distributed was determined on the basis of certain "objective" standards, such as fertility, number and quality of population, and the like. Following this trend, the Congress of Vienna, upon the suggestion of Metternich, appointed a special statistical commission; it was charged with evaluating the territories under discussion by the "objective" standard of number, quality, and type of populations.[26] The delimitation of territory thus became a kind of mathematical exercise. The idea of the "good frontier," developed in the last decades of the nineteenth century in Germany with regard to Russia's territorial aspirations, had a somewhat similar connotation. The idea of the "scientific tariff" attempted to introduce science into foreign trade, building in part upon ideas put forth in the early nineteenth century by Friedrich List. The theory and practice of international plebiscites are also typical manifestations of the rationalist approach to international problems; here the will of the majority is the scientific test according to which sovereignty over territory is to be determined. In the thirties, Major Lefebure advanced his theories on "scientific disarmament." "Geopolitics" endeavoured to put foreign policy as a whole on a scientific basis.

It was only after the First World War that this tendency to reduce political problems to scientific propositions won general acceptance. "Reason is at last becoming an independent agency," wrote Lord Allen of Hartwood, "influencing the conduct of men. This is due to the coming of science. . . . Feeling himself now to be the master of nature, his mind is beginning to work rationally instead of superstitiously. When forming an opinion he observes the phenomena around him and draws his conclusions. From that moment mind begins to be an independent agency of influence. It can now therefore be considered as a political force, whereas that has never previously been possible in the history of civilization. During the last thirty years this has begun to influence public opinion."[27]

Thus began what can properly be called the age of the scientific approach to international affairs, and the end is not yet in sight. Preceded by the Hague Conferences and hundreds of smaller peace congresses, governments themselves embarked on a program of feverish activity unprecedented in recorded history, with the purpose of solving all international problems through scientific methods. The governments, the League of Nations, and private groups vied with each other in organizing international conferences, in encouraging teach-

---

[26]For details see Charles Dupuis, *Le Principe d'équilibre et le Concert Européen* (Paris: Perrin et Cie, 1909), pp. 38ff, 60 ff.

[27]"Pacifism: Its Meaning and Its Task," in Gooch, *op. cit.*, pp. 22, 23.

ing and research, and in publishing hundreds of volumes to cure the ills of humanity in a scientific way. We have recently witnessed widespread efforts to find a scientific solution for the problems of the postwar world. These are the latest, but probably not the last, manifestation of this modern intellectual trend.[28]

Our age is forever searching for the philosophers' stone, the magic formula, which, mechanically applied, will produce the desired result and thus substitute for the uncertainties and risks of political action the certitude of rational calculation. However, what the seekers after the magic formula want is simple, rational, mechanical; what they have to deal with is complicated, irrational, incalculable. As a consequence they are compelled, in order to present at least the semblance of scientific solutions, to simplify the reality of international politics and to rely upon what one might call the "method of the single cause."

The abolition of war is obviously the fundamental problem confronting international thought. To solve the problem one must clearly first determine its cause or causes. What makes a solution appear so difficult for the nonrationalist mind is the *variety* of causes involved—causes which have their roots in the innermost recesses of the human heart. Were it possible to reduce all those multiple, complex factors to a single cause—one capable of rational formulation—the solution of the problem of war would no longer seem impossible. This is what liberal foreign policy has been trying to do since its very inception; and since the heyday of the League of Nations most people would take it for lack of creative thought if a statesman or political thinker did not have a "constructive" plan as a remedy for the "single cause."

Are not the remnants of feudalism the great single cause making for war in this world? Let us do away with aristocratic government everywhere, the classical liberals would say, and we will have peace. In practical politics this general proposition was frequently narrowed down to more special remedies intended to meet particular situations. Thus, as we have seen, Bentham and the Benthamites pointed to the struggle for colonies as the main cause for war; they advocated abstention from colonial policy as a remedy for war. For others, tariffs were the source of all evils in the international sphere; to them, free trade was the source of all good. Others would abolish secret treaties and secret diplomacy in general and, through popular control of international policies,

---

[28]Cf. Charles A. Beard, *A Foreign Policy for America* (New York: Alfred A. Knopf, 1940), pp. 98–99: "In line with the new interests, the study of international law and diplomacy was encouraged in institutions of learning. Old-fashioned courses on diplomacy—cold, scholarly performances—were supplemented by courses on international relations, in which emphasis was laid on world peace and the means of promoting it. Books, pamphlets, and articles on pacification were written, published and widely circulated, often with the aid of subventions from peace funds. International peace conferences were organized and provided opportunities for travel and extended discourses. Seldom had college presidents, professors, clergymen, and leaders among women enjoyed such privileges and received such marked consideration at the hands of the general public. It looked as if a new era of usefulness and distinction had been opened for them in the field of great affairs, and they made the most of its opportunities."

secure peace. Is not modern war an outgrowth of imperialism which, in turn, is a result of the contradictions of monopoly capitalism? Hence, let us do away with capitalism, the Marxists would say, and we will no longer have war: socialism is peace.

The same one-track mode of thought is found also in domestic politics. All social evils stem from our ignorance of the laws of economics: the "single tax" takes account of those laws and will solve all social problems. Our economic system is out of joint because the government spends more than it collects: balance the budget and our economic problems will be solved. Bad linguistic habits are at the root of our social evils: with the acquisition of good linguistic habits our social problems will be solved. Emerson, in "New England Reformers," thus described this kind of thinking:

> One apostle thought all men should go to farming; and another, that no man should buy or sell; that the use of money was the cardinal evil; another, that the mischief was in our diet, that we eat and drink damnation. These made unleavened bread, and were foes to the death to fermentation. . . . Others attacked the system of agriculture; the use of animal manures in farming; and the tyranny of man over brute nature; these abuses polluted his food. . . . Even the insect world was to be defended,—that had been too long neglected, and a society for the protection of ground worms, slugs, and mosquitoes was to be incorporated without delay. With these appeared the adepts of homeopathy; of hydropathy, of mesmerism, of phrenology, and their wonderful theories of the Christian miracles! Others assailed particular vocations, as that of the lawyer, that of the merchant, of the manufacturer, of the clergyman, of the scholar. Others attacked the institution of marriage as the fountain of social evils. Others devoted themselves to the worrying of churches and meetings for public worship; and the fertile forms of antinomianism among the elder puritans, seemed to have their match in the plenty of the new harvest of reform.[29]

In the domestic field, however, the "method of the single cause" has been of rather limited theoretical and practical importance; for here, except in periods of collective insanity, immediate personal experience reveals the absurdity of the approach; and the pressure of the affected interests prevents the quack from being mistaken for the saviour.

The utopian internationalist, on the other hand, has no direct contact with the international scene. His thought, if it is sufficiently general, can roam over the globe without ever risking collision with the stark facts of politics. He who would proclaim the Four Freedoms for the United States itself would soon learn from personal experience the enormity of the social and political problems entailed by any attempt at realizing those great principles. By contrast, proclamation of the Four Freedoms "everywhere in the world" is sufficiently general to avoid contact with historic realities and political facts.

The reformer without responsibility finds in the armory of modern international thought what he is looking for. That one panacea is frequently inconsist-

---

[29] Ralph Waldo Emerson, *Essays: Second Series* (Boston: Houghton Mifflin, 1899), pp. 204–205.

ent with another need not trouble him. For since the "single cause" is an arbitrary abstraction from a multitude of actual causes, one abstraction and, hence, one "single cause" is as good as the next one. Since, furthermore, the hunt for the "single cause" derives from a vague desire to contribute something to the betterment of human affairs rather than from a fixed resolve to intervene in a definite political situation in a definite way, virtually any general explanation of the ills of the world and any general plan to remedy them will satisfy the psychic need involved.

Hence, the great hunting ground for the "single cause" and the "scientific formula" to remedy it has been the international scene, while their great season was the two decades between the world wars.[30] International society is not organized; thus "international organization"—in its abstract rationality a kind of legal counterpart to the utopian systems of eighteenth- and nineteenth-century philosophy—became the scientific formula which, since the leading pacifist and Nobel Prize winner, A. H. Fried, propounded it at the beginning of the century, has been the credo of a whole school of thought. Others would look to material remedies. Are not wars being fought with arms? Let us prohibit or at least reduce armaments, and war will no longer be possible or at least will be less likely. Others, again, would combine different remedies, defending the combination—"on scientific grounds"—as the only appropriate one. Thus the French Radical-Socialist party advocated "security, arbitration, disarmament" as logical successive steps for the establishment of permanent peace; whereas the French Socialists reversed the sequence and swore to the exclusive scientific value of the formula "security through arbitration and disarmament." French foreign policy has been especially productive in abstract schemes which, like the "plan Briand," the "plan Laval," the "plan Tardieux," the "plan Herriot," or the "plan Paul-Boncour," pretended to give in one legal formula a scientific solution to the problems of European security.

In other quarters, especially since the crisis of 1929, the "single cause" of international unrest has been found in the economic field. Restrictions on international trade, the lack of raw materials, and insufficient international purchasing power drive nations to war, so the argument ran. Then let us find a scientific formula for reciprocal trade agreements, for the redistribution of raw materials, and for the floating of international loans—and there will be peace. Faced by the imperialistic aspirations of the thirties, it was reasoned that whenever nations cannot change the status quo peacefully, they will try to change it by war; thus peaceful change, scientifically defined, would make war unnecessary. Since bankers' fears for their investments was responsible for our involvement in the First World War, let us outlaw loans to belligerents: we shall thus escape participation in the next one. More recently, it has been "discovered" that national sovereignty is responsible for war; it follows that the pooling of national sovereignties in a world federation or at least in a federation

---

[30]See Kenneth W. Thompson, *Ethics, Functionalism and Power in International Politics: The Crisis in Values* (Baton Rouge, Louisiana: Louisiana University Press, 1979), pp. 35–45.

of the democracies is a scientific solution to the problem of war and peace. Thus our era is always in search of the scientific formula, but an obstinate reality again and again makes the solution of today the fallacy of tomorrow.

The "scientific" era of international relations resulted in the substitution of supposedly scientific standards for genuine political evaluations; in some cases this went so far as to impede, if not entirely destroy, the ability to make any intelligent political decisions at all. Power, however limited and qualified, is the value which international politics recognizes as supreme. The test to which international political decisions must be subject refers, therefore, to the measure in which those decisions affect the distribution of power. The question which Richelieu, Hamilton (no less than Jefferson, for that matter), or Disraeli would ask before they acted on the international scene was: Does this decision increase or decrease the power of this and other nations? The question of the international "scientist" is different. Since for him the history of international affairs amounts to a succession of scientific problems, correctly or incorrectly handled by informed or misinformed officials, the supreme value is not power but truth. The quest for and the defense of power then become aberrations from the scientific attitude, which looks for causes and remedies. If we do not like the way things are, let us look for its cause and change things by changing the cause. There is essentially nothing to fight for; there is always something to analyze, to understand, and to reform.

How was it possible for the modern mind to make the belief in the all-embracing powers of science the *controlling force* of its foreign policy? Here again, the answer is to be found in the general premises of rationalistic philosophy, seemingly verified in its universal assumptions by domestic experience. The victory of liberalism in the domestic field led to a peculiar narrowing of the political, and a corresponding widening of the nonpolitical, sphere; and thus the latter was open to detached rational examination. Objectives which formerly had been seen as the prize in the struggle for political power were now approached in a dispassionate, matter-of-fact way and mastered in accordance with the specific techniques of economics, administration, or law. First the natural sciences and religion had freed themselves from political domination and had established their autonomy. Then liberalism, by conquering the state, freed an ever increasing domain from direct political domination; finally, liberalism seemed to expel even politics from the realm of the state and to make statecraft itself a science. Commerce and industry were the first to win their autonomy under reason. That which for the physiocrats was still a political program, unsuccessfully suggested to the political powers of the day, was for Adam Smith already a system of scientific truths verified by experience, the practical implications of which no reasonable man could escape. Political tribunals were replaced by independent courts composed of judges trained to render justice according to the principles of legal science. Antiquated and arbitrary election systems favoring certain political groups made way for scientific devices which would secure full and equal representation for all citizens. The civil service system put the selection of government personnel on an objective, nonpolitical basis. Today, legislative reforms are increasingly prepared by committees of experts who seem to be influenced largely by scientific instead of political considerations. Taxation, administration, and insurance become "scientific" in approach; and, finally, there is no field of governmental activity which would not be regarded as a proper area for the application of "political science."

The use of the scientific method in politics, to which the modern mind was led by its perception of the liberal experience, was and is a political fallacy in domestic affairs. There, however, the refined mechanism of political pressure and self-interest serves as an automatic check on doctrinaire excess. In the international field such a mechanism, acting directly upon the individual, does not exist. It is here, therefore, that the belief in the limitless power of the scientific formula has become particularly prolific—and particularly ineffective. For it is here that the panaceas engendered by this belief have no connection whatsoever with the forces which determine the actual course of events. Events will, therefore, either follow their course as though all those proposals by international commissions of experts and other rationalist-utopian devices had never been invented. Or those devices will be applied in an exceptional instance and will then produce effects unforeseen by their promoters and frequently disastrous to them—such as the sanctions against Italy during the Italo-Ethiopian war. Yet, as a supreme irony, this school of thought attempts to monopolize for itself the virtue of being "practical"; it treats with disdain the rare attempts to base international action on a genuine understanding of the forces determining political reality rather than on the ideal postulates of abstract reason.[31]

---

[31]As far back as 1877 James Lorimer could write in "Le problème final du droit international," *Revue du droit international et de legislation comparée*, IX (1877), p. 184: "Strangely enough, however, these speculations of English utilitarianism, taken as a whole, are of all the dissertations on the subject I know the least useful from the practical point of view." Cf. also Beard, *op. cit.*, p. 129: "Nearly every evil that was inconceivable in internationalist ideology in 1919 came to pass within the span of twenty years. It would seem then that this scheme of thought had been based upon some misconceptions respecting the nature and propensities of men and nations or, if this explanation is invalid, that internationalists had not adopted the correct 'approach' to the goal they had set before themselves. Their image of the world had not corresponded with sufficient exactness to its realities or their methods had been deficient in points of technique. They could, and some of them did, ascribe their defeats to the madness of men and nations but this was a confession that their former premises and actions had been founded upon errors of calculation. In any event the verdict was the same, unless all the blame was to be laid on Americans as the world's greatest scapegoats."

4

The Struggle for Power: Policy of the Status Quo

Domestic and international politics are but two different manifestations of the same phenomenon: the struggle for power. Its manifestations differ in the two different spheres because different moral, political, and social conditions prevail in each. Western national societies show a much greater degree of social cohesion within themselves than among themselves. Cultural uniformity, technological unification, external pressure, and, above all, a hierarchic political organization combine to make the national society an integrated whole set apart from other national societies. In consequence, the domestic political order is, for instance, more stable and less subject to violent change than is the international order.

All history shows that nations active in international politics are continuously preparing for, actively involved in, or recovering from organized violence in the form of war. In the domestic politics of Western democracies, on the other hand, organized violence as an instrument of political action on an extensive scale has become a rare exception. Yet as a potentiality it exists here, too, and at times the fear of it in the form of revolution and internal disorders has exerted an important influence upon political thought and action.[1] The difference between domestic and international politics in this respect is one of degree and not of kind.

All politics, domestic and international, reveals three basic patterns; that is, all political phenomena can be reduced to one of three basic types. A political policy seeks either to keep power, to increase power, or to demonstrate power.

To these three typical patterns of politics, three typical international poli-

---

[1]This is true especially of the nineteenth century, as Guglielmo Ferrero has pointed out in *The Principles of Power* (New York: G. P. Putnam's Sons, 1942).

cies correspond. A nation whose foreign policy tends toward keeping power and not toward changing the distribution of power in its favor pursues a policy of the status quo. A nation whose foreign policy aims at acquiring more power than it actually has, through a reversal of existing power relations—whose foreign policy, in other words, seeks a favorable change in power status—pursues a policy of imperialism. A nation whose foreign policy seeks to demonstrate the power it has, either for the purpose of maintaining or increasing it, pursues a policy of prestige.[2] It should be noted that these formulations are of a provisional nature and are subject to further refinement.[3]

The concept "status quo" is derived from *status quo ante bellum*, a diplomatic term referring to the usual clauses in peace treaties which provide for the evacuation of territory by enemy troops and its restoration to the prewar sovereignty. Thus the peace treaties with Italy[4] and Bulgaria[5] terminating the Second World War provide that "all armed forces of the Allied and Associated Powers shall be withdrawn" from the territory of the particular nation "as soon as possible and in any case not later than ninety days from the coming into force of the present Treaty." That is, within this time limit the *status quo ante bellum* shall be reestablished with regard to this territory.[6]

The policy of the status quo aims at the maintenance of the distribution of power which exists at a particular moment in history. One might say that the policy of the status quo fulfills the same function for international politics that a conservative policy performs for domestic affairs. The particular moment in history which serves as point of reference for a policy of the status quo is

---

[2]It is not a departure from this threefold pattern of international politics when sometimes a nation gives up power without being physically compelled to do so, as Great Britain did with regard to India in 1947 and as the United States has done on several occasions with regard to Latin-American countries. In such cases a nation acts like a military commander who may retreat under certain circumstances, because his front is overextended or his lines of communication are threatened or because he wants to concentrate his forces for an attack. Similarly, a nation may retreat from an exposed power position it cannot hope to hold very long. Or it may exchange one kind of control for another kind, e.g., military for political control, political for economic control, or vice versa (the substitution of the Good Neighbor policy for the policy of the "big stick" is a case in point). Or a change in the objectives of its foreign policy may require concentration of effort at another point. In any case, the fact that it gives up power voluntarily cannot be taken to mean that it is not interested in power, any more than the retreat of a military commander proves that he is not interested in military victory.

[3]It must especially be pointed out that these different patterns of international policies do not of necessity correspond to conscious motivations in the mind of statesmen or supporters of the respective foreign policies. Statesmen and supporters may not even be aware of the actual character of the policies they pursue and support. More particularly, a nation may intend to pursue a policy of the status quo, while actually, without being aware of it, it is embarking upon a policy of imperialism. Thus it has been said of the British that they acquired their empire in a "fit of absent-mindedness." In what follows on this point in the text we are exclusively concerned with the actual character of the policies pursued and not with the motives of those who pursue them.

[4]See Article 73, *New York Times*, January 18, 1947, p. 26.

[5]See Article 20, ibid., p. 32.

[6]For a great number of older examples, see Coleman Phillipson, *Termination of War and Treaties of Peace* (New York: E. P. Dutton and Company, 1916), pp. 223 ff.

frequently the end of a war, when the distribution of power has been codified in a treaty of peace. This is so because the main purpose of peace treaties is to formulate in legal terms the shift in power which victory and defeat in the preceding war have brought about, and to insure the stability of the new distribution of power by means of legal stipulations. Thus it is typical for a status quo policy to appear as defense of the peace settlement that terminated the last general war. The European governments and political parties that pursued a policy of the status quo from 1815 to 1848 did so in defense of the peace settlement of 1815, which terminated the Napoleonic Wars. The main purpose of the Holy Alliance, which these governments concluded in 1815, was the maintenance of the status quo as it existed at the conclusion of the Napoleonic Wars. In consequence it functioned mainly as a guarantor of the peace treaty, that is, the Treaty of Paris of 1815.

In this respect, the relation between the policy in defense of the status quo of 1815, the Treaty of Paris, and the Holy Alliance is similar to the relation between the policy in favor of the status quo of 1918, the peace treaties of 1919, and the League of Nations. The distribution of power as it existed at the end of the First World War found its legal expression in the peace treaties of 1919. It became the main purpose of the League of Nations to maintain peace by preserving the status quo of 1918 as it had been formulated in the peace treaties of 1919. Article 10 of the Covenant of the League, obligating its members "to respect and preserve as against external aggression the territorial integrity and existing political independence of all members of the League," recognized as one of the purposes of the League the maintenance of the territorial status quo as established by the peace treaties of 1919. Consequently, in the period between the two world wars the struggle for and against the status quo was in the main fought either by defending or opposing the territorial provisions of the Treaty of Versailles and their guarantee in Article 10 of the Covenant of the League. It was, therefore, only consistent from their point of view that the nations chiefly opposed to the status quo established in 1919 should sever their connections with the League of Nations—Japan in 1932, Germany in 1933, Italy in 1937.

It is not only in peace treaties and international organizations supporting them that the policy of the status quo manifests itself. Nations desiring to maintain a certain distribution of power may use as their instrument special treaties, such as "The Nine Power Treaty relating to Principles and Policies to be followed in Matters concerning China," signed at Washington, February 6, 1922,[7] and the "Treaty of Mutual Guarantee between Germany, Belgium, France, Great Britain, and Italy," signed at Locarno, October 16, 1925.[8]

The Nine Power Treaty transformed the American policy of the "open door" in China into a multilateral policy that the nations mostly interested in trade with China, as well as China itself, pledged themselves to uphold. Its

---

[7]United States *Treaty Series*, No. 671 (Washington, 1923).

[8]*American Journal of International Law*, Vol. 20 (1926), Supplement, p. 22.

main purpose was to stabilize the distribution of power with regard to China which existed at the time between the contracting nations. This meant that the special rights which certain nations, especially Great Britain and Japan, had acquired in certain parts of Chinese territory, such as Manchuria and various ports, should not only remain intact but that no new special rights should be ceded by China to any of the contracting parties.

The Locarno Treaty of mutual guarantee endeavored to supplement the general guarantee of the territorial status quo of 1918, contained in Article 10 of the Covenant of the League, with a special one with respect to the western frontiers of Germany. Article I of the Treaty expressly referred to the guarantee of "the maintenance of the territorial status quo resulting from the frontiers between Germany and Belgium and between Germany and France."

Alliance treaties, in particular, frequently have the function of preserving the status quo in certain respects. Thus, after the victorious conclusion of the war against France, and the foundation of the German Empire in 1871, Bismarck tried to protect the newly won dominant position of Germany in Europe by alliances intended to prevent a war of revenge on the part of France. In 1879, Germany and Austria concluded an alliance for mutual defense against Russia, and, in 1894, France and Russia entered into a defensive alliance against the German-Austrian combination. The mutual fear lest the other alliance be intent upon changing the status quo while professing to maintain it was one of the main factors in bringing about the general conflagration of the First World War.

The alliance treaties that France concluded with the Soviet Union, Poland, Czechoslovakia, and Rumania in the period between the two world wars were intended to maintain the status quo, mainly in view of possible German attempts to change it. Similar treaties between Czechoslovakia, Yugoslavia, and Rumania, and the treaty between Czechoslovakia and the Soviet Union, had the same purpose. The ineffectiveness of these alliances when they were put to the test from 1935 to 1939 was one of the reasons for Germany's attack on Poland in 1939. The British-Polish Alliance of April 5, 1939, was the last attempt, before the outbreak of hostilities, to preserve at least the territorial status quo on the eastern German frontier. Today the alliances that the Soviet Union has concluded with the countries of Eastern Europe and those that the countries of Western Europe have concluded among themselves and with the United States aim similarly at the maintenance of the status quo as it was established in these respective European regions by the distribution of power at the end of the Second World War.

The manifestation of the policy of the status quo which has had the greatest importance for the United States and has been the cornerstone of its foreign relations is the Monroe Doctrine. A unilateral declaration made by President Monroe in his annual message to Congress on December 2, 1823, the Doctrine lays down the two essential principles of any status quo policy. On the one hand, it stipulates respect on the part of the United States for the existing distribution of power in the Western Hemisphere: "With the existing colonies or dependencies of any European power we have not interfered and shall not interfere." On the other hand, it proclaims resistance on the part of the United States to any change of the existing distribution of power by any non-American nation: "But with the governments who have declared their independence, and maintain it . . . we could not view any interposition for the purpose of oppressing them, or controlling in any other manner their destiny, by any European power, in any other light than as the manifestation of an unfriendly disposition towards the United States." As President Franklin D. Roosevelt expressed it in an address before the Governing Body of the Pan-American Union on April 12, 1933: "It [the Monroe Doctrine] was aimed and is aimed against the acquisition in any manner of the control of additional territory in this hemisphere by any non-American power."[9]

We have said that the policy of the status quo aims at the maintenance of the distribution of power as it exists at a particular moment in history. This does not mean that the policy of the status quo is necessarily opposed to any change whatsoever. While it is not opposed to change as such, it is opposed to any change that would amount to a reversal of the power relations among two or more nations, reducing, for instance, A from a first-rate to a second-rate power and raising B to the eminent position A formerly held. Minor adjustments in the distribution of power, however, which leave intact the relative power positions of the nations concerned, are fully compatible with a policy of the status quo. For instance, the purchase of the territory of Alaska by the United States in 1867 did not then affect the status quo between the United States and Russia, since, in view of the technology of communications and warfare at the time, the acquisition by the United States of this then-inaccessible territory did not affect to any appreciable extent the distribution of power between the United States and Russia.

Similarly, by acquiring the Virgin Islands from Denmark in 1917, the United States did not embark upon a policy aiming at a change of the status quo with regard to the Central American republics. While the acquisition of the Virgin Islands greatly improved the strategic position of the United States in so far as the defense of the approaches to the Panama Canal was concerned, it did not change the relative power positions of the United States and the Central American republics. The acquisition of the Virgin Islands may have strengthened the already dominant position of the United States in the Caribbean, yet it did not create it and, therefore, was compatible with a policy of the status quo. One might even say that, by strengthening the preponderance of the United States over the Central American republics, it actually reinforced the existing distribution of power and thus served the purposes of a policy of the status quo.

Beginning in 1962, the Soviet Union undertook to extend its influence significantly through the emplacement of missiles on Cuba. The Kennedy ad-

---

[9] *Roosevelt's Foreign Policy, 1933–41. F.D.R.'s Unedited Speeches and Messages* (New York: Wilfred Funk, Inc., 1942), p. 4.

ministration weighed the possible alternative courses of action it might take to remove the missiles, including an air strike; eventually it chose a policy of blockade and quarantine. The Soviets withdrew their missiles as the result of a Kennedy-Khrushchev agreement but continued to support the Castro regime with massive economic and military assistance. Meanwhile Cuba sought to increase its own ideological influence in the Caribbean and in Central America. By the 1980s, Cuban and Soviet military assistance and military personnel were identified in countries such as Grenada and Nicaragua. Leaving aside the question of popular support for Cuban intervention in these countries, the question which confronted American policymakers was the extent to which the status quo was threatened. Did independent Cuban intervention threaten the status quo? Was Cuban action as a surrogate for the Soviets the real threat? Was Soviet involvement a violation of the Monroe Doctrine and the Kennedy-Khrushchev agreement and itself a threat to the status quo? Successive administrations, beginning with that of John F. Kennedy, were forced to address this question. On October 25, 1983, the Reagan administration invaded Grenada—ostensibly to protect the lives of about 1,000 Americans on the island, but actually because Grenada was seen as an arsenal for military action masterminded by the Cubans and by Soviet advisors there and elsewhere in the Caribbean. Observers continued to ask whether Cuban and Soviet activities had constituted a true threat to the status quo in the region; conflicting answers were put forth in Europe and the United States as President Reagan's policy came under critical scrutiny. The standard for judging Cuban-Soviet involvement and for determining the response of American policymakers was whether an important shift in the distribution of power, and hence of the status quo, was taking place.

5

The Struggle for Power: Imperialism

WHAT IMPERIALISM IS NOT

An objective analysis of the acquisition of the Virgin Islands by the United States might show that it was part of a policy of the status quo in that region. Nevertheless, these and similar moves toward strengthening the position of the United States in the Caribbean have been decried as imperialistic by many observers. Such observers have used the term "imperialistic" not for the purpose of characterizing objectively a particular type of foreign policy, but as a term of opprobrium by which a policy to which the observer is opposed can be discredited. This arbitrary use of the term for polemical purposes has become so widespread that today "imperialism" and "imperialistic" are indiscriminately applied to any foreign policy, regardless of its actual character, to which the user happens to be opposed.

Anglophobes will refer to British imperialism as an actuality in 1980, as they did in 1940 or in 1914. Russophobes will call imperialistic whatever the Russians do in foreign affairs. The Soviet Union considered all participants in the Second World War as waging an imperialistic war until it was attacked by Germany in 1941; the war it then had to fight became anti-imperialistic by definition. To enemies and critics of the United States everywhere, "American imperialism" is a standard term. To add to the confusion, certain economic and political systems and economic groups, such as bankers and industrialists, are indiscriminately identified with imperialistic foreign policies.

In this process of indiscriminate usage the term "imperialism" has lost all concrete meaning. Everybody is an imperialist to someone who happens to take exception to his foreign policies. Under such circumstances it becomes the task of theoretical analysis to break with popular usage in order to give the term an ethically neutral, objective, and definable meaning that at the same time is useful for the theory and practice of international politics.[1]

Before we ask what imperialism actually is, let us ask first what imperialism is not but is most often supposed to be. The three most popular misconceptions require our attention.

1. Not every foreign policy aiming at an increase in the power of a nation is necessarily a manifestation of imperialism. We have already disposed of this misconception in our discussion of the policy of the status quo.[2] We defined imperialism as a policy that aims at the overthrow of the status quo, at a reversal of the power relations between two or more nations. A policy seeking only adjustment, leaving the essence of these power relations intact, still operates within the general framework of a policy of the status quo.

The view that imperialism and any purposeful increase in power are identical is held mainly by two distinct groups. Those who are opposed on principle to a particular nation and its policies, such as Anglophobes, Russophobes, and anti-Americans, regard the very existence of the object of their phobia as a threat to the world. Whenever a country thus feared sets out to increase its power, those who fear it must view the increase in power as a stepping-stone to world conquest; that is, as manifestation of an imperialistic policy. On the other hand, those who, as heirs of the political philosophy of the nineteenth century, consider any active foreign policy an evil bound to disappear in the foreseeable future, will condemn a foreign policy that seeks an increase in power. They will identify that foreign policy with what is for them the paradigm of evil—imperialism.

2. Not every foreign policy aiming at the preservation of an empire that already exists is imperialism. It is widely believed that whatever a nation, such as Great Britain, China, the Soviet Union, or the United States, does in order to maintain its preponderant position in certain regions is imperialistic. Thus imperialism becomes identified with the maintenance, defense, and stabilization of an empire already in existence rather than with the dynamic process of acquiring one. Yet, while it may make sense to apply the term "imperialism" to the domestic policies of an existing empire, it is confusing and misleading to apply the term to international policies of an essentially static and conservative character; for in international politics imperialism is contrasted with the policy of the status quo and, hence, has a dynamic connotation. The history of what is commonly called "British imperialism" is instructive in this regard.

The idea of British imperialism had its origin in Great Britain itself. It was

---

[1]The term is frequently used as synonymous with any kind of colonial expansion, as, for instance, in Parker Thomas Moon, *Imperialism and World Politics* (New York: The Macmillan Company, 1926). Such use is unobjectionable from a theoretical point of view, so long as it implies no general theory of the nature of expansionist policies as such. Since in the text we are concerned with the general characteristics of international policies of expansion, it is obvious that a concept limited to the phenomena of colonial expansion is too narrow for our purposes.

[2]On this point see the discussion in Chapter 4.

used for the first time by the Conservatives under Disraeli in the campaign for the elections of 1874. The idea of British imperialism, as conceived by Disraeli and developed later by Joseph Chamberlain and Winston Churchill, was opposed to what the Conservatives called the cosmopolitanism and internationalism of the Liberals. It found its concrete expression in the political program of "imperial federation." The most important points of this program were: (1) the unification and integration of Great Britain and its possessions into a unified empire with the aid of protective tariffs, (2) the reservation of free colonial land to Englishmen, (3) unified armed forces, and (4) a central representative organ in London.

When this "imperialistic" program was postulated and put into effect, the territorial expansion of Great Britain had in the main come to an end. The program of British "imperialism" was, therefore, essentially a program of consolidation, not of expansion. It sought to secure and exploit what had already been appropriated. It endeavored to stabilize the distribution of power which had been brought about by the creation of the British Empire.

When Kipling justified British imperialism as "the white man's burden," the burden was already shouldered. Since the 1870s, British "imperialism"— that is, British foreign policy with regard to Britain's overseas possessions—was in the main a policy of the status quo and not imperialistic at all in the exact meaning of the term. Yet the anti-imperialists in Great Britain and elsewhere, accepting the imperialistic slogans of Disraeli and Chamberlain at face value and mistaking the effects of imperialism for imperialism itself, opposed the British policy of exploitation and consolidation, especially in Africa and India, as "imperialistic." In fact, when Churchill refused in 1942 "to preside over the liquidation of the British Empire," he was speaking not as an imperialist but as a conservative in foreign affairs, a defender of the status quo of empire.

British "imperialism" and its opponents are the outstanding examples of the confusion between the consolidation and defense of empire, on the one hand, and imperialism, on the other. But they are not the only examples. When we speak of the Roman Empire and of Roman imperialism, we think naturally of the period of Roman history which starts with Augustus, the first emperor governing what was then called for the first time *imperium Romanum*. Yet, when Augustus gave Rome and its possessions the constitution of an empire, the expansion of Rome had essentially come to an end. The foreign policy of the Republic, from the Punic Wars to its overthrow by Julius Caesar, had indeed been imperialistic in the exact meaning of the term. In that period, the political face of the earth had been changed and made Roman. The foreign policy of the emperors and their perpetual wars served the main purpose of securing and protecting what had been conquered before. Not unlike the "imperialistic" policies of Great Britain from the time of Disraeli to Churchill, Roman foreign policy was one of conservation, of the status quo. When there were conquests, as under Trajan for instance, these policies served to make the empire and Roman supremacy secure.

The same is essentially true of the territorial aspects of American "imperialism" from the beginning of the twentieth century to the Second World War. The great debate for and against American imperialism which raged during the first decades of the century followed the great imperialistic expansion of the nineteenth century. The policy which was the subject of that debate was essentially a policy of consolidation, of protection, of exploration; that is, a policy of the status quo. When William Graham Sumner, in 1898, referred to the American policy of territorial expansion as "the conquest of the United States by Spain,"[3] he referred to a policy that was already consummated. When Senator Albert J. Beveridge declared that "God has made us adepts in government that we may administer government among savage and senile peoples,"[4] he endeavored to justify dominion already established rather than to support expansion planned for the future.

Thus, in both Great Britain and the United States, much of the modern debate on imperialism follows after the process of imperialistic expansion, condemning or justifying it in retrospect. In terms of actual policies to be pursued in the future, the debate is concerned primarily with the result of imperialistic policies; that is, the administration and safeguarding of empire. The explanation is not hard to find. The great debate started in Great Britain with the Conservative exaltation of the British Empire, a kind of British counterpart to the nationalism of the continent. The British Empire was a colonial empire and, as such, it became the prototype of modern empire. In consequence, the acquisition and exploitation of colonies became synonymous with empire, which thus received primarily, if not exclusively, an economic connotation. This economic connotation gave rise to the most extensive, most systematic, and also most popular body of thought which has sought to explain imperialism in modern times: the economic theories of imperialism. Here we find the third of the misconceptions that have obscured the true nature of imperialism.

ECONOMIC THEORIES OF IMPERIALISM

The Marxist, Liberal, and "Devil" Theories of Imperialism

The economic theories of imperialism have been developed in three different schools of thought: the Marxist, the liberal, and one that has aptly been called the "devil" theory[5] of imperialism.

The Marxist theory of imperialism rests upon the conviction, which is the foundation of all Marxist thought, that all political phenomena are the reflection of economic forces. Consequently, the political phenomenon of imperialism is the product of the economic system in which it originates—that is, capitalism.

---

[3]See previous quotation, page 41, note 2.

[4]Speech in the Senate, January 9, 1900, reprinted in Ruhl J. Bartlett, *The Record of American Diplomacy*, 4th ed. (New York: Alfred A. Knopf, 1964), p. 385.

[5]Charles A. Beard, *The Devil Theory of War* (New York: The Vanguard Press, 1936); see also *The New Republic*, Vol. 86 (March 4, 11, 18, 1936).

Capitalist societies, according to the Marxist theory, are unable to find within themselves sufficient markets for their products and sufficient investments for their capital. They have, therefore, a tendency to enslave even larger noncapitalist and, ultimately, even capitalist areas in order to transform them into markets for their surplus products and to give their surplus capital opportunities for investment.

The moderate Marxists, such as Kautsky and Hilferding, believed that imperialism was a policy of capitalism and that, therefore, an imperialistic policy was a matter of choice toward which capitalism might be more or less inclined according to circumstances. Lenin[6] and his followers, especially Bukharin,[7] on the other hand, identified imperialism and capitalism outright. Imperialism is identical with capitalism in its last—that is, monopoly—stage of development. According to Lenin, "Imperialism is capitalism in that phase of its development in which the domination of monopolies and finance-capital has established itself; in which the export of capital has acquired very great importance; in which the division of the world among the big international trusts has begun; in which the partition of all the territory of the earth amongst the great capitalist powers has been completed."[8]

In the eyes of the Marxists, capitalism is the main evil and imperialism only its necessary or probable manifestation. The liberal school, of which John A. Hobson[9] is the chief representative, is mainly concerned with imperialism in which it finds the result, not of capitalism as such, but of certain maladjustments within the capitalist system. In conformity with Marxism, the liberal school diagnoses as the root of imperialism the surplus of goods and capital which seek outlets in foreign markets. Yet, according to Hobson and his school, imperialist expansion is not the inevitable and not even the most rational method of disposing of these surpluses. Since the surpluses are the result of the maldistribution of purchasing power, the remedy lies in the expansion of the home market through economic reforms, such as increase in purchasing power and elimination of oversavings. It is this belief in a domestic alternative to imperialism which in the main distinguishes the liberal school from Marxism.

The "devil" theory of imperialism operates on a much lower intellectual level than do its two companion theories. It is widely held by pacifists and has become a stock-in-trade of Communist propaganda. It may be said to have been the official philosophy of the Nye Committee, which in 1934–36 investigated on behalf of the United States Senate the influence of financial and industrial

---

[6]*Collected Works* (New York: International Publishers, 1927), Vol. XVIII; *Selected Works* (New York: International Publishers, 1935), Vol. V.

[7]*Imperialism and World Economy* (New York: International Publishers, 1929). Of the writers who, aside from those mentioned in the text, have particularly influenced the development of the Marxist theory of imperialism, Rosa Luxemburg and Fritz Sternberg ought to be mentioned; cf. the latter's *The Coming Crisis* (New York: The John Day Company, 1946).

[8]*Imperialism, the Highest Stage of Capitalism* (New York: International Publishers, 1933), p. 72.

[9]*Imperialism* (London: G. Allen & Unwin, 1938).

interests on the intervention of the United States in the First World War. The publicity which the proceedings of this committee received made the "devil" theory of imperialism for a time the most popular explanation of foreign affairs in the United States. The simplicity of the theory contributed much to its popularity. It identified certain groups that obviously profited from war, such as manufacturers of war matériel (the so-called munitions makers), international bankers ("Wall Street"), and the like. Since they profited from war, they must be interested in having war. Thus the war profiteers transform themselves into the "war mongers," the "devils" who plan wars in order to enrich themselves.

While the extreme Marxists equate capitalism and imperialism, and while the moderate Marxists and the disciples of Hobson see in imperialism the result of maladjustments within the capitalist system, for the adherents of the "devil" theory imperialism and war in general amount to nothing but a conspiracy of evil capitalists for the purpose of private gain.

Criticism of These Theories

All economic explanations of imperialism, the refined as well as the primitive, fail the test of historic experience. The economic interpretation of imperialism erects a limited historic experience, based on a few isolated cases, into a universal law of history. It is indeed true that in the late nineteenth and twentieth centuries a small number of wars were waged primarily, if not exclusively, for economic objectives. The classic examples are the Boer War of 1899–1902 and the Chaco War between Bolivia and Paraguay from 1932–35. The main responsibility of British gold mining interests for the Boer War can hardly be doubted. The Chaco War is considered by some to have been primarily a war between two oil companies for the control of oil fields. Even in the Persian Gulf war in 1991, the war was fought for multiple objectives, not economics alone.

But during the entire period of mature capitalism, no war, with the exception of the Boer War, was waged by major powers exclusively or even predominately for economic objectives. The Austro-Prussian War of 1866 and the Franco-German War of 1870, for instance, had no economic objectives of any importance. They were political wars, indeed imperialistic wars, fought for the purpose of establishing a new distribution of power, first in favor of Prussia within Germany and then in favor of Germany within the European state system. The Crimean War of 1854–56, the Spanish-American War of 1898, the Russo-Japanese War of 1904–05, the Turko-Italian War of 1911–12, and the several Balkan Wars show economic objectives only in a subordinate role, if they show them at all. The two world wars were certainly political wars, whose stake was the domination of Europe, if not of the world. Naturally, victory in these wars brought economic advantages and, more particularly, defeat brought in its wake economic losses. But these effects were not the real issue; they were only by-products of the political consequences of victory and defeat.

Still less were these economic effects the motives that determined in the minds of the responsible statesmen the issue of war and peace.

The economic theories of imperialism are thus not supported by the experience of that historic period which they suppose to be intimately connected, if not identical, with imperialism; that is, the period of capitalism. Furthermore, the main period of colonial expansion which the economic theories tend to identify with imperialism precedes the age of mature capitalism and cannot be attributed to the inner contradictions of the decaying capitalist system. In comparison with those of the sixteenth, seventeenth, and eighteenth centuries, the colonial acquisitions of the nineteenth and twentieth centuries are small. The latest phase of capitalism even witnesses the liquidation of empire on a large scale in the form of the retreat from Asia and Africa of Great Britain, France, Portugal, and The Netherlands.

The evidence of history is still more unfavorable to the contentions of the economic theories if one tests the theories against the evidence presented by the precapitalist processes of empire building. The policies that in ancient times led to the foundation of the Egyptian, Assyrian, and Persian empires were imperialistic in the political sense. So were the conquests of Alexander the Great and the policies of Rome in the last century before the Christian era. The Arabian expansion in the seventh and eighth centuries showed all the earmarks of imperialism. Pope Urban II used the typical ideological arguments in support of an imperialistic policy when, in 1095, he expressed to the Council of Clermont the reasons for the First Crusade in these words: "For this land which you inhabit, shut in on all sides by the seas and surrounded by the mountain peaks, is too narrow for your large population; nor does it abound in wealth, and it furnishes scarcely food enough for its cultivators. Hence it is that you murder and devour one another, that you wage war and that very many among you perish in civil strife."[10] Louis XIV, Peter the Great, and Napoleon I were the great imperialists of the modern precapitalist age.

All these imperialisms of precapitalist times share with those of the capitalist period the tendency to overthrow the established power relations and put in their stead the dominance of the imperialistic power. Yet those two periods of imperialism share also the subordination of economic objectives to political considerations.

Alexander the Great and Napoleon I did not embark, any more than did Adolph Hitler, on imperialistic policies for the purpose of personal gain or in order to escape the maladjustment of their economic systems. What they aimed at was exactly the same thing the captain of industry is aiming at when he tries to establish an industrial "empire" by adding enterprise to enterprise until he dominates his industry in a monopolistic or quasimonopolistic manner. What the precapitalist imperialist, the capitalist imperialist, and the "imperialistic"

---

[10]F.A. Ogg, editor, *A Source Book of Medieval History* (New York: American Book Company, 1907), p. 286.

capitalist want is power, not economic gain. The captain of industry is no more driven toward his "imperialistic" goal by economic necessity or personal greed than was Napoleon I. Personal gain and the solution of economic problems through imperialistic expansion are for all of them a pleasant afterthought, a welcome by-product, but not the goal by which the imperialistic urge is attracted.

We have seen that imperialism is not determined by economics, capitalist or otherwise. We shall see now that capitalists per se are not imperialists. According to the economic theories and, more particularly, the "devil" theory, capitalists use governments as their tools in instigating imperialistic policies. Yet the investigation of historic instances cited in support of the economic interpretation shows that in most cases the reverse relationship actually existed between statesmen and capitalists. Imperialistic policies were generally conceived by the governments who summoned the capitalists to support these policies. Thus historic evidence points to the primacy of politics over economics, and "the rule of the financier . . . over international politics" is indeed, in the words of Professor Schumpeter, "a newspaper fairytale, almost ludicrously at variance with facts."[11]

Yet, far from being the instigators, capitalists as a group—aside from certain individual capitalists—were not even enthusiastic supporters of imperialistic policies. The literature and policies of the groups and political parties representing the capitalist element in modern societies are a testimony to the traditional opposition of the merchant and manufacturing classes to any foreign policy that, like imperialism, might lead to war. As Professor Viner has stated:

> It was for the most part the middle classes who were the supporters of pacifism, of internationalism, of international conciliation and compromise of disputes, of disarmament—in so far as these had supporters. It was for the most part aristocrats, agrarians, often the urban working classes, who were the expansionists, the imperialists, the jingoes. In the British Parliament it was spokesmen for the "moneyed interests," for the emerging middle classes in the northern manufacturing districts and for the "City" in London, who were the appeasers during the Napoleonic Wars, during the Crimean War, during the Boer War, and during the period from the rise of Hitler to the German invasion of Poland. In our own country it was largely from business circles that the important opposition came to the American Revolution, to the War of 1812, to the imperialism of 1898, and to the anti-Nazi policy of the Roosevelt administration prior to Pearl Harbor.[12]

---

[11] Joseph Schumpeter, *Business Cycles* (New York and London: McGraw-Hill Book Company, 1939), Vol. 1, p. 495, n. 1.

[12] Jacob Viner, "Peace as an Economic Problem," *International Economics* (Glencoe: The Free Press, 1951), p. 255. Cf. Philip S. Foner, *Business and Slavery: the New York Merchants and the Irrepressible Conflict* (Chapel Hill: University of North Carolina Press, 1941), on the opposition of New York and New England merchants to the Civil War, and Disraeli's statement to Lord Salisbury of September 26, 1876: "All the monied and commercial classes in all countries are against war. . . ." Also significant in this respect is the report that the British Ambassador to Germany sent on the eve of the First World War, June 30, 1914, to his Foreign Office: "I hear in fact from all sides

From Sir Andrew Freeport in the *Spectator* at the beginning of the eighteenth century to Norman Angell's *The Great Illusion* in our time, it has been the conviction of the capitalists as a class and of most capitalists as individuals that "war does not pay," that war is incompatible with an industrial society, that the interests of capitalism require peace and not war. For only peace permits those rational calculations upon which capitalist actions are based. War carries with it an element of irrationality and chaos which is alien to the very spirit of capitalism. Imperialism, however, as the attempt to overthrow the existing power relations, carries with it the inevitable risk of war. As a group then, capitalists were opposed to war; they did not initiate, and only supported with misgivings and under pressure, imperialistic policies that might lead, and many times actually did lead, to war.

How was it possible that a body of doctrine, such as the economic theories of imperialism, which is so completely at variance with the facts of experience, could hold sway over the public mind? Two factors are responsible for the success of that doctrine: the climate of opinion in the Western world and the character of the doctrine itself. We have already pointed to the general tendency of the age to reduce political problems to economic ones.[13] The capitalists and their critics are equally guilty of this fundamental error. The former expected from the development of capitalism, freed from the atavistic fetters of the precapitalist age and following only its own inherent laws, general prosperity and peace. The latter were convinced that these aims could be achieved only through reform or the abolition of the capitalist system. Both camps looked to economic remedies for political problems. Bentham advocated the emancipation of the colonies as the means of doing away with the imperialistic conflicts that lead to war. Proudhon, Cobden, and their disciples saw in tariffs the sole source of international conflicts and reasoned that peace lay in extending free trade.[14]

In our own time we have heard it said that since German, Italian, and Japanese imperialism was born of economic needs, these countries would have refrained from imperialistic policies had they received loans, colonies, and access to raw materials. Poor nations will go to war, so the argument runs, in order to escape economic distress; if the rich nations alleviate their economic afflictions, they will have no reason to go to war. In the classic age of capitalism both the adherents and the opponents of the capitalist system believed that the economic motives which seemed to determine the actions of businessmen were guiding the actions of all men.

The other reason for the ready acceptance of the economic interpretation of imperialism lies in its plausibility. What Professor Schumpeter has said of the

---

that the financial and industrial classes are dead against a war in any shape. . . ." *British Documents on the Origin of the War, 1898–1914* (London: His Majesty's Stationery Office, 1926), Vol. XI, p. 361.

[13]See pages 36 ff. See also Hans J. Morgenthau, *Scientific Man vs. Power Politics* (Chicago: University of Chicago Press, 1946; Phoenix Edition, 1965), pp. 75 ff.

[14]See page 35–36.

Marxist theory of imperialism holds generally true: "A series of vital facts of our time seems to be perfectly accounted for. The whole maze of international politics seems to be cleared up by a single powerful stroke of analysis."[15] The mystery of so threatening, inhuman, and often murderous a historic force as imperialism, the theoretical problem of defining it as a distinctive type of international politics, the practical difficulty, above all, of recognizing it in a concrete situation and of counteracting it with adequate means—all this is reduced to either the inherent tendencies or the abuses of the capitalist system. Whenever the phenomenon of imperialism presents itself for either theoretical understanding or practical action, the simple scheme will provide an almost automatic answer that puts the mind at ease.

DIFFERENT TYPES OF IMPERIALISM

The true nature of imperialism as a policy devised to overthrow the status quo can best be explained by a consideration of certain typical situations that favor imperialistic policies and that, given the subjective and objective conditions necessary for an active foreign policy, will almost inevitably produce a policy of imperialism.

Three Inducements to Imperialism

Victorious War

When a nation is engaged in war with another nation, it is very likely that the nation which anticipates victory will pursue a policy that seeks a permanent change of the power relations with the defeated enemy. The nation will pursue this policy regardless of what the objectives were at the outbreak of the war. It is the objective of this policy of change to transform the relation between victor and vanquished which happens to exist at the end of the war into the new status quo of the peace settlement. Thus a war that was started by the victor as a defensive war—for the maintenance of the prewar status quo—transforms itself with the approaching victory into an imperialistic war; that is, for a permanent change in the status quo.

The "Carthaginian Peace," by which the Romans changed their power relations with the Carthaginians permanently in their favor, has become the byword for the kind of peace settlement which tends to perpetuate the relation between victor and vanquished as it exists at the conclusion of hostilities. The Treaty of Versailles and its companion treaties, terminating the First World War, had in the eyes of many observers a similar character. The expansion of the Soviet sphere of influence into Eastern Europe after World War II, especially as recognized in the Helsinki Accords, is a further example. A policy that

---

[15]Joseph Schumpeter, *Capitalism, Socialism, and Democracy* (New York and London: Harper and Brothers, 1947), p. 51.

aims at a peace settlement of this kind must, according to our definition, be called imperialistic. It is imperialistic because it tries to replace the prewar status quo, when approximately equal or at least not thoroughly unequal powers oppose each other, with a postwar status quo where the victor becomes the permanent master of the vanquished.

Lost War

This very status of subordination, intended for permanency, may easily engender in the vanquished a desire to turn the scales on the victor, to overthrow the status quo created by his victory, and to change places with him in the hierarchy of power. In other words, the policy of imperialism pursued by the victory is likely to call forth a policy of imperialism on the part of the vanquished. If he is not forever ruined or else won over to the cause of the victor, the vanquished will want to regain what he has lost and, if possible, gain more.

The typical example of imperialism conceived as a reaction against the successful imperialism of others is German imperialism from 1935 to the end of the Second World War. The European status quo of 1914 was characterized by a concert of great powers, consisting of Austria, France, Germany, Great Britain, Italy, and Russia. The victory of the Allies and the subsequent peace treaties created a new status quo that was the fruition of the imperialistic policies of France. This new status quo established the hegemony of France, exercised in alliance with most of the newly created nations of Eastern and Central Europe.

German foreign policy from 1919 to 1935 operated seemingly within the framework of that status quo, while secretly preparing for its overthrow. It tried to win concessions for Germany, but it nevertheless accepted, at least for the time being and with mental reservations, the power relations established by the Treaty of Versailles. It did not openly challenge these power relations; rather, it aimed at adjustments that left their essence intact. Such was particularly the character of the "policy of fulfillment"—that is, fulfillment of the Treaty of Versailles—which the Republic of Weimar pursued. It was this attempt to improve the international position of Germany while accepting at least temporarily the status quo of Versailles that aroused the violent opposition of nationalists and National Socialists. After the National Socialists had come to power in 1933 and stabilized their regime domestically, they abrogated in 1935 the disarmament provisions of the Treaty of Versailles. In 1936, in violation of the same treaty, they occupied the Rhineland and declared void the demilitarization of the German territory adjacent to the German-French frontier. With these moves the foreign policy of National Socialist Germany became openly imperialistic; for these were the first in a series of moves that expressed Germany's resolution no longer to accept the status quo of Versailles as basis for its foreign policy, but to work for the overthrow of that status quo.

Weakness

Another typical situation that favors imperialistic policies is the existence of weak states or of politically empty spaces, that are attractive and accessible to a strong state. This is the situation out of which colonial imperialism grew. It is also the situation that made possible the transformation of the original federation of thirteen American states into a continental power. Napoleon's as well as Hitler's imperialism had partly this character, the latter's particularly in the period of the "blitzkrieg" of 1940. During the closing phase of the Second World War and the decade following it, imperialism growing out of the relations between strong and weak nations was exemplified by the relations between the Soviet Union and the nations of Eastern Europe. The attractiveness of power vacuums as an incentive to imperialism is at least a potential threat to the survival of many of the new nations of Asia and Africa, deficient as they are in the most important elements of power.

Three Goals of Imperialism

As imperialism grows out of three typical situations, so imperialism moves toward three typical objectives. The objective of imperialism can be the domination of the whole politically organized globe; that is, a world empire. Or it can be an empire or hegemony of approximately continental dimensions. Or it can be a strictly localized preponderance of power. In other words, the imperialistic policy may have no limits but those set by the power of resistance of the prospective victims, or it may have geographically determined limits, such as the geographical boundaries of a continent, or it may be limited by the localized aims of the imperialistic power itself.

World Empire

The outstanding historic examples of unlimited imperialism are the expansionist policies of Alexander the Great, Rome, the Arabs in the seventh and eighth centuries, Napoleon I, and Hitler. They all have in common an urge toward expansion which knows no rational limits, feeds on its own successes and, if not stopped by a superior force, will go on to the confines of the political world.[16] This urge will not be satisfied so long as there remains anywhere a possible object of domination—a politically organized group of men which by

---

[16]Hobbes has given the classical analysis of this unlimited desire for power in the *Leviathan*, Chapter XI (Everyman's Library), pp. 49 ff. "So that in the first place, I put for a generall inclination of all mankind, a perpetuall and restlesse desire of Power after power, that ceaseth only in Death. And the cause of this, is not alwayes that a man hopes for a more intensive delight, that he has already attained to; or that he cannot be content with a moderate power: but because he cannot assure the power and means to live well, which he hath present, without the acquisition of more. And from hence it is, that Kings, whose power is greatest, turn their endeavours to the assuring it at home by Lawes, or abroad by Wars: and when that is done, there succeedeth a new desire; in some, of Fame from new conquest; in others, of ease and sensuall pleasure; in others, of admiration, or being flattered from excellence in some art, or other ability of the mind."

its very independence challenges the conqueror's lust for power. It is, as we shall see, exactly the lack of moderation, the aspiration to conquer all that lends itself to conquest, characteristic of unlimited imperialism, which in the past has been the undoing of the imperialistic policies of this kind. The only exception is Rome, for reasons that will be discussed later.[17]

Continental Empire

The type of geographically determined imperialism is most clearly presented in the policies of European powers to gain a predominant position on the European continent. Louis XIV, Napoleon III, and William II are cases in point. The kingdom of Piedmont under Cavour seeking the domination of the Italian peninsula in the 1850s, the different participants in the Balkan Wars of 1912 and 1913 aspiring to hegemony in the Balkans, Mussolini trying to make the Mediterranean an Italian lake—these are examples of geographically determined imperialism on a less than continental basis. The American policy of the nineteenth century, consisting in the gradual expansion of American rule over the better part of the North American continent is primarily, but not exclusively, determined by the geographic limits of a continent; for the United States has not attempted to bring Canada and Mexico under its domination, although it would have been able to do so. Continental imperialism is here modified by its limitation to a localized section of the continent.

The same mixed type of imperialism constitutes the essence of American foreign policy toward the Western Hemisphere as a whole. The Monroe Doctrine, by postulating for the Western Hemisphere a policy of the status quo with regard to non-American powers, erected a protective shield behind which the United States could establish its predominance within that geographic region. Within these geographic limits, however, American policy was not always uniformly imperialistic. Toward the Central American republics and certain countries of South America it was at times frankly imperialistic, but in its dealings with some other countries, such as Argentina and Brazil, it sought only to maintain the existing superiority of the United States, which was the result of a kind of natural process rather than of a deliberate American policy. Even though the United States has had the power to impose its superiority upon these countries in the form of actual hegemony, it chose not to do so. Here again we find a localized imperialism within the general framework of a geographically limited policy.

Local Preponderance

The prototype of localized imperialism is to be found in the monarchical policies of the eighteenth and nineteenth centuries. In the eighteenth century, Frederick the Great, Louis XV, Maria Theresa, Peter the Great, and Catherine II were the moving forces of this kind of foreign policy. In the nineteenth century, Bismarck was the master of this imperialistic policy, which seeks to

---

[17]See page 343 ff.

overthrow the status quo and to establish political preponderance within self-chosen limits. The difference between such a localized imperialistic policy, continental imperialism, and unlimited imperialism is the difference between the foreign policies of Bismarck, William II, and Hitler. Bismarck wanted to establish Germany's preponderance in Central Europe; William II, in all of Europe; Hitler, in the whole world. The traditional objectives of Russian imperialism, such as control of Finland, Eastern Europe, the Balkans, the Dardanelles, and Iran, are also of a localized nature.

The limits of this type of imperialism are not, as in the case of the geographically limited type, primarily a product of the objective facts of nature beyond which it would be either technically difficult or politically unwise to go. On the contrary, they are primarily the result of a free choice among several alternatives, one of which might be a policy of the status quo, another continental imperialism, a third localized imperialism. In the eighteenth century the third alternative recommended itself because the existing concert of powers, each of about the same strength, discouraged any attempt at continental imperialism. The experience of Louis XIV showed how hazardous such an attempt could be. Furthermore, eighteenth-century imperialism was motivated mainly by considerations of monarchical power and glory, not by the mass emotions of modern nationalism. These considerations operated within a common framework of monarchical traditions and European civilization which imposed upon the actors on the political scene a moral restraint necessarily absent in periods of religious or nationalistic crusades.

In the nineteenth century, the element of choice characteristic of the policy of localized imperialism is paramount in the history of Bismarck's foreign policy. First, he had to overcome the opposition of the Prussian conservatives who favored a policy of the status quo for Prussia over Bismarck's policy of localized imperialism aiming at hegemony within Germany. When victorious wars had made Bismarck's policy feasible, it had to be defended against those who now wanted to go beyond the limits Bismarck had set for Prussian and later German hegemony. The dismissal of Bismarck by William II in 1890 marked the end of localized and the beginning of at least a tendency toward continental imperialism as the foreign policy of Germany.

Three Methods of Imperialism

Just as there are three types of imperialism with respect to the situations from which imperialism typically arises, and three types of imperialism in view of its objectives, so a triple distinction is to be made regarding the typical means employed by imperialistic policies. Accordingly, we must distinguish between military, economic, and cultural imperialism. A widespread popular misconception confuses these three methods with the objectives of imperialism, as though economic imperialism, for instance, aimed at nothing but economic exploitation of other peoples. This misconception has its origin in the economic theories of imperialism as well as in the neglect of the power element in international relations, referred to above.[18] In truth, military imperialism seeks military conquest; economic imperialism, economic exploitation of other peoples; cultural imperialism, the displacement of one culture by another—but always as means to the same imperialistic end. That end is always the overthrow of the status quo; that is, the reversal of the power relations between the imperialist nation and its prospective victims. This immutable end is served by military, economic, and cultural means, either alone or in combination. It is with these means that we are here concerned.

Military Imperialism

The most obvious, the most ancient, and also the crudest form of imperialism is military conquest. The great conquerors of all times have also been the great imperialists. The advantage of this method, from the point of view of the imperialistic nation, lies in the fact that the new power relations resulting from military conquest can as a rule be changed only by another war instigated by the vanquished nation, with the odds normally against the latter. Napoleon I might have relied upon the sole power of the ideas of the French Revolution to establish the hegemony of France in Europe and in the world; that is, he might have chosen cultural imperialism instead of military conquest. On the other hand, if he could make and hold military conquests, he would reach his imperialistic goal more quickly and derive from the process of conquering that maximum of personal satisfaction which victory in combat gives to the victor. Yet the very condition under which this statement is alone correct indicates the great drawback of military conquest as a method of imperialism: war is a gamble; it may be lost as well as won. The nation that starts war for imperialistic ends may gain an empire and keep it, as Rome did. Or it may gain it and, in the process of trying to gain still more, lose it, as in Napoleon's case. Or it may gain it, lose it, and fall victim to the imperialism of others, as in the case of National Socialist Germany and of Japan. Military imperialism is a gamble played for the highest stakes.

Economic Imperialism

Economic imperialism is less obtrusive and also generally less effective than the military variety and is, as a rational method of gaining power, a product of modern times. As such, it is a concomitant of the age of mercantilist and capitalist expansion. Its outstanding modern example is what is called "dollar diplomacy." It has also played an important role in the history of British and French imperialism. British influence in Portugal since the beginning of the eighteenth century has been powerfully supported by economic control. British supremacy in the Arab world was the result of economic policies for which the term "oil diplomacy" is not misplaced. Similarly, the Arab discovery of the political uses of oil has given the oil-producing Arab nations unprecedented power over the industrial nations importing Arab oil. The pre-

---

[18]See pages 30 ff.

dominant influence France exercised in countries such as Rumania in the period between the two world wars was to a considerable extent based upon economic factors.

The common characteristic of the policies we call economic imperialism is their tendency, on the one hand, to overthrow the status quo by changing the power relations between the imperialist nation and others and, on the other hand, to do so not through the conquest of territory but by way of economic control. If a nation cannot or will not conquer territory for the purpose of establishing its mastery over other nations, it can try to achieve the same end by establishing its control over those who control the territory. The Central American republics, for instance, are all sovereign states; they possess all the attributes of sovereignty and display the paraphernalia of sovereignty. But, their economic life being almost completely dependent upon exports to the United States, these nations, unless they receive significant support from another source, are unable to pursue for any length of time policies of any kind, domestic or foreign, to which the United States would object.

The nature of economic imperialism as an unobtrusive, indirect, but fairly effective method of gaining and maintaining domination over other nations is particularly striking where two rival imperialisms compete with economic means for control over the same government. The century-old competition between Great Britain and Russia for control of Iran, though carried on for a long time predominantly by military means, may serve as an example. Professor P. E. Roberts described this situation in Iran, then called Persia, before the First World War:

> Russia presses on her from the north, Great Britain from the south, though the influence of the two powers is very different. Great Britain holds in her hands the bulk of the foreign trade of southern Persia, and claims a general control of the whole Asiatic coastline from Aden eastwards to Baluchistan. . . . Great Britain has never coveted territorial possessions. . . . The development of navigation of the Volga and the construction of the Transcaspian railway have given to Russia the bulk of the trade with northern Persia. But the commercial weapons of Russia are a monopoly and prohibition. She has laid an interdict upon the making of railroads in Persian territory, and has often opposed measures which might regenerate the country.[19]

Only "the commercial and political rivalry of Great Britain" seemed to bar the way to the complete absorption of Iran into the Russian orbit.

During the period of economic and political rivalry between Great Britain and Russia in that region, the foreign policies, and frequently also the domestic policies, of the Iranian government faithfully reflected the intensity of the economic, and sometimes military, pressures that the rival powers brought to bear. When Russia promised or granted economic advantages that Great Britain failed to match, or when Russia threatened to withdraw advantages it had

---

[19]*Cambridge Modern History* (New York: The Macmillan Company, 1910), Vol. XII, p. 491.

granted, Russian influence increased, and vice versa. Russia did not dare realize its territorial ambitions with regard to Iran. Great Britain had none. But both tried to control the Iranian government, which in turn controls oil fields as well as the road to India.

Cultural Imperialism[20]

What we suggest calling cultural imperialism is the most subtle and, if it were ever to succeed by itself alone, the most successful of imperialistic policies. It aims not at the conquest of territory or at the control of economic life, but at the conquest and control of the minds of men as an instrument for changing the power relations between two nations. If one could imagine the culture and, more particularly, the political ideology, with all its concrete imperialistic objectives, of State A conquering the minds of all the citizens determining the policies of State B, State A would have won a more complete victory and would have founded its supremacy on more stable grounds than any military conqueror or economic master. State A would not need to threaten or employ military force or use economic pressure in order to achieve its ends; for that end, the subservience of State B to its will, would have already been realized by the persuasiveness of a superior culture and a more attractive political philosophy.

This is, however, a hypothetical case. Cultural imperialism generally falls short of a victory so complete as to make other methods of imperialism superfluous. The typical role cultural imperialism plays in modern times is subsidiary to the other methods. It softens up the enemy, it prepares the ground for military conquest or economic penetration. Its typical modern manifestation is the fifth column, and one of its two outstanding modern successes is to be found in the operations of the National Socialist fifth columns in Europe before the outbreak and at the beginning of the Second World War. Its success was most spectacular in Austria, where in 1938 a pro-National Socialist government invited the German troops to occupy the country. Its success was considerable in France, where a number of influential citizens, inside and outside the government, had been converted to the National Socialist philosophy and its international objectives. It is hardly an exaggeration to say that these countries were already partly conquered by means of cultural imperialism before military conquest finished the task. Great Britain, by interning at the outbreak of the Second World War all known National Socialists and their sympathizers within its borders, paid tribute to the danger that cultural penetration presented for the prospective victims of German imperialism.

---

[20]What is described under this heading goes frequently by the name of ideological imperialism, the term "ideological" referring particularly to the contest of political philosophies. Two reasons, however, seem to make it advisable to use the term "cultural" instead. On the one hand, the term "cultural" comprises all kinds of intellectual influences, political and otherwise, that serve as means for imperialistic ends. On the other hand, we are using the term "ideological" in Chapter 7 in its specific sociological sense, and it would only make for confusion if we used the same term here in its general popular meaning.

The other outstanding example of cultural imperialism in our time, antedating and surviving the National Socialist fifth column, is the Communist International. In its heyday, directed from Moscow, it guided and controlled the Communist parties in all countries and saw to it that the policies pursued by the national Communist parties were in accord with the foreign policy of the Soviet Union. To the extent that Communist parties gained influence in particular nations, the influence of the Soviet Union over these nations increased, and where Communist parties gained control of national governments, the Russian government, controlling the Communist parties, controlled these national governments.

The technique used by the Soviet Union for establishing its control over the countries of Eastern Europe provides a classic example of the organic interconnectedness between cultural imperialism and the other forms of imperialistic conquest. In those countries the promotion of Communism through Communist parties, directed from Moscow, was a mere means to the end of Russian domination and was co-ordinated with other means serving the same end. Thus military conquest was the foundation for the Russian domination of Eastern Europe. Supporting and in part supplanting it was Russian control over the economic life of Eastern Europe, and the consequent economic dependence of Eastern Europe upon the Soviet Union. Finally, the Soviet Union endeavored to substitute loyalty to Communism and, in consequence, to the Soviet Union for the loyalties the peoples of Eastern Europe have traditionally felt to their respective nations, religions, and parties, endeavoring thus to make them willing tools of Russian policies.

The competition between the Soviet Union and China for the domination of the world Communist movement and for predominant influence in the uncommitted nations, too, uses primarily the instruments of cultural imperialism. The two major Communist nations derive their claim to dominant influence from the assertion that each of them is the true heir of Marx and Lenin, while the other is a heretic supporting the enemies of Communism. Wherever governments and political movements adhere to Communist doctrine, this argument is a source of power for the one of the two major Communist nations that can make the argument credible.

The cultural imperialism of totalitarian governments is well disciplined and highly organized; for these governments are able, because of their totalitarian character, to exert strict control and guiding influence over the thoughts and actions of their citizens and foreign sympathizers. While the technique of cultural imperialism has been perfected by the totalitarians and has been forged into the effective political weapon of the fifth column, the use of cultural sympathy and political affinities as weapons of imperialism is almost as old as imperialism itself. The histories of ancient Greece and Renaissance Italy are replete with episodes in which imperialistic policies were executed through association with political sympathizers in the enemy ranks rather than through military conquests. In modern times religious organizations, associated or identified with governments, have played an important role in imperialistic policies of a cultural character. Typical in this respect are the imperialistic policies of Czarist Russia, which used the dual position of the Czar as head of the Russian government and of the Orthodox Church for the purpose of extending the power of Russia to the followers of the Orthodox faith in foreign countries. That Russia was able in the nineteenth century to succeed Turkey as the preponderant power in the Balkans is largely due to the cultural imperialism that used the Orthodox Church as a weapon of Russian foreign policy.

In the secular field, *la mission civilisatrice* of France has been a potent weapon of French imperialism. The deliberate use of the attractive qualities of French civilization for the purposes of French foreign policy was one of the cornerstones of French imperialism in the countries adjacent to the eastern Mediterranean before the First World War. The wave of public sympathy throughout the world, which came to the aid of France in both world wars, was the fruit of cultural imperialism, which in turn strengthened the French military imperialism of the later, victorious years of both world wars. Cultural imperialism in the form of the diffusion of a national culture is incomparably less mechanical and disciplinary, but not necessarily less effective, than the totalitarian kind. While the latter makes use primarily of the affinities of political philosophy, the former impresses the intellectually influential groups of a foreign country with the attractive qualities of a civilization until these groups tend to find the political objectives and methods of that civilization equally attractive.

We have already pointed out that cultural imperialism generally plays a role subsidiary to the military and economic varieties. Similarly, while economic imperialism sometimes stands by itself, it frequently supports military policies. On the other hand, while military imperialism is able to conquer without the support of nonmilitary methods, no dominion can last that is founded upon nothing but military force. Thus the conqueror will not only prepare for military conquests by economic and cultural penetration. He will also found his empire not upon military force alone, but primarily upon the control of the livelihood of the conquered and upon the domination of their minds. And it is in that most subtle yet most important task that, with the exception of Rome, all the great imperialists, from Alexander to Napoleon and Hitler, have failed. Their failure to conquer the minds of those whom they had conquered otherwise proved to be the undoing of their empires. The ever-renewed coalitions against Napoleon, the revolts of the Poles against the Russians throughout the nineteenth century, the struggle of the underground against Hitler, and the fights of Ireland and India for freedom from British rule are the classic examples in modern times of that ultimate problem which few imperialistic policies have been able to solve.

The share of economic and cultural imperialism in the over-all international activities of governments has greatly increased since the Second World War. It has done so for two reasons. On the one hand, military imperialism pursued openly and on a large scale is no longer a rational instrument of foreign policy since it carries within itself the risk of escalation into a self-destructive nuclear war. Thus a nation bent upon the imperialistic expansion of its power will often substitute economic and cultural methods for military ones. On the other hand, the disintegration of the colonial empires into a great number of weak states, many of which must rely for their very survival upon outside assistance, opens up new opportunities for imperialistic nations to expand their power by economic and cultural means. Thus China, the Soviet Union, and the United States use their economic and cultural resources in order to compete with each other for the expansion of their respective power into the so-called uncommitted third of the world or at least for preventing the other nations to expand theirs. The weakness of the new nations offers them the opportunity, and the unacceptable risk of nuclear war has transformed that opportunity into a rational necessity.

HOW TO DETECT AND COUNTER AN IMPERIALISTIC POLICY

The preceding considerations lead to the fundamental question that confronts the public officials responsible for the conduct of foreign policy as well as citizens trying to form an intelligent opinion on international issues. This question concerns the character of the foreign policy pursued by another nation and, in consequence, the kind of foreign policy that ought to be adopted with regard to it. Is the foreign policy of the other nation imperialistic, or is it not? In other words, does it seek to overthrow the existing distribution of power, or does it only contemplate adjustments within the general framework of the existing status quo? The answer to that question has determined the fate of nations, and the wrong answer has often meant deadly peril or actual destruction; for upon the correctness of that answer depends the success of the foreign policy derived from it. While it would be fatal to counter imperialistic designs with measures appropriate to a policy of the status quo, it would be only a little less risky to deal with a policy seeking adjustments within the status quo as though it were imperialistic. The classic example of the former error is the appeasement of Germany in the late thirties. The other error had a decisive influence upon the foreign policies of the great European powers in the decades before the outbreak of the First World War.

The Problem of Policy: Containment, Appeasement, Fear

As the policies of imperialism and the status quo are fundamentally different in nature, so must the policies designed to counter them be fundamentally different. A policy adequate to counter a policy of the status quo cannot be sufficient to meet a policy of imperialism. A policy of the status quo which seeks adjustments within the existing over-all distribution of power can be dealt with by a policy of give and take, of balance, of compromise: a policy, in short, that makes use of the techniques of adjustment within a given overall distribution of power in order to gain a maximum of advantage and to get by with a minimum of loss. Imperialism, which seeks to overthrow the existing distribution of power, must at the very least be countered by a policy of containment which, in defense of the existing distribution of power, calls a halt to further aggression, expansion, or other disturbances of the status quo on the part of the imperialistic nation. The policy of containment erects a wall, either a real one, such as the Great Wall of China or the French Maginot Line, or an imaginary one, such as the line of military demarcation drawn in 1945 between the Soviet orbit and the Western world. It says in effect to the imperialistic nation: "Thus far and no farther," warning it that a step beyond the line entails the virtual certainty of war.

Appeasement is a foreign policy that attempts to meet the threat of imperialism with methods appropriate to a policy of the status quo. Appeasement tries to deal with imperialism as though it were a policy of the status quo. It errs in transferring a policy of compromise from a political environment favorable to the preservation of the status quo, where it belongs, to an environment exposed to imperialistic attack, where it does not belong. One might say that appeasement is a corrupted policy of compromise, made erroneous by mistaking a policy of imperialism for a policy of the status quo.

It is important to note, in view of the contemporary tendency to use the term "appeasement" indiscriminately as a term of opprobrium, that appeasement and imperialism are logically correlated. In other words, a policy of appeasement on the one side presupposes a policy of imperialism on the other side. If we say that State A pursues with respect to State B a policy of appeasement, we are at the same time saying that State B pursues with respect to State A a policy of imperialism. If the latter statement is incorrect, the former is meaningless.

The appeaser sees in the successive demands of the imperialistic power rationally limited objectives which in themselves are compatible with the maintenance of the status quo and must be disposed of either on their intrinsic merits or by way of compromise. His error lies in not seeing that the successive demands, far from being self-contained and growing from specific grievances, are but the links of a chain at the end of which stands the overthrow of the status quo. The conciliation of antagonistic policies on the basis of legal or moral principles or through a diplomatic bargain is indeed the great task of a diplomacy that operates on both sides within the recognized limits of the status quo. Since both sides accept the existing distribution of power, both sides can afford to settle their differences either on the basis of principle or through compromise; for whatever the settlement may be, it will not affect the basic distribution of power between them.

The situation is, however, different when one or both sides have imperialistic designs; that is, when they seek a fundamental change in the existing distribution of power. Then the settlement of the respective demands on the basis of legal or moral principles or through bargaining methods, in disregard of the influence the settlement might have upon the distribution of power, amounts to a piecemeal change in the power relations in favor of the imperialistic nation. For the latter will always be favored by compromise and will be careful in choosing the grounds for its demands so that principle will favor it, too. Ultimately, these piecemeal changes will add up to the reversal of the power relations in favor of the imperialistic nation. The imperialistic nation will have won a bloodless, yet decisive, victory over an opponent who did not know the difference between compromise and appeasement.

Germany started its imperialistic policies openly in 1935 with the repudiation of the disarmament provisions of the Treaty of Versailles, pointing to the failure of the other nations to disarm and to the increase in French and Russian armaments. Taken by itself and in disregard of an ulterior objective, the argument was not without merit in the light of the legal principle of equality. Apart from paper protests and paper alliances, the only tangible reaction to this first German step on the road to empire was the conclusion three months later of the Anglo-German Naval Agreement, in which Great Britain conceded to Germany a naval force of not more than 35 per cent that of Great Britain. Both the reoccupation of the Rhineland by Germany in 1936 and its denunciation of the international control of its waterways later in the same year found support in the legal principle of equality, if one accepted the professed rational limits of the demands as the actual ones. The annexation of Austria in 1938 could easily be defended by the principle of national self-determination, which had also been one of the professed war aims of the Allied powers in the First World War.

Later in 1938 Germany demanded the German parts of Czechoslovakia. The Munich settlement granted the German demands. When Hitler, shortly before the settlement of Munich, declared that the German parts of Czechoslovakia were the last territorial demands Germany had to make in Europe, he was really saying that the annexation of these territories was an end in itself, self-contained within its own rational limits. He pretended that German policy operated within the general framework of the European status quo and was not intent upon overthrowing it, and that the other European powers ought to view German foreign policy in that light and deal with it correspondingly. It was only by the end of March 1939, five months before the outbreak of the Second World War, that the annexation of the whole of Czechoslovakia and the territorial demands on Poland convinced the Western powers that what had appeared to be a policy of the status quo had really been from the beginning a policy of imperialism, of continental, if not world, dimensions.

At that moment, the distribution of power in Europe was already changed in favor of Germany. It was changed to such an extent that a further increase in German power could not be prevented short of war. Germany had become strong enough to challenge openly the status quo of Versailles, and the prestige—that is, the reputation for power—of the nations identified with the order of Versailles had sunk so low that they were unable to defend what was left of the status quo by mere diplomatic means. They could either surrender or go to war. Thus the appeasers of 1938 became either the quislings (if they deemed resistance to German imperialism hopeless) or the heroes of 1939–45 (if they thought that resistance was morally required regardless of the outcome or that it had even a chance to succeed). The final catastrophe, and the tragic choices with which the catastrophe confronted the actors on the international scene, were predetermined by that initial error which responded to a policy of imperialism as though it were a policy of the status quo.

Once a policy of containment has succeeded in checking a policy of imperialism, or the latter has run its course either because it has reached its objective or has exhausted itself, containment (a policy of uncompromising resistance) might well make way to compromise (a policy of give and take). Such a policy, nefarious when it seeks to appease imperialism, becomes a virtue when it aims at accommodating a policy of the status quo which has left its imperialistic aspiration behind. It was this distinction to which Sir Winston Churchill referred when he said on December 14, 1950, in the House of Commons:

> The declaration of the Prime Minister that there will be no appeasement also commands almost universal support. It is a good slogan for the country. It seems to me, however, that in this House it requires to be more precisely defined. What we really mean, I think, is no appeasement through weakness or fear. Appeasement in itself may be good or bad according to the circumstances. Appeasement from weakness and fear is alike futile and fatal. Appeasement from strength is magnanimous and noble and might be the surest and perhaps the only path to world peace.

The other fundamental error into which those responsible for the conduct of foreign affairs are most likely to fall is the reverse of the one thus far discussed. It mistakes a policy of the status quo for a policy of imperialism. By doing so, State A resorts to certain measures defensive in intent, such as armaments, bases, alliances, with respect to State B. The latter, in turn, resorts to countermeasures, for it now sees State A embarking upon a policy of imperialism. These countermeasures strengthen the initial misapprehension, on the part of State A, of State B's policies, and so forth. Ultimately, either both countries correct their errors with regard to their respective policies or else the ever increasing mutual suspicions, feeding upon each other, end in war. Out of an initial error there develops a vicious circle. Two or more nations, each only seeking to preserve the status quo, but each convinced of the imperialistic designs of the others, find support for their own errors of judgment and action in the errors of the others. In such a situation nothing but an almost superhuman effort will deflect the trend of events from a catastrophic denouement.

The history of European diplomacy between the Franco-German War of 1870 and the outbreak of the First World War in 1914 illustrates this situation. After the victorious conclusion of the War of 1870 and the foundation of the German Empire, German foreign policy was mainly defensive. It was concerned with the maintenance of the position Germany had acquired in Europe and with the danger, Bismarck's famous *cauchemar des coalitions*, that a hostile coalition, especially between France and Russia, might challenge that position.

The Triple Alliance between Germany, Austria, and Italy was the instrument of that defensive policy. It was served also by the Reinsurance Treaty with Russia in which Russia and Germany pledged each other neutrality if either became involved in war with a third power.

After the dismissal of Bismarck in 1890, William II decided to let the Reinsurance Treaty lapse, primarily because of the fear that its continuation might alienate Austria and thus destroy the Triple Alliance. Russia then (in 1891 and 1894) entered into agreements with France which were defensive in character and obviously inspired by fear of the intentions of the Triple Alliance. The provisions of the Military Convention of 1894, in particular, anticipated the possible transformation of the Triple Alliance from a defensive into an imperialistic instrument. Thus the Convention was to remain a force as long as the Triple Alliance. The main provisions of the Convention made the following stipulations: If France were attacked by Germany or by Italy supported by Germany, Russia would give military aid to France. France would do the same in respect to Russia if the latter were attacked by Germany or by Austria supported by Germany. In case of the mobilization of the forces of the Triple Alliance, France and Russia would mobilize their forces without delay.

First, the fear of hostile alliances led to the formation of the Triple Alliance. Then, the fear of the latter's dissolution led to the severance by Germany of the friendly relations with Russia. Finally, the fear of the intentions of the Triple Alliance brought about the Franco-Russian Alliance. It was the mutual fears of these two defensive alliances, and the general insecurity created by the erratic character of the imperialistic utterances of William II, that inspired the diplomatic maneuvers during the two decades before the First World War. These maneuvers sought either new combinations destructive of existing alignments or the support of powers, thus far aloof, for the existing alliances. In the end, the general conflagration in 1914 was made inevitable by the fear that the other side would change the power relations decisively in its favor if not forestalled by such a change in one's own favor. In the two antagonistic blocs, Russia and Austria especially were animated by this fear. The fear of the other's suspected imperialism bred imperialism in reaction, which, in turn, gave substance to the original fear.

The distorting effects of mutual fear are particularly pronounced when antagonistic foreign policies are overlaid with world-embracing ideologies[21] to which the foreign policies actually pursued may or may not correspond. Thus the Communist ideology of world revolution and of the Communization of the world creates in non-Communist nations the fear that the foreign policies of Communist nations are of necessity at the service of a world-wide imperialism. In consequence, every move a country such as the Soviet Union or China makes on the chessboard of international politics is not judged on its own merits but in terms of imperialistic ideology. On the other hand, since Communist philosophy assumes that capitalistic nations are by nature warlike and "imperialistic,"

---

[21]For the explanation of the concept, see Chapter 7.

Western professions of dedication to law and order and opposition to aggression and subversion are interpreted by Communist nations as mere ideological disguises of imperialistic policies.

This mythological perception of reality on both sides calls forth policies seeking to contain the imperialism of the other side, and these policies confirm in the minds of all concerned the original mythological interpretation. The great powers are thus trapped in a vicious circle. First, fear makes them interpret reality in terms of an ideology on which that fear can feed. Then, the measures they take to protect themselves from what may be an imaginary danger confirm the other side in its fears and misinterpretation of reality. Then, countermeasures are taken against these measures, carrying a similar confirmation, and so forth. Thus the fear of one side sustains the fear of the other, and vice versa. Enmeshed in mutual fear and engaged in an arms race which seeks to still those fears, neither side is capable of putting the original assumption of imperialism to the test of actual experience. What was originally a mythological perception of reality has now become a self-fulfilling prophecy: the policies engendered by mutual fear appear to provide empirical evidence for the correctness of the original assumption.[22]

The Problem of Detection

Appeasement, which is the attempt to compromise with an imperialism not recognized as such, and the fear that creates imperialism where there is none—these are the two wrong answers, the two fatal mistakes an intelligent foreign policy must try to avoid. Such an intelligent foreign policy, which recognizes imperialism where it exists and determines its specific nature, is confronted with five difficulties, and they are all of a formidable character.

The first and most fundamental difficulty was pointed out by Bukharin, the foremost exponent of the Communist doctrine from Lenin's death to the great purges in the mid-thirties. Arguing against the non-economic explanation of imperialism, he summarized it thus: "Imperialism is a policy of conquest. But not every policy of conquest is imperialism."[23] The statement is indeed correct and squares with what we have said previously about the distinction between a policy of conquest operating within the existing status quo and one seeking to overthrow it.[24] To make this distinction in a concrete situation presents a formidable difficulty. How was one to know with any degree of certainty what Hitler's ultimate objectives were? From 1935 on, he made demand after demand, each of which in itself could be fully reconciled with a policy of the status quo, yet each of which might be a stepping-stone on the road to empire. The individual steps in themselves were ambiguous and, therefore, did not reveal

---

[22]Cf. John H. Kautsky, "Myth, Self-fulfilling Prophecy, and Symbolic Reassurance in the East-West Conflict," *The Journal of Conflict Resolution*, Vol. IX, No. 1 (March 1965), pp. 1 ff.

[23]N. I. Bukharin, *Imperialism and World Economy* (New York: International Publishers, 1929), p. 114

[24]See pages 55 ff.

the actual nature of the policy of which they formed the elements. Where could one, then, have found an answer to our question?

One might have found it, however tentative and open to doubt, in two of the three typical situations that we pointed out as favoring imperialistic policies. The desire to overthrow the status quo of the Treaty of Versailles had been from the very beginning one of the main points of the National Socialist program, which in 1933 became the official program of the German government. In view of this objective, one might have been able to foresee that the German government would pursue a foreign policy seeking its realization as soon as it had a chance to do so; that is, as soon as the nations identified with the status quo of the Treaty of Versailles were no longer able or willing to defend that status quo effectively.

This initial and fundamental difficulty is aggravated by the fact that a policy which starts out seeking adjustments within the existing distribution of power may change its character either in the course of its success or in the process of its frustration. In other words, the ease with which the original objectives are reached within the established distribution of power may suggest to the expanding nation that it is dealing with weak or irresolute antagonists and that a change in the existing power relations can be achieved without great effort or risk. Thus the appetite may come with the eating, and a successful policy of expansion within the status quo may overnight transform itself into a policy of imperialism. The same may be true of an unsuccessful policy of expansion within the status quo. A nation frustrated in its limited objectives, which do not seem to be attainable within the existing power relations, concludes that it must change these power relations if it is to make sure that it gets what it wants.

Where a policy is couched in purely territorial terms, the nature of the territorial objectives will sometimes indicate the nature of the policy pursued. The objective may, for instance, be a strategic point, the acquisition of which may in itself change the power relations in that particular region. No such help can be expected and, therefore, an additional difficulty must be met where a foreign policy uses mainly the vehicles of economic or cultural penetration. These methods, too, are ambiguous in view of the character of the policy they serve, but their ambiguity is much greater than that of the military method, which has defined territorial objectives. Economic and cultural expansion are generally without a clearly defined locale. They address themselves to a wide variety of ill-defined persons. And, furthermore, they are practiced on a wide scale by an indefinite number of nations. To identify economic or cultural expansion as instruments of imperialism in contrast to identical policies that have no hidden power objective beyond the explicit cultural and economic ones and, hence, are not imperialistic, is indeed a difficult task. Here again reference to the typical situations favorable to imperialistic policies will be of help.

The active economic policies Switzerland has been pursuing in the international sphere have never had an imperialistic tinge. British foreign-trade policies at times have had an imperialistic character with respect to certain countries. Today their end is in the main purely economic; that is, they try to obtain for the inhabitants of the British Isles the necessities of life. They aim at economic survival through favorable trade balances, not at the maintenance or acquisition of political power over foreign nations. It is only with regard to certain strategic regions, such as Egypt and Iran, that since the end of the Second World War British economic policies have at times been subordinated to political considerations. Some of these considerations might have acquired, or under certain conditions will acquire, an imperialistic character.

The cultural penetration of Latin America by Spain was generally bound to be without imperialistic significance, for the military weakness of Spain in relation to the United States forbade any thought of changing the power relations in Latin America in Spain's favor. The cultural mission of France has been in certain countries and at certain times an end in itself. Under different circumstances and in other countries it has been subordinated to imperialistic aims. Here, too, the character of economic and cultural expansion may change with a change in the political situation. When the opportunity beckons, the "reservoir of good will" or a preponderant position in the foreign trade of another country, which a nation has acquired as ends in themselves, may suddenly become sources of political power and potent instruments in the struggle for power. But when circumstances change again, they may lose that quality just as suddenly.

When all these difficulties have been overcome and a foreign policy has been correctly identified as imperialistic, yet another difficulty presents itself. It concerns the kind of imperialism with which one has to deal. A successful localized imperialism may find in its success an incentive to spread wider and wider until it becomes continental or worldwide. More particularly, a country may find it necessary, in order to stabilize and secure a local preponderance, to acquire preponderance of power on an even greater scale, and it may feel fully secure only in a worldwide empire. There is frequently in imperialism a dynamic force, rationalized in aggressive or defensive terms, that proceeds from a limited region to a continent and from there to the world. The Macedonian Empire under Philip and Alexander and Napoleonic imperialism were of this kind. On the other hand, a policy of worldwide imperialism, opposed by superior force, may retreat to a geographically determined region or be satisfied with local preponderance. Or it may lose its imperialistic tendencies altogether and transform itself into a policy of the status quo. The development from geographically determined to localized imperialism and from there to the permanent loss of imperialistic tendencies altogether can be traced in the history of Swedish imperialism in the seventeenth and eighteenth centuries.

Thus the evaluation of imperialistic tendencies and, consequently, of the policies countering them is never definitive. Both policies and counterpolicies are ever subject to re-evaluation and reformulation. But the framers of foreign policy are always exposed to the temptation to take a particular pattern of imperialistic expansion or of any other type of foreign policy as permanent and to pursue a foreign policy adapted to that pattern even when the pattern has changed. A worldwide imperialism requires countermeasures different from those which are adequate for one that is localized, and a nation that counters the latter with measures appropriate to the former will bring on the very dangers it tries to avoid. In this necessity to recognize quickly a change in the imperialistic policy of another nation lies another difficulty and, in the failure to adapt one's own foreign policy quickly to such change, another source of error.

Finally, imperialism poses a problem that it shares with all foreign policy—presenting it, however, in a particularly acute manner. This is the problem of detecting the true nature of a foreign policy behind its ideological disguises. The actors on the international scene rarely present the foreign policy they are pursuing for what it is, and a policy of imperialism almost never reveals its true face in the pronouncements of those who pursue it. The true nature of the policies pursued disappears behind a veil of ideological disguises. The reasons why this must be so and the typical shapes these ideologies take will be discussed in Chapter 7 of this book. How difficult it is to distinguish between the appearance of a foreign policy and its essence will become apparent in the course of that discussion.

6

The Struggle for Power: Policy of Prestige

The policy of prestige has rarely been recognized in modern political literature for what it is: the third of the basic manifestations of the struggle for power on the international scene. The reasons for this neglect are threefold. The policy of prestige shares this neglect with the subtle and intangible relationships the understanding of which, as we have seen,[1] has suffered from the predominant theoretical and practical concern with the material aspect of power in the form of force, actual or threatened. Furthermore, the policy of prestige has used as one of its main vehicles the aristocratic forms of social intercourse practiced in the diplomatic world. That world, with its ceremonial rules, its quarrels about rank and precedence, and its empty formalisms, is the very antithesis of the democratic way of life. Even those not fully persuaded that power politics is nothing but an elitist atavism have been inclined to see in the policy of prestige as practiced by diplomats an anachronistic game, frivolous and farcical and devoid of any organic connection with the business of international politics.

Finally, prestige, in contrast to the maintenance and acquisition of power, is but rarely an end in itself. More frequently, the policy of prestige is one of the instrumentalities through which the policies of the status quo and of imperialism try to achieve their ends. This makes it easy to conclude that the policy of prestige is not important and does not deserve systematic discussion.

Actually, the policy of prestige, however exaggerated and absurd its uses may have been at times, is as intrinsic an element of the relations between nations as the desire for prestige is of the relations between individuals. Here again it becomes obvious that international and domestic politics are but dif-

---

[1] See page 32.

84

ferent manifestations of one and the same social fact. In both spheres, the desire for social recognition is a potent dynamic force determining social relations and creating social institutions. The individual seeks confirmation, on the part of his fellows, of the evaluation he puts upon himself. It is only in the tribute others pay to his goodness, intelligence, and power that he becomes fully aware of, and can fully enjoy, what he deems to be his superior qualities. It is only through his reputation for excellence that he can gain the measure of security, wealth, and power he regards to be his due. Thus, in the struggle for existence and power—which is, as it were, the raw material of the social world—what others think about us is as important as what we actually are. The image in the mirror of our fellows' minds (that is, our prestige), rather than the original, of which the image in the mirror may be but the distorted reflection, determines what we are as members of society.

It is, then, a necessary and important task to see to it that the mental picture other people form of one's position in society at least represents faithfully the actual situation, if it does not excel it. This is exactly what the policy of prestige is about. Its purpose is to impress other nations with the power one's own nation actually possesses, or with the power it believes, or wants the other nations to believe, it possesses. Two specific instrumentalities serve this purpose: diplomatic ceremonial in the widest meaning of the term, and the display of military force.

DIPLOMATIC CEREMONIAL

Two episodes from the life of Napoleon show clearly the symbols through which the power position of a ruler, representing a nation, expresses itself in ceremonial forms. One shows Napoleon at the summit of his power, the other indicates that he had left that summit behind.

In 1804, when Napoleon was about to be crowned Emperor by the Pope, each of the two rulers had a vital interest in demonstrating his superiority over the other. Napoleon was successful in asserting his superiority, not only by putting the crown on his head with his own hands instead of letting the Pope do it, but also by a ceremonial device that the Duke of Rovigo, one of Napoleon's generals and minister of police, reports in his memoirs:

> He went to meet the Pope on the road to Nemours. To avoid ceremony, the pretext of a hunting-party was assumed; the attendants, with his equipages, were in the forest. The Emperor came on horseback and in a hunting-dress, with his retinue. It was at the half-moon on the top of the hill that the meeting took place. There the Pope's carriage drew up; he got out at the left door in his white costume: the ground was dirty; he did not like to step upon it with his white silk shoes, but was obliged to do so at last.
>
> Napoleon alighted to receive him. They embraced; and the Emperor's carriage, which had been purposely driven up, was advanced a few paces, as if from the carelessness of the driver; but men were posted to hold the two doors open:

at the moment of getting in, the Emperor took the right door, and an officer of the court handed the Pope to the left, so that they entered the carriage by the two doors at the same time. The Emperor naturally seated himself on the right; and this first step decided without negotiation upon the etiquette to be observed during the whole time that the Pope was to remain at Paris.[2]

The other episode occurred in 1813 in Dresden, after the defeat in Russia, when Napoleon was threatened by a coalition of all of Europe, a coalition that shortly afterward would inflict upon him the disastrous defeat of Leipzig. In an interview lasting nine hours, Napoleon tried to restrain the Austrian Chancellor, Metternich, from joining the coalition against him. Metternich treated Napoleon as a doomed man, while Napoleon acted like the master of Europe, which he had been for a decade. After a particularly stormy exchange, Napoleon, as if to test his superiority, dropped his hat, expecting the spokesman of the hostile coalition to pick it up. When Metternich feigned not to see it, it must have become clear to both men that a decisive change had occurred in the prestige and power of the victor of Austerlitz and Wagram. Metternich summed up the situation when he told Napoleon at the end of the discussion that he was sure Napoleon was lost.

The relations between diplomats lend themselves naturally as instruments for a policy of prestige, for diplomats are the symbolic representatives of their respective countries.[3] The respect shown them is really shown their countries; the respect shown by them is really shown by their countries; the insult they give or receive is really given or received by their countries. History abounds with examples illustrating these points and the importance attributed to them in international politics.

In most courts it was the custom to have foreign ambassadors introduced to the sovereign by ordinary officials while royal ambassadors were introduced by princes. When in 1698 Louis XIV had the Ambassador of the Republic of Venice introduced by the Prince of Lorraine, the Grand Council of Venice asked the French Ambassador to assure the King that the Republic of Venice would be forever grateful for that honor and the Council sent a special letter of thanks to Louis XIV. Through that gesture France indicated that it regarded the Republic of Venice to be as powerful as a kingdom, and it was for that new prestige that Venice showed its gratitude. At the papal court the Pope used to receive the diplomatic representatives of different types of states in different halls. Ambassadors of crowned heads and of Venice were received in the *Sala Reggia*, the representatives of other princes and of republics in the *Sala Ducale*. The Republic of Genoa is said to have offered the Pope millions in order to have its representatives received in the *Sala Reggia* instead of in the *Sala Ducale*. The Pope, however, refused to grant the request because of the opposition of Venice, which did not want Genoa to be treated on equal terms with herself. Equality of treatment would have meant equality of prestige—that is, reputation for power—and to this the state superior in prestige could not consent.

---

[2]*Memoirs of the Duke of Rovigo* (London, 1828), Vol. 1, Part II, p. 73.
[3]For the different functions of diplomats, see Chapter 24.

At the end of the eighteenth century, it was still the custom at the court of Constantinople that ambassadors and members of their suites who presented themselves to the Sultan were grabbed by the arms by court officials and their heads bent down. After the customary exchange of speeches between ambassador and Prime Minister, the court officials exclaimed: "Praise be to the Eternal that the infidels must come and give homage to our gloriously brilliant sceptre." The humiliation of the representatives of foreign countries was intended to symbolize the inferiority in power of the countries they represented.

Under President Theodore Roosevelt, all diplomatic representatives were received together on the first of January in order to present their congratulations to the President. President Taft changed the arrangement and ordered that ambassadors and ministers be received separately. When the Spanish Minister, who had not been informed of this change, appeared on January 1, 1910, at the White House for the reception of the ambassadors he was refused admission. Whereupon the Spanish government recalled the minister and protested to the government of the United States. A nation that had just lost its empire and passed to the rank of a third-rate power insisted at least upon the prestige commensurate with its former greatness.

In 1946, when the Foreign Minister of the Soviet Union was seated at a victory celebration in Paris in the second row, while the representatives of other great powers sat in the first, he left the meeting in protest. A nation that for long had been a pariah in the international community had attained the unquestioned position of a great power and insisted upon the prestige due to its new status. At the Potsdam Conference of 1945, Churchill, Stalin, and Truman were unable to agree on who should enter the conference room first; finally they entered through three different doors at the same time. These three political leaders symbolized the respective power of their nations. Consequently, the precedence accorded to one of them would have given his nation a prestige of superiority over the other two which the latter were not willing to concede. Since they claimed equality of power, they were bound to be concerned with upholding the prestige in which that equality found its symbolic expression.

To cite two examples: France, since DeGaulle opposed the supranational tendencies of the European Communities, objected

> to the traditional style—striped pants, morning coat and champagne—in which Dr. Walter Hallstein, president of the Common Market Commission, has been receiving ambassadors presenting their credentials.
>
> Paris feels that such a ceremony creates the impression that Dr. Hallstein is equal in rank, for the purpose of receiving ambassadors' credentials, to a chief of state, such as President deGaulle.
>
> The French contend that the commission is not a government and the ceremony should be toned down. This is one aspect of French opposition to the so-called supra-national features of the European communities. France views them as groups of sovereign states.[4]

---

[4]*The New York Times*, May 4, 1966, p. 16.

The peace negotiations among the United States, the South and North Vietnam governments, and the National Liberation Front (Viet Cong) which were supposed to have started in November 1968 were delayed for ten weeks because of a dispute over the shape of the conference table. North Vietnam proposed a square table, or four tables arranged in a circular or diamond pattern, or a plain round table forming a complete unbroken circle. The United States, on the other hand, proposed two half oval tables placed against each other to form a broken oval, or two half-circular tables to form a broken circle, or two half-circular tables, separated somewhat from each other, with two rectangular tables for secretaries between them. As concerns the last proposal, the United States made the concession that the two half-circular tables could be pushed together to adjoin the secretarial tables between them. However, the secretarial tables would have to jut out a few inches on either side from the curved tables.[5] Finally, a circular table without nameplates, flags or markings was agreed upon. Two rectangular tables, measuring about 3 feet by 4½ feet, were to be placed 18 inches from the circular table at opposite sides.

What lay behind these seemingly absurd proceedings? North Vietnam insisted upon the recognition of the Viet Cong as an independent negotiating party. The United States wanted the recognition of its assumption, basic to its long-held conception of the war, that the Viet Cong were a mere extension of the North Vietnamese regime. Thus the controversy over the shape of the table was a symbolic manifestation of the substance of the conflict. Was the Vietnam War the result of the aggression of the North Vietnamese, using the Viet Cong as its instrument, or was the Viet Cong a genuine popular force, aided and abetted but not created by the North Vietnamese? The shape of the table, one way or other, would have prejudged that substantive issue. The shape finally agreed upon appeared to leave that issue in abeyance.

The political importance of the entertainment in which all diplomats vie with each other is well illustrated by these excerpts from an article dealing with the Washington social scene:

> Now the question of whether foreign embassies actually *buy* anything for their countries with all this entertainment is naturally moot. There is no check on it. But most ambassadors pursue their social rounds with dead seriousness and regard it as one of the most important and productive aspects of their job. They are probably right.
>
> After all, propriety severely constricts the activities of an ambassador in the capital to which he is accredited. Certainly an ambassador doesn't want to be seen on the Hill, mingling with Congressmen or publicly registering reaction to the tone and tenor of legislative debates. Yet he must get about enough to receive accurate impressions of American affairs and officials, and in turn leave some impress of his own and his country's character on the public mind. For this, the social avenue is almost his only approach, and unless he is attractive and adept in the salon, he will not be of much use to his country in the chancery. . . .

---

[5]*The New York Times*, December 14, 1968, p. 2.

Because the Latin Americans throw the biggest and most expensive parties in Washington, and appear to profit the least thereby, there is a tendency to write them off as mere playboys. That is a mistake. What the Latinos are striving for, above all, is prestige, a place of equality in the family of American nations; and who can say that by parading not only their wealth but their good manners and bright, zestful minds in a series of unrivaled entertainments they are not accomplishing something toward that end?[6]

The policy of prestige as the policy of demonstrating the power a nation has or thinks it has, or wants other nations to believe it has, finds a particularly fruitful field in the choice of a locality for international meetings. When many antagonistic claims compete with each other and cannot be reconciled through compromise, the meeting-place is frequently chosen in a country that does not participate in the competition for prestige. For this reason, The Hague in the Netherlands and Geneva in Switzerland have been favored meeting-places for international conferences. Frequently, the shift from one favorite meeting-place to another symbolizes a shift in the preponderance of power. During the better part of the nineteenth century, most international conferences were held in Paris. But the Congress of Berlin of 1878, held in the capital of the re-established German Empire after its victory over France, demonstrated to all the world Germany's new prestige of being the preponderant power on the European continent. Originally, the Soviet Union opposed the choice of Geneva as headquarters of the United Nations; for Geneva, the former headquarters of the League of Nations, was symbolic of the low point in Russian prestige in the period between the two world wars. When the distribution of power within the United Nations, meeting in New York in the aftermath of the Second World War, showed the Soviet Union in what appeared to be a permanent minority, confronted with a majority under American leadership, it advocated the transfer of the headquarters of the United Nations to Geneva, which carried no symbolic reference to American supremacy. That in 1972 President Nixon met the Chinese Prime Minister, Chou En-lai, in Peking and not in Washington or at some neutral place has a symbolic significance for the shifts that the nations concerned believe to have occurred in the distribution of power in Asia and in the world.

Normally a nation that has a preponderance of power in a particular field or region insists that international conferences dealing with matters concerning that field or region meet within, or at least close to, its territory. Thus most international conferences dealing with maritime questions have been held in London. International conferences concerned with Japan have met either in Washington or in Tokyo. Most international conferences concerned with the future of Europe after the Second World War have been held either on Russian territory, such as Moscow and Yalta, or in territory occupied by the Soviet Union, such as Potsdam, or in the proximity of Russian territory, such as

---

[6] "R.S.V. Politics," *Fortune*, February 1952, p. 120. (Used by permission of *Fortune*. Copyright Time Inc., 1952.)

Teheran. Yet, by the end of 1947, the political situation had changed to such an extent that President Truman could declare with considerable emphasis that he would meet Stalin nowhere but in Washington.[7]

DISPLAY OF MILITARY FORCE

Besides the practices of diplomacy, the policy of prestige uses military demonstrations as means to achieve its purpose. Since military strength is the obvious measure of a nation's power, its demonstration serves to impress the others with that nation's power. Military representatives of foreign nations are, for instance, invited to peacetime army and navy maneuvers, not in order to let them in on military secrets, but to impress them and their governments with the military preparedness of the particular nation. The invitation of foreign observers to the two atomic bomb tests in the Pacific in 1946 was intended to fulfill a similar purpose. The foreign observer was, on the one hand, to be impressed by the naval might of the United States and with American technological achievements. "Twenty-one observers from the United Nations Atomic Energy Control Commission," reported the *New York Times*, ". . . agreed today that the United States was bombing a group of ships larger than many of the world's navies."[8] On the other hand, the foreign observer was to see for himself what the atomic bomb could do above and under water and how superior in military strength a nation that had the monopoly of the atomic bomb was bound to be in comparison with nations that did not have it.

Because of the high mobility of navies, which are able to bring the flag and the power of a nation to the four corners of the globe and because of the great impressiveness of their appearance, naval demonstrations have in the past been a favorite instrument of the policy of prestige. The visit in 1891 of the French fleet to the Russian port of Kronstadt and the return visit in 1893 of the Russian fleet to the French port of Toulon mark a turning point in the political history of the world; for these mutual visits demonstrated to the world a political and military solidarity between France and Russia which was not long in crystallizing into a political and military alliance. The periodical dispatch, on the part of the great maritime powers, of naval squadrons to the ports of the Far East demonstrated to the peoples of that region the superiority of Western power. The United States has from time to time sent warships to Latin-American ports in order to remind the nations concerned that in the Western Hemisphere American naval power is supreme.

Whenever the claims of a maritime power were challenged in colonial or semicolonial regions either by the natives or by competing powers, these nations would dispatch warships to the region as symbolic representatives of the power of the country. A famous example of this kind of policy of prestige is the

---

[7]*New York Times*, December 19, 1947, p. 1; July 27, 1948, p. 1; February 4, 1949, p. 1.
[8]Ibid., July 1, 1946, p. 3.

visit William II paid in 1905 on board a German warship to Tangier, a port of Morocco, for the purpose of counteracting French claims on that state. The Mediterranean cruises American naval squadrons have been making since the Second World War to Italian, Greek, and Turkish ports are the unmistakable reply to Russian aspirations in that region. The selection of the most exposed regions of Western Europe for maneuvers by the combined forces of the Western allies is intended to demonstrate to the Soviet Union and to the allies themselves the military power of the Atlantic Alliance and the resolution to use this power in defense of the status quo in Western Europe.

The most drastic form of the military type of the policy of prestige is partial or total mobilization. Mobilization as an instrument of the policy of prestige may be obsolete today, since the war of the future will in all probability require total preparedness at all times. In the past, however, and as late as 1938 and 1939, the calling to the colors either of certain classes of the reserves or of all those subject to military service has been a potent instrument of the policy of prestige. When, for instance, in July 1914, Russia mobilized its army, followed by the mobilization of the Austrian, German, and French forces, and when France and Czechoslovakia mobilized their armies in September 1938, and France its army again in March and September 1939, the purpose was always to demonstrate to friend and foe alike one's own military strength and one's resolution to use that strength in support of one's political ends. President Bush did this with the National Guard and reserves in Desert Shield.

Here prestige—reputation for power—is employed both as a deterrent to and as preparation for war. It is hoped that the prestige of one's own nation will be great enough to deter the other nations from going to war. At the same time it is hoped that, if this policy of prestige should fail, the mobilization of the armed forces before the actual outbreak of war will put one's own nation in the most advantageous military position possible under the circumstances. At that point, political and military policy tend to merge and become two different aspects of one and the same policy. We shall have further occasion to point to the intimate relations between foreign and military policy in times of peace as well as of war.[9]

TWO OBJECTIVES OF THE POLICY OF PRESTIGE

The policy of prestige has two possible ultimate objectives: prestige for its own sake, or much more frequently, prestige in support of a policy of the status quo or of imperialism. While in national societies prestige is frequently sought for its own sake, it is rarely the primary objective of foreign policy. Prestige is at most the pleasant by-product of foreign policies whose ultimate objectives are not the reputation for power but the substance of power. The individual members of a national society, protected as they are in their existence and social

---

[9]See Chapters 9, 18, 25.

position by an integrated system of social institutions and rules of conduct, can afford to indulge in the competition for prestige as a kind of harmless social game. But nations, which as members of the international society must in the main rely upon their own power for the protection of their existence and power position, can hardly neglect the effect that a gain or loss of prestige will have upon their power position on the international scene.

It is therefore not by accident that, as we have already pointed out, observers of international affairs who underrate the importance of power tend to take questions of prestige lightly. And it is likewise not by accident that only foolhardy egocentrics are inclined to pursue a policy of prestige for its own sake. In modern times, William II and Mussolini are cases in point. Intoxicated with newly acquired domestic power, they regarded international politics as a kind of personal sport where in the exaltation of one's own nation and in the humiliation of others one enjoyed one's own personal superiority. By doing so, however, they confused the international with the domestic scene. At home, the demonstration of their power, or at least of its appearance, would be at worst nothing more than harmless foolishness. Abroad, such a demonstration is a play with fire that will consume the player who does not have the power commensurate with his belief or his pretense. One-man governments—that is, absolute monarchies or dictatorships—tend to identify the personal glory of the ruler with the political interests of the nation. In view of the successful conduct of foreign policy, this identification is a serious weakness, for it leads to a policy of prestige for its own sake, neglectful of the national interests at stake and of the power available to support them. American policy in Indochina from 1965 to 1975 could well be seen in the light of this analysis.

The function the policy of prestige fulfills for the policies of the status quo and of imperialism grows out of the very nature of international politics. The foreign policy of a nation is always the result of an estimate of the power relations as they exist among different nations at a certain moment of history and as they are likely to develop in the immediate and distant future. The foreign policy of the United States, for instance, is based upon an evaluation of the power of the United States in relation to, let us say, the power of Great Britain, the Soviet Union, and Argentina, and of the probable future development of the power of these different nations. Likewise, the foreign policies of Great Britain, the Soviet Union, and Argentina are based upon similar evaluations, which are constantly subjected to review for the purpose of bringing them up to date.

It is the primary function of the policy of prestige to influence these evaluations. If, for instance, the United States could impress its power upon the Latin-American nations to such an extent as to convince them that its predominance in the Western Hemisphere was unchallengeable, its policy of the status quo in the Western Hemisphere would not be likely to be challenged, and its success would thus be assured. The relative political stability Europe enjoyed during the twenties and in the beginning of the thirties was due mainly to the prestige of France as the strongest military power in the world. German imperialism owes its triumphs in the late thirties mainly to a successful policy of prestige. This policy was able to convince the nations interested in the maintenance of the status quo of Germany's superiority, if not invincibility. For instance, the showing of documentary films of the "blitzkrieg" in Poland and France to foreign audiences composed preferably of military and political leaders clearly served this purpose. Whatever the ultimate objectives of a nation's foreign policy, its prestige—its reputation for power—is always an important and sometimes a decisive factor in determining success or failure of its foreign policy. A policy of prestige is, therefore, an indispensable element of a rational foreign policy.

The Cold War, which dominated the relations of the Western world and the Soviet bloc during the two decades following the Second World War, was fought primarily with the weapons of prestige. The United States and the Soviet Union endeavored to impress each other with their military might, technological achievements, economic potential, and political principles in order to weaken each other's morale and deter each other from taking an irrevocable step toward war. Similarly, they tried to impress their allies, the members of the hostile alliance, and the uncommitted nations with these same qualities. Their aim was to keep the allegiance of their own allies, weaken the unity of the hostile coalition, and win the support of the uncommitted nations.

Prestige has become particularly important as a political weapon in an age in which the struggle for power is fought not only with the traditional methods of political pressure and military force, but in large measure as a struggle for the minds of men. In wide areas of Asia, the Middle East, Africa, and Latin America, the Cold War was fought primarily in terms of competition between two rival political philosophies, economic systems, and ways of life. This is another way of saying that in these regions prestige—reputation for performance and power—has become the main stake for which political warfare is waged. The chief instruments of this struggle are propaganda, which seeks to increase the prestige of one's own side and deflate that of the enemy, and foreign aid, which intends to impress the recipient nation with the economic and technological proficiency of the aid's provider.

A policy of prestige attains its very triumph when it gives the nation pursuing it such a reputation for power as to enable it to forgo the actual employment of the instrument of power. Two factors make that triumph possible: reputation for unchallengeable power and reputation for self-restraint in using it. Of this rare combination the Roman and the British empires and the Good Neighbor policy of the United States, when it prevailed, are the classic examples.

The longevity of the Roman Empire, in contrast to the fate of quick dissolution which generally befalls imperial structures of similar dimensions, was due primarily to the profound respect in which the name of a Roman was held within its confines. Rome was superior in political acumen and military strength to any one of the component parts of the Empire. By making the burden of superiority as easy as possible to bear, it deprived its subject peoples of the incentive to rid themselves of Roman domination. At worst one or the other of the subject peoples might revolt, but there was never incentive enough for the formation of a coalition sufficiently strong to challenge Rome. Isolated revolts would be dealt with swiftly and efficiently by preponderant Roman power, thus increasing Rome's prestige for power. The contrast between the dismal fate of those who dared to challenge Rome, and the peaceful and prosperous existence, under the protection of the Roman law, of those who remained loyal, increased Rome's reputation for moderation in the exercise of its power.

The same reputation for power tempered by self-restraint was one of the foundation stones of the British Empire. Observers have marveled at the ability of a few thousand British officials to dominate hundreds of millions of Indians, not to speak of the voluntary ties of loyalty which kept the self-governing dominions united in the Empire. But the ignominious defeats Great Britain suffered in the Second World War at the hands of Japan shattered forever its reputation for unchallengeable power. And the cry for national liberation, raised by the subject races throughout Asia, drowned out the memory of a tolerant rule mellowed by age and wisdom. When that twofold prestige was gone and the resources to maintain the Empire by sheer force had become unavailable, the Asiatic part of the British Empire did not for long survive the prestige of Britain.

During the era of the Good Neighbor policy, the hegemony of the United States in the Western Hemisphere reposed likewise upon the reputation for unchallengeable power rather than upon its actual exercise. The superiority of the United States in the Western Hemisphere was so obvious and overwhelming that prestige alone was sufficient to assure the United States the position among the American republics commensurate with its power. The United States even at times could afford to forgo insistence upon the prestige that was its due, because the self-restraint thus manifested made its hegemony more tolerable to its neighbors to the south. Thus the United States made a point, from the inauguration of the Good Neighbor policy, to have Pan-American conferences meet in Latin-American countries rather than in the United States. Since in the Western Hemisphere the United States had the substance of unchallengeable power, it deemed it the better part of wisdom not to insist upon all the manifestations of the prestige that go with such overwhelming power, and to allow some other country in the Western Hemisphere to enjoy at least the appearances of power in the form of prestige. Only with the decline of the Organization of American States and a shift in American policy did this outlook begin to change.

THREE CORRUPTIONS OF THE POLICY OF PRESTIGE

For a nation to pursue a policy of prestige is, however, not enough. It can do too much or too little in this respect, and in either case it will run the risk of failure. It does too much when, insecure in the awareness of its power, it invests a particular move with a measure of prestige out of all proportion to its actual importance. The prestige of a nation is not determined by the success or failure of a particular move at a particular moment in history. Quite to the contrary, it reflects the sum total of a nation's qualities and actions, of its successes and failures, of its historic memories and aspirations. The prestige of a nation is very much like the credit of a bank. A bank with large, proven resources and a record of successes can afford what a small and frequently unsuccessful competitor cannot: to make a mistake or suffer a setback. Its known power is big enough for its prestige to survive such reverses. The same is true of nations.

The pages of history are full of instances of nations which, secure in their possession of great power and recognized as such by their peers, have suffered defeat or retreated from exposed positions without suffering a loss in prestige. When was the prestige of France higher: when it fought wars in Indochina and Algeria which it could neither win nor thought it could afford to lose, or after it had liquidated these losing enterprises? And how much, in the long run, did American prestige suffer from the debacle of the Bay of Pigs in 1962? When France demonstrated the wisdom and courage to liquidate two losing enterprises on which it had staked its "honor," its prestige rose to heights it had not attained since the beginning of the Second World War, and the Bay of Pigs has weighed little in the scales of American prestige, heavy as they are with power and successes. Nations must take care not to confound ephemeral fluctuations of public opinion with the lasting foundations of national power and prestige. Prestige in a particular instance, then, like the power it mirrors, must be seen in the context of a nation's over-all power and prestige. The greatness of the latter is reflected in the former, and the deficiencies of the former are compensated for by the latter.

A nation also does too much when it paints an exaggerated picture of its power and thus attempts to gain a reputation for power which exceeds the power it actually possesses. In that case, it builds its prestige upon the appearances of power rather than upon its substance. Here the policy of prestige transforms itself into a policy of bluff. Its outstanding example in recent history is the policy of Italy from the Ethiopian War of 1935 to the African campaign of 1942. Embarking upon a policy of imperialistic expansion with the purpose of making the Mediterranean an Italian lake, Italy during the Ethiopian War and the Spanish Civil War of 1936–39 dared defy Great Britain, then the foremost naval power on earth and the predominant power in the Mediterranean. It did so by creating the impression that it was a military power of the first order. Italy was successful in this policy so long as no other nation dared to put its pretense of power to the actual test. When this test came, it revealed the contrast between Italy's reputation for power, deliberately created by a number of propagandistic devices, and its actual power. It unmasked its policy of prestige as a policy of bluff.

The essence of a policy of bluff is well illustrated in the theater device of letting a score of extras, dressed as soldiers, walk about the stage, disappear behind the scenery, and come back again and again, thus creating the illusion of a great number of marching men. While the ignorant and the gullible will easily be deceived by this appearance of armed might, the informed and detached observer will not fall victim to the deception. And if the stage directions require that the "army" give battle to another "army" the bluff becomes patent to anyone. Here the policy of bluff is reduced to its essentials, and its mechanics are demonstrated in elemental form. It is easy for the policy of bluff to succeed in the short run, but in the long run it can succeed only if it is able to postpone forever the test of actual performance, and this even the highest quality of statecraft cannot assure.

The best that luck and political wisdom can do is to use the initial success of a policy of bluff for the purpose of bringing the actual power of one's nation up to its reputed quality. While the other nations are bluffed into giving that power undeserved consideration, time is gained for bringing prestige and actual power into harmony. A nation, therefore, that has fallen behind in the competition for power, especially in the field of armaments, might try to conceal its weakness behind a policy of bluff while at the same time endeavoring to overcome its handicap. When Great Britain, in the autumn and winter of 1940–41, was actually open to invasion, its prestige, far exceeding at that time its actual military strength, was probably the most important single factor deterring the Germans from the attempt to invade its territory. Subsequently, while maintaining the appearance of its defensive strength, it was able to acquire actual defensive strength. It must, however, be noted that luck came to the assistance of that policy of bluff in the form of Hitler's military mistakes, and that this policy was not so much freely chosen by Great Britain as forced upon it as a desperate last resort by an almost irresistible necessity.[10]

While it thus remains true that it is generally a mistake in international politics to engage in a policy of bluff, it is no less a mistake to go to the other extreme and be satisfied with a reputation for power which is inferior to the actual power possessed. The outstanding examples of this "negative policy of prestige" are the United States and the Soviet Union in the period between the two world wars and, more particularly, in the first years of the Second World War.

At the outbreak of the Second World War, the United States was already potentially the most powerful nation on earth, and it had openly declared its opposition to the imperialism of Germany and Japan. Nevertheless, Germany and Japan proceeded very much as though the United States as a first-rate power did not exist at all. The significance of the attack on Pearl Harbor in view of this discussion lies in the implied expression of contempt for the military

---

[10]One can safely say that in the two most critical periods of its history Great Britain owed its salvation, at least in part, to its prestige. When in 1797 all of Europe was at Napoleon's feet and France concentrated all its efforts upon the destruction of Great Britain, a mutiny broke out in the British fleet. For a time two loyal ships were all that stood between the continent and the British Isles. In the winter of 1940–41, Great Britain was, for however different reasons, similarly helpless. In both situations, the awe in which the British name was held was one of the factors deterring its enemies from an attack that the distribution of material power greatly favored.

strength of the United States. The reputation for power of the United States—
that is, its prestige—was so low that Japan could base its war plans upon the
assumption that American military strength would not recover from the blow
of Pearl Harbor in time to influence the outcome of the war. American prestige
was so low that Germany and Italy, instead of trying to keep the United States
out of the European war, seemed almost eager to bring it in by declaring war
against it on December 10, 1941. Hitler is quoted as having declared in 1934:
"The American is no soldier. The inferiority and decadence of this allegedly
New World is evident in its military inefficiency."[11]

So enormous a depreciation was primarily due to what can almost be called
the absence of an American policy of prestige in so far as reputation for military
power is concerned. Far from demonstrating to the other nations what the
human and material potentialities of the United States could mean in terms of
military power, the United States seemed almost anxious to prove to the world
its unwillingness, if not inability, to transform those enormous potentialities
into actual instruments of war. Thus the United States invited neglect and
attack from its enemies, failure for its policies, mortal danger to its vital interests.

The Soviet Union had to cope with similar results not because it neglected,
but because it failed in, its policy of prestige. Throughout the period between
the two world wars, the reputation of the Soviet Union for power was low.
While Germany, France, and Great Britain at times tried to secure Russian
support for their foreign policies, no nation had a sufficiently high opinion of the
power of the Soviet Union to overcome the aversion to Russian political ideology and the fear of its spreading through the rest of Europe. When, for instance,
during the Czechoslovakian crisis of 1938 France and Great Britain were confronted with the alternative of either approving the imperialistic expansion of
Germany or trying to check it with the aid of the Soviet Union, the latter's
prestige was so low that the Western European powers rejected its proffered
co-operation without much hesitation. The military prestige of the Soviet Union
reached its lowest point during the campaign against Finland in 1939–40, when
little Finland seemed able to hold its own against the Russian giant. That lack
of prestige was one of the factors that convinced the German general staff as
well as the general staffs of the allied nations that the Soviet Union would be
unable to withstand a German attack.

For a wise foreign policy, however, such discrepancy between prestige and
actual power ought not to be a matter of indifference. For if the Soviet Union
had appeared to be as powerful in 1938 or 1939 or 1941 as it actually was—that
is, if its prestige had then been commensurate with its power—the policies of
the other nations with respect to the Soviet Union might easily have been
different, and the destiny of the Soviet Union and of the world might have been
different as well. Whether today the Soviet Union is as strong as it seems to be,

---

[11]Hermann Rauschning, *The Voice of Destruction* (New York: G. P. Putnam's Sons, 1940), p.
71.

or stronger, or weaker, is a question of fundamental importance for both the Soviet Union and the rest of the world. The same is true of the United States and of any other nation playing an active role in international politics. To demonstrate to the rest of the world the power one's own nation possesses, revealing neither too much nor too little, is the task of a wisely conceived policy of prestige.

7

The Ideological
Element in
International Policies

THE NATURE OF POLITICAL IDEOLOGIES[1]

It is a characteristic aspect of all politics, domestic as well as international, that frequently its basic manifestations do not appear as what they actually are—manifestations of a struggle for power. Rather, the element of power as the immediate goal of the policy pursued is explained and justified in ethical, legal, or biological terms. That is to say: the true nature of the policy is concealed by ideological justifications and rationalizations.

The deeper the individual is involved in the power struggle, the less likely he is to see the power struggle for what it is. The words which Hamlet addresses to his mother might be addressed with equal lack of success to all hungry for power:

> . . . Mother, for love of grace,
> Lay not that flattering unction to your soul,
> That not your trespass, but my madness speaks.

---

[1] The concept of ideology is frequently used in the general sense of philosophic, political, and moral convictions; we are dealing with the subject matter referred to by this general concept of ideology in later parts of this book. The concept of ideology used in this chapter corresponds to what Karl Mannheim has called "particular ideology." See Karl Mannheim, *Ideology and Utopia* (New York: Harcourt, Brace and Company, 1936), p. 49: "The particular conception of ideology is implied when the term denotes that we are sceptical of the ideas and representations advanced by our opponent. They are regarded as more or less conscious disguises of the real nature of a situation, the true recognition of which would not be in accord with his interests. These distortions range all the way from conscious lies to half-conscious and unwitting disguises; from calculated attempts to dupe others to self-deception." See also p. 238: "The study of ideologies has made it its task to unmask the more or less conscious deceptions and disguises of human interest groups, particularly those of political parties."

Or, as Tolstoy puts it in *War and Peace:*

> When a man acts alone, he always carries within him a certain series of considerations, that have, as he supposes, directed his past conduct, and that serve to justify to him his present action, and to lead him to make projects for his future activity.
>
> Assemblies of men act in the same way, only leaving to those who do not take direct part in the action to invent consideration, justifications, and projects concerning their combined activity.
>
> For causes, known or unknown to us, the French began to chop and hack at each other. And to match the event, it is accompanied by its justification in the expressed wills of certain men, who declare it essential for the good of France, for the cause of freedom, of equality. Men cease slaughtering one another, and that event is accompanied by the justification of the necessity of centralisation of power, of resistance to Europe, and so on. Men march from west to east, killing their fellow-creatures, and this event is accompanied by phrases about the glory of France, the baseness of England, and so on. History teaches us that those justifications for the event are devoid of all common sense, that they are inconsistent with one another, as, for instance, the murder of a man as a result of the declaration of his rights, and the murder of millions in Russia for the abasement of England. But those justifications have an incontestable value in their own day.
>
> They remove moral responsibility from those men who produce the events. At the time they do the work of brooms, that go in front to clear the rails for the train: they clear the path of men's moral responsibility. Apart from those justifications, no solution could be found for the most obvious question that occurs to one at once on examining any historical event; that is, How did millions of men come to combine to commit crimes, murders, wars, and so on?[2]

The actor on the political scene cannot help "playing an act" by concealing the true nature of his political actions behind the mask of a political ideology. The more removed the individual is from a particular power struggle, the more likely he is to understand its true nature. So it is not by accident that foreigners have often a better understanding of the politics of a particular country than have the natives, and that scholars are better equipped than politicians to understand what politics is all about. On the other hand, politicians have an ineradicable tendency to deceive themselves about what they are doing by referring to their policies not in terms of power but in terms of either ethical and legal principles or biological necessities. In other words, while all politics is necessarily pursuit of power, ideologies render involvement in that contest for power psychologically and morally acceptable to the actors and their audience.

These legal and ethical principles and biological necessities fulfill a dual function in the sphere of international politics. They are either the ultimate goals of political action, of which we have spoken before[3]—that is, those ultimate objectives for the realization of which political power is sought—or they are the pretexts and false fronts behind which the element of power, inherent

---

[2]Epilogue, Part II, Chapter VII.
[3]See pages 30 ff.

in all politics, is concealed. These principles and necessities may fulfill one or the other function, or they may fulfill them both at the same time. A legal and ethical principle, such as justice, for example, or a biological necessity, such as an adequate standard of living, may be the goal of a foreign policy, or it may be an ideology, or it may be both at the same time. Since we are not concerned here with the ultimate goals of international politics, we shall deal with ethical and legal principles and biological necessities only in so far as they perform the function of ideologies.

These ideologies are not the accidental outgrowth of the hypocrisy of certain individuals who need only to be replaced by other, more honest individuals in order to make the conduct of foreign affairs more decent. Disappointment always follows such expectations. The members of the opposition who were most vocal in exposing the deviousness of Franklin D. Roosevelt's or Churchill's foreign policies shocked their followers, once they had become responsible for the conduct of foreign affairs, by their own use of ideological disguises. It is the very nature of politics to compel the actor on the political scene to use ideologies in order to disguise the immediate goal of his action. The immediate goal of political action is power, and political power is power over the minds and actions of men. Yet those who have been chosen as the prospective object of the power of others are themselves intent upon gaining power over others. Thus the actor on the political scene is always at the same time a prospective master and a prospective subject. While he seeks power over others, others seek power over him.

To this ambivalence of man as a political being corresponds the ambivalence of his moral evaluation of this condition. He will consider his own desire for power as just and will condemn as unjust the desire of others to gain power over him. Since the end of the Second World War, the Russians have found their own designs for power justified by considerations of their own security. But they have condemned as "imperialistic" and preparatory to world conquest the expansion of American power. The United States has put a similar stigma on Russian aspirations, while it views its own international objectives as necessities of national defense. As John Adams put it:

> Power always thinks it has a great soul and vast views beyond the comprehension of the weak and that it is doing God's service when it is violating all His laws. Our passions, ambitions, avarice, love and resentment, etc., possess so much metaphysical subtlety and so much overpowering eloquence that they insinuate themselves into the understanding and the conscience and convert both to their party.

The ambivalence of this evaluation, characteristic of the approach of all nations to the problem of power, is again inherent in the very nature of international politics. The nation that dispensed with ideologies and frankly stated that it wanted power and would, therefore, oppose similar aspirations of other nations, would at once find itself at a great and perhaps decisive disadvantage in the struggle for power. That frank admission would, on the one hand, unite the other nations in fierce resistance to a foreign policy so unequivocally stated and would thereby compel the nation pursuing it to employ more power than would otherwise be necessary. On the other hand, that admission is tantamount to flouting openly the universally accepted moral standards of the international community and would thereby put the particular nation in a position where it would be likely to pursue its foreign policy halfheartedly and with a bad conscience. To rally a people behind the government's foreign policy and to marshal all the national energies and resources to its support, the spokesman of the nation must appeal to biological necessities, such as national existence, and to moral principles, such as justice, rather than to power. This is the only way a nation can attain the enthusiasm and willingness to sacrifice without which no foreign policy can pass the ultimate test of strength.

Such are the psychological forces that inevitably engender the ideologies of international policies and make them weapons in the struggle for power on the international scene. A government whose foreign policy appeals to the intellectual convictions and moral valuations of its own people has gained an incalculable advantage over an opponent who has not succeeded in choosing goals that have such appeal or in making the chosen goals appear to have it. Ideologies, like all ideas, are weapons that may raise the national morale and, with it, the power of one nation and, in the very act of doing so, may lower the morale of the opponent. The enormous contribution Woodrow Wilson's Fourteen Points made to the victory of the Allies in the First World War by strengthening the morale of the Allies and weakening the morale of the Central Powers is the classic example of the importance of the moral factor for international politics.[4]

TYPICAL IDEOLOGIES OF FOREIGN POLICIES

It follows from the nature of international politics that imperialistic policies resort practically always to ideological disguises, whereas status quo policies more frequently can be presented as what they actually are. It also follows from this nature that certain types of ideologies are coordinated with certain types of international policies.

Ideologies of the Status Quo

A policy of the status quo can often afford to reveal its true nature and dispense with ideological disguises, because the status quo has already, by virtue of its very existence, acquired a certain moral legitimacy. What exists must have something in its favor; otherwise it would not exist. As Demosthenes put it:

> For no one would go to war as readily for aggrandizement as for the defense of his own possessions; but while all men fight desperately to keep what they are in

---

[4]On the problem of national morale in general, see pages 149 ff.

danger of losing, it is not so with aggrandizement; men make it, indeed, their aim, but if prevented, they do not feel thay have suffered any injustice from their opponents.[5]

Since a nation that pursues a policy of the status quo seeks the preservation of the power it already has, it may avoid the need to allay the resentment of other nations and its own scruples. This is especially so when the preservation of the territorial status quo is not open to moral or legal attack and when national power has by tradition been exclusively used for the preservation of this status quo. Such nations as Switzerland, Denmark, Norway, and Sweden do not need to hesitate to define their foreign policies in terms of the maintenance of the status quo, since this status quo is generally recognized as legitimate. Other nations, such as Great Britain, France, Yugoslavia, Czechoslovakia, and Rumania, which in the period between the two world wars in the main pursued a policy of the status quo, could not afford simply to declare that their foreign policies aimed at the defense of their possessions. Since the legitimacy of the status quo of 1919 was itself being challenged within and without these nations, they had to invoke moral principles able to meet that challenge. Peace and international law fulfilled that purpose.

Peace and international law are eminently qualified to serve as ideologies for a policy of the status quo. Since imperialistic policies, by disturbing the status quo, frequently lead to war and must always take the possibility of war into account, a foreign policy that proclaims pacifism as its guiding principle is by the same token anti-imperialistic and supports the maintenance of the status quo. By expressing in pacifist terms the objectives of the policy of the status quo, a statesman puts the stigma of war-mongering upon his imperialistic opponents, clears his and his countrymen's conscience of moral scruples, and can hope to win the support of all countries interested in the maintenance of the status quo.[6]

International law fulfills a similar ideological function for policies of the status quo. Any legal order tends to be primarily a static social force. It defines a certain distribution of power and offers standards and processes to ascertain and maintain it in concrete situations. Domestic law, through a highly developed system of legislation, judicial decisions, and law enforcement, allows for adaptations and sometimes even considerable changes within the general distribution of power. International law, in the absence of such a system making for lawful change, is, not only primarily but essentially, by dint of its very nature, a static force. The invocation of international law, of "order under law," of "ordinary legal processes" in support of a particular foreign policy, therefore, always indicates the ideological disguise of a policy of the status quo. More particularly, when an international organization, such as the League of Nations, has been established for the purpose of maintaining a particular status quo,

---

[5]Demosthenes, *For the Liberty of the Rhodians*, sections 10–11.

[6]See page 112, on the recent transformation of the ideology of peace; see also pages 231 ff.

support of that organization becomes tantamount to support of that particular status quo.

Since the end of the First World War, it has become rather common to make use of such legalistic ideologies in justification of a policy of the status quo. While the alliances of former periods of history have not disappeared, they tend to become "regional arrangements" within an over-all legal organization. The "maintenance of the status quo" yields to the "maintenance of international peace and security." A number of states that have the same interest in the maintenance of the status quo will be likely to protect their common interests against a threat from a particular source not by a "Holy Alliance" but by a "system of collective security" or a "treaty of mutual assistance." Since changes in the status quo are frequently brought about at the expense of small nations, defense of the rights of small nations, such as of Belgium in 1914 and Finland and Poland in 1939, becomes under appropriate conditions another ideology of the policy of the status quo.

Ideologies of Imperialism

A policy of imperialism is always in need of an ideology; for, in contrast to a policy of the status quo, imperialism always has the burden of proof. It must prove that the status quo it seeks to overthrow deserves to be overthrown and that the moral legitimacy which in the minds of many attaches to things as they are ought to yield to a higher principle of morality calling for a new distribution of power. Thus, in the words of Gibbon: "For every war a motive of safety or revenge, of honor or zeal, of right or convenience, may be readily found in the jurisprudence of conquerors."[7]

In so far as the typical ideologies of imperialism make use of legal concepts, they cannot well refer to positive international law; that is, to international law as it actually is. As we have seen, the static character of international law makes it the natural ideological ally of the status quo. The dynamic quality of imperialism requires dynamic ideologies. In the domain of law it is the doctrine of natural law—that is, of the law as it ought to be—that fits the ideological needs of imperialism. Against the injustices of international law as it exists, symbolizing the status quo, the imperialistic nation will invoke a higher law that corresponds to the requirements of justice. Thus National Socialist Germany based its demands for the revision of the status quo of Versailles primarily upon the principle of equality which the Treaty of Versailles was said to have violated. The demand for colonies, for instance, of which the Treaty of Versailles had deprived Germany completely, and the demand for the revision of that treaty's provisions for unilateral disarmament, were derived from the same principle.

When the imperialistic policy is not directed against a particular status quo resulting from a lost war, but grows from a power vacuum inviting conquest, moral ideologies that make it an unavoidable duty to conquer take the

---

[7] *The Decline and Fall of the Roman Empire* (The Modern Library Edition), Vol. II, p. 1235.

place of the appeal to a just natural law against an unjust positive law. Then to conquer weak peoples appears as "the white man's burden," the "national mission," "manifest destiny," a "sacred trust," a "Christian duty." Colonial imperialism, in particular, has frequently been disguised by ideological slogans of this kind, such as the "blessings of Western civilization," which it was the mission of the conqueror to bring to the colored races of the earth. The Japanese ideology of the East Asiatic "co-prosperity zone" carries the similar connotation of a humanitarian mission. Whenever a political philosophy, held with the fervor of a religious faith, coincides with an imperialistic policy, it becomes a ready instrument of ideological disguise. Arab imperialism during the period of Arab expansion justified itself as the fulfillment of religious duty. Napoleonic imperialism swept over Europe under the banner of "Liberty, Equality, Fraternity." Russian imperialism, especially in its aspirations for Constantinople and the Dardanelles, has successively or simultaneously made use of the Orthodox faith, Pan-Slavism, world revolution, and defense from capitalist encirclement.

In modern times, especially under the influence of the social philosophies of Darwin and Spencer, the ideologies of imperialism have preferred biological arguments. Transferred to international politics, the philosophy of the survival of the fittest sees in the military superiority of a strong nation over a weak one a natural phenomenon that makes the latter the preordained object of the former's power. According to this philosophy, it would be contrary to nature if the strong did not dominate the weak and if the weak tried to be the equal of the strong. The strong nation has a right to a "place in the sun"; it is the "salt of the earth." As the famous German sociologist Werner Sombart discovered in the First World War, the Germanic "hero" must necessarily win out over the British "shopkeeper." That the inferior races should serve the master race is a law of nature that only villains and fools will oppose; slavery and extermination are the latter's just dessert.

Communism, fascism, and Nazism, as well as Japanese imperialism, have given these biological ideologies a revolutionary turn. The nations that nature has appointed to be the masters of the earth are kept in inferiority by the trickery and violence of the naturally inferior nations. The vigorous but poor "have-nots" are cut off from the riches of the earth by the wealthy but decadent "haves." The proletarian nations, inspired by ideals, must fight the capitalist nations defending their moneybags. The ideology of overpopulation found particular favor with Germany, Italy, and Japan before the Second World War. The Germans are a "people without space" who, if they cannot obtain "living space," must "suffocate" and, if they cannot obtain sources of raw materials, must "starve." With different variations, this ideology was used in the thirties also by Italy and Japan to justify their expansionist policies and to disguise their imperialistic goals.[8]

---

[8]The purely ideological character of the claim for colonies, justified in the period between the two world wars by Germany, Italy, and Japan with population pressure and economic distress, is

The most widely practiced disguise and justification of imperialism has, however, always been the ideology of anti-imperialism.[9] It is so widely used because it is the most effective of all ideologies of imperialism. As, according to Huey Long, fascism will come to the United States in the guise of antifascism, so imperialism has come to many a country in the guise of anti-imperialism. In 1914 as well as in 1939, both sides went to war in order to defend themselves against the imperialism of the other side. Germany attacked the Soviet Union in 1941 in order to forestall the latter's imperialistic designs. Since the end of the Second World War, American and British as well as Russian and Chinese foreign policy has been justified by the imperialistic objectives of other nations. By thus presenting one's own foreign policy, regardless of its actual character, as anti-imperialistic—that is, defensive and protective of the status quo—one gives one's own people that good conscience and confidence in the justice of their own cause without which no people can support its foreign policy whole-heartedly and fight successfully for it. At the same time one may confound the enemy who, ideologically less well prepared, may no longer be certain on which side justice is to be found.

The economic demands that the nations of the "Third World" have presented contain a strong ideological element. The responsibility for the economic distress of many of these nations, which must be attributed to a variety of reasons, such as natural poverty, irrational economic policies, corruption, and incompetence, is typically laid at the door of the developed rich and industrial nations. One stark and disquieting fact gives the concept of North-South confrontation a semblance of plausibility: the extreme differences in the standard of living between the industrial nations and those of the Third World. From that supposed causal responsibility follows the moral responsibility to make amends for the evils previously wrought and to contribute to a more equal future distribution of the world's wealth. The most salient case in point is the

---

clearly demonstrated by the relevant population and economic statistics. The four African colonies of Germany covered 930,000 square miles and had, in 1914, a population of almost twelve million, of which only 20,000 were white. It was pointed out at that time that more Germans were living in the city of Paris than in all of Germany's colonies combined. After Eritrea had been an Italian colony for fifty years, the 2,000 square miles of territory most suitable for settlement contained about 400 Italian inhabitants. The Japanese colonies of Korea and Formosa absorbed within a period of forty years less than one year's increase of the Japanese population.

As for the economic importance of colonies to their mother countries, the figures are eloquent in the case of Germany and Italy. The imports from, and the exports to, the German colonies amounted in 1913 to 0.5 per cent of the total German imports and exports. In 1933, the imports from the Italian colonies were 1.6 per cent of the total imports, and the exports to them were 7.2 per cent of all the exports from Italy; a considerable portion of the latter must have consisted of war material. Only for Japan were its colonies of paramount economic importance, its trade with them in 1934 amounting to almost 25 per cent of its total trade (23.1 per cent of the total imports, 22 per cent of the total exports). See Royal Institute of International Affairs, *The Colonial Problem* (London, New York, Toronto: Oxford University Press, 1937), especially p. 287.

[9]A variant of the ideology of anti-imperialism is the ideology of anti-power politics. According to this ideology, other nations are motivated in their policies by aspirations for power, while one's own nation, free from such base motives, pursues purely ideal objectives.

unequal distribution of food, causing excess and gluttony in the industrial nations and chronic undernourishment and even famine in many countries of the Third World. However, both the causal and the moral nexus between abundance in the industrial world and want in the Third World are open to serious question.

Throughout history mankind has been divided by drastic differences in standards of living. What sets the present situation apart is the awareness of these differences by the advantaged and disadvantaged members of mankind owing to the modern technologies of communication. That awareness coincides with the ascendancy of the principle of equality, both of opportunity and condition, throughout the world. Hence the aspirations of the disadvantaged to a narrowing of the gap between the rich and the poor—and the moral embarrassment of the rich in the face of these aspirations.

It goes without saying that these aspirations and the attendant moral embarrassment—both incapable of satisfaction or relief on a worldwide scale— are extensively used as ideological justifications and rationalizations for specific political aims in the service of concrete national interests. These aims are naturally directed toward changes in the status quo at the expense of the rich and in favor of the poor. The former, aware of the existing extreme inequality, and persuaded by the moral principle which condemns it, are at an obvious disadvantage in defining and promoting their own interests; they must do so, as it were, with a bad conscience, no longer fully convinced of the rightness of their case. Faced with the claim to economic equality, they are in a morally helpless position, one similar to that in which the Western democracies found themselves in 1938 when confronted with the German claim to a part of Czechoslovakia, advanced in the name of the moral principle of national self-determination.

The moral argument in favor of the equalization of the standard of living throughout the world appears as a special application of the general argument in support of humanitarian aid to nations in distress. The United States has accepted this obligation in theory and practice. However, the situation providing a moral justification for humanitarian aid differs fundamentally from the one calling for equalization of the standard of living throughout the world. Humanitarian aid is justified by a sudden natural catastrophe, the consequences of which the affected country finds hard to remedy with its own resources alone. The worldwide differences in the standard of living are the result of a complex of natural, cultural, economic, and political factors. Outside intervention may be able to modify such differences in specific instances, but it cannot expect to eliminate them throughout the world. It is this impossibility to achieve—even with the best of intentions and the most extensive commitment of resources—what is presumed to be morally required that negates the moral obligation. The principle of Roman law *ultra vires nemo obligatur* (beyond his ability nobody is obligated) applies also to presumed moral obligations.

The supposed moral obligation for the industrialized, rich nations to raise the standard of living of the nonindustrialized, poor nations throughout the world is grounded in the causal relationship which is presumed to exist between the policies and the high standard of living of the former and the low standard of living of the latter. However, the assumption of a simple causal relationship of this kind is a myth. The colonialists, imperialists, and capitalists perform here the function of the devil to whom the evils of underdevelopment can be traced. In truth, these evils have multiple causes, of which colonialism, imperialism, and capitalism are, at best, only one.

The elimination of inequalities in food supply is, then, not only—and not even primarily—a matter of agricultural technology and collective generosity, but of political interest and will. In many societies the perpetuation of poverty, of which the scarcity of food is a striking manifestation, is not just another unfortunate accident to be remedied by technological reform, but the result of deliberate social, economic, and political choices. If one wants to rid the world of hunger, one has to rid these societies of the arrangements that have caused it. More likely than not, that means radical reform—if not revolution. Whether the political elites of Third World nations are willing to follow their own rhetoric is a matter of controversy.

Thus the terms in which the so-called North-South conflict is fought out between the have and the have-not nations of the world in good measure conceal and at the same time justify a conflict between the traditionally powerful and the new politically weak nations whose main real object is exactly a new distribution of power.

Ambiguous Ideologies

The ideology of anti-imperialism draws its effectiveness from its ambiguity. It confounds the observer, who cannot always be sure whether he is dealing with an ideology of imperialism or with the true expression of a policy of the status quo. This confounding effect is present whenever an ideology is not made to order, as it were, for a particular type of policy, but can be worn by the defenders of the status quo as well as by the promoters of imperialism. Traditionally, and more particularly in the eighteenth and nineteenth centuries, the balance of power has been used as an ideological weapon by the defenders of the status quo and the promoters of imperialism. In our time, the ideologies of national self-determination and of the United Nations have performed a similar function. Since the beginning of the Cold War, they have been joined to an ever increasing extent by the ideologies of peace, relaxation of tensions, détente.

The principle of national self-determination, as conceived by Woodrow Wilson, justified the liberation of the Central and Eastern European nationalities from foreign domination. Theoretically it was opposed not only to the status quo of empire, but also to imperialism of any kind, either on the part of the old imperial powers—Germany, Austria, and Russia—or on the part of the liberated small nations. Yet the destruction of the old imperial order at once called forth, still in the name of self-determination, new imperialisms. Those of Poland, Czechoslovakia, Rumania, and Yugoslavia are as outstanding as they were inevitable; for the power vacuum left by the breakdown of the old imperial order had to be filled and the newly liberated nations were there to fill it. As soon as they had installed themselves in power, they invoked the selfsame principle of national self-determination in defense of the new status quo. This principle was their most potent ideological weapon from the end of the First to the end of the Second World War.

It was by a stroke of propagandistic genius that Hitler hit upon the principle of national self-determination in order to disguise and justify his policies of territorial expansion. The German minorities of Czechoslovakia and Poland, under the banner of national self-determination, were now to play the same role in undermining the national existence of Czechoslovakia and Poland which the Czech, Slovak, and Polish nationalities, under the same ideological banner, had played in undermining the national existence of the Austrian-Hungarian Empire. With their own ideological weapon turned against them, the benefactors of the status quo of Versailles had no ideology, except the one of law and order, with which to defend that status quo. Thus Austria and Czechoslovakia were surrendered, and Poland was exposed to mortal danger. After the settlement of Munich granted the German demands with regard to Czechoslovakia, the London *Times*, making the German ideology its own, declared: "Self-determination, the professed principle of the Treaty of Versailles, has been invoked by Herr Hitler against its written text, and his appeal has been allowed."[10] Rarely, if ever, has modern history offered a more striking example of the importance of ideologies in international politics and of the confounding effect of an ambiguous ideology aptly employed.

The ideology of national self-determination also plays a crucial part in the conflict between Israel and the Arab states. The Arab claims of national self-determination, in order to do them justice, must be put in the political context from which they have risen and within which they are supposed to operate. Arab claims for Palestinian self-determination must be seen in the context of the continuous opposition of most Arabs to the existence not only of the state of Israel but of Jewish settlements within the territory of Palestine. In other words, recognition of Israel as a state is incompatible with the claim to national self-determination of the Palestinian Arabs. For their claim is based not only upon the West Bank of the Jordan but—as innumerable pronouncements of the Palestine Liberation Organization (PLO) claim—upon the whole territory on which the state of Israel has been erected. Thus the principle of national self-determination on behalf of the Palestinian Arabs reveals itself as an ideological disguise for the unchanging aspiration of Arabs to destroy the state of Israel and establish an Arab state in its place. When Francis I of France was asked why he always made war against Charles V of Hapsburg, he replied: "Because both of us want the same thing, Italy." The same reply, substituting Palestine for Italy, could be given by the leaders of Israel and the PLO.

---

[10]London *Times*, September 28, 1938.

The United Nations was intended at its inception to serve as an instrument of China, France, Great Britain, the Soviet Union, and the United States, and of their allies, for maintaining the status quo as established by the victory of these nations in the Second World War. But in the years immediately following the conclusion of the Second World War, this status quo proved to be only provisional and subject to contradictory interpretations and claims by the different nations. The ideology of the United Nations is, therefore, used by these different nations for the purpose of justifying their particular interpretations and disguising their particular claims. All nations appear as the champions of the United Nations, and quote its Charter in support of the particular policies they are pursuing. These policies being contradictory, the reference to the United Nations and its Charter becomes an ideological device justifying one's own policy in the light of generally accepted principles and at the same time concealing its true character. Its ambiguity makes this ideology a weapon with which to confound one's enemies and strengthen one's friends.

Since the end of the Second World War, the ideologies of peace, relaxation of tensions, and détente have to an ever increasing extent come to perform a similar function. In view of the general fear of a third world war, fought with the modern weapons of mass destruction, no government can expect to gain support for its foreign policies from its own and other peoples if it cannot convince them of its peaceful intentions. Thus "peace congresses," "peace offensives," and "peace crusades" have become standard weapons of propaganda in the Cold War. These well-nigh universal professions of peaceful intentions are meaningless as references to the actual foreign policies pursued, since it can well be taken for granted that, in view of the incalculable destructiveness of modern war, all nations would rather pursue their aims by peaceful means than by war. Yet by the same token these professions perform two important political functions. They tend to conceal the actual policies pursued behind a veil of professed peaceful purposes. They also tend to attract support of men of good will everywhere for these policies, whatever they may actually be, since they are presented as aiming at the preservation of peace, a goal that men of good will everywhere ardently desire.

Similar considerations apply to the well-nigh universal commitment to disarmament, especially in its "general and complete" form. An end to the armaments race is widely considered desirable on humanitarian, political, and economic grounds. But it is obvious from the experience of the last two decades that the political conditions of the world make disarmament impossible.[11] When, in view of this complete failure of all attempts at disarmament of any kind, governments declare as their policy "general and complete" disarmament, they are actually making an ideological appeal to the nations of the world yearning for peace and relief from the burdens of competitive armaments. This

[11]See for an extensive discussion of the reasons for the failure of disarmament below, Chapter 18.

appeal serves the purpose of making the foreign policies actually pursued more acceptable to the other nations than they might otherwise be.

THE PROBLEM OF RECOGNITION

To see through these ideological disguises and grasp behind them the actual political forces and phenomena is, then, one of the most important and most difficult tasks for the student of international politics. This task is important because, unless it is done, it is impossible to determine correctly the character of the foreign policy with which one happens to deal. The recognition of imperialistic tendencies and of their particular character depends upon a clear distinction between the ideological pretense that generally disavows imperialistic aspirations altogether and the actual objectives of the policies pursued. To make this distinction correctly is difficult because of the general difficulty of detecting the true meaning of any human action apart from what the actor believes or feigns it to mean. This general problem is aggravated by two other difficulties peculiar, at least in their generality, to international politics. One is to distinguish a boast or bluff indicative of a policy of prestige from an ideological disguise of actual imperialism. The other is to discover behind an ideology of the status quo or of localized imperialism the true meaning of the policy actually pursued.

We have already had occasion to refer to the foreign policy of William II, which conveyed through its language and manifestations the impression of being openly imperialistic while it was actually a strange mixture of imperialistic designs and neurotic boastfulness. Conversely, the true imperialistic essence of the foreign policies of Hitler and Mussolini was not generally recognized up to the late thirties, being explained away as mere bluff and boastfulness for home consumption. To determine the true character of a foreign policy behind its deliberate or unconscious ideological disguise becomes particularly difficult when the ideologies of the status quo are used as a disguise. The period following the Second World War offers striking examples of this difficulty in the foreign policies of the United States and the Soviet Union.

Both nations have expressed the objectives of their foreign policies in the almost identical terms of status-quo ideologies. Both the Soviet Union and the United States have proclaimed that they have no territorial ambitions beyond the line of military demarcation which was established by the agreements of Teheran, Yalta, and Potsdam and through understandings among the military commanders at the end of the war; that they want to see free and democratic governments established everywhere; that they are guided by considerations of security and national defense; and that it is the capitalist or Communist imperialism of the other side against which they are compelled, in spite of their own wishes, to defend themselves.

Most Americans and most Russians are obviously convinced that these statements are a faithful expression of the true character of their countries' foreign policy. Yet they cannot both be right, while one or the other or both may be wrong. For it may be that the Soviet Union misunderstands the foreign policy of the United States or that the United States misunderstands the foreign policy of the Soviet Union, or that both misunderstand each other. The solution of this riddle upon which the fate of the world may well depend is not to be sought in the character of the ideologies alone, but in the sum total of the factors determining the foreign policy of a nation. Of this, more will be said later.[12]

---

[12]See Part Ten.

PART THREE

National Power

8

The Essence of National Power

WHAT IS NATIONAL POWER?

We have said that by power we mean the power of man over the minds and actions of other men, a phenomenon to be found whenever human beings live in social contact with one another. We have spoken of the "power of a nation" or of "national power" as though the concept were self-evident and sufficiently explained by what we have said about power in general. Yet, while it can be easily understood that individuals seek power, how are we to explain the aspirations for power in the collectives called nations? What is a nation? What do we mean when we attribute to a nation aspirations and actions?

A nation as such is obviously not an empirical thing. A nation as such cannot be seen. What can be empirically observed are only the individuals who belong to a nation. Hence, a nation is an abstraction from a number of individuals who have certain characteristics in common, and it is these characteristics that make them members of the same nation. Besides being a member of a nation and thinking, feeling, and acting in that capacity, the individual may belong to a church, a social or economic class, a political party, a family, and may think, feel, and act in these capacities. Apart from being a member of all these social groups, he is also a human being pure and simple, and thinks, feels, and acts in that capacity. Therefore, when we speak in empirical terms of the power or of the foreign policy of a certain nation, we can only mean the power or the foreign policy of certain individuals who belong to the same nation. As Marcel Proust put it: "The life of nations merely repeats, on a larger scale, the lives of their component cells; and he who is incapable of understanding the mystery, the reactions, the laws that determine the movements of the individual, can never hope to say anything worth listening to about the struggles of nations."

Yet this poses another difficulty. The power or the foreign policy of the

115

United States is obviously not the power or the foreign policy of all the individuals who belong to the nation called the United States of America. The fact that the United States emerged from the Second World War as the most powerful nation on earth has not affected the power of the great mass of individual Americans. It has, however, affected the power of all those individuals who administer the foreign affairs of the United States and, more particularly, speak for and represent the United States on the international scene. For a nation pursues foreign policies as a legal organization called a state, whose agents act as the representatives of the nation in international affairs. They speak for it, negotiate treaties in its name, define its objectives, choose the means for achieving them, and try to maintain, increase, and demonstrate its power. They are the individuals who, when they appear as representatives of their nation on the international scene, wield the power and pursue the policies of their nation. It is to them that we refer when we speak in empirical terms of the power and of the foreign policy of a nation.

How, then, does it come about that the great mass of the individual members of a nation, whose individual power is not affected by the vicissitudes of national power, identify themselves with the power and the foreign policies of their nation, experience this power and these policies as their own, and do so with an emotional intensity often surpassing the emotional attachment to their individual aspirations for power? By asking this question, we are posing the problem of modern nationalism. In preceding periods of history, the collectivity with whose power and aspirations for power the individual identified himself was determined by ties of blood, of religion, or of common loyalty to a feudal lord or prince. In our time the identification with the power and policies of the nation has largely superseded or, in any case, overshadows those older identifications. How is this phenomenon of modern nationalism to be explained?

We have learned from our discussion of the ideologies of foreign policies that in the mind of the individual the power aspirations of others bear the stigma of immorality. While this attitude has one of its roots in the desire of the prospective victim of the power of others to defend his freedom against this threat, the other root grows from the attempt of society as a whole to suppress and keep in bounds individual aspirations for power. Society has established a network of rules of conduct and institutional devices for controlling individual power drives. These rules and devices either divert individual power drives into channels where they cannot endanger society, or else they weaken them or suppress them altogether. Law, ethics, and mores, innumerable social institutions and arrangements, such as competitive examinations, election contests, sports, social clubs, and fraternal organizations—all serve that purpose.

In consequence, most people are unable to satisfy their desire for power within the national community. Within that community, only a relatively small group permanently wields power over great numbers of people without being subject to extensive limitations by others. The great mass of the population is to a much greater extent the object of power than it is its wielder. Not being able to find full satisfaction of their desire for power within the national boundaries, the people project those unsatisfied aspirations onto the international scene. There they find vicarious satisfaction in identification with the power drives of the nation. When the citizen of the United States thinks of the power of his country, he experiences the same kind of exaltation the citizen of Rome must have felt when, identifying himself with Rome and its power and by the same token contrasting himself with the stranger, he would say: *"Civis Romanus sum."* When we are conscious of being members of a very powerful nation, the nation whose industrial capacity and material wealth are unsurpassed, we flatter ourselves and feel a great pride. It is as though we all, not as individuals but collectively, as members of the same nation, owned and controlled so magnificent a power. The power our representatives wield on the international scene becomes our own and the frustrations we experience within the national community are compensated for by the vicarious enjoyment of the power of the nation.

These psychological trends, operating within the individual members of a nation, find support in the rules of conduct and in the institutions of society itself. Society restrains aspirations for individual power within the national community and puts the mark of opprobrium upon certain power drives pointing toward individual aggrandizement. But it encourages and glorifies the tendencies of the great mass of the population, frustrated in its individual power drives, to identify itself with the nation's struggle for power on the international scene. Power pursued by the individual for his own sake is considered an evil to be tolerated only within certain bounds and in certain manifestations. Power disguised by ideologies and pursued in the name and for the sake of the nation becomes a good for which all citizens must strive. The national symbols, especially in so far as they have reference to the armed forces and the relations with other nations, are instruments of that identification of the individual with the power of the nation. The ethics and mores of society tend to make that identification attractive by holding out rewards and threatening punishments.

Thus it is not by accident that certain groups of the population are either the most militant supporters of the national aspirations for power in the international field, or else refuse to have anything to do with them at all. These are the groups which are primarily the object of the power of others and are most thoroughly deprived of outlets for their own power drives or are most insecure in the possession of whatever power they may have within the national community. The lower middle classes especially, such as the white-collar workers, but also the main bulk of the laboring masses,[1] identify themselves completely with the national aspirations for power. Or else—and here the main example is the revolutionary proletariat in the heyday of Marxism, particularly in Europe—they do not identify themselves with national aspirations at all. While the latter

---

[1]They have, in terms of power, less to lose and more to gain from nationalistic foreign policies than any other group of the population, with the exception of the military.

group has thus far been of small concern for the foreign policies of the United States, the former has taken on ever greater importance.

It is here, then, that one must seek the roots of modern nationalism and the explanation for the increasing ferocity with which foreign policies are pursued in modern times. The growing insecurity of the individual in Western societies, especially in the lower strata, and the atomization of Western society in general have magnified enormously the frustration of individual power drives. This, in turn, has given rise to an increased desire for compensatory identification with the collective national aspirations for power. These increases have been quantitative as well as qualitative.

ROOTS OF MODERN NATIONALISM

Until the time of the Napoleonic Wars, only very small groups of the population identified themselves with the foreign policies of their nation. Foreign policies were truly not national but dynastic policies, and the identification was with the power and the policies of the individual monarch rather than with the power and the policies of a collectivity, such as the nation. As Goethe put it in a significant passage of his autobiography: "We all felt for Fredrick [the Great], but what did we care for Prussia?"

"These [scientific] societies," wrote Thomas Jefferson to John Hollins on February 19, 1809, "are always at peace, however their nations may be at war. Like the republic of letters, they form a great fraternity spreading over the whole earth, and their correspondence is never interrupted by any civilized nation."

With the Napoleonic Wars began the period of national foreign policies and wars; that is, the identification of the great masses of the citizens of a nation with national power and national policies, replacing identification with dynastic interests. Talleyrand pointed to that change when he said to Czar Alexander in 1808: "The Rhine, the Alps, and the Pyrénées are the conquests of France; the rest, of the Emperor; they mean nothing to France." Up to the First World War it was doubtful to what degree the members of the European socialist parties identified themselves with the power and policies of their respective nations. Yet the full participation in that war of the main bulk of the workers in all belligerent countries demonstrated the identification of practically the whole population with the power and policies of their respective nations.

Retreat from Nationalism: Apparent and Real

The Second World War has, however, brought about a certain retrogression from that maximum of identification which the First World War witnessed. That retrogression took place on the top and at the base of the social pyramid. On the one hand, small yet powerful profascist groups of intellectual, political, and military leaders in Great Britain and France either refused to identify themselves with their countries or even preferred to identify themselves with the national enemy. The leaders who felt this way were insecure in their power positions, especially in view of the initial political and military weakness of their countries, and the enemy alone seemed to be able to assure them their positions on top of the social pyramid. On the other hand, the French Communists, owing allegiance to both France and the Soviet Union, were able to identify themselves fully with their nation only after the German attack on the Soviet Union in 1941 had brought both allegiances into play. The German attack on France alone was unable to rouse them to active opposition to the invader. But the German attack on the Soviet Union made France and the Soviet Union allies in a common cause and allowed the French Communists to oppose in the German invaders of France the common enemy of France and the Soviet Union alike. The identification of the French Communists with French national policies was predicated upon the identity of those policies with Russian interests and policies. This Communist allegiance to foreign interests and policies, to take precedence over the national ones, was a universal phenomenon that, as such, was a challenge to the cohesion of the nation state and to its very existence.[2]

This disintegration of national solidarity can hardly be called a retreat from nationalism, for it exchanges loyalty to a foreign nation for loyalty to one's own. The Communist Frenchman, as it were, transformed himself into a Russian nationalist who supports the policies of the Soviet Union. What is new in this nationalism is its inconsistency in demanding identification with one—foreign —nation while denying the claims of other nations to the loyalty of their citizens.

It testifies to the strength of national solidarity that even this transfer of loyalty from one's own nation to another one, which is the fountainhead of a worldwide political movement, has proven to be an ephemeral interlude. For we are witnessing the revival of national solidarity in Communist governments and movements, which have begun in differing degrees to put their respective national interests ahead of the interests of the Soviet Union. The monolithic world-Communist movement, directed by, and at the service of, the Soviet Union, has been replaced by "polycentrism," in which national loyalties and interests take precedence over the affinities of political philosophy. With the revolutions of 1989, this trend reached fulfillment.

However, the aftermath of the Second World War has brought into being a genuine retrogression from nationalism in the form of a movement toward the unification of Western Europe. This movement has thus far to its credit several concrete achievements in terms of working supranational organizations, including the European Coal and Steel Community, the Common Market (European Economic Community), and the development of a European Community. Two experiences have given birth to the movement toward European unification: the destructiveness of the Second World War and the political, military, and

---

[2]See also Chapter 23.

economic decline of Europe in its aftermath. The supporters of this movement cannot help concluding from these experiences that, in Western Europe 'at least, the nation state is an obsolescent principle of political organization which, far from assuring the security and power of its members, condemns them to impotence and ultimate extinction either by each other or by their more powerful neighbors. Only the future will show whether this acute sense of insecurity, not only of the individuals but also of the national societies to which they belong, will lead to political creativity in the form of the political, military, and economic unification of Europe, or to political impotence in the form of a retreat into "neutralism"—that is, the renunciation of an active foreign policy altogether—or to political desperation in the form of a more intense identification with the individual nations.

A force that runs counter to the revival of nationalism is the growing recognition by statesmen, intellectuals, and technical experts that certain fundamental problems posed by the modern technologies of transportation, communications, and warfare transcend the interests and the ability to solve of any single nation, however powerful. The control of nuclear energy, the protection and restoration of the natural environment, the supply of food and raw materials are problems of this kind. They cannot be solved by an individual nation competing with other nations for national advantage. All nations, or a considerable number of them, have a common interest in the solution of these problems, which interest ought to be reflected in common policies transcending particular national interests. While some small elites have become aware of this novel element in world politics and are trying to come intellectually to terms with it, the actual conduct of national foreign policies has hardly been affected by it. To the contrary, it testifies to the undiminished strength of nationalism that organizations, such as the United Nations and its specialized agencies, created for the purpose of realizing the common interests of the nations of the world, have been seized by competing nationalisms for the purpose of serving competing national interests.

Personal Insecurity and Social Disintegration

Qualitatively, the emotional intensity of the identification of the individual with his nation stands in inverse proportion to the stability of the particular society as reflected in the sense of security of its members. The greater the stability of society and the sense of security of its members, the smaller are the chances for collective emotions to seek an outlet in aggressive nationalism, and vice versa.[3] The revolutionary wars of France in the last decade of the eighteenth century and the wars of liberation against Napoleon from 1812–15 are the first examples in modern times of mass insecurity, induced by the instability of domestic societies and leading to emotional outbursts in the form of fervent mass iden-

---

[3]These collective emotions may, of course, seek an outlet in aggressiveness within the nation as well; that is, in the form of class struggle, revolution, urban violence, and civil war.

tifications with aggressive foreign policies and wars. Social instability became acute in Western civilization during the nineteenth century. It became permanent in the twentieth century as a result of the emancipation of the individual from the ties of tradition, especially in the form of religion, of the increased rationalization of life and work, and of cyclical economic crises. The insecurity of the groups affected by these factors found an emotional outlet in fixed and emotionally accentuated nationalistic identifications. As Western society became ever more unstable, the sense of insecurity deepened and the emotional attachment to the nation as the symbolic substitute for the individual became ever stronger. Under the impact of the world wars, revolutions, concentration of economic, political, and military power, and the economic crises of the twentieth century it reached the fervor of a secular religion. Contests for power now took on the ideological aspects of struggles between good and evil. Foreign policies transformed themselves into sacred missions. Wars were fought as crusades, for the purpose of bringing the true political religion to the rest of the world.

This relation between social disintegration, personal insecurity, and the ferocity of modern nationalistic power drives can be studied to particular advantage in German fascism, where these three elements were more highly developed than anywhere else. The general tendencies of the modern age toward social disintegration were driven to extremes in Germany by a conjunction of certain elements in the national character favoring the extremes rather than mediating and compromising positions, and by three events that weakened the social fabric of Germany to such an extent as to make it an easy prey for the consuming fire of National Socialism.

The first of these events was the defeat in the First World War, coinciding with a revolution that was held responsible not only for the destruction of traditional political values and institutions, but for the loss of the war itself. The revolution naturally brought loss of power and insecurity in social status to those who had been at or near the top of the social hierarchy under the monarchy. Yet the social situation of large masses of the population was similarly affected by the impact of the idea that defeat and revolution were both the result of treacherous machinations of domestic and foreign enemies working for the destruction of Germany. Thus it was widely held that Germany was not only "encircled" by foreign enemies, but that its own body politic was shot through with invisible hostile organisms, sapping its strength and bent upon destroying it.

The second event was the inflation of the early twenties which proletarized economically large sectors of the middle classes and weakened, if not destroyed, in the people at large the traditional moral principles of honesty and fair dealing. The middle classes, in protest against their economic proletarization, embraced the most antiproletarian and nationalistic ideologies available. The lower strata of the middle classes especially had always derived at least a limited satisfaction from their superiority to the proletariat. When they viewed the social pyramid as a whole, they had always to look up much farther than they were able to look down. Yet, while they were not actually at the bottom of the social pyramid, they were uncomfortably close to it. Hence their frustrations and insecurity and their predisposition for the nationalistic identification. Now inflation pushed them down to the bottom, and in the desperate struggle to escape social and political identification with the amorphous mass of the proletariat they found succor in the theory and practice of National Socialism. For National Socialism offered them lower races to look down upon and foreign enemies to feel superior to and conquer.

Finally, the economic crisis of 1929 brought all the different groups of the German people in different ways face to face with the actual or threatened loss of social status and intellectual, moral, and economic insecurity. The workers were faced with actual or threatened permanent unemployment. Those groups of the middle classes who had recovered from the economic devastation of inflation were losing what they had regained. The industrialists had to cope with increased social obligations and were haunted by the fear of revolution. National Socialism focused all those fears, insecurities, and frustrations upon two foreign enemies: The Treaty of Versailles and bolshevism, and their alleged domestic supporters. It channeled all those thwarted emotions into one mighty stream of nationalistic fanaticism. Thus National Socialism was able to identify in a truly totalitarian fashion the aspirations of the individual German with the power objectives of the German nation. Nowhere in modern history has that identification been more complete. Nowhere has that sphere in which the individual pursues his aspirations for power for their own sake been smaller. Nor has the force of the emotional impetus with which that identification transformed itself into aggressiveness on the international scene been equaled in modern civilization.

While the transformation of individual frustrations into collective identification with the nation has never in modern history been more comprehensive and intensive than it was in National Socialist Germany, nevertheless the German variety of modern nationalism differs in degree rather than in kind from the nationalism of other great powers, such as that of the Soviet Union or of the United States. In the Soviet Union the great mass of the population has no opportunity to satisfy its power drives within the domestic society. The average Russian worker and peasant has nobody to look down upon, and his insecurity is intensified by the practices of the police state as well as by a low standard of living. Here, too, a totalitarian regime projects these frustrations, insecurities, and fears onto the international scene where the individual Russian finds in the identification with "the most progressive country in the world," "the fatherland of socialism," vicarious satisfaction for his aspirations for power. The conviction, seemingly supported by historic experience, that the nation with which he identifies himself is constantly menaced by capitalist enemies serves to elevate his personal fears and insecurities onto the collective plane. His personal fears are thus transformed into anxiety for the nation. Identification with the nation thus serves the dual function of satisfying individual power drives and alleviating individual fears by projecting both onto the international scene.

In the United States, the process by which national power is appropriated by the individual and experienced as his own resembles by and large the typical pattern as it developed in Western civilization during the nineteenth century. This is to say, the identification of the individual with the power and the foreign policies of the nation proceeds largely in terms of the typical frustrations and insecurities of the middle class. Yet American society is to a much greater extent a middle-class society than any other society in Western civilization. More importantly, whatever class distinctions there may be tend to be mitigated, if not resolved, in American society by the common denominator of middle-class values and aspirations. The identification of the individual with the nation in terms of middle-class frustrations and aspirations is, therefore, almost as predominant and typical in American society as the proletarian identification is in the Soviet Union. On the other hand, the relatively great mobility of American society opens to the great masses of the population avenues for social and economic improvement. These opportunities have in the past, at least in normal times, tended to keep rather low the emotional intensity of that identification as compared with the corresponding situations in the Soviet Union and in National Socialist Germany.[4]

New factors have, however, arisen in recent times with the increasing atomization of society, the threat of world revolution as symbolized by international Communism, the relative disappearance of geographical isolation, and the danger of nuclear war. Thus, in the last quarter of the twentieth century, intensified individual frustrations and anxieties have called forth a more intensive identification, on the part of the individual, with the power and the foreign policies of the nation. If, therefore, the present trend toward ever-increasing domestic frustration and international instability is not reversed, the United States is likely to partake to a growing extent in those tendencies in modern culture which have found their most extreme manifestations in Soviet Russia and National Socialist Germany, tendencies that make for an ever more complete and intensive identification of the individual with the nation. In this completeness and intensity of identification we have one of the roots of the ferocity and ruthlessness of modern foreign policies where national aspirations for power clash with each other, supported by virtually total populations with an unqualified dedication and intensity of feeling which in former periods of history only the issues of religion could command.

---

[4]Intense nationalistic identification in the United States has been associated in the past mainly with antagonism, on the part of the most insecure sector of the middle class, against certain ethnic groups, such as the Negro or the latest wave of proletarian immigrants.

9

Elements of National Power

What are the factors that make for the power of a nation vis-à-vis other nations? What are the components of what we call national power? If we want to determine the power of a nation, what factors are we to take into consideration? Two groups of elements have to be distinguished: those which are relatively stable, and those which are subject to constant change.

GEOGRAPHY

The most stable factor upon which the power of a nation depends is obviously geography. For instance, the fact that the continental territory of the United States is separated from other continents by bodies of water three thousand miles wide to the east and more than six thousand miles wide to the west is a permanent factor that determines the position of the United States in the world. It is a truism to say that the importance of this factor today is not what it was in the times of George Washington or President McKinley. But it is fallacious to assume, as is frequently done, that the technical development of transportation, communications, and warfare has eliminated altogether the isolating factor of the oceans. This factor is certainly much less important today than it was fifty or a hundred years ago, but from the point of view of the power position of the United States it still makes a great deal of difference that the United States is separated from the continents of Europe and Asia by wide expanses of water instead of bordering directly on, let us say, France, China, or Russia. In other words, the geographical location of the United States remains a fundamental factor of permanent importance which the foreign policies of all nations must take into account, however different its bearing upon political decisions might be today from what it was in other periods of history.

Similarly, the separation of Great Britain from the European continent by a small body of water, the English Channel, is a factor that Julius Caesar could no more afford to overlook than could William the Conqueror, Philip II, Napoleon, or Hitler. However much other factors may have altered its importance throughout the course of history, what was important two thousand years ago is still important today, and all those concerned with the conduct of foreign affairs must take it into account.

What is true of the insular location of Great Britain is true of the geographic position of Italy. The Italian-peninsula is separated from the rest of Europe by the high mountain massif of the Alps, and while the valleys of the Alps descend gradually southward toward the north Italian plain, they precipitate abruptly toward the north. This geographical situation has been an important element in the political and military considerations of Italy and of other nations with regard to Italy. For, under all conditions of warfare of which we know, this geographical situation has made it extremely difficult to invade Central Europe from Italy, while it has made it much less difficult to invade Italy from the north. In consequence, invasions of Italy have been much more frequent than invasions by Italy. From Hannibal in the Punic Wars to General Clark in the Second World War, this permanent geographical factor has determined political and military strategy.

The Pyrenees have fulfilled for the international position of Spain a somewhat different, but no less permanent, function. It has been said that Europe ends at the Pyrenees. The Pyrenees, by making Spain difficult of access to the outside world, have indeed functioned as a barrier shutting Spain off from the main stream of the intellectual, social, economic, and political developments that transformed the rest of Europe. Spain has also been by-passed by most of the great political and military conflagrations of continental Europe. This position on the sidelines of continental politics is at least partially the result of that geographical seclusion provided by the mountain barrier of the Pyrenees.

Finally, let us consider the geographical situation of the Soviet Union. The Soviet Union constitutes an enormous land mass that extends over one seventh of the land area of the earth and is two and one-half times as large as the territory of the United States. While it is about five thousand miles by air from the Bering Straits to Koenigsberg, the capital of what was formerly East Prussia, now called Kaliningrad, it is half that distance from Murmansk at the Barents Sea to Ashkhabad at the northern frontier of Iran. This territorial extension is a permanent source of great strength which has thus far frustrated all attempts at military conquest from the outside. This enormous land mass dwarfed the territory conquered by foreign invaders in comparison with what still remained to be conquered.

Conquest of a considerable portion of a country without prospects for speedy recovery usually breaks the will to resist of the conquered people. This is, as we have seen, the political purpose of military conquests. Similar conquests—especially if, as under Napoleon and Hitler, they did not have a limited objective, but aimed at the very existence of Russia as a nation—had a rather stimulating effect upon Russian resistance. For not only were the conquered parts of Russia small in comparison with those which were left in Russian hands, but the task of the invader became more difficult with every step he advanced. He had to keep an ever greater number of troops supplied over ever lengthening lines of communication deep in a hostile country. Thus geography has made the conquest of Russian territory, as soon as the objectives of such conquest became ill defined and tended to become unlimited, a liability for the conqueror rather than an asset. Instead of the conqueror's swallowing the territory and gaining strength from it, it is rather the territory that swallows the conqueror, sapping his strength.

The possibility of nuclear war has enhanced the importance of the size of territory as a source of national power. In order to make a nuclear threat credible, a nation requires a territory large enough to disperse its industrial and population centers as well as its nuclear installations. The conjunction between the large radius of nuclear destruction and the relatively small size of their territories imposes a severe handicap upon the ability of the traditional nation states, such as Great Britain and France, to make a nuclear threat credible. Thus it is the quasi-continental size of their territory which allows nations, such as the United States, the Soviet Union, and China, to play the role of major nuclear powers.

Another geographical factor, however, constitutes at the same time a weakness and an asset for the international position of the Soviet Union. We are referring to the fact that neither high mountains nor broad streams separate the Soviet Union from its western neighbors and that the plains of Poland and Eastern Germany form a natural continuation of the Russian plain. There exists, then, no natural obstacle to invasion on the western frontier of Russia, either on the part of the Soviet Union or on the part of the Soviet Union's western neighbors. Thus, from the fourteenth century to the present, White Russia and the westernmost part of Russia proper have been the scene of continuous thrusts and counterthrusts and a field of battle where Russia and its western neighbors met. The lack of a natural frontier—that is, of a frontier predetermined, like the Italian or the Spanish, by geographical factors—has been a permanent source of conflict between Russia and the West. Similarly, yet for the opposite reason, the possibility of such a frontier between France and Germany in the form of the Rhine, to which France always aspired and which it had rarely the strength to attain, has been a permanent source of conflict between those two countries since the times of the Romans. As concerns Russia, the bolshevist foreign minister Vishinsky summed up the transcendent importance of geography when he said, upon being reproached for following a Czarist policy on the Dardanelles: "If a warship has to sail from the Mediterranean to the Black Sea, it must pass through the Dardanelles whether the government in Moscow is Czarist or Communist."[1]

---

[1]Quoted after Denis Healey, *Neutrality* (London: Ampersand Ltd., 1955), p. 36.

NATURAL RESOURCES

Another relatively stable factor that exerts an important influence upon the power of a nation with respect to other nations is natural resources.

Food

To start with the most elemental of these resources, food: a country that is self-sufficient, or nearly self-sufficient, has a great advantage over a nation that is not and must be able to import the foodstuffs it does not grow, or else starve. It is for this reason that the power and, in times of war, the very existence of Great Britain, which before the Second World War grew only 30 percent of the food consumed in the British Isles, has always been dependent upon its ability to keep the sea lanes open over which the vital food supplies had to be shipped in. Whenever its ability to import food was challenged, as in the two world wars through submarine warfare and air attacks, the very power of Great Britain was challenged, and its survival as a nation put in jeopardy.

For the same reason, Germany, though to a much smaller extent deficient in foodstuffs than Great Britain, in order to survive a war was bound to pursue three principal goals, either severally or in combination: first, the avoidance of a long war through a speedy victory before its food reserves were exhausted; second, the conquest of the great food-producing areas of eastern Europe; and third, the destruction of British seapower, which cut Germany off from access to overseas sources of food. In both world wars, Germany was unable to attain the first and third objectives. It reached the second goal in the First World War too late to be of decisive effect. Thus the Allied blockade, by imposing upon the German people privations that sapped their will to resist, was one of the essential factors in the victory of the Allies. In the Second World War, Germany became virtually self-sufficient with regard to food, not primarily through conquest, but through the deliberate starvation and the outright killing of millions of people in conquered territories.

A deficiency in home-grown food has thus been a permanent source of weakness for Great Britain and Germany which they must somehow overcome, or face the loss of their status as great powers. A country enjoying self-sufficiency, such as the United States, need not divert its national energies and foreign policies from its primary objectives in order to make sure that its populations will not starve in war. Since such countries are reasonably free from worry on that count, they have been able to pursue much more forceful and single-minded policies than otherwise would have been possible. Self-sufficiency in food has thus always been a source of great strength.

Conversely, permanent scarcity of food is a source of permanent weakness in international politics. Of the truth of this observation, India was the prime example before the so-called green revolution drastically increased its food supply. The scarcity of food from which India suffered was the result of two factors: the increase in population, outstripping the supply of food, and the insufficiency of exports to pay for the import of the food necessary to make up the deficit. This dual imbalance, which made the ever-present threat of mass starvation one of the main concerns of government, put an insuperable handicap upon any active foreign policy India might have wanted to pursue. Regardless of the other assets of national power which were at its disposal, the deficiencies in food compelled it to act in its foreign policy from weakness rather than from strength. The same observation applies with particular force to the nations of the Third World that continuously live under the threat of famine and the actuality of undernourishment without most of any of the other assets which go into the making of national power. These are the so-called "basket cases" that are limited to hoping that international generosity will help them to survive the next famine.

Self-sufficiency in food, or lack of it, is a relatively stable factor in national power, but it is sometimes, as the example of contemporary India shows, subject to decisive changes. There may be changes in the consumption of food brought about by changing conceptions of nutrition. There may be changes in the technique of agriculture which may increase or decrease the output of agricultural products. The outstanding examples of the influence of changes in the agricultural output upon national power are, however, to be found in the disappearance of the Near East and of North Africa as power centers and in the descent of Spain from a world power to a third-rate power.

The agricultural systems of the Near East and North Africa were all founded upon irrigation. Even though it can hardly be proved that the decline in the national power of Babylon, of Egypt, and of the Arabs was concomitant with the disorganization of their irrigation systems, this much is certain—the decay of their systems of agriculture made irreparable the decline of their national power. For the disappearance of regulated irrigation transformed the better part of the arable land of these regions into deserts. It was only in Egypt that the natural irrigation of the Nile preserved a certain measure of fertility even after artificial irrigation had broken down.

As for Spain, while one dates the decline of its power from the destruction of the Armada by Great Britain in 1588, its political downfall became definite only after misrule in the seventeenth and eighteenth centuries had destroyed considerable sections of its arable land through large-scale deforestation. In consequence, wide regions of northern and central Spain were transformed into virtual deserts.

Raw Materials

What holds true of food is of course also true of those natural resources which are important for industrial production and, more particularly, for the waging of war. The absolute and relative importance natural resources in the form of raw materials have for the power of a nation depends necessarily upon the technology of the warfare practiced in a particular period of history. Before the large-scale mechanization of warfare, when hand-to-hand fighting was the prevalent military technique, other factors, such as the personal qualities of the individual soldier, were more important than the availability of the raw materials with which his weapons were made. In that period of history which extends from the beginning of historic time well into the nineteenth century, natural resources played a subordinate role in determining the power of a nation. With the increasing mechanization of warfare, which since the industrial revolution has proceeded at a faster pace than in all preceding history, national power has become more and more dependent upon the control of raw materials in peace and war. It is not by accident that the two most powerful nations today, the United States and the Soviet Union, come closest to being self-sufficient in the raw materials necessary for modern industrial production, and control at least the access to the sources of those raw materials which they do not themselves produce.

As the absolute importance of the control of raw materials for national power has increased in proportion to the mechanization of warfare, so certain raw materials have gained in importance over others. This has happened whenever fundamental changes in technology have called for the use of new materials or the increased use of old ones. In 1936, a statistician rated the share of a number of basic minerals in industrial production for military purposes and assigned them the following values: coal, 40; oil, 20; iron, 15; copper, lead, manganese, sulphur, 4 each; zinc, aluminum, nickel, 2 each.[2] Half a century before, the share of coal would certainly have been considerably greater, since as a source of energy it had at that time only small competition from water and wood and none from oil. The same would have been true of iron which then had no competition from light metals and such substitutes as plastics. Great Britain, which was self-sufficient in coal and iron, was the one great world power of the nineteenth century.

The influence the control of raw materials can exert upon national power and the shifts in the distribution of power which it can bring about are demonstrated in our own day most strikingly by the case of uranium. Only a few years ago the control or lack of control of uranium deposits was entirely irrelevant for the power of a nation. The author we have quoted above,[3] writing in 1936, did not even mention this mineral in his evaluation of the relative military importance of minerals. The release of atomic energy from the uranium atom and the use of that energy for warfare have at once modified the actual and potential hierarchy of nations in view of their relative power. Nations that control deposits of uranium, such as Canada, Czechoslovakia, the Soviet Union, the Union of South Africa, and the United States, have risen in the power calculations. Others that neither possess nor have access to deposits of that mineral have fallen in terms of relative power.

---

[2]Ferdinand Friedensburg, *Die mineralischen Bodenschätze als weltpolitische and militärische Machtfaktoren* (Stuttgart: F. Enke, 1936), p. 175.

[3]See preceding note.

The Power of Oil

Since the First World War, oil as a source of energy has become more and more important for industry and war. Most mechanized weapons and vehicles are driven by oil; consequently, countries that possess considerable deposits of oil have acquired an influence in international affairs which in some cases can be attributed primarily, if not exclusively, to that possession. "One drop of oil," said Clemenceau during the First World War, "is worth one drop of blood of our soldiers." The emergence of oil as an indispensable raw material has brought about a shift in the relative power of the politically leading nations. The Soviet Union has become more powerful since it is self-sufficient in this respect, while Japan has grown considerably weaker, since it is completely lacking in oil deposits.

Aside from its location as the land bridge of three continent, the Near East is strategically important because of the oil deposits of the Arabian peninsula. Control over them traditionally has been an important factor in the distribution of power, in the sense that whoever is able to add them to his other sources of raw materials adds that much strength to his own resources and deprives his competitors proportionately. It is for this reason that Great Britain, the United States and, for a time, France embarked in the Near East upon what has aptly been called "oil diplomacy": that is, the establishment of spheres of influence giving them exclusive access to the oil deposits in certain regions.

Yet oil is no longer one of many raw materials important in the measurement of a nation's power. It is now a material factor whose very possession threatens to overturn centuries-old patterns of international politics. The embargo on oil by the oil-producing states in the winter of 1973–74, together with the drastic rise in the price of oil, suddenly clarified certain basic aspects of world politics which we might have understood theoretically, but which were brought home in earnest by the drastic change in power relations brought on by the new politics of oil.

Traditionally a functional relationship has existed between political, military, and economic power. That is to say, political power has been throughout history a function of military and—in recent times more particularly—of economic power. Take for instance the expansion of Europe into what later became the colonial areas of the Western Hemisphere, Africa, and Asia. That expansion was primarily due to a technological gap between the colonial powers and the colonized nations. In other words, the conquest of India by Great Britain (much inferior in manpower and in many other aspects of national power) was largely made possible by Great Britain's possession of a higher technology which, when transformed into military power, the Indian states could not resist.

Those relationships of a functional nature between technology and economic power, on the one hand, and political and military power, on the other, have been disturbed—one might even say destroyed—by the recent use of oil as a political weapon. Many of those oil-producing states are states only by way of what might be called semantic courtesy. Measured in terms of natural resources, they have nothing but sand and oil. But it is the oil which seemingly overnight has made those small plots on the map which we call states important and even powerful factors in world politics. In other words, a state which has nothing to go on by way of power, which is lacking in all the elements which traditionally have gone into the making of national power, suddenly becomes a powerful factor in world politics because it has one important asset—oil. This is indeed an event which is of revolutionary importance for world politics.

Two basic factors in our period of history have made possible this divorce of political power from military and industrial-technological power. (1) Free trade between the private producers and consumers of certain raw materials and monopolistically controlled trade through colonial and semicolonial arrangements by the consumer governments has been replaced by monopolistic or quasi-monopolistic controls on the part of the producer governments acting in concert. Formerly the consumers could keep the price low through colonial arrangements and the control of consumption; now the producers can keep the price high by controlling production. (2) Formerly producers and consumers of raw materials were tied together by complementary interests, the balance of which favored the consumer. The latter's needs were limited as compared with the number of potential producers and the quantity of raw materials available. The consumer had, accordingly, a choice among several producers to buy from, and also of the quantity to buy from the several producers chosen. Today, what was once a buyer's market has become a seller's market. The consumption of raw materials has enormously increased, not only in absolute terms—between 1760 and 1913 imports of food and raw materials to Great Britain increased seventy-fold—but also relative to available resources. Thus oil has become the lifeblood of industrially advanced nations, many of which are completely (*e.g.,* Japan) or in considerable measure (*e.g.* the nations of Western Europe) dependent upon imports from other nations.

The power which oil bestows is, first of all, the result of the technological development of modern industrial nations. Twenty or fifty years ago oil did not bestow such power upon producing nations because the use of oil as the lifeblood of modern industry was limited. When nations which have large deposits of oil are able to co-operate and co-ordinate policies, as the oil-exporting states were during the fall of 1973, they can apply a stranglehold to the consuming nations; they can impose political conditions which the consuming nations can refuse to meet only at the risk of enormous political, economic, and social dislocations.

A state which is powerless in all other respects, which is not a major force in terms of traditional power, can exert enormous—and under certain conditions even decisive—power over nations which have all the implements of power at their disposal except one—deposits of oil. Thus a nation like Japan, one of the foremost industrial nations of the world and potentially a great power, is completely dependent upon the supply of oil from abroad. If for some reason the oil-producing nations were to impose a total embargo upon Japan, they could destroy her political, economic, and social fabric, and if they were to connect that threat of a total embargo with political conditions, they could impose their will upon Japan. They could reduce Japan to the status of satellite, a dependency of the oil-producing nations. To a certain extent those nations have already tasted that power. During the Middle Eastern war of October, 1973, they forced Japan and the nations of Western Europe (which are only partially dependent on the import of oil) to take certain political steps which they would not have taken on their own initiative, but which they felt they had to take under the circumstances because otherwise they would have risked political, social, and economic ruin.

It is not only the quasi-monopoly which the oil-producing nations acting in concert have on the supply of oil which has caused such dislocation. It is particularly, and in the long run more importantly, the control (whether actual or potential) they exert over the price of oil that has become one of the main factors of instability in the world economy and one of the main sources of inflation. The inflationary tendencies which were already at work in the industrial nations of the world were greatly aggravated by the fourfold increase in the price of oil in 1973 and the further doubling of the wellhead price in 1978.

It is important to note that this situation is potentially of a permanent nature. As long as the oil-producing nations co-operate against the consuming nations, as long as there is no competition among them for markets or for economic or political advantages, they will be able to impose virtually any conditions on the oil-consuming nations, just as they did in the wake of the 1973 war. In the case of a country like Japan it would be suicide to refuse such conditions. In the case of other nations, such as the United States, whose main sources of energy are domestic, it would mean severe discomfort of the kind already experienced in 1973. The nations of Western Europe, for example West Germany, whose main sources of petroleum come from abroad, would face catastrophe if they attempted to defy those nations upon whom they depend for oil.

While there is no way of destroying this stranglehold short of war, there is a way of mitigating its results. It lies in weakening the monopolistic or quasi-monopolistic position of the oil-producing nations by strengthening the position of the oil-consuming ones. The latter fall into two categories: those like Japan, who are utterly dependent upon the importation of oil, and for whom therefore the access to foreign oil is a matter of life and death; and those like the United States, who, by virtue of domestic sources of energy, can be inconvenienced and harmed, but not mortally wounded, by the political manipulation of oil. The latter are able to protect themselves from the more severe consequences of such manipulation by limiting the importation of oil, by restricting its domestic use, by stockpiling reserves, and by embarking upon a crash program, after the model of the Manhattan Project for the discovery of nuclear fission, to develop alternative sources of energy. The very existence of such a four-pronged policy would have a salutary effect upon all concerned. It would strengthen the morale of the oil consumers and give pause to the producers.

Such a policy would also lay the psychological and material groundwork for a policy of sharing between those consumers who possess considerable domestic sources of energy and those who lack them. For the oil producers are able to strike at a consumer, such as the United States, not only directly by cutting off its supply, but also indirectly by bringing its principal allies, such as the Federal Republic of Germany and Japan, to their knees. Thus the United States is doubly vulnerable to the political manipulation of oil, and it must meet that dual threat by making itself as quickly and as much as possible independent of foreign oil supplies and by making a fraction of its domestic resources available to its most endangered allies.

Finally, if one looks at this situation created by the political use of oil from an over-all point of view, one realizes that it is the specific result of what we identified earlier as the main characteristic of contemporary world politics: the disjunction between the organizational structures and political processes through which we act on the world scene, on the one hand, and the objective conditions under which humanity lives, on the other. Thus one is struck by the utter irrationality of leaving the control of nuclear power which can destroy mankind to sovereign nation states. The same applies to entrusting the control of oil—which can destroy in a different way (less dramatically but almost as thoroughly) the civilization of the highly developed industrial nations—to so-called nation states which are sovereign only in a very limited sense. The states belonging to the "nuclear club" are no longer, and the oil-producing states have never been, capable of performing the functions for which government is established in the first place, that is, to protect and promote the life, liberty, and happiness of its citizens. Their power is essentially destructive.

INDUSTRIAL CAPACITY

The example of uranium illustrates, however, the importance of another factor for the power of a nation—industrial capacity. The Congo has vast deposits of high-grade uranium. Yet, while this fact has increased the value of that country as a prize of war and, therefore, its importance from the point of view of military strategy, it has not affected the power of the Congo in relation to other nations. For the Congo does not have the industrial plant to put the uranium deposits to industrial and military use. On the other hand, for Great Britain, Canada, and the United States, as for Czechoslovakia and the Soviet Union, the possession of uranium signifies an enormous increase in power. In these countries the industrial plants exist or can be built, or they can easily be used in a neighboring country, where uranium can be transformed into energy to be employed in peace and war.

The same situation can be exemplified by coal and iron. The United States and the Soviet Union have drawn a good deal of their national strength from the possession of vast amounts of these two raw materials because they possess also industrial plants that can transform them into industrial products. The

Soviet Union has built its plant, and is still in the process of building it, at enormous human and material sacrifices. It is willing to make the sacrifices because it recognizes that without the industrial plant it cannot build and maintain a military establishment commensurate with its foreign policy. Without this plant the Soviet Union cannot play the important part in international politics which it intends to play.

India follows the United States and the Soviet Union closely as a depository of coal and iron. Its reserves of iron ore in the two provinces of Bihar and Orissa alone are estimated at 2.7 billion tons. Furthermore, India's output of manganese, which is indispensable for the production of steel, was a million tons as early as 1939, topped only by the output of the Soviet Union. But despite these riches in raw materials, without which no nation can attain first rank in modern times, India cannot be classified today as a first-rate power even faintly comparable to the United States and the Soviet Union. The reason for this lag between the potentialities and actualities of power, which concerns us in the context of this discussion (others will be mentioned later), is the lack of an industrial establishment commensurate with the abundance of raw materials. While India can boast of a number of steel mills, such as the Tata Iron Works, which are among the most modern in existence, it has no per capita productive capacity, especially for finished products, that can be compared with even one of the second-rate industrial nations. In 1980, fewer than six million Indians—less than one per cent of the total population—were employed in industry. So we see that India possesses, in the abundance of some of the key raw materials, one of the elements that go into the making of national power, and to that extent it may be regarded as a potentially great power. Actually, however, it will not become a great power as long as it is lacking in other factors without which no nation in modern times can attain the status of a great power. Of these factors industrial capacity is one of the most important.

The technology of modern warfare transportation and communications has made the over-all development of heavy industries an indispensable element of national power. Since victory in modern war depends upon the number and quality of highways, railroads, trucks, ships, airplanes, tanks, and equipment and weapons of all kinds, from mosquito nets and automatic rifles to oxygen masks and guided missiles, the competition among nations for power transforms itself largely into competition for the production of bigger, better, and more implements of war. The quality and productive capacity of the industrial plant, the know-how of the working man, the skill of the engineer, the inventive genius of the scientist, the managerial organization—all these are factors upon which the industrial capacity of a nation and, hence, its power depend.

Thus it is inevitable that the leading industrial nations should be identical with the great powers, and a change in industrial rank, for better or for worse, should be accompanied or followed by a corresponding change in the hierarchy of power. So long as Great Britain as an industrial nation had no equal, it was the most powerful nation on earth, the only one that deserved to be called a world power. The decline of France as a power in comparison with Germany, which was unmistakable after 1870 and was only seemingly and temporarily arrested during the decade following the First World War, was in part but the political and military manifestation of the industrial backwardness of France and of the industrial predominance of Germany on the European continent.

The Soviet Union, while having been potentially always a great power, became one in fact only when it entered the ranks of the foremost industrial powers in the thirties, and it became the rival of the United States as the other superpower only when it acquired in the fifties the industrial capacity for waging nuclear war. Similarly, the potential of China as a great power will only be realized if and when it acquires a similar industrial capacity. When the United States was at the height of its power in the forties, the *Economist* of London related that power to American economic strength by saying:

> In any comparison of potential resources of the Great Powers the United States, even before Hitler's war, far outstripped every other nation in the world in material strength, in scale of industrialization, in weight of resources, in standards of living, by every index of output and consumption. And the war, which all but doubled the American national income while it either ruined or severely weakened every other Great Power, has enormously increased the scale upon which the United States now towers above its fellows. Like mice in the cage of an elephant, they follow with apprehension the movements of the mammoth. What chance would they stand if it were to begin to throw its weight about, they who are in some danger even if it only decides to sit down?[4]

This drastic increase in the importance of industrial capacity for national power has also accentuated the traditional distinction between great and small powers. The very term "superpower" points to an unprecedented accumulation of power in the hands of a few nations, which sets these nations apart not only from the small ones but from the traditional great powers as well. What distinguishes the superpowers from all other nations, aside from their ability to wage all-out nuclear war and absorb a less than all-out nuclear attack, is their virtual industrial self-sufficiency and their technological capacity to stay abreast of the other nations. By the same token, the dependence of the nations of the third and fourth rank upon the nations of the first rank, which we can call superpowers, has also drastically increased. The military power of the former depends to a sometimes decisive extent upon the willingness of the latter to supply them with modern weapons and the implements of modern communications and transportation. Without this supply many of them would be helpless in confrontation with an enemy thus supplied.

MILITARY PREPAREDNESS

What gives the factors of geography, natural resources, and industrial capacity their actual importance for the power of a nation is military preparedness. The

---

[4]*Economist*, May 24, 1947, p. 785. (Reprinted by permission.)

dependence of national power upon military preparedness is too obvious to need much elaboration. Military preparedness requires a military establishment capable of supporting the foreign policies pursued. Such ability derives from a number of factors of which the most significant, from the point of view of our discussion, are technological innovations, leadership, and the quantity and quality of the armed forces.

Technology

The fate of nations and of civilizations has often been determined by a differential in the technology of warfare for which the inferior side was unable to compensate in other ways. Europe, in the period of its expansion from the fifteenth through the nineteenth century, carried its power on the vehicle of a technology of warfare superior to that of the Western Hemisphere, Africa, and the Near and Far East. The addition of infantry, firearms, and artillery to the traditional weapons in the fourteenth and fifteenth centuries spelled a momentous shift in the distribution of power in favor of those who used those weapons before their enemies did. The feudal lords and independent cities, who in the face of these new weapons continued to rely upon cavalry and the castles which until then had been practically immune against direct attack, now found themselves suddenly dislodged from their position of preponderance.

Two events illustrate dramatically this shift in power which politically and militarily marks the end of the Middle Ages and the beginning of the modern era of history. First, in the battles of Morgarten in 1315 and of Laupen in 1339, armies composed of Swiss infantry inflicted disastrous defeats upon feudal cavalry, demonstrating that foot soldiers recruited from the common people were superior to an aristocratic and expensive army of equestrians. The second is the invasion of Italy in 1494 by Charles VIII of France. With infantry and artillery, Charles VIII broke the power of the proud Italian city-states, until then secure behind their walls. The seemingly irresistible destructiveness of these new techniques of warfare made an indelible impression upon contemporaries, some of which is reflected in the writings of Machiavelli and other Florentine writers of the time.[5]

The twentieth century has thus far witnessed four major innovations in the technique of warfare. They gave at least a temporary advantage to the side that used them before the opponent did, or before he was able to protect himself against them. First, the submarine was used in the First World War by Germany primarily against British shipping and seemed to be capable of deciding the war in favor of Germany until Great Britain found in the convoy an answer to that menace. Second, the tank was used in considerable and concentrated numbers by the British, but not by the Germans, in the closing phase of the

---

[5]See the account by Felix Gilbert, "Machiavelli: The Renaissance of the Art of War," in *Makers of Modern Strategy*, edited by Edward Mead Earle (Princeton: Princeton University Press, 1944), pp. 8, 9.

First World War, giving the Allies one of their assets for victory. Third, strategic and tactical co-ordination of the air force with the land and naval forces contributed greatly to the German and Japanese superiority in the initial stages of the Second World War. Pearl Harbor and the disastrous defeats that the British and the Dutch suffered at the hands of the Japanese on land and at sea in 1941 and 1942 were the penalties to be paid for technological backwardness in the face of a more progressive enemy. If one reads the somber review of British defeats which Churchill gave in the secret session of Parliament on April 23, 1942,[6] one is struck by the fact that all these defeats on land, on the sea, and in the air have one common denominator: the disregard or misunderstanding of the change in the technology of warfare brought about by air power. Finally, nations which possess nuclear weapons and the means to deliver them have an enormous technological advantage over their competitors.

However, the availability of nuclear weapons also results in two extraordinary paradoxes, referred to above, as concerns its bearing upon national power. Both paradoxes stem from the enormous destructiveness of nuclear weapons. It is by virtue of that destructiveness that a quantitative increase in nuclear weapons, in contrast to conventional ones, does not of necessity signify a corresponding increase in national power. Once a nation possesses all the nuclear weapons necessary to destroy all the enemy targets it has chosen for destruction, taking all possible contingencies, such as a first strike by the enemy, into consideration, additional nuclear weapons will not increase that nation's power.[7]

The other paradox lies in the inverse relationship between the degree of destructiveness of nuclear weapons and their rational usability. High-yield nuclear weapons are instruments of indiscriminate mass destruction and can therefore not be used for rational military purposes. They can be used to deter a war by threatening total destruction; but they cannot be used to fight a war in a rational manner. A nation armed with nothing but high-yield nuclear weapons could draw very little political power from its military posture; for it would have no military means by which to impose its will upon another nation, aside from threatening it with total destruction.

If such a nation has a second-strike nuclear capability, it will threaten total destruction in return and then the two threats either will cancel each other out or will lead to the mutual destruction of the belligerents. If the threatened nation has no nuclear means of retaliation, it will either suffer total destruction or surrender unconditionally as did Japan in 1945 after Hiroshima and Nagasaki had been destroyed by nuclear bombs. In other words, the threatening nation could wipe the nonnuclear nation off the face of the earth, either piecemeal, city by city, or in one devastating blow, but it could not subtly adapt the degree of military pressure to be used to the degree of psychological resistance to be overcome. The absence of conventional weapons, susceptible to such subtle

---

[6]*Winston Churchill's Secret Session Speeches* (New York: Simon and Schuster, 1946), pp. 53 ff.
[7]Cf. below, pages 280 ff.

adaptations, and the sole reliance upon high-yield nuclear weapons would make a nation less powerful than it would be if it possessed a combination of high-yield nuclear weapons for the purpose of deterrence and an armory of conventional weapons usable for the ordinary purposes of warfare. Hence the paradox that in order to make nuclear weapons usable one must reduce their yield to approximate that of conventional weapons.

Leadership

Aside from the timely use of technological innovations, the quality of military leadership has always exerted a decisive influence upon national power. The power of Prussia in the eighteenth century was primarily a reflection of the military genius of Frederick the Great and of the strategic and tactical innovations introduced by him. The art of warfare had changed between the death of Frederick the Great in 1786 and the battle of Jena in 1806 when Napoleon destroyed the Prussian army, which in itself was then as good and strong as it had been twenty years before. But, what was more important, military genius was lacking in its leaders who were fighting the battles of Frederick the Great all over again. On the other side military genius was in command, employing new ideas in strategy and tactics. This factor decided the issue in favor of France.

The Maginot Line psychology of the French general staff in the period between the two world wars has become a byword for faulty strategic thinking. While the tendencies of modern technology, especially its trend toward mechanization of transportation and of communications, pointed toward the probability of a war of movement, the French general staff continued to think in terms of the trench warfare of the First World War. The German general staff, on the other hand, fully alive to the strategic potentialities of mechanized warfare, planned its campaigns in terms of unprecedented mobility. The conflagration of these two conceptions, not only in France but also in Poland and the Soviet Union, produced in the "blitzkrieg" a superiority of German power which brought Germany close to final victory. The intellectual shock and the military and political devastation caused by the onslaught of Hitler's panzers and dive bombers upon the Polish cavalry in 1939 and upon the immobile French army in 1940 ushered in a new period of military history, similar to the one initiated by Charles VIII's invasion of Italy in 1494. But, while the Italian states had nobody to fall back on in order to recover their strength, in the Second World War the superior technology of the United States and the superior manpower of the Soviet Union turned Hitler's innovations to his destruction.

Quantity and Quality of Armed Forces

The power of a nation in military terms is also dependent upon the quantity of men and arms and their distribution among the different branches of the military establishment. A nation may have a good grasp of technological innovations in warfare. Its military leaders may excel in the strategy and tactics appropriate to the new techniques of war. Yet such a nation may be militarily and, in consequence, also politically weak if it does not possess a military establishment that in its over-all strength and in the strength of its component parts is neither too large nor too small in view of the tasks it may be called upon to perform. Must a nation, in order to be strong, possess a large army or is its power not impaired by having, at least in peacetime, only small land forces, composed of highly trained, heavily armed specialized units? Have battle-ready forces-in-being become more important than trained reserves? Have large surface navies become obsolete, or do aircraft carriers still fulfill a useful purpose? How large a military establishment can a nation afford in view of its resources and commitments? Does concern for national power require large-scale peacetime production of aircraft and other mechanized weapons, or should a nation, in view of rapid changes in technology, spend its resources on research and on the production of limited quantities of improved types of weapons?

Whether a nation gives the right or the wrong answer to such questions of a quantitative character has obviously a direct bearing upon national power. Can decision in war be forced by one new weapon, such as artillery, as was thought at the turn of the fifteenth century, or the submarine, as the Germans thought in the First World War, or the airplane, as was widely believed in the period between the two world wars, or the inter-continental guided missiles, as many believe today? The wrong answers given to some of these questions by Great Britain and France in the period between the two world wars preserved for them the semblance of power in terms of the traditional military conceptions. But those errors brought them to the brink of final defeat in the course of the Second World War, whose military technique required different answers to these questions. Upon the quality of the answers we give to these and similar questions today will depend the future power of the United States in relation to other nations.

POPULATION

When we turn from material factors and those compounded of material and human elements to the purely human factors that determine the power of a nation, we have to distinguish quantitative and qualitative components. While among the latter we count national character, national morale, and the quality of diplomacy and of government in general, the former needs to be discussed in terms of size of population.

Distribution

It would, of course, not be correct to say that the larger the population of a country the greater the power of that country. For if such an unqualified correlation existed between size of population and national power, China, whose population is estimated as being over 1 billion people,[8] would be the most powerful nation on earth, followed by India with about 730 million. The Soviet Union with about 272 million and the United States with 234 million would run third and fourth, respectively. Though one is not justified in considering a country to be very powerful because its population is greater than that of most other countries, it is still true that no country can remain or become a first-rate power which does not belong to the more populous nations of the earth. Without a large population it is impossible to establish and keep going the industrial plant necessary for the successful conduct of modern war; to put into the field the large number of combat groups to fight on land, on the sea, and in the air; and, finally, to fill the cadres of the troops, considerably more numerous than the combat troops, which must supply the latter with food, means of transportation and communication, ammunition, and weapons. It is for this reason that imperialistic countries stimulate population growth with all kinds of incentives, as did Nazi Germany and Fascist Italy, and then use that growth as an ideological pretext for imperialistic expansion.

A comparison between the population of the United States and that of Australia and Canada will make clear the relation between size of population and national power. Australia has today, in an area of somewhat less than three million square miles, a population of about fifteen million, while the Canadian population, in an area of close to three and one-half million square miles, amounts to twenty-four and one-half million. The United States, on the other hand, in an area between that of Australia and Canada, has a population of 234 million, more than fifteen times larger than Australia's and nearly ten times larger than Canada's. With the population of either Australia or Canada, the United States could never have become the most powerful nation on earth. The waves of mass immigration in the nineteenth and the first two decades of the twentieth centuries brought to the United States this element of national power. Had the Immigration Law of 1924, limiting immigration to the United States to 150,000 persons a year, been enacted a hundred or even fifty years earlier, thirty-six or twenty-seven million people, respectively, would have been prevented from settling in the United States, and they and their descendants would have been lost to the United States.

In 1824, the population of the United States amounted to close to eleven million. By 1874, it had risen to forty-four million; by 1924, to 114 million. During that century the share of immigration in the growth of the American population was on the average close to 30 per cent, approaching 40 per cent in the period from 1880 to 1910. In other words, the most spectacular rise in American population coincides with the absolute and relative peaks of immigration. Free immigration from 1824 and, more particularly, from 1874 to 1924 is mainly responsible for the abundance of manpower which has meant so much

---

[8]All population figures, unless indicated otherwise, are derived from the information reported in the U.S. Census Bureau Report for mid-June 1983, *New York Times*, September 4, 1983, p. A9.

for the national power of the United States in war and peace. Without this immigration, it is unlikely that the population of the United States would amount to more than half of what it actually is today. In consequence, the national power of the United States would be inferior to what 234 million people make it today.

Since size of population is one of the factors upon which national power rests, and since the power of one nation is always relative to the power of others, the relative size of the population of countries competing for power and, especially, the relative rate of their growth deserve careful attention. A country inferior in size of population to its competitor will view with alarm a declining rate of growth if the population of its competitor tends to increase more rapidly. Such has been the situation of France with regard to Germany between 1870 and 1940. During that period, the population of France increased by four million, whereas Germany registered a gain of twenty-seven million. While in 1800 every seventh European was a Frenchman, in 1930 only every thirteenth was a Frenchman. In 1940, Germany had at its disposal about fifteen million men fit for military service, whereas France had only five million.

On the other hand, ever since the unification in 1870, Germany has viewed sometimes with alarm, and always with respect, the Russian population figures, which show a greater rate of increase than Germany's. Looking at the situation as it existed at the outbreak of the First World War solely from the point of view of population trends, Germany could feel that time was on Russia's side, and France could feel that time was on the side of Germany, while both Austria and Russia, for other reasons already alluded to,[9] could believe that postponement of the conflict would favor the opponent. Thus all the protagonists, with the exception of Great Britain, had reasons of their own to prefer a war in 1914 to a peaceful settlement which they could not regard as definite, but only as a breathing spell before the unavoidable settling of accounts.

As the shifts in the distribution of power within Europe in recent history have been roughly duplicated by the changes in population trends, so the emergence of the United States as the great power center of the West, taking the place of Western and Central Europe, can be read in the population figures of the respective countries. In 1870, the population of France as well as of Germany exceeded that of the United States. Yet, in 1940, the population of the United States had increased by 100 million while the combined increase in the populations of France and Germany in the same period amounted to only thirty-one million.

It is thus obvious that a nation cannot be the first rank without a population sufficiently large to create and apply the material implements of national power. On the other hand, it has become obvious only in recent times that a large population can also exert a drastically negative influence upon national power. This has happened in so-called underdeveloped nations, such as India and Egypt, whose populations have greatly increased, by virtue of a decrease

---

[9] See pages 80 and 81.

in the mortality rates, while their food supply did not keep pace with the increase in population. These countries were continually faced with the threat of famine and with the need to take care of large masses of undernourished and diseased people. They had to divert scarce resources from the development of their national power to the feeding and care of their populations. The largeness of their population, far from being an asset for their national power, is an obstacle to its development. For such nations, to bring the number of their population into harmony with their resources is a necessity, and if resources cannot be increased, population control is a precondition of national power.[10]

Trends

It is obvious from what has been said thus far that in trying to assess the future distribution of power the prediction of population trends plays an important role. All other factors remaining approximately equal, a considerable decline in the manpower of a nation in comparison with its competitors on the international scene spells a decline in national power, and a considerable increase, under similar conditions, amounts to a gain in national strength. When, toward the end of the nineteenth century, the British Empire was the only world power in existence, its population amounted to about 400 million; that is, approximately one fourth of the total population of the world. In 1946, it came close to 550 million. Since India's population was then estimated at 400 million, these figures illustrate the enormous loss in national power, in terms of size of population alone, which Great Britain suffered in the loss of India.

From the point of view of population, the position of the United States will continue to show considerable strength in comparison with Western Europe because of the latter's anticipated small increases. But compared with the population trend in Latin America, the position of the United States is well on its way to deterioration. Latin America shows the greatest rate of increase of any major region in the world. In 1900, Latin America had an estimated sixty-three million inhabitants to seventy-five million for the United States. The population of Argentina alone more than doubled between 1914 and 1965 and is now almost twenty-eight million. In the same period the population of the United States has only risen from 99 to 234 million.

It is, however, not sufficient to know the over-all population figures of different countries in order to assess correctly the influence of the population factor upon national power. The age distribution within a given population is an important element in power calculations. All other things being equal, a nation with a relatively large population of maximum potential usefulness for military and productive purposes (roughly between twenty and forty years of age) will have an edge in power over a nation in whose population the older age groups predominate.

It must be pointed out, however, that the projection of population trends

---

[10]Cf. above page 127.

is hazardous even without the interference of war or natural catastrophes. The estimates of population trends which were made in the forties painted a rather pessimistic picture of the increase of the American population as compared with that of the Soviet Union. Yet today the population of the United States exceeds by a wide margin the number that some population experts of great repute expected it to reach by 1975. Even in a field whose scientific accuracy appears to be relatively high, the prediction of national power is beset with uncertainties. But these uncertainties do not affect the importance of population trends for the development of national power. Nor can they diminish the active concern of statesmen with the population trends of their own nations.

Echoing Augustus and his successors on the throne of the Roman Empire, Sir Winston Churchill, as British Prime Minister, expressed this concern when he said in his radio address of March 22, 1943:

> One of the most somber anxieties which beset those who look thirty, or forty, or fifty years ahead, and in this field one can see ahead only too clearly, is the dwindling birth-rate. In thirty years, unless present trends alter, a smaller working and fighting population will have to support and protect nearly twice as many old people; in fifty years the position will be worse still. If this country is to keep its high place in the leadership of the world, and to survive as a great power that can hold its own against external pressures, our people must be encouraged by every means to have larger families.

NATIONAL CHARACTER

Its Existence

Of the three human factors of a qualitative nature which have a bearing on national power, national character and national morale stand out both for their elusiveness from the point of view of rational prognosis and for their permanent and often decisive influence upon the weight a nation is able to put into the scales of international politics. We are not concerned here with the question of what factors are responsible for the development of a national character. We are only interested in the fact—contested but (it seems to us) incontestable, especially in view of the anthropological concept of the "culture pattern"—that certain qualities of intellect and character occur more frequently and are more highly valued in one nation than in another. To quote Coleridge:

> . . . But that there is an invisible spirit that breathes through a whole people, and is participated by all, though not by all alike; a spirit which gives a color and character both to their virtues and vices, so that the same action, such I mean as are expressed by the same words, are yet not the same in a Spaniard as they would be in a Frenchman, I hold for an undeniable truth, without the admission of which all history would be a riddle. I hold likewise that the difference of nations, their

relative grandeur and meanness, all, in short, which they are or do,—(not indeed at one particular time, under the accidental influence of a single great man, as the Carthaginians under the great Xantippus, and afterwards under their own Hannibal,) but all in which they persevere, as a nation, through successions of changing individuals, are the result of this spirit; . . .[11]

These qualities set one nation apart from others, and they show a high degree of resiliency to change. A few examples, taken at random, will illustrate the point.

Is it not an incontestable fact that, as John Dewey[12] and many others have pointed out, Kant and Hegel are as typical of the philosophic tradition of Germany as Descartes and Voltaire are of the French mind, as Locke and Burke are of the political thought of Great Britain, as William James and John Dewey are of the American approach to intellectual problems? And can it be denied that these philosophic differences are but expressions, on the highest level of abstraction and systematization, of fundamental intellectual and moral traits that reveal themselves on all levels of thought and action and that give each nation its unmistakable distinctiveness? The mechanistic rationality and the systematic perfection of Descartes' philosophy reappear in the tragedies of Corneille and Racine no less than in the rationalistic fury of Jacobin reform. They reappear in the sterility of the academic formalism that characterizes much of the contemporary intellectual life of France. They reappear in the scores of peace plans, logically perfect but impracticable, in which French statecraft excelled in the period between the two world wars. On the other hand, the trait of intellectual curiosity which Julius Caesar detected in the Gauls has remained throughout the ages a distinctive characteristic of the French mind.

Locke's philosophy is as much a manifestation of British individualism as Magna Carta, due process of law, or Protestant sectarianism. In Edmund Burke, with his undogmatic combination of moral principle and political expediency, the political genius of the British people reveals itself as much as in the Reform Acts of the nineteenth century or the balance-of-power policies of Cardinal Wolsey and Canning. What Tacitus said of the destructive political and military propensities of the Germanic tribes fitted the armies of Frederick Barbarossa no less than those of William II and of Hitler. It fits, too, the traditional rudeness and clumsy deviousness of German diplomacy. The authoritarianism, collectivism, and state worship of German philosophy have their counterpart in the tradition of autocratic government, in servile acceptance of any authority so long as it seems to have the will and force to prevail, and, concomitant with it, the lack of civil courage, the disregard of individual rights, and the absence of a tradition of political liberty. The description of the American national character, as it emerges from Tocqueville's *Democracy in Amer-*

---

[11]Samuel Taylor Coleridge, *Essays on his own Times* (London: William Pickering, 1850), Vol. II, pp. 668–9.

[12]*German Philosophy and Politics* (New York: G. P. Putnam's Sons, 1942), *passim.*

ica, has not been deprived of its timeliness by the intervention of more than a century. The indecision of American pragmatism between an implicit dogmatic idealism and reliance upon success as a measure of truth is reflected in the vacillations of American diplomacy between the Four Freedoms and the Atlantic Charter, on the one hand, and "dollar diplomacy," on the other.

The Russian National Character

As for Russia, the juxtaposition of two experiences, almost a century apart, will provide striking proof of the persistence of certain intellectual and moral qualities.

Bismarck wrote in his memoirs:

> At the time of my first stay in St. Petersburg, in 1859, I had an example of another Russian peculiarity. During the first spring days it was then the custom for everyone connected with the court to promenade in the Summer Garden between Paul's Palace and the Neva. There the Emperor had noticed a sentry standing in the middle of a grass plot; in reply to the question why he was standing there, the soldier could only answer, "Those are my orders." The Emperor therefore sent one of his adjutants to the guard-room to make inquiries; but no explanation was forthcoming except that a sentry had to stand there winter and summer. The source of the original order could no longer be discovered. The matter was talked of at court, and reached the ears of the servants. One of them, an older pensioner, came forward and stated that his father had once said to him as they passed the sentry in the Summer Garden: "There he is, still standing to guard the flower, on that spot the Empress Catherine once noticed a snowdrop in bloom unusually early, and gave orders that it was not to be plucked." This command had been carried out by placing a sentry on the spot, and ever since then one had stood there all the year round. Stories of this sort excite our amusement and criticism, but they are an expression of the elementary force and persistence on which the strength of the Russian nature depends in its attitude towards the rest of Europe. It reminds us of the sentinels in the flood at St. Petersburg in 1825, and in the Shipka Pass in 1877; not being relieved, the former were drowned, the latter frozen to death at their posts.[13]

Time magazine of April 21, 1947, contains the following report:

> Down Potsdam's slushy Berlinerstrasse stumbled twelve haggard men. . . . Their faces had the pale, creased look of prisoners. Behind them trudged a stubby, broad-faced Russian soldier, Tommy gun crooked in his right arm, the wide Ukrainian steppe in his blue eyes.
>
> Approaching the Stadtbahn station, the group met a stream of men and women hurrying home from work.
>
> An angular, middle-aged woman suddenly sighted the twelve men. She stopped in her tracks, stared wide-eyed at them for a full minute. Then she

---

[13]*Bismarck, the Man and Statesman, being the Reflections and Reminiscences of Otto, Prince von Bismarck,* translated under the supervision of A. J. Butler (New York and London: Harper and Brothers, 1899), Vol. I, p. 250.

dropped her threadbare market bag, flew across the street in front of a lumbering charcoal-burning truck and threw herself with a gasping cry upon the third prisoner. Prisoners and passers-by paused and gaped dumbly at the two Rodinesque figures fingering the backs of each other's rough coats and mumbling hysterically: "*Wohin?*" "*. . . weiss nicht.*" "*Warum?*" "*. . . weiss nicht.*"

Slowly the Russian walked around his charges and approached the couple. Slowly a grin covered his face. He tapped the woman on the back. She shuddered. Rigid apprehension spread over the faces of the onlookers, but the Russian rumbled soothingly: "*Keine Angst. Keine Angst.*" (No fear. No fear.) Then he waved the muzzle of his Tommy gun toward the prisoner, who instinctively recoiled a step, and asked: "*Dein Mann?*"

"*Ja,*" replied the woman, tears streaming down her cheeks.

"*Gu-ut,*" grunted the Russian, wrinkling his nose, "*Nimm mit,*" and he gave the bewildered prisoner a gentle shove toward the sidewalk.

The spectators exhaled a mass sigh of relief as the couple stumbled off deliriously, hand in hand. Eleven prisoners, muttering to each other, pushed on down the street past the muttering crowd: "Unpredictable Russians . . . incredible . . . I can't understand . . . I don't understand the Russians."

The Russian shuffled along stoically, gripping a long papirosa between yellow stained teeth as he fished in a pocket for matches. Suddenly his face clouded. He hitched the Tommy gun higher under his arm, took a dirty piece of paper from the wide, ragged sleeve of his shinel, and scowled at it. After a few steps he stuffed the paper back carefully, stared for a moment at the bent backs of the prisoners, then searched the strained faces of a new load of commuters just leaving the station.

With no fuss, the Russian stepped up to a youngish man with a briefcase under his arm and a dirty brown felt hat pulled over his ears, and commanded: "*Eeh, Du! Komm!*" The German froze, casting a terrified glance over his shoulder at the frightened stream of men and women who were trying not to see or hear. The Russian waved his Tommy gun and curled his lip. "*Komm!*" He pushed his petrified recruit roughly into the gutter.

Again the prisoners were twelve. The Russian's face relaxed. With a third sputtering match he lighted his papirosa and placidly blew smoke toward the tense Germans scurrying home through the gathering dusk.[14]

Between these two episodes a great revolution intervened, interrupting the historic continuity on practically all levels of national life. Yet the traits of the Russian national character emerged intact from the holocaust of that revolution. Even so thorough a change in the social and economic structure, in political leadership and institutions, in the ways of life and thought has not been able to affect the "elementary force and persistence" of the Russian character which Bismarck found revealed in his experience and which reveal themselves in the Russian soldier of Potsdam as well.

To illustrate the same continuity of the national character, let us consider the following excerpts from diplomatic dispatches sent by an American diplomat from Russia to the Department of State:

> During the last year it has been evident that the policy of Russia toward foreigners and their entrance into the empire was becoming more and more stringent.

---

[14]*Time*, April 21, 1947, p. 32. (Used by permission of *Time*. Copyright Time, Inc., 1947.)

I heard of several Americans last summer who were unable to procure visas.
. . . This arises mainly from political considerations and a fear of foreign influence
upon the popular mind. To this it may be added that there is a strong anti-foreign
party in Russia whose policy would exclude all foreigners except for mere purposes
of transient commerce. . . .

The position of a minister here is far from being pleasant. The opinion prevails
that no communication, at least of a public nature, is safe in the post office but is
opened and inspected as a matter of course. . . . The opinion also prevails that
ministers are constantly subjected to a system of espionage and that even their
servants are made to disclose what passed in their households, their conversations,
associations, etc. . . .

Secrecy and mystery characterize everything. Nothing is made public that is
worth knowing.

A strange superstition prevails among the Russians that they are destined to
conquer the world. Appeals to the soldiery founded on this idea of fatality and its
glorious rewards are seldom made in vain. To a feeling of this sort has been
attributed that remarkable patience and endurance which distinguish the Russian
soldier in the midst of the greatest privations.

. . . Nothing is more striking to an American on his first arrival here than the
rigor of the police.

These impressions were gathered, not, as one might expect, in recent years
by Ambassadors Kennan, Bohlen, or Thompson, but in 1851–52 by Neill S.
Brown, then United States Minister to Russia.

National Character and National Power

National character cannot fail to influence national power; for those who act for
the nation in peace and war, formulate, execute, and support its policies, elect
and are elected, mold public opinion, produce and consume—all bear to a
greater or lesser degree the imprint of those intellectual and moral qualities
which make up the national character. The "elementary force and persistence"
of the Russians, the individual initiative and inventiveness of the Americans,
the undogmatic common sense of the British, the discipline and thoroughness
of the Germans are some of the qualities which will manifest themselves, for
better or for worse, in all the individual and collective activities in which the
members of a nation may engage. In consequence of the differences in national
character, the German and Russian governments, for instance, have been able
to embark upon foreign policies that the American and British governments
would have been incapable of pursuing, and vice versa. Antimilitarism, aversion to standing armies and to compulsory military service are permanent traits
of the American and British national character. Yet the same institutions and
activities have for centuries stood high in the hierarchy of values of Prussia,
from where their prestige spread over all of Germany. In Russia the tradition
of obedience to the authority of the government and the traditional fear of the
foreigner have made large permanent military establishments acceptable to the
population.

Thus the national character has given Germany and Russia an initial advantage in the struggle for power, since they could transform in peacetime a greater portion of their national resources into instruments of war. On the other hand, the reluctance of the American and British peoples to consider such a transformation, especially on a large scale and with respect to manpower, except in an obvious national emergency, has imposed a severe handicap upon American and British foreign policy. Governments of militaristic nations are able to plan, prepare, and wage war at the moment of their choosing. They can, more particularly, start a preventive war whenever it seems to be most propitious for their cause. Governments of pacifist nations, of which the United States was the outstanding example until the end of the Second World War, are in this respect in a much more difficult situation and have much less freedom of action. Restrained as they are by the innate antimilitarism of their peoples, they must pursue a more cautious course in foreign affairs. Frequently the military strength actually at their disposal will not be commensurate with the political commitments that their concern for the national interest imposes upon them. In other words, they will not have the armed might sufficient to back up their policies. When they go to war, they may well do so on the terms of their enemies. In the past they have had to rely upon other traits in the national character and upon other compensating factors, such as geographical location and industrial potential, to carry them over the initial period of weakness and inferiority to ultimate victory. Such can be the effects, for good or evil, of the character of a nation.

The observer of the international scene who attempts to assess the relative strength of different nations must take national character into account, however difficult it may be to assess correctly so elusive and intangible a factor. Failure to do so will lead to errors in judgment and policies, such as the depreciation of the recuperative force of Germany after the First World War and the underestimation of Russian staying power in 1941–42. The Treaty of Versailles could restrict Germany in all the other implements of national power, such as territory, sources of raw materials, industrial capacity, and military establishment. But it could not deprive Germany of all those qualities of intellect and character which enabled it within a period of two decades to rebuild what it had lost and to emerge as the strongest single military power in the world. The virtually unanimous opinion of the military experts who in 1942 gave the Russian army only a few more months of resistance may have been correct in purely military terms, such as military strategy, mobility, industrial resources, and the like. Yet this expert opinion was obviously mistaken in underrating that factor of "elementary force and persistence" which better judgment has recognized as the great source of Russian strength in its dealings with Europe. The pessimism that in 1940 denied Great Britain a chance for survival had its roots in a similar neglect or misreading of the national character of the British people.

We have already mentioned in another context the contempt in which American power was held by the German leaders before the Second World War.[15] It is interesting to note that exactly the same mistake, and for the same

---

[15]See page 99.

reason, was made by the German leaders during the First World War. Thus, in October 1916, the German Secretary of the Navy estimated the significance of the United States joining the Allies to be "zero," and another German minister of that period declared in a parliamentary speech, after the United States had actually entered the war on the side of the Allies: "The Americans cannot swim and they cannot fly, the Americans will never come." In both cases, the German leaders underestimated American power by paying attention exclusively to the quality of the military establishment at a particular moment, to the antimilitarism of the American character, and to the factor of geographical distance. They disregarded completely the qualities of the American character, such as individual initiative, gift for improvisation, and technical skill, which, together with the other material factor and under favorable conditions, might more than outweigh the disadvantages of geographical remoteness and of a dilapidated military establishment.

On the other hand, the belief of many experts, at least until the battle of Stalingrad in 1943, in the invincibility of Germany drew its strength from the material factors as well as from certain aspects of the German national character which seemed to favor total victory. These experts neglected other aspects of the national character of the German people, in particular their lack of moderation. From the emperors of the Middle Ages and the princes fighting the Thirty Years' War to William II and Hitler, this lack of moderation has proved to be the one fatal weakness of the German national character. Unable to restrain goals and action within the limits of the possible, the Germans have time and again squandered and ultimately destroyed the national power of Germany built upon other material and human factors.

NATIONAL MORALE

More elusive and less stable, but no less important than all the other factors in its bearing upon national power, is what we propose to call national morale. National morale is the degree of determination with which a nation supports the foreign policies of its government in peace or war. It permeates all activities of a nation, its agricultural and industrial production as well as its military establishment and diplomatic service. In the form of public opinion, it provides an intangible factor without whose support no government, democratic or autocratic, is able to pursue its policies with full effectiveness, if it is able to pursue them at all. Its presence or absence and its qualities reveal themselves particularly in times of national crisis, when either the existence of the nation is at stake or else a decision of fundamental importance must be taken upon which the survival of the nation might well depend.

Its Instability

While certain traits of the national character may easily manifest themselves in the national morale of the people at a certain moment of history, such as the common sense of the British, the individualism of the French, the tenacity of the Russians, no conclusion can be drawn from the character of a nation as to what the morale of that nation might be under certain contingencies. Their national character seems to qualify the American people to a particular degree for playing the role of a first-rate power under the conditions of the twentieth century. Yet nobody can foresee with any degree of certainty what the national morale of the American people would be like under the conditions of hardship and disintegration which prevailed in the different belligerent countries of Europe and Asia during certain phases of the Second World War and of the postwar years. Nor is there a way of anticipating the reactions of the British people to a repetition of the experiences of the Second World War. They stood up under the "blitz" and V-weapons once. Could they stand up under them a second time? And what about nuclear weapons? Similar questions can be asked of all nations, and no rational answers are forthcoming.

American national morale, in particular, has been in recent years the object of searching speculation at home and abroad; for American foreign policy and, through it, the weight of American power in international affairs is to a peculiar degree dependent upon the moods of American public opinion, as they express themselves in the votes of Congress, election results, polls, and the like. Would the United States join the United Nations and stay with it despite disappointments? Would Congress support the economic and military assistance program for Europe, and for how long would it vote billions for foreign aid throughout the world? How far were the American people willing to go in supporting South Korea, and under what conditions would they continue to do so? Would they be willing to cope indefinitely with the liabilities, risks, and frustrations attributed to the Soviet Union, without either relaxing their efforts or trying to end it all by drastic action? The main factor upon which the answers to these questions depended or depend is the state of national morale at the decisive moment.

The national morale of any people will obviously break at a certain point. The breaking point is different for different people and under different circumstances. Some peoples will be brought close to the breaking point by tremendous and useless losses in war, such as the French after the Nivelle offensive in 1917 in the Champagne. One great defeat will suffice to undermine the national morale of others, such as the defeat the Italians suffered in 1917 at Caporetto, which cost them three hundred thousand men in prisoners and the same number in deserters. The morale of others, such as the Russians in 1917, will break under the impact of a combination of tremendous war losses in men and territory and the mismanagement of an autocratic government. The morale of others will only slowly decline and, as it were, corrode at the edges—not break at all in one sudden collapse, even when exposed to a rare combination of governmental mismanagement, devastation, invasion, and a hopeless war situation. Such was the case of the Germans in the last stage of the Second World War, when a number of military leaders and former high officials gave up the lost cause while the masses of the people fought on until practically the moment of Hitler's suicide. The persistence of German morale in 1945 under most unfavorable circumstances illustrates dramatically the unpredictability of such collective reactions. Under much less severe circumstances the national morale of Germany collapsed in November 1918, a precedent that should have presaged a similar collapse of German morale some time in the summer of 1944, after the Allied invasion of France. Tolstoy gives in *War and Peace* a vivid analysis of the independent importance of morale for military success:

> Military science assumes that the relative strength of forces is identical with their numerical proportions. Military science maintains that the greater the number of soldiers, the greater their strength. *Les gros bataillons ont toujours raison.*
>
> To say this is as though one were in mechanics to say that forces were equal or unequal simply because the masses of the moving bodies were equal or unequal.
>
> Force (the volume of motion) is the product of the mass into the velocity.
>
> In warfare the force of armies is the product of the mass multiplied by something else, an unknown x.
>
> Military science, seeing in history an immense number of examples in which the mass of an army does not correspond with its force, and which small numbers conquer large ones, vaguely recognizes the existence of this unknown factor, and tries to find it sometimes in some geometrical disposition of the troops, sometimes in the superiority of the weapons, and most often in the genius of the leaders. But none of those factors yield results that agree with the historical facts.
>
> One has but to renounce the false view that glorifies the effect of the activity of the heroes of history in warfare in order to discover this unknown quantity, x.
>
> X is the spirit of the army, the greater or less desire to fight and to face dangers on the part of all men composing the army, which is quite apart from the question whether they are fighting under leaders of genius or not, with cudgels or with guns that fire thirty times a minute. The men who have the greater desire to fight always put themselves, too, in the more advantageous position for fighting. The spirit of the army is the factor which multiplied by the mass gives the product of the force. To define and express the significance of this unknown factor, the spirit of the army, is the problem of science.
>
> This problem can only be solved when we cease arbitrarily substituting for that unknown factor x the conditions under which the force is manifested, such as the plans of the general, the arming of the men and so on, and recognize this unknown factor in its entirety as the greater or less desire to fight and face danger. Then only by expressing known historical facts in equations can one hope from comparison of the relative value of this unknown factor to approach its definition. Ten men, or battalions or divisions are victorious fighting with fifteen men or battalions or divisions, that is, they kill or take prisoner all of them while losing four of their own side, so that the loss has been four on one side and fifteen on the other. Consequently, four on one side have been equivalent to fifteen on the other, and consequently $4x = 15y$. Consequently $\dfrac{x}{y} = \dfrac{15}{4}$. This equation does not give us the value of the unknown factors, but it does give us the ratio between their values. And from the reduction to such equations of various historical units (battles, campaigns, periods of warfare) a series of numbers are obtained, in which there must be and may be discovered historical laws.[16]

---

[16]Leo Tolstoy, *War and Peace*, Part XIV, Chapter II.

The Quality of Society and Government as Decisive Factors

While national morale is subjected to its ultimate test in war, it is important whenever a nation's power is brought to bear on an international problem. It is important partly because of the anticipated effects of national morale upon military strength, partly because national morale influences the determination with which the government pursues its foreign policies. Any segment of the population which feels itself permanently deprived of its rights and of full participation in the life of the nation will tend to have a lower national morale, to be less "patriotic" than those who do not suffer from such disabilities. The same is likely to be true of those whose vital aspirations diverge from the permanent policies pursued by the majority or by the government. Whenever deep dissensions tear a people apart, the popular support that can be mustered for a foreign policy will always be precarious and will be actually small if the success or failure of the foreign policy has a direct bearing upon the issue of the domestic struggle.

Autocratic governments, which in the formulation of their policies do not take the wishes of the people into account, cannot rely upon much popular support for their foreign policies. Such was the case in countries like Czarist Russia and the Austrian monarchy. The example of Austria is particularly instructive. Many of the foreign policies of that country, especially with respect to the Slavic nations, aimed at weakening the latter in order better to be able to keep in check the Slavic nationalities living under Austrian rule. In consequence, these Slavic nationalities tended to be at best indifferent to the foreign policies of their own government and at worst to support actively the policies of Slavic governments directed against their own. Thus it is not surprising that during the First World War whole Slavic units of the Austro-Hungarian army went over to the Russians. The government dared to use other such units only against non-Slavic enemies, such as the Italians. For similar reasons, during the First World War the German army used Alsatian units against the Russians, and Polish units against the French.

The Soviet Union had a similar experience of lack of morale during the Second World War when large contingents composed in the main of Ukrainians and Tartars deserted to the Germans. Great Britain had the same experience with India, whose national energies supported but unwillingly and with reservations the foreign policies of its alien master—if they did not, like Bose and his followers during the Second World War, come to the assistance of the alien master's enemy. Napoleon and Hitler had to learn to their dismay that among the spoils of foreign conquest popular support of the conqueror's policies is not necessarily to be found. The amount and strength of the support Hitler, for instance, found among the conquered peoples of Europe was in inverse ratio to the quality of the national morale of the particular people.

Any country with deep and unbridgeable class divisions will find its national morale in a precarious state. French power ever since the thirties has suffered from this weakness. From the time of Hitler's ascent to power, the vacillating foreign policies of the French governments, following each other in rapid succession and concealing their impotence behind the ideologies of a status quo they were unwilling and incapable of defending, has already weakened the national morale of the French people as a whole. The crises of 1938–39, with the ever renewed threat of war and general mobilizations to meet it, followed by Hitler's successes, demobilizations, and an increasingly precarious peace, had contributed powerfully to the general decay of French morale. While there was decay everywhere, there was actual collapse only in two important sectors of French society. On the one hand, faced with social legislation limiting their powers, considerable groups of the French upper classes rallied to the cry: "Rather Hitler (the enemy dictator) then Blum (the French Socialist)!" Although Hitler threatened the position of France in Europe and its very existence as a nation, these groups were unable to give wholehearted support to the French foreign policy opposing Hitler. After the conquest of France they favored the domination of France by Hitler rather than its liberation from the foreign dictator. On the other hand, the Communists, for different reasons, undermined the national morale of France so long as Hitler fought only the capitalists of the West. It was only after he had attacked the Soviet Union that they contributed new strength to French national morale by fighting in the forefront of the resistance against the invader.

However unpredictable the quality of national morale, especially at a moment of great crisis, there are obvious situations where national morale is likely to be high, while under certain different conditions the odds are in favor of a low state of national morale. One can say, in general, that the more closely identified a people are with the actions and objectives of their government— especially, of course, in foreign affairs—the better are the chances for national morale to be high, and vice versa. Thus it can surprise only those who mistakenly think of the modern totalitarian state in terms of the autocracies of the eighteenth and nineteenth centuries that in Nazi Germany national morale was high almost to the last. It declined slowly rather than breaking in one sudden collapse as it did in November 1918. The great bulk of the Russian people, despite the greatest hardships in war and peace, have consistently shown a high degree of national morale.

The modern totalitarian state has been able to fill the gap between government and people, a gap that was typical of the monarchies of the eighteenth and nineteenth centuries, through the use of democratic symbols, totalitarian control of public opinion, and policies actually or seemingly benefiting the people. Practically all national energies flow into the channels chosen by the government, and the identification of the individual with the state, which we have recognized as one of the characteristics of modern politics,[17] reaches under the stimulation of totalitarianism the intensity of religious fervor. There-

---

[17]See pages 118 ff.

fore, so long as totalitarian governments are or seem to be successful, or can at least hold out hope for success, they can count upon the determined support of their peoples for the foreign policies they pursue.

What totalitarianism can achieve only by force, fraud, and deification of the state, democracy must try to accomplish through the free interplay of popular forces, guided by a wise and responsible government. Where the government is unable to prevent the degeneration of this interplay into class, racial, or religious conflicts, tending to split the national community into warring groups, national morale is likely to be low, at least among the victimized groups if not among the people as a whole. The policies of France before and during the Second World War illustrate this point. So does the weakness of the foreign policies in peace and war of countries where feudal aristocracies or autocratic dictators control the government and oppress the people. The governments of such nations can never choose and pursue their foreign objectives with any degree of determination, even at the risk of war, because they can never be sure of the support of their peoples. They constantly fear lest the domestic opposition exploit difficulties and reverses in the international field for the purpose of overthrowing the regime. Where, however, a government speaks as the mouthpiece, and acts as the executor, of the popular will, national morale is likely to reflect the real identity between popular aspirations and governmental actions. The national morale of Denmark under the German occupation from 1940 to the end of the Second World War and the bravery of the Norwegians against the invading Germans illustrate this point no less strikingly than did the national morale of Germany until the defeat at Stalingrad.

In the last analysis, then, the power of a nation, in view of its national morale, resides in the quality of its government. A government that is truly representative, not only in the sense of parliamentary majorities, but above all in the sense of being able to translate the inarticulate convictions and aspirations of the people into international objectives and policies, has the best chance to marshal the national energies in support of those objectives and policies. The adage that free men fight better than slaves can be amplified into the proposition that nations well governed are likely to have a higher national morale than nations poorly governed. The quality of government is patently a source of strength or weakness with respect to most of the factors upon which national power depends, especially in view of the influence the government exerts upon natural resources, industrial capacity, and military preparedness. For the quality of national morale, the quality of government takes on a special importance. Whereas it operates upon the other elements of national power as one among several influences, all more or less manageable by human action, it is the only tangible factor among intangibles which accounts for the quality of national morale. Without national morale, national power is either nothing but material force or else a potentiality that awaits its realization in vain. Yet the only means of deliberately improving national morale lies in the improvement of the quality of government. All else is a matter of chance.

THE QUALITY OF DIPLOMACY[18]

Of all the factors that make for the power of a nation, the most important, however unstable, is the quality of diplomacy. All the other factors that determine national power are, as it were, the raw material out of which the power of a nation is fashioned. The quality of a nation's diplomacy combines those different factors into an integrated whole, gives them direction and weight, and awakens their slumbering potentialities by giving them the breath of actual power. The conduct of a nation's foreign affairs by its diplomats is for national power in peace what military strategy and tactics by its military leaders are for national power in war. It is the art of bringing the different elements of the national power to bear with maximum effect upon those points in the international situation which concern the national interest most directly.

Diplomacy, one might say, is the brains of national power, as national morale is its soul. If its vision is blurred, its judgment defective, and its determination feeble, all the advantages of geographical location, of self-sufficiency in food, raw materials, and industrial production, of military preparedness, of size and quality of population will in the long run avail a nation little. A nation that can boast of all these advantages, but not of a diplomacy commensurate with them, may achieve temporary successes through the sheer weight of its natural assets. In the long run, it is likely to squander the natural assets by activating them incompletely, haltingly, and wastefully for the nation's international objectives.

In the long run, such a nation must yield to one whose diplomacy is prepared to make the most of whatever other elements of power are at its disposal, thus making up through its own excellence for deficiencies in other fields. By using the power potentialities of a nation to best advantage, a competent diplomacy can increase the power of a nation beyond what one would expect it to be in view of all the other factors combined. Often in history the Goliath without brains or soul has been smitten and slain by the David who had both. Diplomacy of high quality will bring the ends and means of foreign policy into harmony with the available resources of national power. It will tap the hidden sources of national strength and transform them fully and securely into political realities. By giving direction to the national effort, it will in turn increase the independent weight of certain factors, such as industrial potential, military preparedness, national character, and morale. It is for this reason that national power is apt to rise to its height fulfilling all its potentialities, particularly in times of war, when ends and means of policy are clearly laid out.

The United States, in the period between the two world wars, furnishes a striking example of a potentially powerful nation playing a minor role in world affairs because its foreign policy refused to bring the full weight of its potential

---

[18]By the term "diplomacy," as used in the following pages, we refer to the formation and execution of foreign policy on all levels, the highest as well as the subordinate. On the subject matter discussed here, see also Part Ten.

strength to bear upon international problems. As far as the power of the United States on the international scene was concerned, the advantages of geography, natural resources, industrial potential, and size and quality of population might as well have not existed at all, for American diplomacy proceeded as though they did not exist.

The transformation American foreign policy has undergone since the end of the Second World War seemed to have answered definitively the question whether, and to what extent, American diplomacy is willing and able to transform the potentialities of national power into political actualities. Yet at the beginning of that period, in an article significantly entitled, "Imperialism or Indifference," the London *Economist* still doubted the answer. After enumerating the factors that, taken by themselves, would make the United States the most powerful nation on earth, the *Economist* continued:

> But though these things are essential ingredients, they are not all that it takes to make a Great Power. There must also be the willingness, and the ability, to use economic resources in support of national policy. The rulers of Soviet Russia . . . are not likely, at least for a generation to come, to have nearly as good cards in their hands as the Americans. But the nature of their system of concentrated power and iron censorship enables them to play a forcing game. The Americans' hand is all trumps; but will any of them ever be played? And for what purpose?[19]

The classic example of a country that, while in other respects hopelessly outclassed, returned to the heights of power chiefly by virtue of its brilliant diplomacy is France in the period from 1890 to 1914. After is defeat in 1870 at the hands of Germany, France was a second-rate power, and Bismarck's statecraft, by isolating it, kept it in that position. With Bismarck's dismissal in 1890, Germany's foreign policy turned away from Russia and was unwilling to alleviate Great Britain's suspicion. French diplomacy took full advantage of those mistakes of German foreign policy. In 1894, France added a military alliance to the political understanding reached with Russia in 1891; in 1904 and 1912, it entered into informal agreements with Great Britain. The configuration of 1914, which found France aided by potent allies and Germany deserted by one (Italy) and burdened with the weakness of the others (Austria-Hungary, Bulgaria, Turkey) was in the main the work of a galaxy of brilliant French diplomatists: Camille Barrère, Ambassador to Italy, Jules Cambon, Ambassador to Germany, Paul Cambon, Ambassador to Great Britain, Maurice Paléologue, Ambassador to Russia.

In the period between the two world wars, Rumania owed its ability to play a role in international affairs much superior to its actual resources chiefly to the personality of one man, its Foreign Minister Titulescu. Similarly, so small and precariously located a country as Belgium owed a great deal of the power it was able to exercise during the nineteenth century to two shrewd and active kings, Leopold I and Leopold II. Spanish diplomacy in the seventeenth, and

---

[19]*Economist*, May 24, 1947, p. 785. (Reprinted by permission.)

Turkish diplomacy in the nineteenth century were able for a time to compensate for the decline of national power in other respects. The ups and downs of British power are closely connected with changes in the quality of British diplomacy. Cardinal Wolsey, Castlereagh, and Canning signify the summits of British diplomacy as well as of British power, while Lord North and Neville Chamberlain stand for the decline of both. What would the power of France have been without the statecraft of Richelieu, Mazarin, and Talleyrand? What would Germany's power have been without Bismarck? Italy's without Cavour? And what did the power of the young American republic not owe to Franklin, Jefferson, Madison, Jay, the Adamses, its ambassadors and secretaries of state?

Nations must rely upon the quality of their diplomacy to act as a catalyst for the different factors that constitute their power. In other words, these different factors, as they are brought to bear upon an international problem by diplomacy, are what is called a nation's power. Therefore it is of the utmost importance that the good quality of the diplomatic service be constant. And constant quality is best assured by dependence upon tradition and institutions rather than upon the sporadic appearance of outstanding individuals. It is to tradition that Great Britain owes the relative constancy of its power from Henry VIII to the First World War. Whatever the whims and shortcomings of its kings and ministers may have been, the traditions of its ruling class and, in recent times, its professional foreign service were able, a few notable exceptions notwithstanding, to mold the prerequisites of national power, with which Great Britain was endowed, into the greatness of its actual power. It is no accident that when, due to the diplomacy of Stanley Baldwin and Neville Chamberlain, British power reached its lowest point in centuries, the professionals of the Foreign Office had little influence upon the conduct of British foreign policy, and that the two men mainly responsible for it were, in terms of family tradition, businessmen and newcomers to the aristocracy that for centuries had ruled Great Britain. In Winston Churchill, the scion of a ruling family, the aristocratic traditions were again brought to bear upon the national power of Great Britain. Today the institutional excellence of the British foreign service reveals itself in the skill with which Great Britain has brought its commitments all over the world into harmony with the reduced resources of its national power.

On the other hand, Germany owed its power to the demoniac genius of two men, Bismarck and Hitler. Since Bismarck's personality and policies made it impossible for traditions and institutions to develop that might have been able to perpetuate the intelligent conduct of Germany's foreign policy, his disappearance from the political scene in 1890 was the signal for a deep and permanent drop in the quality of German diplomacy. The consequent deterioration of Germany's international position culminated in the military predicament with which the First World War confronted it. In the case of Hitler, the strength and weakness of German diplomacy lay in the mind of the Führer himself. The victories German diplomacy won from 1933 to 1940 were the victories of one man's mind, and the deterioration of that mind was a direct cause of the disasters that marked the last years of the Nazi regime. The national suicide of Germany in the last months of the Second World War, when military resistance had become a futile gesture paid for in hundreds of thousands of lives and the ruin of cities, and Hitler's suicide in the last stage of the war—the self-extinction, in other words, of Germany's national power and of the life of its leader—were both the work of one man. That man was unfettered by those traditions and institutional safeguards by which healthy political systems try to provide for continuity in the quality of diplomacy and thus tend to inhibit the spectacular successes of genius as well as the abysmal blunders of madmen.

So far as continuity in the quality of the conduct of foreign affairs is concerned, the United States stands between the continuous high quality of British diplomacy and the traditional low quality, interrupted by short-lived triumphs, of German foreign policy. With an unchallengeable superiority in material and human resources at its disposal, American diplomacy in the Western Hemisphere could not fail to be successful in some measure, regardless of the quality of its foreign policy. The same has been true to a lesser degree in the relations between the United States and the rest of the world. The "big stick" in the form of the material superiority of the United States spoke its own language, regardless of whether American diplomacy spoke in a soft or loud voice, in articulate or confused terms, with or without a clearly conceived purpose. The brilliance of the first decades of American diplomacy was followed by a long period of mediocrity, if not ineptitude, interrupted under the impact of great crises by three brief periods of great achievements under Woodrow Wilson, Franklin D. Roosevelt, and Harry Truman. While American diplomacy was thus lacking in the institutional excellence of the British, it had the benefit of material conditions that even poor statecraft could hardly dissipate. Furthermore, it could draw upon a national tradition, formulated in Washington's Farewell Address and, more particularly, in the Monroe Doctrine. The guidance of this tradition would protect a poor diplomacy from catastrophic blunders and make a mediocre diplomacy look better than it actually was. Unanswered is the question whether such a tradition can save American diplomacy from a crusading ideological approach.

THE QUALITY OF GOVERNMENT

The best conceived and most expertly executed foreign policy, drawing upon an abundance of material and human resources, must come to naught if it cannot draw also upon good government. Good government, viewed as an independent requirement of national power,[20] means three things: balance between, on the one hand, the material and human resources that go into the making of national power and, on the other, the foreign policy to be pursued; balance

---

[20]We have already spoken of the quality of government as a requirement of national morale; see pages 152 ff.

among those resources; and popular support for the foreign policies to be pursued.

The Problem of Balance Between Resources and Policy

Good government, then, must start by performing two different intellectual operations. First, it must choose the objectives and methods of its foreign policy in view of the power available to support them with a maximum chance of success. A nation that sets its sights too low, forgoing foreign policies well within the reach of its power, abdicates its rightful role in the council of nations; the United States fell into that error in the interwar period. A nation may also set its sights too high and pursue policies that cannot be successfully executed with the available power; this was the error which the United States committed during the peace negotiations in 1919. As Lloyd George put it: "The Americans appeared to assume responsibility for the sole guardianship of the Ten Commandments and for the Sermon on the Mount; yet, when it came to a practical question of assistance and responsibility, they absolutely refused to accept it." A nation may try to play the role of a great power without having the prerequisites for doing so, and will court disaster, as Poland did in the interwar period. Or, being a great power, it may embark upon a policy of unlimited conquest, overtaxing its strength; the unsuccessful world-conquerors, from Alexander to Hitler, illustrate that point.

Thus the national power available determines the limits of foreign policy. There is only one exception to that rule, and that is when the very existence of the nation is at stake. Then the policy of national survival overrides the rational considerations of national power, and the emergency reverses the normal relationship between policy and considerations of power, establishing the primacy of the former. A nation is then called upon to subordinate all other interests to that of survival and to make a national effort that rationally could not have been expected of it. This is what Great Britain did in the fall and winter of 1940–41.

The Problem of Balance Among Resources

Once a government has brought its foreign policy into balance with the power available to it, it must bring the different elements of national power into balance with each other. A nation does not necessarily attain the maximum of national power because it is very rich in natural resources, possesses a very large population, or has built an enormous industrial and military establishment. It attains that maximum when it has at its disposal a sufficient quantity and quality, in the right admixture, of those resources of power which will allow it to pursue a given foreign policy with a maximum chance of success. Great Britain, when it was at the summit of its power, was deficient in many of the elements of national power, such as natural resources, size of population, and ground troops. Yet it had developed to unchallengeable supremacy that one element of national power, the navy, which was a perfect instrument for the

British policy of overseas expansion, and at the same time assured the uninter-rupted flow from abroad of those raw materials and foodstuffs without which Great Britain could not have survived. In view of this policy, of the available natural resources, and of the geographic location, a large population and a standing army would have been for Great Britain a handicap rather than an asset. On the other hand, had Great Britain continued to pursue a policy of continental expansion, as it did during the better part of the Middle Ages, it would have been in need of both.

A large population is a source of weakness rather than of strength, as the example of India has shown us,[21] if it cannot be adequately fed with the available resources. The hasty building of great industrial and military estab-lishments by totalitarian methods creates certain elements of national power, but in its very process destroys others, such as national morale and the physical resilience of the population; the developments in the Soviet satellites of Eastern Europe are a case in point. To plan for a military establishment that is too big to be supported by the available industrial capacity, and hence can be built and maintained only at the price of galloping inflation, economic crisis, and deterio-ration of morale, is to plan for national weakness rather than for power. In a national emergency, when the very existence of the nation is at stake, the American government, for instance, can and must offer the people guns instead of butter; if it cannot make a case for such an emergency, it must strike a balance between military and civilian requirements by allocating a fair share of the economic product for civilian consumption. Another government, such as the Chinese or Korean, might not need to take such considerations of civilian welfare into account. In other words, a government in its building of national power cannot be oblivious to the character of the nation it governs. One nation will revolt against hardships that another nation will take patiently in its stride, and sometimes a nation will surprise the world and itself by the sacrifices it willingly makes for the defense of its interests and its existence.

The Problem of Popular Support

A contemporary government, especially one subject to democratic control, has only performed part of its task when it has established the two types of balances which we have discussed above. Another task, perhaps the most difficult of all, still lies ahead of it. It must secure the approval of its own people for its foreign policies and the domestic ones designed to mobilize the elements of national power in support of them. That task is difficult because the conditions under which popular support can be obtained for a foreign policy are not necessarily identical with the conditions under which a foreign policy can be successfully pursued. As Tocqueville put it, with special reference to the United States:

> Foreign politics demand scarcely any of those qualities which are peculiar to a democracy; they require, on the contrary, the perfect use of almost all those in

---

[21]See pages 127, 128.

which it is deficient. Democracy is favorable to the increase of the internal resources of a state; it diffuses wealth and comfort, promotes public spirit, and
fortifies the respect for law in all classes of society: all these are advantages which
have only an indirect influence over the relations which one people bears to
another. But a democracy can only with great difficulty regulate the details of an
important undertaking, persevere in a fixed design, and work out its execution in
spite of serious obstacles. It cannot combine its measures with secrecy or await
their consequences with patience. . . .

The propensity that induces democracies to obey impulse rather than prudence, and to abandon mature design for the gratification of a momentary passion,
was clearly seen in America on the breaking out of the French Revolution. It was
then as evident to the simplest capacity as it is at the present time that the interest
of the Americans forbade them to take any part in the contest which was about to
deluge Europe with blood, but which could not injure their own country. But the
sympathies of the people declared themselves with so much violence in favor of
France that nothing but the inflexible character of Washington and the immense
popularity which he enjoyed could have prevented the Americans from declaring
war against England. And even then, the exertions which the austere reason of that
great man made to repress the generous but imprudent passions of his fellow
citizens nearly deprived him of the sole recompense which he ever claimed, that
of his country's love. The majority reprobated his policy, but it was afterwards
approved by the whole nation.[22]

Thinking required for the successful conduct of foreign policy can be
diametrically opposed to the rhetoric and action by which the masses and their
representatives are likely to be moved. The peculiar qualities of the statesman's
mind are not always likely to find a favorable response in the popular mind. The
statesman must think in terms of the national interest, conceived as power
among other powers. The popular mind, unaware of the fine distinctions of the
statesman's thinking, reasons more often than not in the simple moralistic and
legalistic terms of absolute good and absolute evil. The statesman must take the
long view, proceeding slowly and by detours, paying with small losses for great
advantage; he must be able to temporize, to compromise, to bide his time. The
popular mind wants quick results; it will sacrifice tomorrow's real benefit for
today's apparent advantage.

If Tocqueville's point is well taken, the kind of thinking required for the
successful conduct of foreign policy will at times be opposed to considerations
by which people are moved. A foreign policy that is passionately and overwhelmingly supported by public opinion cannot be assumed for that reason
alone to be good foreign policy. On the contrary, the harmony between foreign
policy and public opinion may well have been achieved at the price of surrendering the principles of good foreign policy to the unsound preferences of public
opinion.

In the American case these inherent difficulties are aggravated by the fact

---

[22]Alexis de Tocqueville, *Democracy in America* (New York: Alfred A. Knopf, 1945), Vol. I, pp.
234–5.

that the United States is almost continuously recovering from the last elections or preparing for the next one. Especially in the latter case, the temptation is overwhelming for an administration to seek to gain electoral advantage by catering to the preferences of public opinion, regardless of foreign policy. Thus one requirement of the statesman's art is to steer a middle course between respect for the perennial principles of sound foreign policy and the fickle preferences of public opinion.

These considerations shed an illuminating light upon the apparent paradox of President Jimmy Carter, who emerged from the Democratic primaries in 1980 as virtually unbeatable in his appeal to the electorate, yet under his leadership the United States had suffered a string of humiliating defeats in its relations with other nations. The most spectacular of these defeats was the continuing captivity of fifty hostages in Iran. By foreswearing from the outset any form of violence in response to this outrage, Carter deprived himself of any leverage against Iran. The disadvantages he was able to threaten Iran with, primarily economic sanctions, were bound to be ineffective. The advantages he could offer (such as economic and military aid) did not outweigh, in the eyes of the Iranians, the risks and liabilities American largesse would entail. Thus the United States stood helpless—in a situation which in most other periods of American history would have called forth swift action to settle the issue, even at the risk of some American lives.

But the President, by putting the emphasis on saving American lives by peaceful means, hit upon a sympathetic chord in American public opinion. Carter did what Wilson had allegedly done before: "He kept us out of war." He did so without abandoning the most visible and sentimental American objective: saving those fifty American lives. It apparently did not occur to public opinion or to the President that the leader responsible for American foreign policy has a duty not only to preserve lives, but also to preserve the long-term interests of the nation.

The same mixture of rhetorical commitment and political inaction has secured public support for our policies toward the Soviet Union and assured their ineffectiveness at the same time. Regardless of one's interpretation of the significance of the Soviet military takeover of Afghanistan, the belligerent verbal reaction of the President was out of all proportion to the actual measures taken in response to that takeover.

Yet while that belligerence may have surprised the Russians, the absence of action commensurate with that rhetoric did nothing to induce a change in their policies. The Russians will go as far as they can without provoking the United States into a nuclear confrontation. Positive cases in point are the Cuban missile crisis and the successive Berlin crises; a negative confirmation of this thesis was the extended military occupation of Afghanistan.

However, the President's belligerent stance appeared to be a great success in domestic politics. The President who had declared his intention to make the protection and promotion of human rights the cornerstone of his foreign policy spoke to the Soviet Union in the language of John Foster Dulles. Public-opinion polls registered overwhelming popular approval: once again, a futile foreign policy was compensated for by domestic triumph. Here, however, Mr. Carter encountered another dilemma, superimposed upon the one between foreign policy and domestic politics. It evolved from the rational unacceptability of nuclear confrontation.

The need of great powers to defend and promote their interests by the use of force as a last resort implies in the case of the United States and the Soviet Union the possibility of using nuclear weapons as an instrument of force. Yet the use of nuclear weapons not as a single, isolated demonstration, as at Hiroshima and Nagasaki, but as normal instruments of warfare would mean the destruction of all the belligerents as viable societies. Nuclear weapons thus used—in contrast to conventional weapons—would not be a rational means to the rational ends of foreign policy, but instruments of desperation denoting suicide and genocide. This was the second fundamental dilemma Carter faced.

The anarchic character of the international system forced him, following a convention coterminous with history, to contemplate resort to physical violence as the ultimate factor in the settlement of international issues. Yet the irrationality of the all-out use of such violence made him shrink from the use even of conventional violence lest it might escalate into nuclear war. Thus in an international crisis today the President acts with utmost caution, if he acts at all, and he compensates for the lack of effective action with belligerent talk. In this tendency, President Carter did not stand alone.

Popular support is the precondition of the President's stewardship of foreign policy. The creation of a public opinion supporting him, even at the sacrifice of some elements of foreign policy, is a task which a President can only shun at the risk of losing office and, with it, his ability to pursue any foreign policy at all. The question to which Carter's conduct gave rise concerned not the need of a compromise between the requirements of a sound foreign policy and the demands of public opinion, but the point at which the compromise was to be made. Aside from faulting him for ignorance and incompetence, the critics maintained that he surrendered too many principles of a sound foreign policy to the demands of public opinion. The issue was not whether the President ought to pursue the national interest regardless of the possibility of nuclear war, but where to draw the line between concern for the national interest and fear of nuclear war. The question was whether Carter, in his anxiety to stay as far away as possible from nuclear war, had not needlessly sacrificed important national interests.

Confronted with this dilemma between a good foreign policy and a bad one that public opinion demands, a government must avoid two pitfalls. It must resist the temptation to sacrifice what it considers good policy upon the altar of public opinion, abdicating leadership and exchanging short-lived political advantage for the permanent interests of the country. It must also avoid widening the unavoidable gap between the requirements of good foreign policy and the preferences of public opinion. It widens that gap if, shunning tolerable compromise with the preferences of public opinion, it sticks in every detail to a foreign policy it considers to be right, and sacrifices public support to the stubborn pursuit of that policy.

Instead, the government, to be successful in its foreign and domestic policies alike, must comply with three basic requirements. It must recognize that the conflict between the requirements of good foreign policy and the preferences of public opinion is in the nature of things and, hence, unavoidable, and that it can perhaps be narrowed, but it can never be bridged, by concessions to the domestic opposition. Second, the government must realize that it is the leader and not the slave of public opinion; that public opinion is not a static thing to be discovered and classified by public-opinion polls as plants are by botanists, but that it is a dynamic, ever changing entity to be continuously created and recreated by informed and responsible leadership; that it is the historic mission of the government to assert that leadership lest it be the demagogue who asserts it.[23] Third, it must distinguish between what is desirable in its foreign policy and what is essential, and while it may be willing to compromise with public opinion on nonessentials, it must fight, even at the risk of its own fortunes, for what it regards to be the irreducible minimum of good foreign policy.

A government may have a correct understanding of the requirements of foreign policy and of the domestic politics to support them, but if it fails in marshaling public opinion behind these policies, its labors will be in vain, and all the other assets of national power of which the nation can boast will not be used to best advantage. Of this truth the policies of contemporary democratic governments, including those of the United States, offer abundant proof.[24]

Domestic Government and Foreign Policy

It is not enough, however, for a government to marshal national public opinion behind its foreign policies. It must also gain the support of the public opinion of other nations for its foreign and domestic policies. This requirement is a reflection of the changes that have occurred in recent times in the character of foreign policy. Foreign policy is being pursued in our time not only with the traditional weapons of diplomacy and military might, but also with the novel weapon of propaganda. For the struggle for power on the international scene

---

[23]Lord Norwich, who as Mr. Duff Cooper occupied in the interwar period important cabinet posts and other government positions, puts his finger on the common misunderstanding of public opinion and the government's relation to it when he says in his memoirs (*Old Men Forget* [London: Hart-Davis, 1953]) of Neville Chamberlain: "The Prime Minister's main mistake seems to me to be two. He believes public opinion is what the "Times" tells him it is—and he believes Conservative opinion is what the Chief Whip says it is." Unfortunately, this passive acceptance of what somebody says public opinion wants has become—and not only in the England of the interwar period—one of the main obstacles to good foreign policy.

[24]This theme has been elaborated in Hans J. Morgenthau, "The Conduct of Foreign Policy," *Aspects of American Government*, Sydney Bailey, editor (London: The Hansard Society, 1950), pp. 99 ff.; and *In Defense of the National Interest* (New York: Alfred A. Knopf, 1951; Washington, D.C.: University Press of America, 1982), pp. 221 ff.

is today not only a struggle for military supremacy and political domination, but in a specific sense a struggle for the minds of men. The power of a nation, then, depends not only upon the skill of its diplomacy and the strength of its armed forces but also upon the attractiveness for other nations of its political philosophy, political institutions, and political policies. This is true in particular of the United States and the Soviet Union, who compete with each other not only as the two political and military superpowers but also as the foremost representatives of two different political philosophies, systems of government, and ways of life.

Thus whatever these superpowers—and this is true also, in a lesser degree, of other nations—do or do not do, achieve or fail to achieve, in their domestic and foreign policies has a direct bearing upon their standing as these representatives and, hence, upon their power. A nation, for instance, that embarked upon a policy of racial discrimination could not help losing the struggle for the minds of the colored nations of the earth. An underdeveloped nation that could increase in a spectacular fashion the health, literacy, and standard of living of its people would thereby have achieved a considerable increase in its power in other underdeveloped regions of the world.

At this point, then, as at others to be mentioned later,[25] the traditional distinction between foreign and domestic policies tends to break down. One might almost be tempted to say that there are no longer any purely domestic affairs, for whatever a nation does or does not do is held for or against it as a reflection of its political philosophy, system of government, and way of life. A domestic achievement that is intelligible to other nations in terms of their aspirations cannot fail to increase the power of the nation; a domestic failure, equally intelligible, is bound to decrease it.

---

[25]See pages 271–273.

10

Evaluation of National Power

THE TASK OF EVALUATION

It is the task of those responsible for the foreign policy of a nation and of those who mold public opinion with regard to international affairs to evaluate correctly the bearing of these factors upon the power of their own nation and of other nations as well, and this task must be performed for both the present and the future. What is the influence of the unification of the armed services upon the quality of the military establishment of the United States? What effect will the use of nuclear energy have upon the industrial capacity of the United States and of other nations? How will the industrial capacity, military strength, and national morale of China develop after Deng's death? How has the hostility of China and Pakistan influenced the national morale of India? What is the significance of the revival of a German army for the national power of Germany? Has reeducation changed the national character of Germany and Japan? How has the national character of the people of Argentina reacted upon the political philosophies, methods, and objectives of successive military and civilian regimes? In what ways does the advancement of the Russian sphere of influence to the Elbe River affect the geographical position of the Soviet Union? Will this or that reorganization or change in the personnel of the State Department strengthen or weaken the quality of American diplomacy? What about a reunified Germany? These are some of the questions which must be answered correctly if a nation's foreign policy is to be successful.

Yet these questions referring to changes in one particular factor are not the most difficult to answer. There are others which concern the influence of changes in one factor upon other factors, and here the difficulties increase and the pitfalls multiply. What is, for instance, the import of the modern technology of warfare for the geographical position of the United States? How, in other words, do guided missiles and supersonic planes affect the geographical isolation of the United States from other countries? To what degree will the United States lose, and to what degree will it retain, its traditional inviolability to overseas attack? What do the same technological developments mean in view of the geography of Russian territory? To what extent have these factors reduced the protective function of the wide expanses of the Russian plains? And what, in this context, of the protection the Channel has afforded Great Britain since the beginning of British history? What will the industrialization of Brazil, China, and India signify for the military strength of these countries? What is the relative importance of the American army, navy, and air force in view of changes in the technology of warfare? What does the anticipated rate of increase of the American population in the next two decades and the more rapid increase of the populations of Latin America, India, and China portend for the industrial capacity and military strength of the respective nations? How will fluctuations in industrial production affect the national morale of the United States, the Soviet Union, Germany, Great Britain, and France? Will the British national character preserve its traditional qualities under the impact of the fundamental changes which the industrial capacity, military strength, and geographical isolation of Great Britain are undergoing? Will independence for the countries of eastern Europe strengthen national morale?

The task of the analyst of national power does not, however, stop here. He must yet try to answer another group of questions of a still higher order of difficulty. These questions concern the comparison of one power factor in one nation with the same or another power factor in another nation. In other words, they concern the relative weight of changes in the individual components of the power of different nations for the over-all power relations of these different nations. If one considers, for instance, the relative power of the United States and the Soviet Union at a particular moment, let us say in 1991, the question arises of how the different power factors on either side add up and to which side, and in what respects, they give a superiority in power. To what extent does the quantitatively and qualitatively superior industrial capacity of the United States compensate for the probable inferiority of its land forces? What are the respective strengths and weaknesses of the highly concentrated American industrial and population centers, with their great vulnerability to air attack and their great ease of communication, and of the dispersed Russian centers, partly secret in location and character, yet faced with great difficulties in transportation? What power did the Soviet Union derive from the exposure of Western Europe to ideological and military penetration from the East? What weakness does it suffer from its exposure to air and naval attack from the Pacific? What is the significance, in terms of the respective power positions, of the pluralistic operation in the United States of groups subservient to Soviet foreign policy, and of the changing character of Soviet public opinion? What is the impact upon the national power of the United States of a democratic form of government and of a nontotalitarian economic system in comparison with the political and economic organization of the Soviet Union?

These and similar questions must be asked and answered with regard to all nations that play an active role on the international scene. The relative influence of the different factors upon national power must be determined with regard to all nations that compete with each other in the field of international politics. Thus one ought to know whether France is stronger than Italy and in what respects. One ought to know what the assets and liabilities in terms of the different power factors of India or China are with respect to the Soviet Union, of Japan with regard to the United States, of Argentina with regard to Chile, and so on.

The task of power computation is still not completed. In order to gain at least an approximately true picture of the distribution of power among several nations, the power relations, as they seem to exist at a particular moment in history, must be projected into the future. To achieve this it is not enough to ask oneself: What are the power relations between the United States and the Soviet Union at this moment, and what are they likely to be two years hence? Decisions on international matters based upon, and referring to, the power relations between the United States and the Soviet Union cannot wait for measurements of power every two years. They must be made every day. And everyday changes, however small and imperceptible at first, in the factors making for national power add an ounce of strength to this side and take a grain of might away from the other.

On the relatively stable foundation of geography the pyramid of national power rises through different gradations of instability to its peak in the fleeting element of national morale. All the factors we have mentioned, with the exception of geography, are in constant flux, influencing each other and influenced in turn by the unforeseeable intervention of nature and man. Together they form the stream of national power, rising slowly and then flowing on a high level for centuries, as in Great Britain, or rising steeply and falling sharply from its crest, as was the case in Germany; or, as in the United States and the Soviet Union, rising steeply and facing the uncertainties of the future. To chart the course of the stream and of the different currents that compose it, and to anticipate the changes in their direction and speed, is the ideal task of the observer of international politics.

It is an ideal task and, hence, incapable of achievement. Even if those responsible for the foreign policy of a nation were endowed with superior wisdom and unfailing judgment, and could draw upon the most complete and reliable sources of information, there would be unknown factors to spoil their calculations. They could not foresee such natural catastrophes as famines and epidemics, such man-made catastrophes as wars and revolutions, as well as inventions and discoveries, the rise and disappearance of intellectual, military, and political leaders, the thoughts and actions of such leaders, not to speak of the imponderables of national morale. In short, even the wisest and best informed of men would still have to face all the contingencies of history and of nature. Actually, however, the assumed perfection in intellect and information is never available. Not all the men who inform those who make decisions in foreign affairs are well informed, and not all the men who make decisions are

POPULATION DENSITIES OF THE U.S. AND THE U.S.S.R.

This map was originally drafted by Charles R. Jones under the direction of Hans J. Morgenthau, and reflects post–World War II data available at the time. It is intended to provide a rough cross-section of population densities for the United States and the Soviet Union. Current precise data for the Soviet Union are unavailable.

Areas of the United States and the Soviet Union are shown in correct relation

U.S. 3,022,000 Sq. Mi. (approx.)

U.S.S.R.—8,300,000 Sq. Mi. (approx.)

Density of population per square mile:

Over 250
125–250
25–125
2–25
under 2

wise. Thus the task of assessing the relative power of nations for the present and for the future resolves itself into a series of hunches, of which some will certainly turn out to be wrong while others may be proved by subsequent events to have been correct. The success or failure of a foreign policy, in so far as it depends upon such power calculations, is determined by the relative importance of the right and wrong hunches made by those responsible for a particular foreign policy of a particular nation, as well as by those who conduct the foreign affairs of other nations. Sometimes the mistakes in the assessment of power relations committed by one nation are compensated for by the mistakes committed by another. Thus the success of the foreign policy of a nation may be due less to the accuracy of its own calculations than to the greater errors of the other side.

TYPICAL ERRORS OF EVALUATION

Of all the errors that nations can commit in evaluating their own power and the power of other nations, three types are so frequent and illustrate so well the intellectual pitfalls and practical risks inherent in such evaluations that they deserve some further discussion. The first disregards the relativity of power by erecting the power of one particular nation into an absolute. The second takes for granted the permanency of a certain factor that has in the past played a decisive role, thus overlooking the dynamic change to which most power factors are subject. The third attributes to one single factor a decisive importance, to the neglect of all the others. In other words, the first error consists in not correlating the power of one nation to the power of other nations, the second consists in not correlating actual power at one time to possible power at some future time, and the third consists in not correlating one power factor to others of the same nation.

The Absolute Character of Power

When we refer to the power of a nation by saying that this nation is very powerful and that nation is weak, we always imply a comparison. In other words, the concept of power is always a relative one. When we say that the United States is at present one of the two most powerful nations on earth, what we are actually saying is that if we compare the power of the United States with the power of all other nations, as they exist at present, we find that the United States is more powerful than all others save one.

It is one of the most elemental and frequent errors in international politics to neglect this relative character of power and to deal instead with the power of a nation as though it were an absolute. The evaluation of the power of France in the period between the two world wars is a case in point. At the conclusion of the First World War, France was the most powerful nation on earth from a military point of view. France was so regarded up to the very moment in 1940 when its actual military weakness became obvious in a crushing defeat. The newspaper headlines from the beginning of the Second World War in September 1939 to the defeat of France in the summer of 1940 tell most eloquently the story of that misjudgment of French military power. During that period of the so-called phony war the German armies were supposed not to dare to attack the French because of the latter's superior strength, and on numerous occasions the French were reported to have broken through the German lines. At the root of that misjudgment there was the misconception that the military power of France was not relative to the military power of other nations, but something absolute. French military strength, taken by itself, was at least as great in 1939 as it was in 1919; France was therefore believed to be as strong a nation in 1939 as it had been in 1919.

The fatal error of that evaluation lies in the unawareness of the fact that in 1919 France was the strongest military power on earth only in comparison with other nations, of which its closest competitor, Germany, was defeated and disarmed. The supremacy of France as a military power was, in other words, not an intrinsic quality of the French nation which might be ascertained in the same way in which one might detect the national characteristics of the French people, their geographic location, and natural resources. That supremacy was, on the contrary, the result of a peculiar power configuration; that is, of the comparative superiority of France as a military power over the other nations. The quality of the French army as such had indeed not decreased between 1919 and 1939. Measured in numbers and quality of troops, artillery, airplanes, and staff work, French military power had not deteriorated. Thus even so keen an expert on international affairs as Sir Winston Churchill, comparing the French army of the late thirties with the French army of 1919, could declare in 1937 that the French army was the only guarantee of international peace.

He and most of his contemporaries compared the French army of 1937 with the French army of 1919, which had gained its reputation from comparison with the German army of the same year, instead of comparing the French army of 1937 with the German army of the same year. Such a comparison would have shown that the power configuration of 1919 was reversed in the late thirties. While the French military establishment still was essentially as good as it had been in 1919, Germany's armed forces were now vastly superior to the French. What exclusive concern with French armed might—as if it were an absolute quality—could not reveal, a comparison of the relative military strength of France and Germany might have indicated, and grave errors in political and military judgment might thus have been avoided.

A nation that at a particular moment in history finds itself at the peak of its power is particularly exposed to the temptation to forget that all power is relative. It is likely to believe that the superiority it has achieved is an absolute quality to be lost only through stupidity or neglect of duty. A foreign policy based on such assumptions runs grave risks, for it overlooks the fact that the superior power of that nation is only in part the outgrowth of its own qualities, while it is in part the result of the qualities of other nations compared with its own.

The predominance of Great Britain from the end of the Napoleonic Wars to the beginning of the Second World War was due mainly to its insular protection from attack and its quasi-monopolistic control of the main sea lanes of the world. In other words, Great Britain during that period of history had in comparison with other nations two advantages no other nation possessed. Great Britain's insular location has not changed and its navy is still one of the most powerful in the world. But other nations have acquired weapons, such as nuclear bombs and guided missiles, that obviate to a considerable extent the two advantages from which the power of Great Britain grew. This change in the power position of Great Britain sheds light upon the tragic dilemma that confronted Neville Chamberlain in the years before the Second World War. Chamberlain understood the relativity of Britain's power. He knew that not even victory in war could stop its decline. It was Chamberlain's ironic fate that his attempts to avoid war at any price made war inevitable, and that he was forced to declare the war he dreaded as the destroyer of British power. It is, however, a testimony to the wisdom of British statecraft that since the end of the Second World War, British foreign policy has by and large been conscious of the decline of British power relative to the power of other nations. British statesmen have been aware of the fact that while the British navy, taken by itself, may be as strong as it was ten years ago and the channel is as broad and unruly as it always was, other nations have increased their power to such an extent as to deprive those two British assets of much of their effectiveness.

The Permanent Character of Power

The second typical error impairing the evaluation of national power is related to the first one, but proceeds from a different intellectual operation. While it may be well aware of the relativity of power, it singles out a particular power factor or power relation, basing the estimate upon the assumption that this factor or relation is immune to change.

We have already had occasion to refer to the miscalculation that up to 1940 saw in France the first military power on earth. Those who held this view erected French power as they had experienced it at the end of the First World War into a permanent quality of France which seemed impervious to historic change, forgetting that the eminence of that power in the twenties was the result of comparison and that it would have to be tested by comparison in order to ascertain its quality in 1940. Conversely, when the actual weakness of France revealed itself in military defeat, there developed a tendency in France and elsewhere to expect that weakness to endure. France was treated with neglect and disdain as though it were bound to be weak forever.

The evaluation of Russian power has followed a similar pattern, but in reverse historical order. From 1917 to the battle of Stalingrad in 1943, the Soviet Union was treated as if its weakness at the beginning of the twenties was bound to persist whatever change might occur in other fields. Thus the British military mission that was sent to Moscow in the summer of 1939 to conclude a military alliance with the Soviet Union, in anticipation of the approaching war with Germany, conceived its task with a view of Russian power which might have been justified ten or twenty years before. This miscalculation was an important element in the mission's failure. On the other hand, immediately after the victory of Stalingrad and under the impact of the Soviet Union's aggressive foreign policy, the belief in the permanent invincibility of the Soviet Union and in the permanency of its predominance in Europe was widely held as a dogma.

There is a seemingly ineradicable inclination in our attitude toward the Latin-American countries to assume that the unchallengeable superiority of the colossus of the North, which has existed since the nations of the Western Hemisphere won their independence, was almost a law of nature which population trends, industrialization, political and military developments might modify but could not basically alter. Similarly, since for centuries the political history of the world has been determined by members of the white races, while the colored races were in the main the objects of that history, it is difficult for members of all races alike to visualize a situation where the political supremacy of the white races might no longer exist; where, indeed, the relation between the races might even be reversed. It is especially the demonstration of seemingly irresistible military power which exerts a strange fascination over the minds of those who are given to hasty prophecies rather than to cautious analysis. It makes them believe that history has come to a standstill, as it were, and that today's holders of unchallengeable power cannot fail to enjoy this power tomorrow and the day after. Thus, when in 1940 and 1941 the power of Germany was at its peak, it was widely believed that German domination of Europe was established forever. When the hidden strength of the Soviet Union startled the world in 1943, Stalin was saluted as the future master of Europe and Asia. In the postwar years the American monopoly of the atomic bomb gave rise to the conception of the "American Century," a world dominion based upon unchallengeable American power.[1]

The root of all those tendencies to believe in the absolute character of power or to take the permanency of a particular power configuration for granted lies in the contrast between the dynamic, ever changing character of the power relations between nations, on the one hand, and the human intellect's thirst for certainty and security in the form of definite answers, on the other. Confronted with the contingencies, ambiguities, and uncertainties of the international situation, we search for a definite comprehension of the power factors upon which our foreign policy is based. We all find ourselves in the position of Queen Victoria, who after dismissing Palmerston, whose unpredictable moves on the international scene had exasperated her, asked her new Prime Minister, John Russell, for "a regular programme embracing these dif-

---

[1]The most spectacular contemporary victim of the fallacy of the permanent character of power is James Burnham. See George Orwell, "Second Thoughts on James Burnham," *Polemic*, No. 3, May 1946, pp. 13 ff.; "James Burnham Rides Again," *Antioch Review*, Vol. 7, No. 2, Summer 1947, pp. 315 ff.

ferent relations with other powers." The answers we receive are not always so wise as the one John Russell gave Queen Victoria. "It is very difficult," he replied, "to lay down any principles from which deviations may not frequently be made."[2] Yet a misguided public opinion is only too prone to blame statesmen for such deviations, deeming compliance with principles, without regard for the distribution of power, to be a virtue rather than a vice.

What the observer of international politics needs in order to reduce to a minimum the unavoidable errors in the calculations of power is a creative imagination, immune from the fascination that the preponderant power of the moment so easily imparts, able to detach itself from the superstition of an inevitable trend in history, open to the possibilities for change which the dynamics of history entail. A creative imagination of this kind would be capable of that supreme intellectual achievement of detecting under the surface of present power relations the germinal developments of the future, combining the knowledge of what is with the hunch as to what might be, and condensing all these facts, symptoms, and unknowns into a chart of probable future trends which is not too much at variance with what actually will happen.

The Fallacy of the Single Factor

The third typical error in assessing the power of different nations—attributing to a single factor an overriding importance, to the detriment of all the others—can best be illustrated in three of its manifestations most consequential in modern times: geopolitics, nationalism, and militarism.

Geopolitics

Geopolitics is a pseudoscience erecting the factor of geography into an absolute that is supposed to determine the power, and hence the fate, of nations. Its basic conception is space. Yet, while space is static, the peoples living within the spaces of the earth are dynamic. According to geopolitics, it is a law of history that peoples must expand by "conquering space," or perish, and that the relative power of nations is determined by the mutual relation of the conquered spaces. This basic conception of geopolitics was first expressed in a paper by Sir Halford Mackinder, "The Geographical Pivot of History," read before the Royal Geographical Society in London in 1904. "As we consider this rapid review of the broader currents of history, does not a certain persistence of geographical relationship become evident? Is not the pivot region of the world's politics that vast area of Euro-Asia which is inaccessible to ships, but in antiquity lay open to the horse-riding nomads, and is today to be covered with a network of railways?" This is the "Heartland" of the world which stretches from the Volga to the Yangtze and from the Himalayas to the Arctic Ocean. "Outside the pivot area, in a great inner crescent, are Germany,

---

[2]Robert W. Seton Watson, *Britain in Europe, 1789–1914* (New York: The Macmillan Company, 1937), p. 53.

Austria, Turkey, India and China, and in an outer crescent, Britain, South Africa, Australia, the United States, Canada and Japan." The "World-Island" is composed of the continents of Europe, Asia, and Africa, around which the lesser land areas of the world are grouped. From this geographical structure of the world geopolitics draws the conclusion that "Who rules east Europe commands the Heartland; who rules the Heartland commands the World-Island; who rules the World-Island commands the World."[3]

Mackinder, on the basis of this analysis, foresaw the emergence of Russia, or whatever nation would control the territory described above, as the dominating world power. The German geopoliticians, under the leadership of General Haushofer, who exerted an important influence upon the power calculations and foreign policies of the Nazi regime, were more specific. They postulated an alliance with the Soviet Union or else the conquest of Eastern Europe by Germany in order to make Germany the predominant power on earth. It is obvious that this postulate cannot be directly inferred from the geopolitical premise. Geopolitics only tells us what space is destined, because of its location relative to other spaces, to harbor the master of the world. It does not tell us to what particular nation that mastery will fall. Thus the German school of geopolitics, eager to demonstrate that it was the mission of the German people to conquer the "Heartland," the geographical seat of world dominion, combined the geopolitical doctrine with the argument of population pressure. The Germans were a "people without space," and the "living space" that they must have in order to live beckoned to be conquered in the empty plains of Eastern Europe.

Geopolitics, as presented in the writings of Mackinder and Fairgrieve, had given a valid picture of one aspect of the reality of national power, a picture seen from the exclusive, and therefore distorting, angle of geography. In the hands of Haushofer and his disciples, geopolitics was transformed into a kind of political metaphysics to be used as an ideological weapon in the service of the national aspirations of Germany.[4]

Nationalism

Geopolitics is the attempt to understand the problem of national power exclusively in terms of geography, and degenerates in the process into a political metaphysics couched in a pseudoscientific jargon. Nationalism tries to explain national power exclusively or at least predominantly in terms of national character, and degenerates in the process into the political metaphysics of

---

[3]Sir Halford J. Mackinder, *Democratic Ideals and Reality* (New York: Henry Holt and Company, 1919), p. 150.

[4]The ideological connotations of isolationism and the solidarity of the Western Hemisphere are akin to geopolitics in that they derive a conception of foreign policy from distorted or fictional geographical factors. The distortion of isolationism has already been pointed out in the text; as to the fictional character of the geographical unity of the Western Hemisphere, see Eugene Staley, "The Myth of the Continents," in *Compass of the World*, edited by Hans W. Weigert and Vilhjalmur Stefansson (New York: The Macmillan Company, 1944), pp. 89–108.

racism. As geographical location is for geopolitics the one determinant of national power, so membership in a nation is for nationalism a similar determinant. Membership in a nation may be defined in terms of language, culture,
common origin, race, or in the decision of the individual to belong to the nation.
But no matter how it is defined, the membership always entails as its essence
partaking in certain qualities, called the national character, which the members
of a particular nation have in common and by which they are differentiated
from the members of other nations. The preservation of the national character
and, more particularly, the development of its creative faculties is the supreme
task of the nation. In order to fulfill this task, the nation needs power that will
protect it against other nations and will stimulate its own development. In other
words, the nation needs a state. "One nation—one state" is thus the political
postulate of nationalism; the nation state is its ideal.

But though the nation needs the power of the state for the sake of its
preservation and development, the state needs the national community in order
to maintain and increase its power. Particularly in the nationalistic philosophy
of Germany—in the writings of Fichte and Hegel, for instance—the national
character or spirit appears as the soul, and the political organization of the state
as the body, of the national community, which needs both in order to fulfill its
mission among the other national communities. The feeling of affinity, the
participation in a common culture and tradition, the awareness of a common
destiny, which are of the essence of national sentiment and patriotism, are
transformed by nationalism into a political mysticism in which the national
community and the state become superhuman entities, apart from and superior
to their individual members, entitled to absolute loyalty and, like the idols of
old, deserving of the sacrifice of men and goods.

This mysticism reaches its apogee in the racist worship of the national
character. The nation is here identified with a biological entity, the race, which,
so long as it remains pure, produces the national character in all its strength and
splendor. The dilution of the race through the admixture of alien elements
corrupts the character of the nation and thus weakens the power of the state.
The homogeneity of the nation and the purity of the race thus appear as the
very essence of national power, and for the latter's sake national minorities
must either be absorbed or ejected. In the end, the national character of one's
own nation comes to be regarded as the repository of all those qualities—
courage, loyalty, discipline, industry, endurance, intelligence, and faculty for
leadership—the possession of which justifies the exercise of supreme power
over other nations and at the same time makes the exercise of such power
possible. The overestimation of the qualities of one's own nation, which is
characteristic of all nationalism, leads in the concept of the master race to the
very idolatry of the national character. The master race is, by virtue of the
superior quality of its national character, destined to rule the world. It has by
virtue of these qualities the potential power to exercise world-wide dominion,
and it is the task of statesmanship and of military conquest to transform those
slumbering potentialities into the actualities of world empire.

The intellectual and political excesses of nationalism and of its degenerate offspring, racism, have shocked and repelled the non-nationalistic mind to a much greater degree than have the excesses of geopolitics. The latter have in the main been limited to Germany, and were perpetrated in an esoteric language. The excesses of nationalism, on the other hand, are the logical outgrowth of a secular religion that has engulfed in the fanaticism of holy wars of extermination, enslavement, and world conquest only certain countries, yet has left its mark on many everywhere. Since nationalism has singled out the national character as the pivot of its political philosophy, program, and action, critical observers have frequently tended to go to the other extreme and have denied the existence of a national character altogether. Intent upon demonstrating the mythical and subjective essence of nationalism, they have been anxious to show that its alleged empirical basis, the national character, is also nothing but a myth.

One can readily agree with the critics of nationalism and racism that the allegedly inevitable determination of the national character by the "blood"— that is, the common biological characteristics of the members of a certain group—is a political fabrication without any basis in fact. One can also agree that the absolute constancy of the national character, deriving from the immutability of the qualities of a pure race, belongs in the realm of political mythology. The existence of the United States as a nation and its assimilative powers offer convincing proof of the fallacy of both assertions. On the other hand, to deny altogether the existence of the national character and its bearing upon national power runs counter to the facts of experience, of which we have given a few samples above.[5] Such denial would be an error no less detrimental to a correct assessment of the power of a nation in relation to others than the nationalistic deification of the national character has proved to be.

Militarism

Militarism commits the same type of error with respect to military preparedness which geopolitics and nationalism commit with regard to geography and national character. Militarism is the conception that the power of a nation consists primarily, if not exclusively, in its military strength, conceived especially in quantitative terms. The largest army, the biggest navy, the biggest and fastest air force in the world, superiority in numbers of nuclear weapons become the predominant, if not the exclusive, symbols of national power.

Nations whose military strength lies in navies rather than in large standing armies are wont to point with abhorrence to the militarism of Germany, France, or the Soviet Union without recognizing that they have developed their peculiar brand of militarism. Influenced by writers such as Mahan, they have emphasized out of all proportion the importance of the size and quality of their navies for national power. In the United States there is a widespread tendency to overemphasize the technological aspects of military preparedness, such as

---

[5]See pages 143 ff.

the speed and the range of airplanes and the uniqueness of nuclear weapons. The average German was misled by masses of goose-stepping soldiers. The average Russian experiences the supremacy of Soviet power, derived from space and population, in the throngs filling the vastness of Red Square on May Day. The typical Englishman used to lose his sense of proportion in the presence of the gigantic form of a dreadnought. Many Americans succumbed to the fascination that emanated from the "secret" of the atomic bomb. All these attitudes toward military preparedness have in common the mistaken belief that all that counts, or at least what counts most for the power of a nation, is the military factor conceived in terms of numbers and quality of men and weapons.[6]

From the militaristic error follows inevitably the equation of national power with material force. To speak loudly and carry a big stick, to rephrase Theodore Roosevelt's famous dictum, is indeed the preferred method of militaristic diplomacy. The proponents of this method are unaware that it is sometimes wise to speak softly and carry a big stick; that it is sometimes even wise to leave the big stick at home where it is available when needed. In its exclusive concern with military strength, militarism is contemptuous of the intangibles of power. Without them a powerful nation may frighten other nations into submission or it may conquer by sheer overwhelming force, but it cannot rule what it has conquered; for it cannot gain voluntary acceptance for its rule. In the end, the power of militarism must yield to a power tempered with self-restraint which seeks the effectiveness of national power in the infrequency of its military use. The failures of Spartan, German, and Japanese militarism, compared with the triumphs of the Roman and British policies of empire-building, show the disastrous practical results of that intellectual error which we call militarism.

Thus the error of militarism gives new sharpness to the structure and contours of national power. Militarism—and here is the essence of its error—is unable to understand the paradox that a maximum of material power does not necessarily mean a maximum of over-all national power. A nation that throws into the scale of international politics the maximum of material power it is

---

[6]This aspect of militarism is impressively described by R. H. Tawney, *The Acquisitive Society* (New York: Harcourt, Brace and Company, 1920), p. 44: "Militarism is the characteristic, not of an army, but of a society. Its essence is not any particular quality or scale of military preparation, but a state of mind, which, in its concentration on one particular element in social life, ends finally by exalting it until it becomes the arbiter of all the rest. The purpose for which military forces exist is forgotten. They are thought to stand by their own right and to need no justification. Instead of being regarded as an instrument which is necessary in an imperfect world, they are elevated into an object of superstitious veneration, as though the world would be a poor insipid place without them, so that political institutions and social arrangements and intellect and morality and religion are crushed into a mold made to fit one activity, which in a sane society is a subordinate activity, like the police, or the maintenance of prisons, or the cleansing of sewers, but which in a militarist state is a kind of mystical epitome of society itself.

"Militarism . . . is fetish worship. It is the prostration of men's souls before, and the laceration of their bodies to appease an idol." (Reprinted by permission of the publisher.)

capable of mustering will find itself confronted with the maximum effort of all its competitors to equal or surpass its power. It will find that it has no friends, but only vassals and enemies. Since the emergence of the modern state system in the fifteenth century, no single nation has succeeded in imposing its will for any length of time upon the rest of the world by sheer material force alone. No nation that has tried the ways of militarism has been strong enough to withstand the other nations' combined resistance, which the fear of its superior material power had called into being.

The only nation that in modern times could maintain a continuous position of preponderance owed that position to a rare combination of potential superior power, a reputation for superior power, and the infrequent use of that superior power. Thus Great Britain was able, on the one hand, to overcome all serious challenges to its superiority because its self-restraint gained powerful allies and, hence, made it actually superior. On the other hand, it could minimize the incentive to challenge it because its superiority did not threaten the existence of other nations. When Great Britain stood at the threshold of its greatest power, it heeded the warning of its greatest political thinker—a warning as timely today as when first uttered in 1793:

> Among precautions against ambition, it may not be amiss to take one precaution against our *own*. I must fairly say, I dread our *own* power and our *own* ambition; I dread our being too much dreaded. It is ridiculous to say we are not men, and that, as men, we shall never wish to aggrandize ourselves in some way or other. Can we say that even at this very hour we are not invidiously aggrandized? We are already in possession of almost all the commerce of the world. Our empire in India is an awful thing. If we should come to be in a condition not only to have all this ascendant in commerce, but to be absolutely able, without the least control, to hold the commerce of all other nations totally dependent upon our good pleasure, we may say that we shall not abuse this astonishing and hitherto unheard-of power. But every other nation will think we shall abuse it. It is impossible but that, sooner or later, this state of things must produce a combination against us which may end in our ruin.[7]

---

[7]Edmund Burke, "Remarks on the Policy of the Allies with Respect to France," *Works*, Vol. IV (Boston: Little, Brown, and Company, 1899), p. 457.

PART FOUR

Limitations of
National Power:
The Balance
of Power

11

The Balance of Power

The aspiration for power on the part of several nations, each trying either to maintain or overthrow the status quo, leads of necessity to a configuration that is called the balance of power[1] and to policies that aim at preserving it. We say "of necessity" advisedly. For here again we are confronted with the basic misconception that has impeded the understanding of international politics and has made us the prey of illusions. This misconception asserts that men have a choice between power politics and its necessary outgrowth, the balance of power, on the one hand, and a different, better kind of international relations on the other. It insists that a foreign policy based on the balance of power is one among several possible foreign policies and that only stupid and evil men will choose the former and reject the latter.

It will be shown in the following pages that the international balance of power is only a particular manifestation of a general social principle to which all societies composed of a number of autonomous units owe the autonomy of their component parts; that the balance of power and policies aiming at its preservation are not only inevitable but are an essential stabilizing factor in a society of sovereign nations; and that the instability of the international balance of power is due not to the faultiness of the principle but to the particular conditions under which the principle must operate in a society of sovereign nations.

SOCIAL EQUILIBRIUM

Balance of Power as Universal Concept

The concept of "equilibrium" as a synonym for "balance" is commonly employed in many sciences—physics, biology, economics, sociology, and political

---

[1]The term "balance of power" is used in the text with four different meanings: (1) as a policy aimed at a certain state of affairs, (2) as an actual state of affairs, (3) as an approximately equal distribution of power, (4) as any distribution of power. Whenever the term is used without qualification, it refers to an actual state of affairs in which power is distributed among several nations with approximate equality.

science. It signifies stability within a system composed of a number of autonomous forces. Whenever the equilibrium is disturbed either by an outside force or by a change in one or the other elements composing the system, the system shows a tendency to re-establish either the original or a new equilibrium. Thus equilibrium exists in the human body. While the human body changes in the process of growth, the equilibrium persists as long as the changes occurring in the different organs of the body do not disturb the body's stability. This is especially so if the quantitative and qualitative changes in the different organs are proportionate to each other. When, however, the body suffers a wound or loss of one of its organs through outside interference, or experiences a malignant growth or a pathological transformation of one of its organs, the equilibrium is disturbed, and the body tries to overcome the disturbance by re-establishing the equilibrium either on the same or a different level from the one that obtained before the disturbance occurred.[2]

The same concept of equilibrium is used in a social science, such as economics, with reference to the relations between the different elements of the economic system, e.g., between savings and investments, exports and imports, supply and demand, costs and prices. Contemporary capitalism itself has been described as a system of "countervailing power."[3] It also applies to society as a whole. Thus we search for a proper balance between different geographical regions, such as the East and the West, the North and the South; between different kinds of activities, such as agriculture and industry, heavy and light industries, big and small businesses, producers and consumers, management and labor; between different functional groups, such as city and country, the old, the middle-aged, and the young, the economic and the political sphere, the middle classes and the upper and lower classes.

---

[2]Cf., for instance, the impressive analogy between the equilibrium in the human body and in society in Walter B. Cannon, *The Wisdom of the Body* (New York: W. W. Norton and Company, 1932), pp. 293, 294: "At the outset it is noteworthy that the body politic itself exhibits some indications of crude automatic stabilizing processes. In the previous chapter I expressed the postulate that a certain degree of constancy in a complex system is itself evidence that agencies are acting or are ready to act to maintain that constancy. And moreover, that when a system remains steady it does so because any tendency towards change is met by increased effectiveness of the factor or factors which resist the change. Many familiar facts prove that these statements are to some degree true for society even in its present unstabilized condition. A display of conservatism excites a radical revolt and that in turn is followed by a return to conservatism. Loose government and its consequences bring the reformers into power, but their tight reins soon provoke restiveness and the desire for release. The noble enthusiasms and sacrifices of war are succeeded by moral apathy and orgies of self-indulgence. Hardly any strong tendency in a nation continues to the stage of disaster; before that extreme is reached corrective forces arise which check the tendency and they commonly prevail to such an excessive degree as themselves to cause a reaction. A study of the nature of these social swings and their reversal might lead to valuable understanding and possibly to means of more narrowly limiting the disturbances. At this point, however, we merely note that the disturbances are roughly limited, and that this limitation suggests, perhaps, the early stages of social homeostasis." (Reprinted by permission of the publisher. Copyright 1932, 1939, by Walter B. Cannon.)

[3]John K. Galbraith, *American Capitalism, the Concept of Countervailing Power* (Boston: Houghton Mifflin, 1952).

Two assumptions are at the foundation of all such equilibriums: first, that the elements to be balanced are necessary for society or are entitled to exist and, second, that without a state of equilibrium among them one element will gain ascendancy over the others, encroach upon their interests and rights, and may ultimately destroy them. Consequently, it is the purpose of all such equilibriums to maintain the stability of the system without destroying the multiplicity of the elements composing it. If the goal were stability alone, it could be achieved by allowing one element to destroy or overwhelm the others and take their place. Since the goal is stability plus the preservation of all the elements of the system, the equilibrium must aim at preventing any element from gaining ascendancy over the others. The means employed to maintain the equilibrium consist in allowing the different elements to pursue their opposing tendencies up to the point where the tendency of one is not so strong as to overcome the tendency of the others, but strong enough to prevent the others from overcoming its own. In the words of Robert Bridges:

> Our stability is but balance; and wisdom lies
> In masterful administration of the unforeseen.

Nowhere have the mechanics of social equilibrium been described more brilliantly and at the same time more simply than in *The Federalist*. Concerning the system of checks and balances of the American government, No. 51 of *The Federalist* says:

> This policy of supplying, by opposite and rival interests, the defect of better motives, might be traced to the whole system of human affairs, private as well as public. We see it particularly displayed in all the subordinate distributions of power, where the constant aim is to divide and arrange the several offices in such a manner as that each may be a check on the other—that the private interests of every individual may be a sentinel over the public rights. These inventions of prudence cannot be less requisite in the distribution of the supreme powers of the state.

In the words of John Randolph, "You may cover whole skins of parchment with limitations, but power alone can limit power."[4]

Balance of Power in Domestic Politics

The concept of equilibrium or balance has indeed found its most important application, outside the international field, in the sphere of domestic government and politics.[5] Parliamentary bodies have frequently developed within

---

[4]Quoted after William Cabell Bruce, *John Randolph of Roanoke* (New York and London: G. P. Putnam, 1922), Vol. II, p. 211.

[5]It hardly needs to be pointed out that, while the balance of power is a universal social phenomenon, its functions and results are different in domestic and international politics. The balance of power operates in domestic politics within a relatively stable framework of an integrated society, kept together by a strong consensus and the normally unchallengeable power of a central

themselves a balance of power. A multiparty system lends itself particularly to such a development. Here two groups, each representing a minority of the legislative body, often oppose each other, and the formation of a majority depends upon the votes of a third group. The third group will tend to join the potentially or actually weaker of the two, thus imposing a check upon the stronger one. Even the two-party system of the United States Congress displayed the typical configuration of this checking and balancing process when, in the last years of Franklin D. Roosevelt's administration and during most of Truman's, the Southern Democrats constituted themselves a third party, voting on many issues with the Republican minority. They thus checked not only the Democratic majority in Congress, but also the executive branch, which was also controlled by the Democratic party.[6]

The American government is the outstanding modern example of a governmental system whose stability is maintained by an equilibrium among its component parts. In the words of Lord Bryce:

---

government. On the international scene, where consensus is weak and a central authority does not exist, the stability of society and the freedom of its component parts depend to a much greater extent upon the operations of the balance of power.

Cf. also J. Allen Smith, *The Growth and Decadence of Constitutional Government* (New York: Henry Holt and Company, 1930), pp. 241, 242: "In the absence of any common and impartial agency to interpret international law and supervise international relations, every state is anxious not only to increase its own authority but to prevent, if possible, any increase in the authority of rival states. The instinct of self-preservation, in a world made up of independent nations, operates to make each desire power in order to secure itself against the danger of external aggression. The fact that no country alone is sufficiently strong to feel secure against any possible combination of opposing states makes necessary the formation of alliances and counteralliances through which each state seeks to ensure the needed support in case its safety is menaced from without. This is usually referred to as the struggle to maintain the balance of power. It is merely an application of the check and balance theory of the state to international politics. It is assumed, and rightly so, that if any state should acquire a predominant position in international affairs, it would be a distinct menace to the interests and well-being of the rest of the world. Power, even though it may have been acquired as a means of protection, becomes a menace to international peace as soon as the country possessing it comes to feel stronger than any possible foe. It is no less necessary to maintain the balance of power in international politics, than it is to prevent some special interest from gaining the ascendency in the state. But since this balance of power idea is based on the fear of attack and assumes that every nation should be prepared for war, it can not be regarded as in any real sense a guaranty of international peace." (Reprinted by permission of the publisher.) Cf. also *The Cambridge Modern History*, Vol. V (New York: The Macmillan Co., 1908), p. 276.

[6]Cf. the illuminating discussion of the general problem in John Stuart Mill, *Considerations on Representative Government* (New York: Henry Holt and Company, 1882), p. 142: "In a state of society thus composed, if the representative system could be made ideally perfect, and if it were possible to maintain it in that state, its organization must be such that these two classes, manual laborers and their affinities on one side, employers of labor and their affinities on the other, should be, in the arrangement of the representative system, equally balanced, each influencing about an equal number of votes in Parliament; since, assuming that the majority of each class, in any difference between them, would be mainly governed by their class interests, there would be a minority of each in whom the consideration would be subordinate to reason, justice, and the good of the whole; and this minority of either, joining with the whole of the other, would turn the scale against any demands of their own majority which were not such as ought to prevail." See also page 153, and, concerning the balance of power within federal states, pages 9, 200.

The Constitution was avowedly created as an instrument of checks and balances. Each branch of the government was to restrain the others, and maintain the equipoise of the whole. The legislature was to balance the executive, and the judiciary both. The two houses of the legislature were to balance one another. The national government, taking all its branches together, was balanced against the State governments. As the equilibrium was placed under the protection of a document, unchangeable save by the people themselves, no one of the branches of the national government has been able to absorb or override the others ... each branch maintains its independence and can, within certain limits, defy the others.

But there is among political bodies and offices (i.e. the persons who from time to time fill the same office) of necessity a constant strife, a struggle for existence similar to that which Mr. Darwin has shown to exist among plants and animals; and as in the case of plants and animals so also in the political sphere this struggle stimulates each body or office to exert its utmost force for its own preservation, and to develop its aptitudes in any direction where development is possible. Each branch of the American government has striven to extend its range and its powers; each has advanced in certain directions, but in others has been restrained by the equal or stronger pressure of other branches.[7]

No. 51 of *The Federalist* has laid bare the power structure of this "dynamic equilibrium" or "moving parallelogram of force," as it was called by Charles A. Beard:[8] "... the defect must be supplied, by so contriving the interior structure of the government as that its several constitutional parts may, by their mutual relations, be the means of keeping each other in their proper places. . . . But the great security against a gradual concentration of the several powers in the same department, consists in giving to those who administer each department the necessary constitutional means and personal motives to resist the encroachment of others. . . . The provision for defense must in this, as in all other cases, be made commensurate to the danger of attack. Ambition must be made to counteract ambition. The interest of the man must be connected with the constitutional rights of the place. . . ." The aim of these constitutional arrangements is "to guard one part of the society against the injustices of the other part. Different interests necessarily exist in different classes of citizens. If a majority be reunited by a common interest, the rights of the minority will be insecure."

The author, Madison, expected to safeguard the rights of the minority "by comprehending in the society so many separate descriptions of citizens as will render an unjust combination of a majority of the whole very improbable, if not impracticable. . . . The society itself will be broken into so many parts, interests, and classes of citizens, that the rights of individuals, or of the minority, will be in little danger from interested combinations of the majority." Security will lie "in the multiplicity of interests," and the degree of security "will depend on the number of interests." And Charles A. Beard thus summarizes the philosophy of the American government: "The framers understood that government in action is power. They tried to pit the ambitions, interests, and forces of human

---

[7] *The American Commonwealth* (New York: The Macmillan Company, 1891), Vol. I, pp. 390–1.
[8] *The Republic* (New York: The Viking Press, 1944), pp. 190–1.

beings in the three departments against one another in such a way as to prevent any one set of agents from seizing all power, from becoming dangerously powerful."[9]

One needs only to substitute the terminology of international politics for the concepts used by *The Federalist*, Lord Bryce, and Charles A. Beard in their analysis of the structure and dynamics of the American government, and there emerge the main elements common to both the system of checks and balances of the American Constitution and the international balance of power. In other words, the same motive forces have given rise to the American system of checks and balances and to the international system of the balance of power. Both systems seek to fulfill the same functions for their own stability and the autonomy of their constituent elements, however much they may differ in the means they employ and in the degree to which they realize their aim. Both are subject to the same dynamic processes of change, disequilibrium, and the establishment of a new balance on a different level.

Which are the main patterns of the international balance of power? What are the typical situations out of which it arises and within which it operates? What functions does it fulfill? And to what transformations has it been subjected in recent history?

TWO MAIN PATTERNS OF THE BALANCE OF POWER

Two factors are at the basis of international society: one is the multiplicity, the other is the antagonism of its elements, the individual nations. The aspirations for power of the individual nations can come into conflict with each other—and some, if not most of them, do at any particular moment in history—in two different ways. In other words, the struggle for power on the international scene can be carried on in two typical patterns.

The Pattern of Direct Opposition

Nation A may embark upon an imperialistic policy with regard to Nation B, and Nation B may counter that policy with a policy of the status quo or with an imperialistic policy of its own. France and its allies opposing Russia in 1812, Japan opposing China from 1931 to 1941, the United Nations vs. the Axis from 1941 on, correspond to that pattern. The pattern is one of direct opposition between the nation that wants to establish its power over another nation and the latter, which refuses to yield.

Nation A may also pursue an imperialistic policy toward Nation C, which may either resist or acquiesce in that policy, while Nation B follows with regard

---

[9]Ibid. Cf. also John C. Calhoun, "A Disquisition on Government," in *The Works of John C. Calhoun* (Columbia: A. S. Johnston, 1851), Vol. I, pp. 35–6, 38–9.

to Nation C either a policy of imperialism or one of the status quo. In this case, the domination of C is a goal of A's policy. B, on the other hand, is opposed to A's policy because it either wants to preserve the status quo with respect to C or wants the domination of C for itself. The pattern of the struggle for power between A and B is here not one of direct opposition, but of competition, the object of which is the domination of C, and it is only through the intermediary of that competition that the contest for power between A and B takes place. This pattern was visible, for instance, in the competition between Great Britain and Russia for the domination of Iran, in which the struggle for power between the two countries has repeatedly manifested itself during the last hundred years. It is also clear in the competition for dominant influence in Germany which in the aftermath of the Second World War has marked the relations between France, Great Britain, the Soviet Union, and the United States. The competition between the United States and China or between the Soviet Union and China for control of the countries of Southeast Asia offers another example of the same pattern.

It is in situations such as these that the balance of power operates and fulfills its typical functions. In the pattern of direct opposition, the balance of power results directly from the desire of either nation to see its policies prevail over the policies of the other. A tries to increase its power in relation to B to such an extent that it can control the decisions of B and thus lead its imperialistic policy to success. B, on the other hand, will try to increase its power to such an extent that it can resist A's pressure and thus frustrate A's policy, or else embark upon an imperialistic policy of its own with a chance for success. In the latter case, A must, in turn, increase its power in order to be able to resist B's imperialistic policy and to pursue its own with a chance for success. This balancing of opposing forces will go on, the increase in the power of one nation calling forth an at least proportionate increase in the power of the other, until the nations concerned change the objectives of their imperialistic policies—if they do not give them up altogether—or until one nation gains or believes it has gained a decisive advantage over the other. Then either the weaker yields to the stronger or war decides the issue.

So long as the balance of power operates successfully in such a situation, it fulfills two functions. It creates a precarious stability in the relations between the respective nations, a stability that is always in danger of being disturbed and, therefore, is always in need of being restored. This is, however, the only stability obtainable under the assumed conditions of the power pattern. For we are here in the presence of an inevitable inner contradiction of the balance of power. One of the two functions the balance of power is supposed to fulfill is stability in the power relations among nations; yet these relations are, as we have seen, by their very nature subject to continuous change. They are essentially unstable. Since the weights that determine the relative position of the scales have a tendency to change continuously by growing either heavier or lighter, whatever stability the balance of power may achieve must be precarious and subject to perpetual adjustments in conformity with intervening changes. The other function that a successful balance of power fulfills under these conditions is to insure the freedom of one nation from domination by the other.

Owing to the essentially unstable and dynamic character of the balance, which is not unstable and dynamic by accident or only part of the time, but by nature and always, the independence of the nations concerned is also essentially precarious and in danger. Here again, however, it must be said that, given the conditions of the power pattern, the independence of the respective nations can rest on no other foundation than the power of each individual nation to prevent the power of the other nations from encroaching upon its freedom. The following diagram illustrates this situation:

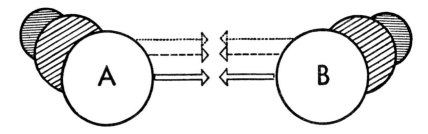

The Pattern of Competition

In the other pattern, the pattern of competition, the mechanics of the balance of power are identical with those discussed. The power of A necessary to dominate C in the face of B's opposition is balanced, if not outweighed, by B's power, while, in turn, B's power to gain dominion over C is balanced, if not outweighed, by the power of A. The additional function, however, that the balance fulfills here, aside from creating a precarious stability and security in the relations between A and B, consists in safeguarding the independence of C against encroachments by A or B. The independence of C is a mere function of the power relations existing between A and B.

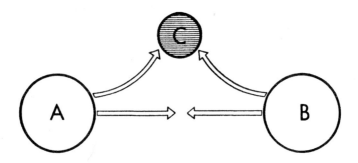

If these relations take a decisive turn in favor of the imperialistic nation—that is, A—the independence of C will at once be in jeopardy:

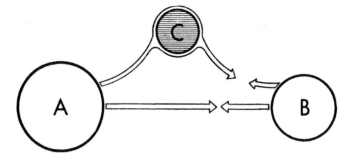

If the status quo nation—that is, B—should gain a decisive and permanent advantage, C's freedom will be more secure in the measure of that advantage:

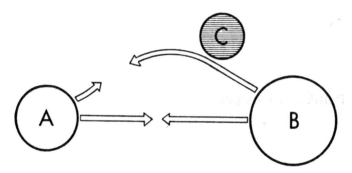

If, finally, the imperialistic nation—A—should give up its imperialistic policies altogether or shift them permanently from C to another objective—that is, D—the freedom of C would be permanently secured:

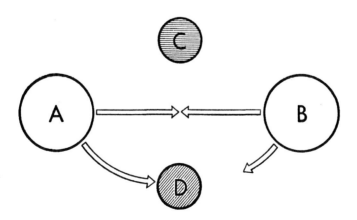

No one has recognized this function of the balance of power to preserve the independence of weak nations more clearly than Edmund Burke. He said in 1791 in his "Thoughts on French Affairs":

> As long as those two princes [the King of Prussia and the German Emperor], are at variance, so long the liberties of Germany are safe. But if ever they should so far understand one another as to be persuaded that they have a more direct and more certainly defined interest in a proportioned mutual aggrandizement than in a reciprocal reduction, that is, if they come to think that they are more likely to be enriched by a division of spoil than to be rendered secure by keeping to the old policy of preventing others from being spoiled by either of them, from that moment the liberties of Germany are no more.[10]

Small nations have always owed their independence either to the balance of power (Belgium and the Balkan countries until the Second World War), or to the preponderance of one protecting power (the small nations of Central and South America, and Portugal), or to their lack of attractiveness for imperialistic aspirations (Switzerland and Spain). The ability of such small nations to maintain their neutrality has always been due to one or the other or all of these factors, e.g., the Netherlands, Denmark, and Norway in the First, in contrast to the Second, World War, and Switzerland and Sweden in both world wars.

The same factors are responsible for the existence of so-called buffer states—weak states located close to powerful ones and serving their military security. The outstanding example of a buffer state owing its existence to the balance of power is Belgium from the beginning of its history as an independent state in 1831 to the Second World War. The nations belonging to the so-called Russian security belt, which stretches along the western and southwestern frontiers of the Soviet Union from Finland to Bulgaria, exist by leave of their preponderant neighbor, whose military and economic interests they serve.

Korea and the Balance of Power

All these different factors have brought to bear successively upon the fate of Korea. Because of its geographic location in the proximity of China, it has existed as an autonomous state for most of its long history by virtue of the control or intervention of its powerful neighbor. Whenever the power of China was not sufficient to protect the autonomy of Korea, another nation, generally Japan, would try to gain a foothold on the Korean peninsula. Since the first century B.C., the international status of Korea has by and large been determined either by Chinese supremacy or by rivalry between China and Japan.

The very unification of Korea in the seventh century was a result of Chinese intervention. From the thirteenth century to the decline of Chinese power in the nineteenth century, Korea stood in a relationship of subservience to China as its suzerain and accepted Chinese leadership in politics and culture. From the end of the sixteenth century Japan, after it had invaded Korea

---

[10]*Works*, Vol. IV (Boston: Little, Brown, and Company, 1889), p. 331.

without lasting success, opposed to the claim of China its own claim to control of the country. Japan was able to make good that claim as a result of its victory in the Sino-Japanese War of 1894–95. Then Japan was challenged in its control of Korea by Russia, and from 1896 on the influence of Russia became dominant. The rivalry between Japan and Russia for control of Korea ended with the defeat of Russia in the Russo-Japanese War of 1904–05. Japanese control of Korea, thus firmly established, was terminated with the defeat of Japan in the Second World War. From then on, the United States replaced Japan as a check upon Russian ambitions in Korea. China, by intervening in the Korean War, resumed its traditional interest in the control of Korea. Thus for more than two thousand years the fate of Korea has been a function either of the predominance of one nation controlling Korea, or of a balance of power between two nations competing for that control.

12

Different Methods of the Balance of Power

The balancing process can be carried on either by diminishing the weight of the heavier scale or by increasing the weight of the lighter one.

DIVIDE AND RULE

The former method has found its classic manifestation, aside from the imposition of onerous conditions in peace treaties and the incitement to treason and revolution, in the maxim "divide and rule." It has been resorted to by nations who tried to make or keep their competitors weak by dividing them or keeping them divided. The most consistent and important policies of this kind in modern times are the policy of France with respect to Germany and the policy of the Soviet Union with respect to the rest of Europe. From the seventeenth century to the end of the Second World War, it has been an unvarying principle of French foreign policy either to favor the division of the German Empire into a number of small independent states or to prevent the coalescence of such states into one unified nation. The support of the Protestant princes of Germany by Richelieu, of the Rhinebund by Napoleon I, of the princes of Southern Germany by Napoleon III, of the abortive separatist movements after the First World War, and the opposition to the unification of Germany after the Second World War—all have their common denominator in considerations of the balance of power in Europe, which France found threatened by a strong German state. Similarly, the Soviet Union from the twenties to the present has consistently opposed all plans for the unification of Europe, on the assumption that the pooling of the divided strength of the European nations into a "Western bloc" would give the enemies of the Soviet Union such power as to threaten the latter's security.

The other method of balancing the power of several nations consists in adding to the strength of the weaker nation. This method can be carried out by two different means: Either B can increase its power sufficiently to offset, if not surpass, the power of A, and vice versa; or B can pool its power with the power of all the other nations that pursue identical policies with regard to A, in which case A will pool its power with all the nations pursuing identical policies with respect to B. The former alternative is exemplified by the policy of compensations and the armament race as well as by disarmament; the latter, by the policy of alliances.

COMPENSATIONS

Compensations of a territorial nature were a common device in the eighteenth and nineteenth centuries for maintaining a balance of power which had been, or was to be, disturbed by the territorial acquisitions of one nation. The Treaty of Utrecht of 1713, which terminated the War of the Spanish Succession, recognized for the first time expressly the principle of the balance of power by way of territorial compensations. It provided for the division of most of the Spanish possessions, European and colonial, between the Hapsburgs and the Bourbons *"ad conservandum in Europa equilibrium,"* as the treaty put it.

The three partitions of Poland in 1772, 1793, and 1795, which in a sense mark the end of the classic period of the balance of power, reaffirm its essence by proceeding under the guidance of the principle of compensations. Since territorial acquisitions at the expense of Poland by any one of the interested nations—Austria, Prussia, and Russia—to the exclusion of the others would have upset the balance of power, the three nations agreed to divide Polish territory in such a way that the distribution of power among themselves would be approximately the same after the partitions as it had been before. In the treaty of 1772 between Austria and Russia, it was even stipulated that "the acquisitions . . . shall be completely equal, the portion of one cannot exceed the portion of the other."

Fertility of the soil and number and quality of the populations concerned were used as objective standards by which to determine the increase in power which the individual nations received through the acquisition of territory. While in the eighteenth century this standard was rather crudely applied, the Congress of Vienna refined the policy of compensations by appointing in 1815 a statistical commission charged with evaluating territories by the standard of number, quality, and type of population.

In the latter part of the nineteenth and the beginning of the twentieth century, the principle of compensations was again deliberately applied to the distribution of colonial territories and the delimitation of colonial or semicolonial spheres of influence. Africa, in particular, was during that period the object of numerous treaties delimiting spheres of influence for the major colonial powers. Thus the competition between France, Great Britain, and Italy for the domination of Ethiopia was provisionally resolved, after the model of the partitions of Poland, by the treaty of 1906, which divided the country into three spheres of influence for the purpose of establishing in that region a balance of power among the nations concerned. Similarly, the rivalry between Great Britain and Russia with respect to Iran led to the Anglo-Russian treaty of 1907, which established spheres of influence for the contracting parties and a neutral sphere under the exclusive domination of Iran. The compensation consists here not in the outright cession of territorial sovereignty, but rather in the reservation, to the exclusive benefit of a particular nation, of certain territories for commercial exploitation, political and military penetration, and eventual establishment of sovereignty. In other words, the particular nation has the right, without having full title to the territory concerned, to operate within its sphere of influence without competition or opposition from another nation. The other nation, in turn, has the right to claim for its own sphere of influence the same abstinence on the part of the former.

Even where the principle of compensations is not deliberately applied, however, as it was in the aforementioned treaties, it is nowhere absent from political arrangements, territorial or other, made within a balance-of-power system. For, given such a system, no nation will agree to concede political advantages to another nation without the expectation, which may or may not be well founded, of receiving proportionate advantages in return. The bargaining of diplomatic negotiations, issuing in political compromise, is but the principle of compensations in its most general form, and as such it is organically connected with the balance of power.

ARMAMENTS

The principal means, however, by which a nation endeavors with the power at its disposal to maintain or re-establish the balance of power are armaments. The armaments race in which Nation A tries to keep up with, and then to outdo, the armaments of Nation B, and vice versa, is the typical instrumentality of an unstable, dynamic balance of power. The necessary corollary of the armaments race is a constantly increasing burden of military preparations devouring an ever greater portion of the national budget and making for ever deepening fears, suspicions, and insecurity. The situation preceding the First World War, with the naval competition between Germany and Great Britain and the rivalry of the French and German armies, illustrates this point.

It is in recognition of situations such as these that, since the end of the Napoleonic Wars, repeated attempts have been made to create a stable balance of power, if not to establish permanent peace, by means of the proportionate disarmament of competing nations. The technique of stabilizing the balance of power by means of a proportionate reduction of armaments is somewhat similar to the technique of territorial compensations. For both techniques require a quantitative evaluation of the influence that the arrangement is likely to exert on the respective power of the individual nations. The difficulties in making such a quantitative evaluation—in correlating, for instance, the military strength of the French army of 1932 with the military power represented by the industrial potential of Germany—have greatly contributed to the failure of most attempts at creating a stable balance of power by means of disarmament. The only outstanding success of this kind was the Washington Naval Treaty of 1922, in which Great Britain, the United States, Japan, France, and Italy agreed to a proportionate reduction and limitation of naval armaments. Yet it must be noted that this treaty was part of an over-all political and territorial settlement in the Pacific which sought to stabilize the power relations in that region on the foundation of Anglo-American predominance.[1]

ALLIANCES

The historically most important manifestation of the balance of power, however, is to be found not in the equilibrium of two isolated nations but in the relations between one nation or alliance of nations and another alliance.

The General Nature of Alliances

Alliances are a necessary function of the balance of power operating within a multiple-state system. Nations A and B, competing with each other, have three choices in order to maintain and improve their relative power positions. They can increase their own power, they can add to their own power the power of other nations, or they can withhold the power of other nations from the adversary. When they make the first choice, they embark upon an armaments race. When they choose the second and third alternatives, they pursue a policy of alliances.

Whether or not a nation shall pursue a policy of alliances is, then, a matter not of principle but of expediency. A nation will shun alliances if it believes that it is strong enough to hold its own unaided or that the burden of the commitments resulting from the alliance is likely to outweigh the advantages to be expected. It is for one or the other or both of these reasons that, throughout the better part of their history, Great Britain and the United States have refrained from entering into peacetime alliances with other nations.

Yet Great Britain and the United States have also refrained from concluding an alliance with each other even though, from the proclamation of the Monroe Doctrine in 1823 to the attack on Pearl Harbor in 1941, they have acted, at least in relation to the other European nations, as if they were allied. Their relationship during that period provides another instance of a situation in

---

[1] The problem of disarmament will be discussed in greater detail in Chapter 18.

which nations dispense with an alliance. It occurs when their interests so obviously call for concerted policies and actions that an explicit formulation of these interests, policies, and actions in the form of a treaty of alliance appears to be redundant.

With regard to the continent of Europe, the United States and Great Britain have had one interest in common: the preservation of the European balance of power. In consequence of this identity of interests, they have found themselves by virtual necessity in the camp opposed to a nation which happened to threaten that balance. And when Great Britain went to war in 1914 and 1939 in order to protect the European balance of power, the United States first supported Great Britain with a conspicuous lack of that impartiality befitting a neutral and then joined her on the battlefield. Had in 1914 and 1939 the United States been tied to Great Britain by a formal treaty of alliance, it might have declared war earlier, but its general policies and concrete actions would not have been materially different than they actually were.

Not every community of interests, calling for common policies and actions, also calls for legal codification in an explicit alliance. Yet, on the other hand, an alliance requires of necessity a community of interests for its foundation.[2] Under what conditions, then, does an existing community of interests require the explicit formulation of an alliance? What is it that an alliance adds to the existing community of interests?

An alliance adds precision, especially in the form of limitation, to an existing community of interests and to the general policies and concrete measures serving them.[3] The interests nations have in common are not typically so precise and limited as to geographic region, objective, and appropriate policies as has been the American and British interest in the preservation of the European balance of power. Nor are they so incapable of precision and limitation as concerns the prospective common enemy. For, while a typical alliance is directed against a specific nation or group of nations, the enemy of the Anglo-American community of interests could in the nature of things not be specified beforehand, since whoever threatens the European balance of power is the enemy. As Jefferson shifted his sympathies back and forth between Napoleon and Great Britain according to who seemed to threaten the balance of power at the time, so during the century following the Napoleonic Wars, Great Britain and the United States had to decide in the light of circumstances ever liable to change who posed at the moment the greatest threat to the balance of power. This blanket character of the enemy, determined not individually but by the function he performs, brings to mind a similar characteristic of collective security, which is directed against the abstractly designed aggressor, whoever he may be.

---

[2]See the quotations from Thucydides and Lord Salisbury, pages 10 and 11.

[3]Glancing through the treaties of alliance of the seventeenth and eighteenth centuries, one is struck by the meticulous precision with which obligations to furnish troops, equipment, logistic support, food, money, and the like, were defined.

The typical interests which unite two nations against a third are both more definite as concerns the determination of the enemy and less precise as concerns the objectives to be sought and the policies to be pursued. In the last decades of the nineteenth century, France was opposed to Germany, and Russia was opposed to Austria, while Austria was allied with Germany against France and Russia. How could the interests of France and Russia be brought upon a common denominator, determining policy and guiding action? How could, in other words, the *casus foederis* be defined so that both friend and foe would know what to expect in certain contingencies affecting their respective interest? It was for the treaty of alliance of 1894 to perform these functions. Had the objectives and policies of the Franco-Russian alliance of 1894 been as clear as were the objectives and policies of Anglo-American cooperation in Europe, no alliance treaty would have been necessary. Had the enemy been as indeterminate, no alliance treaty would have been feasible.

Not every community of interests calling for co-operation between two or more nations, then, requires that the terms of this co-operation be specified through the legal stipulations of a treaty of alliance. It is only when the common interests are inchoate in terms of policy and action that a treaty of alliance is required to make them explicit and operative. These interests, as well as the alliances expressing them and the policies serving them, can be distinguished in five different ways according to: their intrinsic nature and relationship, the distribution of benefits and power, their coverage in relation to the total interests of the nations concerned, their coverage in terms of time, and their effectiveness in terms of common policies and actions. In consequence, we can distinguish alliances serving identical, complementary, and ideological interests and policies. We can further distinguish mutual and one-sided, general and limited, temporary and permanent, operative and inoperative alliances.

The Anglo-American alliance with regard to Europe provides the classic example of an alliance serving identical interests; the objective of one partner—the preservation of the balance of power in Europe—is also the objective of the other. The alliance between the United States and Pakistan is one of many contemporary instances of an alliance serving complementary interests. For the United States it serves the primary purpose of expanding the scope of the policy of containment; for Pakistan it serves primarily the purpose of increasing her political, military, and economic potential vis-à-vis her neighbors.

The pure type of an ideological alliance is presented by the Treaty of the Holy Alliance of 1815 and the Atlantic Charter of 1941. Both documents laid down general moral principles to which the signatories pledged their adherence, and general objectives whose realization they pledged themselves to seek. The Treaty of the Arab League of 1945 provides a contemporary example of an alliance, expressing, since the war against Israel of 1948, primarily ideological solidarity.

Much more typical is the addition of ideological commitments to material ones in one and the same treaty of alliance.[4] Thus the Three Emperors' League of 1873 provided for military assistance among Austria, Germany, and Russia in case of attack on any of them and, at the same time, emphasized the solidarity of the three monarchies against republican subversion. In our times, the ideological commitment against Communist subversion, inserted in treaties of alliance, performs a similar function. The ideological factor also manifests itself in the official interpretation of an alliance, based upon material interests, in terms of an ideological solidarity transcending the limitations of material interests. The conception of the Anglo-American alliance, common before the British invasion of Egypt in 1956, as all-inclusive and world-embracing, based upon common culture, political institutions, and ideals, is a case in point.

As concerns the political effect of this ideological factor upon an alliance, three possibilities must be distinguished. A purely ideological alliance, unrelated to material interests, cannot but be stillborn; it is unable to determine policies or guide actions and misleads by presenting the appearance of political solidarity where there is none. The ideological factor, when it is superimposed upon an actual community of interests, can lend strength to the alliance by marshaling moral convictions and emotional preferences to its support. It can also weaken it by obscuring the nature and limits of the common interests which the alliance was supposed to make precise and by raising expectations, bound to be disappointed, for the extent of concerted policies and actions. For both these possibilities, the Anglo-American alliance can again serve as an example.

The distribution of benefits within an alliance should ideally be one of complete mutuality; here the services performed by the parties for each other are commensurate with the benefits received. This ideal is more likely to be approximated in an alliance concluded among equals in power and serving identical interests; here the equal resources of all, responding to equal incentives, serve one single interest. The other extreme in the distribution of benefits is one-sidedness, a *societas leonia* in which one party receives the lion's share of benefits while the other bears the main bulk of burdens. In so far as the object of such an alliance is the preservation of the territorial and political integrity of the receiving party, such an alliance is indistinguishable from a treaty of guarantee. Complementary interests lend themselves most easily to this kind of disproportion, since they are by definition different in substance and their comparative assessment is likely to be distorted by subjective interpretation. A marked superiority in power is bound to add weight to such interpretations.

The distribution of benefits is thus likely to reflect the distribution of power within an alliance, as is the determination of policies. A great power has a good chance to have its way with a weak ally as concerns benefits and policies, and it is for this reason that Machiavelli warned weak nations against making

---

[4]It ought to be pointed out that the Holy Alliance and the Atlantic Charter usually supplement material commitments contained in separate legal instruments.

alliances with strong ones except by necessity.[5] The relationship between the United States and South Korea exemplifies this situation.

However, this correlation between benefits, policies, and power is by no means inevitable. A weak nation may well possess an asset which is of such great value for its strong ally as to be irreplaceable. Here the unique benefit the former is able to grant or withhold may give it within the alliance a status completely out of keeping with the actual distribution of material power. In recent history, the relationships between the United States and Spain with regard to bases and between the United States and Saudi Arabia with regard to oil come to mind.

The misinterpretation of the Anglo-American alliance, mentioned before, also illustrates the confusion between limited and general alliances. In the age of total war, wartime alliances tend to be general in that they comprise the total interests of the contracting parties both with regard to the waging of the war and the peace settlement. On the other hand, peacetime alliances tend to be limited to a fraction of the total interests and objectives of the signatories. A nation will conclude a multitude of alliances with different nations which may overlap and contradict each other on specific points.

A typical alliance attempts to transform a small fraction of the total interests of the contracting parties into common policies and measures. Some of these interests are irrelevant to the purposes of the alliance, others support them, others diverge from them, and still others are incompatible with them. Thus a typical alliance is imbedded in a dynamic field of diverse interests and purposes. Whether and for how long it will be operative depends upon the strength of the interests underlying it as over against the strength of the other interests of the nations concerned. The value and the chances of an alliance, however limited in scope, must be considered in the context of the over-all policies within which it is expected to operate.

General alliances are typically of temporary duration and most prevalent in wartime; for the overriding common interest in winning the war and securing through the peace settlement the interests for which the war was waged is bound to yield, once victory is won and the peace treaties are signed, to the traditionally separate and frequently incompatible interests of the individual nations. On the other hand, there exists a correlation between the permanency of an alliance and the limited character of the interests it serves; for only such a specific, limited interest is likely to last long enough to provide the foundation for a durable alliance.[6] The alliance between Great Britain and Portugal, concluded in 1703, has survived the centuries because Portugal's interest in the protection of her ports by the British fleet and the British interest in the control of Atlantic approaches to Portugal have endured. Yet it can be stated as a

---

[5] *The Prince*, Chapter 21.

[6] This correlation, however, cannot be reversed. Especially in the seventeenth and eighteenth centuries, limited alliances were frequently concluded *ad hoc;* that is, to counter an attack, to engage in one, or to embark upon a particular expedition. With the passing of the specific occasion in view of which the alliance was concluded, the alliance itself lost its object and came to an end.

general historical observation that while alliance treaties have frequently assumed permanent validity by being concluded "in perpetuity" or for periods of ten or twenty years, they could not have been more durable than the generally precarious and fleeting configurations of common interests which they were intended to serve. As a rule, they have been short-lived.

The dependence of alliances upon the underlying community of interests also accounts for the distinction between operative and inoperative alliances. For an alliance to be operative—that is, able to coordinate the general policies and concrete measures of its members—those members must agree not only on general objectives, but on policies and measures as well. Many alliances have remained scraps of paper because no such agreement was forthcoming, and it was not forthcoming because the community of interests did not extend beyond general objectives to concrete policies and measures. The classic case of an inoperative alliance is that of the United States and France, made inoperable by Washington's Neutrality Proclamation of 1793 after the War of the First Coalition had broken out between France and the monarchies of Europe. Hamilton justified that Proclamation with an argument of general applicability: "There would be no proportion between the mischiefs and perils to which the United States would expose themselves, by embarking in the war, and the benefit which the nature of their stipulation aims at securing to France, or that which it would be in their power actually to render her by becoming a party." The Franco-Russian alliances of 1935 and 1944 and the Anglo-Russian alliance of 1942 are other cases in point. The legal validity of a treaty of alliance and its propagandistic invocation can easily deceive the observer about its actual operational value. The correct assessment of this value requires examination of the concrete policies and measures which the contracting parties have taken in implementation of the alliance.

These considerations are particularly relevant for alliances between a nuclear power (A) and a non-nuclear power (B), directed against another nuclear power (C). Will A risk nuclear destruction at the hands of C in order to honor the alliance with B? The extremity of the risk involved casts doubt upon the operational quality of such an alliance. This doubt, first explicitly raised by DeGaulle, has weakened the alliances between the United States and some of its major allies.

Alliances vs. World Domination

While the balance of power as a natural and inevitable outgrowth of the struggle for power is as old as political history itself, systematic theoretic reflections, starting in the sixteenth century and reaching their culmination in the eighteenth and nineteenth centuries, have conceived the balance of power generally as a protective device of an alliance of nations, anxious for their independence, against another nation's designs for world domination, then called universal monarchy. B, directly threatened by A, joins with C, D, and E, potentially threatened by A, to foil A's designs. Polybius has pointed to the essence of this configuration in his analysis of the relations between the Romans, the Carthaginians, and Hiero of Syracuse:

> The Carthaginians, being shut in on all sides, were obliged to resort to an appeal to the states in alliance with them. Hiero during the whole of the present war had been most prompt in meeting their requests, and was now more complaisant than ever, being convinced that it was in its own interest for securing both its Sicilian dominions and his friendship with the Romans, that Carthage should be preserved, and that the stronger Power should not be able to attain its ultimate object entirely without effort. In this he reasoned very wisely and sensibly, for such matters should never be neglected, and we should never contribute to the attainment by one state of a power so preponderant, that none dare dispute with it even for their acknowledged rights.[7]

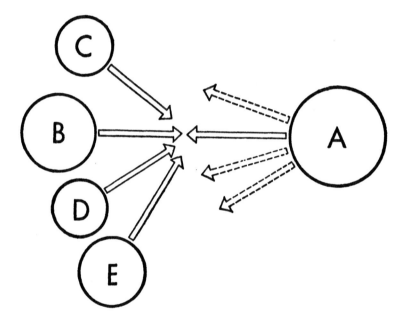

In modern times, Francis Bacon was, after the Florentine statesmen and historians Rucellai and Guicciardini, the first to recognize the essence of the balance of power by way of alliances. In his essay *Of Empire* he says:

> First, for their neighbors, there can no general rule be given (the occasions are so variable), save one which ever holdeth—which is, that princes do keep due sentinel, that none of their neighbors do overgrow so (by increase of territory, by embracing of trade, by approaches, or the like,) as they become more able to annoy them than they were. . . . During that triumvirate of kings, King Henry VIII of England, Francis I, king of France, and Charles V, emperor, there was

---

[7]Polybius I, 83.

such a watch kept that none of the three could win a palm of ground, but the other two would straightways balance it, either by confederation, or, if need were, by a war, and would not in any wise take peace at interest; and the like was done by that League (which Guicciardine saith was the security of Italy,) made between Ferdinando, kind of Naples, Lorenzius Medices, and Ludovicus Sforsa, potentates, the one of Florence, the other of Milan.

The alliances Francis I concluded with Henry VIII and the Turks in order to prevent Charles V of Hapsburg from stabilizing and expanding his empire are the first modern example on a grand scale of the balance of power operating between an alliance and one nation intent upon establishing a universal monarchy. In the second half of the seventeenth century, Louis XIV of France took over the role of the Hapsburgs, and called forth a similar reaction among the European nations. Alliances were formed around England and the Netherlands with the purpose of protecting the European nations from French domination and establishing a new balance of power between France and the rest of Europe.

The wars against the France of 1789 and against Napoleon show the same configuration of one preponderant nation aiming at world domination and being opposed by a coalition of nations for the sake of preserving their independence. The manifesto with which the first coalition initiated these wars in 1792 declared that "no power interested in the maintenance of the balance of power in Europe could see with indifference the Kingdom of France, which at one time formed so important a weight in this great balance, delivered any longer to domestic agitations and to the horrors of disorder and anarchy which, so to speak, have destroyed her political existence." And when these wars approached their conclusion, it was still the purpose of the Allied powers, in the words of the Convention of Paris of April 23, 1814, "to put an end to the miseries of Europe, and to found her repose upon a just redistribution of forces among the nations of which she is composed"; that is, upon a new balance of power. The coalitions that fought the Second World War against Germany and Japan owed their existence to the same fear, common to all their members, of the latter nations' imperialism, and they pursued the same goal of preserving their independence in a new balance of power. Similarly, the Western bi- and multilateral alliances have since the late forties pursued the objective of putting a halt to the imperialistic expansion of the Soviet Union through the creation of a new world balance of power.

Alliances vs. Counteralliances

The struggle between an alliance of nations defending their independence against one potential conqueror is the most spectacular of the configurations to which the balance of power gives rise. The opposition of two alliances, one or both pursuing imperialistic goals and defending the independence of their members against the imperialistic aspirations of the other coalition, is the most frequent configuration within a balance-of-power system.

To mention only a few of the more important examples: the coalitions that fought the Thirty Years' War under the leadership of France and Sweden, on the one hand, and of Austria, on the other, sought to promote the imperialistic ambitions, especially of Sweden and Austria, and, at the same time, to keep the ambitions of the other side in check. The several treaties settling the affairs of Europe after the Thirty Years' War tried to establish a balance of power serving the latter end. The many coalition wars that filled the period between the Treaty of Utrecht of 1713 and the first partition of Poland of 1772 all attempted to maintain the balance that the Treaty of Utrecht had established and that the decline of Swedish power as well as the rise of Prussian, Russian, and British strength tended to disturb. The frequent changes in the alignments, even while war was in progress, have startled the historians and have made the eighteenth century appear to be particularly unprincipled and devoid of moral consideration. It was against that kind of foreign policy that Washington's Farewell Address warned the American people.

Yet the period in which that foreign policy flourished was the golden age of the balance of power in theory as well as in practice. It was during that period that most of the literature on the balance of power was published and that the princes of Europe looked to the balance of power as the supreme principle to guide their conduct in foreign affairs. As Frederick the Great wrote:

> It is easy to see that the political body of Europe finds itself in a violent condition: it has, so to speak, lost its equilibrium and is in a state where it cannot remain for long without risking much. It is with it as it is with the human body which subsists only through the mixture of equal quantities of acids and alkalies; when either of the two substances predominates, the body resents it and its health is considerably affected. And when this substance increases still more, it can cause the total destruction of the machine. Thus when the policy and the prudence of the princes of Europe lose sight of the maintenance of a just balance among the dominant powers, the constitution of the whole body politic resents it: violence is found on one side, weakness on the other; in one, the desire to invade everything, in the other impossibility to prevent it; the most powerful imposes laws, the weakest is compelled to subscribe to them; finally, everything concurs in augmenting the disorder and the confusion; the most powerful, like an impetuous torrent, overflows its banks, carries everything with it, and exposes this unfortunate body to the most disastrous revolutions.[8]

It is true that the princes allowed themselves to be guided by the balance of power in order to further their own interests. By doing so, it was inevitable that they would change sides, desert old alliances, and form new ones whenever it seemed to them that the balance of power had been disturbed and that a realignment of forces was needed to restore it. In that period, foreign policy was indeed a sport of kings, not to be taken more seri-

---

[8]Frederick the Great, "Considerations on the present state of the political body of Europe," *Oeuvres de Frédéric le Grand*, Vol. VIII (Berlin: Rudolph Decker, 1848), p. 24. I have supplied the translation from the French.

ously than games and gambles, played for strictly limited stakes, and utterly devoid of transcendent principles of any kind. Since such was the nature of international politics, what looks in retrospect like treachery and immorality was then little more than an elegant maneuver, a daring piece of strategy, or a finely contrived tactical movement, all executed according to the rules of the game, which all players recognized as binding. The balance of power of that period was amoral rather than immoral. The technical rules of the art of politics were its only standard. Its flexibility, which was its peculiar merit from the technical point of view, was the result of imperviousness to moral considerations, such as good faith and loyalty, a moral deficiency that to us seems deserving of reproach.

From the beginning of the modern state system at the turn of the fifteenth century to the end of the Napoleonic Wars in 1815, European nations were the active elements in the balance of power. Turkey was the one notable exception. Alliances and counteralliances were formed in order to maintain the balance or to restore it. The century from 1815 to the outbreak of the First World War saw the gradual extension of the European balance of power into a world-wide system. One might say that this epoch started with President Monroe's message to Congress in 1823, stating what is known as the Monroe Doctrine. By declaring the mutual political independence of Europe and the Western Hemisphere and thus dividing the world, as it were, into two political systems, President Monroe laid the groundwork for the subsequent transformation of the European into a world-wide balance-of-power system.

This transformation was for the first time clearly envisaged and formulated in the speech George Canning made as British Foreign Secretary to the House of Commons on December 12, 1826. Canning had been criticized for not having gone to war with France in order to restore the balance of power which had been disturbed by the French invasion of Spain. In order to disarm his critics, he formulated a new theory of the balance of power. Through the instrumentality of British recognition of their independence, he included the newly freed Latin-American republics as active elements in the balance. He reasoned thus:

> But were there no other means than war for restoring the balance of power?—Is the balance of power a fixed and unalterable standard? Or is it not a standard perpetually varying, as civilization advances, and as new nations spring up, and take their place among established political communities? The balance of power a century and a half ago was to be adjusted between France and Spain, the Netherlands, Austria, and England. Some years after, Russia assumed her high station in European politics. Some years after that again, Prussia became not only a substantive, but a preponderating monarchy.—Thus, while the balance of power continued in principle the same, the means of adjusting it became more varied and enlarged. They became enlarged, in proportion to the increased number of considerable states—in proportion, I may say, to the number of weights which might be shifted into the one or the other scale. . . . Was there no other mode of resistance,

than by a direct attack upon France—or by a war to be undertaken on the soil of Spain? What, if the possession of Spain might be rendered harmless in rival hands—harmless as regarded us—and valueless to the possessors? Might not compensation for disparagement be obtained . . . by means better adapted to the present time? If France occupied Spain, was it necessary, in order to avoid the consequences of that occupation—that we should blockade Cadiz? No. I looked another way—I saw materials for compensation in another hemisphere. Contemplating Spain, such as our ancestors had known her, I resolved that if France had Spain, it should not be Spain *"with the Indies."* I called the New World into existence, to redress the balance of the Old.[9]

This development toward a world-wide balance of power operating by means of alliances and counteralliances was consummated in the course of the First World War, in which practically all nations of the world participated actively on one or the other side. The very designation of that war as a "world" war points to the consummation of the development.

In contrast to the Second World War, however, the First World War had its origins exclusively in the fear of a disturbance of the European balance of power, which was threatened in two regions: Belgium and the Balkans. Belgium, located at the northeastern frontier of France and guarding the eastern approaches to the English Channel, found itself a focal point of great power competition, without being strong enough to participate actively in that competition. That the independence of Belgium was necessary for the balance of power in Europe was axiomatic. Its annexation by any of the great European nations would of necessity make that nation too powerful for the security of the others. This was recognized from the very moment when Belgium gained its independence with the active support of Great Britain, Austria, Russia, Prussia, and France. These nations, assembled at a conference in London, declared on February 19, 1831, that "They had the right, and the events imposed upon them the duty to see to it that the Belgian provinces, after they had become independent, did not jeopardize the general security and the European balance of power."[10]

In furtherance of that aim, in 1839 the five nations concerned concluded a treaty in which they declared Belgium to be "an independent and perpetually neutral state" under the collective guaranty of the five signatories. This declaration sought to prevent Belgium forever from participating, on one or the other side, in the European balance of power. It was the German violation of Belgium's neutrality which in 1914 crystallized the threat to the balance of power emanating from Germany and enabled Great Britain to justify its participation in the war on the side of France, Russia, and their allies.

The concern of Austria, Great Britain, and Russia in the preservation of the balance of power in the Balkans was concomitant with the weakening of Turkish power in that region. The Crimean War of 1854–56 was fought by an alliance of France, Great Britain, and Turkey against Russia for the purpose of

---

[9]*Speeches of the Right Honourable George Canning* (London, 1836), Vol. VI, pp. 109-11.
[10]*Protocols of Conferences in London Relative to the Affairs of Belgium* (1830–31), p. 60.

maintaining the balance of power in the Balkans. The alliance treaty of March 13, 1854, declared "that the existence of the Ottoman Empire in its present extent, is of essential importance to the balance of power among the states of Europe." The subsequent rivalries and wars, especially the events that led to the Congress of Berlin of 1878 and the Balkan Wars of 1912 and 1913, are all overshadowed by the fear that one of the nations mainly interested in the Balkans might gain an increase in that region out of proportion to the power of the other nations concerned.

In the years immediately preceding the First World War, the balance of power in the Balkans increased in importance; for, since the Triple Alliance between Austria, Germany, and Italy seemed approximately to balance the Triple Entente between France, Russia, and Great Britain, the power combination that gained a decisive advantage in the Balkans might easily gain a decisive advantage in the over-all European balance of power. It was this fear that motivated Austria in July 1914 to try to settle its accounts with Serbia once and for all, and that induced Germany to support Austria unconditionally. It was the same fear that brought Russia to the support of Serbia, and France to the support of Russia. In his telegraphic message of August 2, 1914, to George V of England, the Russian Czar summed the situation up well when he said that the effect of the predominance of Austria over Serbia "would have been to upset balance of power in Balkans, which is of such vital interest to my Empire as well as to those Powers who desire maintenance of balance of power in Europe. . . . I trust your country will not fail to support France and Russia in fighting to maintain balance of power in Europe."[11]

After the First World War, France maintained permanent alliances with Poland, Czechoslovakia, Yugoslavia, and Rumania and, in 1935, concluded an alliance—which was, however, not implemented—with the Soviet Union. This policy can be understood as a kind of preventive balance-of-power policy which anticipated Germany's comeback and attempted to maintain the status quo of Versailles in the face of such an eventuality. On the other hand, the formation in 1936 of an alliance between Germany, Italy, and Japan, called the Axis, was intended as a counterweight against the alliance between France and the Eastern European nations, which would at the same time neutralize the Soviet Union.

Thus the period between the two world wars stands in fact under the sign of the balance of power by alliances and counteralliances, although in theory the principle of the balance of power was supposed to have been superseded by the League of Nations principle of collective security. Yet, actually, collective security, as will be shown later in greater detail,[12] did not abolish the balance of power. Rather, it reaffirmed it in the form of a universal alliance against any potential aggressor, the presumption being that such an alliance

---

[11]*British Documents on the Origins of the War, 1898–1914* (London: His Majesty's Stationery Office, 1926), Vol. XI, p. 276.

[12]See Chapter 19.

would always outweigh the aggressor. Collective security differs, however, from the balance of power in the principle of association by virtue of which the alliance is formed. Balance-of-power alliances are formed by certain individual nations against other individual nations or an alliance of them on the basis of what those individual nations regard as their separate national interests. The organizing principle of collective security is the respect for the moral and legal obligation to consider an attack by any nation upon any member of the alliance as an attack upon all members of the alliance. Consequently, collective security is supposed to operate automatically; that is, aggression calls the counteralliance into operation at once and, therefore, protects peace and security with the greatest possible efficiency. Alliances within a balance-of-power system, on the other hand, are frequently uncertain in actual operation, since they are dependent upon political considerations of the individual nations. The defection of Italy from the Triple Alliance in 1915 and the disintegration of the French system of alliances between 1935 and 1939 illustrate this weakness of the balance of power.

THE "HOLDER" OF THE BALANCE

Whenever the balance of power is to be realized by means of an alliance—and this has been generally so throughout the history of the Western world—two possible variations of this pattern have to be distinguished. To use the metaphor of the balance, the system may consist of two scales, in each of which are to be found the nation or nations identified with the same policy of the status quo or of imperialism. The continental nations of Europe have generally operated the balance of power in this way.

The system may, however, consist of two scales plus a third element, the "holder" of the balance or the "balancer." The balancer is not permanently identified with the policies of either nation or group of nations. Its only objective within the system is the maintenance of the balance, regardless of the concrete policies the balance will serve. In consequence, the holder of the balance will throw its weight at one time in this scale, at another time in the other scale, guided only by one consideration—the relative position of the scales. Thus it will put its weight always in the scale that seems to be higher than the other because it is lighter. The balancer may become in a relatively short span of history consecutively the friend and foe of all major powers, provided they all consecutively threaten the balance by approaching predominance over the others and are in turn threatened by others about to gain such predominance. To paraphrase a statement of Palmerston: While the holder of the balance has no permanent friends, it has no permanent enemies either; it has only the permanent interest of maintaining the balance of power itself.

The balancer is in a position of "splendid isolation." It is isolated by its own choice; for, while the two scales of the balance must vie with each other to add its weight to theirs in order to gain the overweight necessary for success, it must refuse to enter into permanent ties with either side. The holder of the balance waits in the middle in watchful detachment to see which scale is likely to sink. Its isolation is "splendid"; for, since its support or lack of support is the decisive factor in the struggle for power, its foreign policy, if cleverly managed, is able to extract the highest price from those whom it supports. But since this support, regardless of the price paid for it, is always uncertain and shifts from one side to the other in accordance with the movements of the balance, its policies are resented and subject to condemnation on moral grounds. Thus it has been said of the outstanding balancer in modern times, Great Britain, that it lets others fight its wars, that it keeps Europe divided in order to dominate the continent, and that the fickleness of its policies is such as to make alliances with Great Britain impossible. "Perfidious Albion" has become a byword in the mouths of those who either were unable to gain Great Britain's support, however hard they tried, or else lost it after they had paid what seemed to them too high a price.

The holder of the balance occupies the key position in the balance-of-power system, since its position determines the outcome of the struggle for power. It has, therefore, been called the "arbiter" of the system, deciding who will win and who will lose. By making it impossible for any nation or combination of nations to gain predominance over the others, it preserves its own independence as well as the independence of all the other nations, and is thus a most powerful factor in international politics.

The holder of the balance can use this power in three different ways. It can make its joining one or the other nation or alliance dependent upon certain conditions favorable to the maintenance or restoration of the balance. It can make its support of the peace settlement dependent upon similar conditions. It can, finally, in either situation see to it that the objectives of its own national policy, apart from the maintenance of the balance of power, are realized in the process of balancing the power of others.

France under Louis XIV and Italy in the decade before the First World War attempted to play this role of arbiter of the European balance of power. But France was too deeply involved in the struggle for power on the European continent, too much a part of its balance of power, and too much lacking in the commanding superiority to play that role successfully. Italy, on the other hand, had not enough weight to throw around to give it the key position in the balance of power. For this reason it earned only the moral condemnation, but not the respect, that similar policies had brought Great Britain. Only Venice in the sixteenth century and Great Britain since the reign of Henry VIII were able to make the holding of the balance between other nations one of the cornerstones of their foreign policies, using the three methods mentioned above either severally or jointly.

The idea appeared for the first time with reference to the Venetians in a letter written in 1553 by Queen Mary of Hungary to the imperial ambassador in England. She pointed out that the Italians had good reason to oppose France; but, she continued: "You know how they fear the power of the one and of the other of the two princes [Charles V and Francis I] and how they are concerned to balance their power."[13] In the following years, on the occasion of Venice's refusals of French offers of alliance, French statesmen characterized the foreign policy of Venice in similar terms, with special reference to the aspects of isolation and detachment from alliances with either side. In 1554 for instance, Henry II of France was reported by a Venetian ambassador to have explained such refusals by the fear of Venice that in the event of the death of Charles V Spain might become inferior to France; Venice, however, tried to "keep things in balance *(tener le cose in equale stato)*." Another Venetian ambassador reported in 1558 that the French explained the foreign policy of Venice by its suspicion of the increase in power of France and Spain. Venice wanted to prevent "that the balance tip to either side *(que la bilancia non pendesse da alcuna parte)*." The ambassador added that "this policy is being praised and even admired by intelligent people; in these turbulent times the weak find protection nowhere but in the Republic of Venice and therefore all Italians in particular, desire her independence and welcome her armaments."[14]

The classic example of the balancer has, however, been provided by Great Britain. To Henry VIII is attributed the maxim: *cui adhaero praeest* (he whom I support will prevail). He is reported to have had himself painted holding in his right hand a pair of scales in perfect balance, one of them occupied by France, the other by Austria, and holding in his left hand a weight ready to be dropped in either scale. Of England under Elizabeth I it was said "that France and Spain are as it were the Scales in the Balance of Europe and England the Tongue or the Holder of the Balance."[15] In 1624, a French pamphlet invited King Jacob to follow the glorious example of Elizabeth and Henry VIII, "who played his role so well between the Emperor Charles V and King Francis by making himself feared and flattered by both and by holding, as it were, the balance between them."

With the appearance of Louis XIV as a new aspirant for the universal monarchy, it became more and more common, in England and elsewhere, to consider it the English mission to act as "arbiter of Europe" by keeping the Hapsburgs and France in balance. This same standard was applied critically to the foreign policies of Charles II and James II, who made common cause with Louis XIV, the strongest rival of British power, against the Netherlands, and in support of the anti-French policies of William III. With the War of the Spanish Succession, that standard was erected into a dogma, especially in England. It remained, as applied to ever new combinations of powers, practically unchallenged until the Manchester liberals after the middle of the nineteenth century advocated complete and permanent detachment from the affairs of the European continent—that is, isolationism—as the principle of British foreign policy.

---

[13]*Papiers d'État du Cardinal de Granvelle* (Paris, 1843), Vol. IV, p. 121.

[14]Eugeno Albéri, *Le Relazioni degli Ambiasciatori Veneti al Senato*, Series I (Firenze, 1862), Vol. II, pp. 287, 464.

[15]William Camden, *Annales of the History of the Most Renowned and Victorious Princess Elizabeth, Late Queen of England* (London, 1635), p. 196.

As the tradition and practice of British diplomacy, this variety of the balance of power seems to have disappeared only in recent years with the decline of British, and the growth of American and Russian, power. When that tradition and practice were about to disappear, Sir Winston Churchill summarized it most eloquently in a speech to the Conservative Members Committee on Foreign Affairs in March 1936:

> For four hundred years the foreign policy of England has been to oppose the strongest, most aggressive, most dominating Power on the Continent, and particularly to prevent the Low Countries falling into the hands of such a Power. Viewed in the light of history these four centuries of consistent purpose amid so many changes of names and facts, of circumstances and conditions, must rank as one of the most remarkable episodes which the records of any race, nation, state or people can show. Moreover, on all occasions England took the more difficult course. Faced by Philip II of Spain, against Louis XIV under William III and Marlborough, against Napoleon, against William II of Germany, it would have been easy and must have been very tempting to join with the stronger and share the fruits of his conquest. However, we always took the harder course, joined with the less strong Powers, made a combination among them, and thus defeated and frustrated the Continental military tyrant whoever he was, whatever nation he led. Thus we preserved the liberties of Europe, protected the growth of its vivacious and varied society, and emerged after four terrible struggles with an ever-growing fame and widening Empire, and with the Low Countries safely protected in their independence. Here is the wonderful unconscious tradition of British foreign policy. All our thoughts rest in that tradition today. I know of nothing which has occurred to alter or weaken the justice, wisdom, valour and prudence upon which our ancestors acted. I know of nothing that has happened to human nature which in the slightest degree alters the validity of their conclusions. I know of nothing in military, political, economic, or scientific fact which makes me feel that we are less capable. I know of nothing which makes me feel that we might not, or cannot, march along the same road. I venture to put this very general proposition before you because it seems to me that if it is accepted everything else becomes much more simple.
>
> Observe that the policy of England takes no account of which nation it is that seeks the overlordship of Europe. The question is not whether it is Spain, or the French Monarchy, or the French Empire, or the German Empire, or the Hitler regime. It has nothing to do with rulers or nations; it is concerned solely with whoever is the strongest or the potentially dominating tyrant. Therefore we should not be afraid of being accused of being pro-French or anti-German. If the circumstances were reversed, we could equally be pro-German and anti-French. It is a law of public policy which we are following, and not a mere expedient dictated by accidental circumstances, or likes and dislikes, or any other sentiment.[16]

---

[16]Winston S. Churchill. *The Second World War*, Vol. I, *The Gathering Storm* (Boston: Houghton Mifflin Co., 1948), pp. 207–8. (Reprinted by permission of the publisher.)

13

The Structure of the Balance of Power

DOMINANT AND DEPENDENT SYSTEMS

We have spoken thus far of the balance of power as if it were one single system comprehending all nations actively engaged in international politics. Closer observation, however, reveals that such a system is frequently composed of a number of subsystems that are interrelated with each other, but that maintain within themselves a balance of power of their own. The interrelationship between the different systems is generally one of subordination, in the sense that one dominates because of the relatively great weight accumulated in its scales, while the others are, as it were, attached to the scales of that dominant system.

Thus, in the sixteenth century, the dominant balance of power operated between France and the Hapsburgs, while at the same time an autonomous system kept the Italian states in equilibrium. In the latter part of the seventeenth century a separate balance of power developed in Northern Europe out of the challenge with which the rise of Swedish power confronted the nations adjacent to the Baltic Sea. The transformation of Prussia into a first-rate power in the eighteenth century brought about a particular German balance of power, the other scale of which had Austria as its main weight. This autonomous system, "a little Europe within the great," was dissolved only in 1866 with the expulsion of Austria from the Germanic Confederation as a consequence of the Prusso-Austrian War of the same year. The eighteenth century saw also the development of an Eastern balance of power occasioned by the ascendancy of Russia. The partitions of Poland, by virtue of the principle of compensations, between Russia, Prussia, and Austria are the first spectacular manifestations of that new system.

Throughout the nineteenth century until the present day, the balance of power in the Balkans has been of concern to the nations of Europe. As early as 1790 Turkey concluded a treaty with Prussia in which the latter promised to go to war with Austria and Russia "because of the prejudice which the enemies, in crossing the Danube, have brought to the desirable and necessary balance of power." In the latter part of the nineteenth century one began to speak of an African balance of power with reference to a certain equilibrium among the colonial acquisitions of the great powers. Later on, the balance of power in the Western Hemisphere, in the Pacific, in the Far and Near East were added to the diplomatic vocabulary. One even spoke of an "Austrian equilibrium"; and of the Austrian monarchy with its antagonistic nationalities it was said that it "is constrained to apply to itself the rules of conduct which the powers of Europe with their perpetual rivalries follow with regard to each other."[1]

It is not by accident that the autonomy of such local balance-of-power systems is the greater and their subordination to a dominant system the less noticeable, the more removed they are physically from the center of the struggle for power—the more they operate at the periphery of the dominant system, out of reach of the dominant nations. Thus an Italian balance of power could develop during the fifteenth century in relative autonomy, while the great nations of Europe were occupied in other regions. For the better part of the history of Western civilization the different balance-of-power systems of Asia, Africa, and America were entirely independent of the configurations of the European nations, to the point of being hardly known to them.

The balance of power in the Western Hemisphere up to the Second World War and in Eastern Europe until the end of the eighteenth century owe their relative autonomous development to their location at the periphery of the power centers of the time. The partitions of Poland which were intended to preserve the balance of power in Eastern Europe were executed by the directly interested nations without interference of any other nation. The alliance concluded in 1851 between Brazil and Uruguay against Argentina for the purpose of maintaining the balance of power in South America had only a very remote connection with the European balance of power. On the other hand, it has now become possible to speak of an autonomous African balance of power. Since the indigenous peoples of Africa have started to compete for power with each other and with non-African nations, Africa is no longer solely an object of the struggle for power centered elsewhere.

The more intimately a local balance of power is connected with the dominant one, the less opportunity it has to operate autonomously and the more it tends to become merely a localized manifestation of the dominant balance of power. The balance of power within the German Confederation from Frederick the Great to the War of 1866 presents an intermediate situation between full autonomy and complete integration. It combines a certain degree of autonomy with integration into the dominant system. While the equilibrium between Prussia and Austria was, as we have seen,[2] a precondition for the preservation

---

[1]Albert Sorel, *L'Europe et la révolution française* (Paris: E. Plon, 1885), Vol. I, p. 443.
[2]See pages 191–92.

of the liberties of the members of the Germanic Confederation, this equilibrium was also indispensable for the maintenance of the European balance of power as a whole.

The German balance thus fulfilled a dual function: one within its own framework, another for the general system of which it was a part. Conversely, the fusion of Prussia and Austria or the domination of one by the other would not only have been destructive of the independence of the individual German states but would as well have threatened the freedom of the other European nations. "If Europe," as Edmund Burke put it, "does not conceive the independence and the equilibrium of the empire to be in the very essence of the system of balance of power in Europe . . . all the politics of Europe for more than two centuries have been miserably erroneous."[3] The perpetuation of the balance between Prussia and Austria was, therefore, in the interest not only of the other members of the Germanic Confederation but of all European nations.

When, as a consequence of the War of 1866, Prussia and later Germany gained a permanent advantage over Austria which destroyed the balance between the two nations and made Germany predominant in Europe, it became one of the functions of the European balance of power to preserve at least the independence of Austria against infringement by its stronger neighbor. It was in consequence of that permanent European interest that after the First World War the victorious Allies sought by legal, economic, and political measures to prevent the fusion of Austria with Germany. Moreover, it was within the logic of this situation that Hitler regarded the annexation of Austria as a necessary stepping stone on the road toward the overthrow of the European balance of power.

The balance of power in the Balkans has fulfilled a similar function since the last decades of the nineteenth century. Here, too, the maintenance of a balance of power among the Balkan nations has been regarded as a prerequisite for the maintenance of the European balance. Whenever the local balance was threatened, the great nations of Europe intervened in order to restore it. The statement of the Russian Czar at the beginning of the First World War, quoted above,[4] clearly illustrates that connection.

STRUCTURAL CHANGES IN THE BALANCE OF POWER[5]

In recent times the relations between the dominant balance of power and the local systems have shown an ever increasing tendency to change to the detriment of the autonomy of the local systems. The reasons for this development lie in the structural changes that the dominant balance of power has undergone

---

[3]*Works*, Vol. IV (Boston: Little, Brown and Company, 1889), p. 330.
[4]See page 208.
[5]For other structural changes, see pages 204 ff.

since the First World War and that became manifest in the Second. We have already indicated the gradual expansion of the dominant balance-of-power system from Western and Central Europe to the rest of the continent, and from there to other continents, until finally the First World War saw all the nations of the earth actively participating in a world-wide balance of power.

Hand in hand with the consummation of this expansion went a shift of the main weights of the balance from Europe to other continents. At the outbreak of the First World War in 1914, the main weights in the balance were predominantly European: Great Britain, France, and Russia in one scale, Germany and Austria in the other. At the end of the Second World War, the principal weights in each scale were either entirely non-European, as in the case of the United States, or predominantly non-European, as in the case of the Soviet Union. In consequence, the whole structure of the world balance of power has changed. At the end of the First World War and even at the beginning of the Second, the two scales of the balance, so to speak, were still in Europe: only the weights of the scales came from all over the earth. The main protagonists of the power contest and the principal stakes for which it was fought were still predominantly European. To paraphrase the words of George Canning, already quoted, non-European powers were called in only for the purpose of redressing the balance of power of Europe. In Churchill's words of 1940, "The New World, with all its power and might, steps forth to the rescue and the liberation of the Old."

Today the balance of power of Europe is no longer the center of world politics around which local balances would group themselves, either in intimate connection or in lesser or greater autonomy. Today the European balance of power has become a mere function of the world-wide balance of which the United States and the Soviet Union have been the main weights, placed on opposite scales. The distribution of power in Europe is only one of the concrete issues over which the power contests between the United States and the Soviet Union have been waged. The revolution of 1989 may change this, but the exact character of the change can not yet be foreseen.

What is true of the formerly dominant system is true of all the traditional local systems as well. The balance of power in the Balkans, no less than the balances in the Near and Far East, have shared the fate of the general European system. They have become mere functions of the new world-wide balance, mere "theaters" where the power contest between the two great protagonists is fought out. One might say that of all the local balance-of-power systems only the South American system has retained a certain measure of autonomy, protected as it is by the predominance of the United States.

PART FIVE

Limitations of National Power: International Morality and World Public Opinion

14

Morality, Mores, and Law as Restraints on Power

We have seen in the preceding chapter that power is a crude and unreliable method of limiting the aspirations for power on the international scene. If the motivations behind the struggle for power and the mechanisms through which it operates were all that needed to be known about international politics, the international scene would indeed resemble the state of nature described by Hobbes as a "war of every man against every man."[1] International politics would be governed exclusively by those considerations of political expediency of which Machiavelli has given the most acute and candid account. In such a world the weak would be at the mercy of the strong. Might would indeed make right.

Actually, however, the very threat of a world where power reigns not only supreme, but without rival, engenders that revolt against power which is as universal as the aspiration for power itself. To stave off this revolt, to pacify the resentment and opposition that arise when the drive for power is recognized for what it is, those who seek power employ, as we have seen, ideologies for the concealment of their aims. What is actually aspiration for power, then, appears to be something different, something that is in harmony with the demands of reason, morality, and justice. The substance, of which the ideologies of international politics are but the reflection, is to be found in the normative orders of morality, mores, and law.

From the Bible to the ethics and constitutional arrangements of modern democracy, the main function of these normative systems has been to keep aspirations for power within socially tolerable bounds. All ethics, mores, and

---

[1]*Leviathan*, Chapter XIII.

legal systems dominant in Western civilization recognize the ubiquity of power drives and condemn them. Conversely, such political philosophies as Machiavelli's and Hobbes's, which regard the ubiquity of power drives as an ultimate fact of social life, to be accepted rather than condemned and restrained, have met with the disapproval of prevailing opinion. They have lacked the intellectual and practical influence that has made such political philosophies as St. Augustine's and Locke's potent forces in Western civilization.

On the other hand, that very tradition of Western civilization which attempts to restrain the power of the strong for the sake of the weak has been opposed as effeminate, sentimental, and decadent. The opponents have been those who, like Nietzsche, Mussolini, and Hitler, not only accept the will to power and the struggle for power as elemental social facts but glorify their unrestrained manifestations and postulate this absence of restraint as an ideal of society and a rule of conduct for the individual. But in the long run philosophies and political systems that have made the lust and the struggle for power their mainstays have proved impotent and self-destructive. Their weakness demonstrates the strength of the Western tradition that seeks, if not to eliminate, at least to regulate and restrain the power drives that otherwise would either tear society apart or deliver the life and happiness of the weak to the arbitrary will of the powerful.

It is at these two points that morality, mores, and law intervene in order to protect society against disruption and the individual against enslavement and extinction. When a society or certain of its members are unable to protect themselves with their own strength against the power drives of others—when, in other words, the mechanics of power politics are found wanting, as sooner or later they must be—these normative systems try to supplement power politics with their own rules of conduct. This is the message the normative systems give to strong and weak alike: Superior power gives no right, either moral or legal, to do with that power all that is physically capable of doing. Power is subject to limitations, in the interest of society as a whole and in the interest of its individual members, which are not the result of the mechanics of the struggle for power but are superimposed upon that struggle in the form of norms or rules of conduct by the will of the members of society themselves.

Three types of norms or rules of conduct operate in all higher societies: ethics, mores, and law. Their distinctive characteristics have been much debated in the literature of philosophy and jurisprudence. For the purpose of this study it is sufficient to point out that every rule of conduct has two elements: the command and the sanction. No particular command is peculiar to any particular type of norm—"thou shalt not kill" can be a command of ethics, mores, or law. It is the sanction that differentiates these three different types of rules of conduct.

"Thou shalt not kill" is a command of ethics, mores, or law according to whether, in case of its violation, a sanction peculiar to ethics or to mores or to law is applied to punish the violator and prevent further violations. If A kills B and afterward feels pangs of conscience or of remorse, we are in the presence of a sanction peculiar to ethics and, hence, of an ethical norm. If A kills B and unorganized society reacts with spontaneous demonstrations of disapproval, such as business boycott, social ostracism, and the like, we have to do with a sanction peculiar to the mores, and, hence, to a norm of the mores. If, finally, A kills B and organized society reacts in the form of a rational procedure with predetermined police action, indictment, trial, verdict, and punishment, the sanction is of a legal nature and the norm, therefore, belongs in the category of law.

All domestic societies are regulated by an intricate maze of rules of conduct of this kind, supporting or contradicting each other or operating independently. The more important a society considers those interests and values which it tries to safeguard by rules of conduct, the stronger are the sanctions with which it threatens an infraction of its rules. Society exerts its greatest pressure, and therefore has the best chance of enforcing its rules of conduct against its recalcitrant members when it brings all the different kinds of sanctions at its disposal simultaneously to bear upon the infractor of its rules. It is weakest, and therefore its sanctions are most likely to be ineffective, when only one type of sanction supports its interests and values. When one rule of conduct requires an action that another rule of conduct condemns, the fate of the interest or value concerned depends upon the relative strength of the sanctions supporting the contradictory commands.

Against a threat to its own existence by treason or by revolution, or a threat to the existence of its individual members by murder, society marshals all three types of sanction. Thus morality, mores, and law, reinforcing each other, give threefold protection to the life of society and to the lives of the individuals who compose it. The would-be traitor or killer faces the pangs of his conscience, the spontaneous reactions of society in the form, for instance, of ostracism, and the punishment of the law. The same situation prevails where not the existence of society or of its individual members but their property is at stake. Property, too, is surrounded by the triple wall of morality, mores, and law. Between the would-be thief and cheat and the property he covets, society interposes all the sanctions it is able to employ.

Where less highly prized interests and values are at stake, society may call upon only one type of sanction. Thus certain kinds of competitive practices in business and politics, such as lying, are opposed only by morality. The mores will come into play only under extreme conditions; if, for instance, the amount and degree of lying exceed the measure society regards as tolerable. The law will remain silent in the case of ordinary lying, if for no other reason than that no law prohibiting it can be enforced. It will speak only in case of qualified lying, such as perjury and cheating, where the lie threatens interests and values beyond mere truth. The rules of fashion, on the other hand, are enforced exclusively by the mores, for the issues involved are not important enough for morality and law to be concerned about them. It is, finally, the law alone that takes cognizance of violations of traffic regulations. Morality and mores do not participate in their enforcement, for the sanctions of the law are generally sufficient to establish some kind of mechanical order in the realm of traffic.

The problem of the relative strength of different injunctions becomes acute when there is conflict between different rules of conduct. The classic example, much discussed in the literature of jurisprudence, of a conflict between two rules of the same legal system is the prohibition of dueling in the criminal codes of certain European countries, while the military codes of the same countries require officers to settle certain disputes by way of duels. A system of ethics which commands us to obey God rather than man and at the same time to give unto Caesar what is Caesar's presents a similar conflict when a law of the state contradicts one of God's commandments. Conflicts of this kind are particularly frequent in the political sphere. Rival governments—a revolutionary government and a legitimate government, a government in exile and a quisling government—demand obedience from the same group of people. The rules of conduct with which a politician is expected to comply are often at odds with the norms that address all members of society. The ethics and mores of politics are considered to permit greater leeway than the general ethics and mores of society in actions such as "campaign oratory" and political advertising, although concern is growing.

Conflicts between different rules of conduct are decided by the relative pressure the sanctions of the conflicting rules are able to exert upon the will of the individual. Unable to comply with all the norms addressed to him at the same time, he must choose the one to obey and violate the others. The relative strength of these pressures is, in turn, the expression of the relative strength of the social forces that support one set of values and interests against another. The normative order of society whose purpose is to keep the power aspirations of its individual members within socially tolerable bounds is itself in a certain measure the result of social forces contending with each other for the domination of society through their influence, say, on legislation or court decisions.

Social life consists overwhelmingly of continuous reactions, which have become largely automatic, to the pressures society exerts upon its members through its rules of conduct. These rules of conduct watch over the individual from morning till night, molding his actions into conformity with the standards of society. One might even say that society as a dynamic force is nothing but the sum total of its rules of conduct imposing patterns of action upon its members. What we call civilization is in a sense nothing but the automatic reactions of the members of a society to the rules of conduct by which that society endeavors to make its members conform to certain objective standards, to restrain their aspirations for power, and to domesticate and pacify them in all socially important respects. The civilization with which we are here of course mainly concerned—Western civilization—has been to a large extent successful in this endeavor. Western civilization has not, however, as many nineteenth- and twentieth-century writers believed, altogether banished the struggle for power from the domestic scene and replaced it with something different and better, such as co-operation, harmony, permanent peace, nor is it on its way to do so. This misconception of the role that the aspirations and the struggle for power play in politics has been treated in the third chapter of this book.

The best that Western civilization has been able to achieve—which is, as far as we can see, the best that any civilization can achieve—has been to mitigate the struggle for power on the domestic scene, to civilize its means, and to direct it toward objectives that, if attained, minimize the extent to which life, liberty, and the pursuit of happiness of the individual members of society are involved in the struggle for power. More particularly, the crude methods of personal combat have been replaced by the refined instruments of social, commercial, and professional competition. The struggle for power is being fought not with deadly weapons but with competitive examinations, with competition for social distinctions, with periodical elections for public and private offices, and, above all, with competition for the possession of money and of things measurable in money.

In the domestic societies of Western civilization the possession of money has become the outstanding symbol of the possession of power. Through the competition for the acquisition of money the power aspirations of the individual find a civilized outlet in harmony with the rules of conduct laid down by society. The different normative injunctions against homicide and against individual and collective violence of any kind seek to create the normative preconditions for such a civilized redirection of the struggle for power. All the social instrumentalities and institutions relevant to the different competitive devices of society serve the purpose, not of eliminating the struggle for power, but of creating civilized substitutes for the brutality and crudeness of an unlimited and unregulated struggle for power.

Such is, in brief and sketchy outline, the way ethics, mores, and law limit the struggle for power in the domestic societies of Western civilization. And what of international society? What rules of morality, mores, and law are effective on the international scene? What functions do they fulfill for international society? What kind of international ethics, international mores in the form of world public opinion, and international law is there to delimit, regulate, and civilize the struggle for power among nations in the same way the domestic normative systems affect the struggle for power among the members of a domestic society?

15

International Morality

A discussion of international morality must guard agaisnt the two extremes of either overrating the influence of ethics upon international politics or underestimating it by denying that statesmen and diplomats are moved by anything but considerations of material power.

On the one hand, there is the dual error of confounding the moral rules people actually observe with those they pretend to observe, as well as with those which writers declare they ought to observe. "On no subject of human interest, except theology," said Professor John Chipman Gray, "has there been so much loose writing and nebulous speculation as on international law."[1] The same must be said of international morality. Writers have put forward moral precepts that statesmen and diplomats ought to take to heart in order to make relations between nations more peaceful and less anarchic, such as the keeping of promises, trust in the other's word, fair dealing, respect for international law, protection of minorities, repudiation of war as an instrument of national policy. But they have rarely asked themselves whether and to what extent such precepts, however desirable in themselves, actually determine the actions of men. Furthermore, since statesmen and diplomats are wont to justify their actions and objectives in moral terms, regardless of their actual motives, it would be equally erroneous to take those protestations of selfless and peaceful intentions, of humanitarian purposes, and international ideals at their face value. It is pertinent to ask whether they are mere ideologies concealing the true motives of action or whether they express a genuine concern for the compliance of international policies with ethical standards.

On the other hand, there is the misconception, usually associated with the general depreciation and moral condemnation of power politics, discussed earlier,[2] that international politics is so thoroughly evil that it is no use looking for

---

[1] *Nature and Sources of the Law* (New York: The Macmillan Company, 1927), p. 127.
[2] See pages 37 ff.

moral limitations of the aspirations for power on the international scene. Yet, if we ask ourselves what statesmen and diplomats are capable of doing to further the power objectives of their respective nations and what they actually do, we realize that they do less than they probably could and less than they actually did in other periods of history. They refuse to consider certain ends and to use certain means, either altogether or under certain conditions, not because in the light of expediency they appear impractical or unwise but because certain moral rules interpose an absolute barrier. Moral rules do not permit certain policies to be considered at all from the point of view of expediency. Certain things are not being done on moral grounds, even though it would be expedient to do them. Such ethical inhibitions operate in our time on different levels with different effectiveness. Their restraining function is most obvious and most effective in affirming the sacredness of human life in times of peace.

THE PROTECTION OF HUMAN LIFE

Protection of Human Life in Peace

International politics can be defined, as we have seen, as a continuing effort to maintain and to increase the power of one's own nation and to keep in check or reduce the power of other nations. The relative power of nations depends, however, as we have also pointed out,[3] upon the quantity and quality of human beings in terms of size and quality of population, size and quality of military establishment, quality of government, and, more particularly, of diplomacy. Viewed as a series of technical tasks into which moral considerations do not enter, international politics would have to consider as one of its legitimate purposes the drastic reduction or even the elimination of the population of a rival nation, of its most prominent military and political leaders, and of its ablest diplomats. And when international politics was considered exclusively as a technique, without moral significance, for the purpose of maintaining and gaining power, such methods were used without moral scruples and as a matter of course.

According to its official records, the Republic of Venice, from 1415 to 1525, planned or attempted about two hundred assassinations for purposes of its foreign policy. Among the prospective victims were two emperors, two kings of France, and three sultans. The documents record virtually no offer of assassination to have been rejected by the Venetian government. From 1456 to 1472, it accepted twenty offers to kill the Sultan Mahomet II, the main antagonist of Venice during that period. In 1514, John of Ragusa offered to poison anybody selected by the government of Venice for an annual salary of fifteen hundred ducats. The Venetian government hired the man "on trial," as we would say today, and asked him to show what he could do with Emperor Maximilian. In

---

[3]See pages 135 ff.

the same period the cardinals brought their own butlers and wine to a papal coronation dinner for fear they might otherwise be poisoned; this custom is reported to have been general in Rome, without the host's taking offense.

Such methods to attain political ends are no longer widely practiced today. Yet the political motives for employing them exist today as they did when practices of this kind actually prevailed. It is not a matter of indifference for the nations engaged in the competition for power whether or not their competitor can avail itself of the services of outstanding military and political leaders. Thus they may hope that an outstanding leader or governing group will be compelled to give up the reins of power, either through a political upheaval or through infirmity and death. We know now that during the Second World War speculations as to how long Hitler and Mussolini would stay alive, or at least in power, formed an important part of the power calculations of the antifascist alliance, and that the news of President Roosevelt's death revived Hitler's hopes of victory. During the Cold War one factor in American policy toward the Soviet Union had been the expectation that the Soviet regime might disintegrate from within because of the inability of its rulers to keep themselves in power. The technical difficulties of engineering such removals from power by violent means are not greater today than they were in previous periods of history. Such removals are still as desirable and feasible as they always were. What has changed is the influence of civilization, which makes some desirable and feasible policies morally reprehensible and, hence, normally impossible of execution.

The existence and effectiveness of moral restraints became manifest in the reactions to the assassination plots engendered by the Central Intelligence Agency (CIA) of the United States. What the predominant segment of American public opinion objected to was not the lack of success of those attempts but their violation of moral restraints. That such attempts were made at all points to a weakening of moral restraint in a small number of public officials operating in secret. That such moral transgressions met with overwhelming disapproval on moral grounds testifies to the continued validity of such moral norms.

Moral limitations of the same kind protect in times of peace the lives not only of outstanding individuals but also of large groups, even of whole nations whose destruction would be both politically desirable and feasible. In the problem of Germany, as seen both by the Germans and by the rest of the world, modern history provides a striking illustration of the influence of ethics upon international politics. The fundamental fact of international politics from the German point of view has been from Bismarck to Hitler the "encirclement" of Germany by powerful nations in the East and in the West. Bismarck, however ruthless and immoral his particular moves on the chessboard of international politics may have been, rarely deviated from the basic rules of the game which had prevailed in the society of Christian princes of the eighteenth century. It was a fraudulent and treacherous game, but there were a few things no member of that aristocratic society would stoop to do. Thus, confronted with the proximity of Russia and France as a condition of Germany's political existence,

Bismarck accepted the inevitability of the fact and tried to turn it to Germany's advantage by maintaining close relations with Russia and by isolating France.

Hitler, on the other hand, did not recognize the social framework within whose limitations international politics had operated from the end of the Thirty Years' War virtually to his own ascent to power. He was free of the moral scruples that had compelled Bismarck to accept the existence of France and Russia as the inescapable fact upon which to build a German foreign policy. Hitler undertook to change that fact by physically destroying Germany's eastern and western neighbors. Considered as a mere problem of political technique devoid of ethical significance, Hitler's solution was much more thorough and politically expedient than Bismarck's, for it promised to solve the problem of Germany's international position once and for all as far as the eastern and western neighbors of Germany were concerned. Furthermore, in itself Hitler's solution proved to be as feasible as it would have been in Bismarck's time. It might have succeeded had it not been for certain political and military errors that carried Hitler and his policies to destruction and that the political genius of Bismarck might well have avoided.

The German problem, as it presents itself to the non-German world, and especially to the nations threatened with German hegemony, was formulated with brutal frankness by the French statesman Clemenceau when he declared on the occasion of the First World War that there were twenty million Germans too many. This statement points to the inescapable fact, which has confronted Europe and the world since the Franco-German War of 1870, that Germany is by virtue of size and quality of population the most powerful nation of Europe. To reconcile this fact with the security of the other European nations and of the rest of the world is the task of political reconstruction which faced the world after the First World War and which confronted it again after the Second. That, since Clemenceau, the German problem has always been posed in terms that take the existence of "twenty million Germans too many" for granted reveals the same moral limitations on the pursuit of power which we found in Bismarck's foreign policy and which we did not find in Hitler's. For there are two ways of dealing with a problem of international politics such as the German.

One is the method by which the Romans irrevocably solved the Carthaginian problem. It is the method of solving a technical political problem by the appropriate means without regard for any transcendent moral considerations. Since, from the point of view of the power aspirations of Rome, there were too many Carthaginians, Cato would end his every speech by proclaiming: *"Ceterum censeo Carthaginem esse delendam"* ("As for the rest, I am of the opinion that Carthage must be destroyed"). With its destruction the Carthaginian problem, as seen by Rome, was solved forever. No threat to Rome's security and ambition was ever again to rise from the desolate place that once was Carthage. Similarly, if the Germans had been successful in their over-all plans and if their firing-squads and extermination camps could have finished their tasks, the "nightmare of coalitions" would have been forever banished from the minds of German statesmen.

A foreign policy that does not permit mass extermination as a means to its end does not impose this limitation upon itself because of considerations of political expediency. On the contrary, expediency would counsel such a thorough and effective operation. The limitation derives from an absolute moral principle, which must be obeyed regardless of considerations of national advantage. A foreign policy of this kind, therefore, actually sacrifices the national interest where its consistent pursuit would necessitate the violation of a moral principle, such as the prohibition of mass killings in times of peace. This point cannot be too strongly made; for frequently the opinion is advanced that this respect for human life is the outgrowth of "the obligation not to inflict *unnecessary* death or suffering on other human beings, i.e., death or suffering not necessary for the attainment of some higher purpose which is held, rightly or wrongly, to justify a derogation from the general obligation."[4] On the contrary, the fact of the matter is that nations recognize a moral obligation to refrain from the infliction of death and suffering under certain conditions despite the possibility of justifying such conduct in the light of a "higher purpose," such as the national interest.

The fundamental conflict between these two conceptions of international politics, one operating within a framework of morality, the other outside it, is graphically illustrated by an episode Sir Winston Churchill reports in his memoirs. At the Teheran Conference, Stalin raised the issue of the punishment to be inflicted upon the Germans after the war.

> The German General Staff, he said, must be liquidated. The whole force of Hitler's mighty armies depended upon about fifty thousand officers and technicians. If these were rounded up and shot at the end of the war, German military strength would be extirpated. On this I thought it right to say: "The British Parliament and public will never tolerate mass executions. Even if in war passion they allowed them to begin, they would turn violently against those responsible after the first butchery had taken place. The Soviets must be under no delusion on this point."
>
> Stalin however, perhaps only in mischief, pursued the subject. "Fifty thousand," he said, "must be shot." I was deeply angered. "I would rather," I said, "be taken out into the garden here and now and be shot myself than sully my own and my country's honour by such infamy."[5]

Protection of Human Life in War

Similar moral limitations are placed upon international policies in times of war. They concern civilians and combatants unable or unwilling to fight. From the beginning of history through the better part of the Middle Ages, belligerents were held to be free, according to ethics as well as law, to kill all enemies whether or not they were members of the armed forces, or else to treat them

---

[4]E. H. Carr., *The Twenty Years' Crisis, 1919–1939* (London: Macmillan and Company, 1939), p. 196.

[5]Winston S. Churchill, *The Second World War*, Vol. V, *Closing the Ring* (Boston: Houghton Mifflin Co., 1951), pp. 373–4. (Reprinted by permission of the publisher.)

in any way they saw fit. Men, women, and children were often put to the sword or sold into slavery by the victor without any adverse moral reactions taking place. In Chapter IV of Book III of *On the Law of War and Peace,* under the heading "On the Right of Killing Enemies in a Public War and on Other Violence against the Person," Hugo Grotius presents an impressive catalogue of acts of violence committed in ancient history against enemy persons without discrimination. Grotius himself, writing in the third decade of the seventeenth century, still regarded most of them as justified in law and ethics, provided the war was waged for a just cause.[6]

This absence of moral restraints upon killing in war resulted from the nature of war itself. In those times war was considered a contest between all the inhabitants of the territories of the belligerent states. The enemy to be fought was the total number of individuals owing allegiance to a certain lord or living within a certain territory rather than the armed forces of the legal abstraction called a state in the modern sense. Thus every individual citizen of the enemy state became an enemy of every individual citizen of the other side.

Since the end of the Thirty Years' War, the conception has become prevalent that war is not a contest between whole populations, but only between the armies of the belligerent states. In consequence, the distinction between combatants and noncombatants has become one of the fundamental legal and moral principles governing the actions of belligerents. War is considered to be a contest between the armed forces of the belligerent states, and, since the civilian populations do not participate actively in the armed contest, they are not to be made its object. Consequently, it is considered to be a moral and legal duty not to attack, wound, or kill noncombatant civilians purposely. Injuries and death suffered by them as incidents of military operations, such as the bombardment of a town or a battle taking place in an inhabited area, are regretted as sometimes unavoidable concomitants of war. However, to avoid them to the utmost is again considered a moral and legal duty. The Hague Conventions with respect to the Laws and Customs of War on Land of 1899 and 1907, and the Geneva Convention of 1949, gave express and virtually universal legal sanction to that principle.

A corresponding development has taken place with regard to members of the armed forces unwilling or unable to fight. It follows from the conception of war prevailing in antiquity and in the better part of the Middle Ages that no exception to the moral and legal right to kill all enemies could be made for certain categories of disabled combatants. Thus Grotius could still state as the prevailing moral and legal conviction of his time: "The right to inflict injury extends even over captives, and without limitation of time. . . . The right to inflict injury extends even over those who wish to surrender, but whose surrender is not accepted."[7]

Yet, as the logical outgrowth of the conception of war as a contest between

---

[6]See especially § III.
[7]Ibid., § X, XI.

armed forces, the idea developed that only those who are actually able and willing to participate actively in warfare ought to be the object of deliberate armed action. Those who were no longer engaged in actual warfare because of sickness, wounds, or because they had been made prisoners or were willing to be made prisoners ought not to be harmed. This tendency toward the humanization of warfare started in the sixteenth century and culminated in the great multilateral treaties of the nineteenth and early twentieth centuries. Practically all civilized nations have adhered to these treaties. Between 1581 and 1864, 291 international agreements were concluded for the purpose of protecting the lives of the wounded and sick. The Geneva Convention of 1864, superseded by those of 1906, 1929, and 1949, translated into concrete and detailed legal obligations the moral convictions of the age as to the treatment to be accorded to the wounded, the sick, and the medical persons in charge of them. The International Red Cross is both the symbol and the outstanding institutional realization of those moral convictions.

As concerns prisoners of war, their lot was still miserable even in the eighteenth century, although they were as a rule no longer killed, but were treated as criminals and used as objects of exploitation by being released only for ransom. Article 24 of the Treaty of Friendship concluded in 1785 between the United States and Prussia for the first time clearly indicated a change in the moral convictions on that matter. It prohibited the confinement of prisoners of war in convict prisons as well as the use of irons and stipulated their treatment as military personnel. The Hague Conventions of 1899 and 1907, as well as the Geneva Conventions of 1929 and 1949, laid down a detailed system of legal rules intended to assure humane treatment of prisoners of war.

From the same humanitarian concern for the life and sufferings of human beings exposed to the destructiveness of war emanate all the international treaties concluded since the mid-nineteenth century for the purpose of humanizing warfare. They prohibit the use of certain weapons, limit the use of others, define the rights and duties of neutrals—in short, they try to infuse into warfare a spirit of decency and of respect for the common humanity of all its prospective victims and to restrict violence to the minimum compatible with the goal of war; that is, breaking the enemy's will to resist. The Declaration of Paris of 1856 limited maritime warfare. The Declaration of St. Petersburg of 1868 prohibited the use of lightweight projectiles charged with explosives or inflammable substances. The Hague Declaration of 1899 prohibited the use of expanding (dum-dum) bullets. A number of international conventions prohibited gas, chemical, and bacteriological warfare. The Hague Conventions of 1899 and 1907 codified the laws of war on land and sea and the rights and duties of neutrals. The London Protocol of 1936 limited the use of submarines against merchant vessels. And, in our times, attempts are being made to limit nuclear warfare. All these efforts bear witness to the virtually universal growth of a moral reluctance to use unlimited violence as an instrument of foreign policy.

There may be legal arguments against the validity or effectiveness of these international treaties, derived from the wholesale disregard or violations of their prohibitions. Yet this is no argument against the existence of a moral conscience that feels ill at ease in the presence of violence, or at least certain kinds of violence, on the international scene. The existence of such a conscience is attested to by the attempts to bring the practice of states into harmony with moral principles through international agreements. It reveals itself also in the general justifications and excuses defending alleged violations of these agreements in moral terms. Most nations subscribe to legal agreements of this kind and try to live up to them, at least in a certain measure. Therefore, the protestations of innocence or of moral justification with which accusations in such matters are uniformly met are more than mere ideologies. They are the indirect recognition of certain moral limitations, which nations at times completely disregard and frequently violate. Finally, the moral conscience of large groups within a warring nation may revolt against undeniable and flagrant violations of moral and legal limitations upon the conduct of war. Such groups may demonstrate against the war and refuse to support it, thereby testifying to the existence of a moral conscience aware of moral limitations.

Moral Condemnation of War

Finally, since the turn of the century, the attitude toward war itself has reflected an ever-increasing awareness on the part of most statesmen that certain moral limitations restrict the use of war as an instrument of foreign policy. Statesmen have decried the ravages of war and have since the beginning of history justified their own participation in them in terms of self-defense or religious duty. The avoidance of war itself—that is, of any war—has become an aim of statecraft only since the turn of the century. The two Hague Peace Conferences of 1899 and 1907, the League of Nations of 1919, the Briand-Kellogg Pact of 1928 outlawing aggressive war, and the United Nations in our day all have the avoidance of war itself as their ultimate objective.

At the foundation of these and other legal instruments and organizations, of which Part Eight of this book will treat in detail, there is the conviction that war, and especially modern war, is not only a terrible thing to be avoided for reasons of expediency, but also an evil thing to be shunned on moral grounds. The student of the different collections of diplomatic documents concerning the origins of the First World War is struck by the hesitancy on the part of almost all responsible statesmen, with the exception perhaps of those of Vienna and St. Petersburg, to take steps that might irrevocably lead to war. This hesitancy and the almost general dismay among the statesmen when war finally proved to be inevitable contrasts sharply with the deliberate care with which, as late as the nineteenth century, wars were planned and incidents fabricated for the purpose of making war inevitable and placing the blame for starting it on the other side.

In the years preceding the Second World War the policies of the Western powers were animated, to their great political and military disadvantage, by the desire to avoid war at any price. This desire overrode all other considerations of national policy. Similarly, the anxiety of all the great powers without exception to limit the Korean War to the Korean peninsula and thus prevent it from developing into a third world war, and the self-restraint practiced by all of them during the many international crises that have arisen since the end of the Second World War, are striking illustrations of a fundamental change in the attitude toward war. It is especially in the refusal to consider seriously the possibility of preventive war, regardless of its expediency in view of the national interest, that the moral condemnation of war as such has manifested itself in recent times in the Western world. When war comes, it must come as a natural catastrophe or as the evil deed of another nation, not as a foreseen and planned culmination of one's own foreign policy. Only thus might the moral scruples, rising from the violated moral norm that there ought to be no war at all, be stilled, if they can be stilled at all.

International Morality and Total War

Thus, in contrast to antiquity and the better part of the Middle Ages, the modern age places moral limitations upon the conduct of foreign affairs in so far as they might affect the lives of individuals or groups of individuals. However, certain important factors in the present condition of mankind point toward a definite weakening of those moral limitations. Let us remember that the absence of moral limitations with regard to the destruction of life was concomitant with the total character of warfare in which whole populations faced each other as personal enemies. Let us remember, too, that the gradual limitation of killing in war, and its subjection to certain conditions, coincided with the gradual development of limited war in which only armies faced each other as active opponents. With war taking on in recent times, to an ever-greater degree and in different respects, a total character, the moral limitations upon killing are observed to an ever-lessening degree. Indeed, their very existence in the consciences of political and military leaders as well as of the common people becomes ever more precarious and is threatened with extinction.

War in our time has become total in four different respects: (1) with regard to the fraction of the population engaged in activities essential for the conduct of the war, (2) with regard to the fraction of the population affected by the conduct of the war, (3) with respect to the fraction of the population completely identified in its convictions and emotions with the conduct of the war, and (4) with respect to the objective of the war.

Mass armies supported by the productive effort of the majority of the civilian population have replaced the relatively small armies of previous centuries, which consumed only a small portion of the national product. The success of the civilian population in keeping the armed forces supplied may be as important for the outcome of the war as the military effort itself. Therefore, the defeat of the civilian population (the breaking of its ability and will to produce) may be as important as the defeat of the armed forces (the breaking of their ability and will to resist). Thus the character of modern war, drawing its weapons from a vast industrial machine, blurs the distinction between soldier and civilian. The worker, the engineer, the scientist are not innocent bystanders cheering on the armed forces from the sidelines. They are as intrinsic and indispensable a part of the military organization as are the soldiers, sailors, and airmen. Thus a modern nation at war must seek to disrupt and destroy the productive processes of its enemy, and the modern technology of war provides the means for the realization of that aim. The importance of civilian production for modern war and the interest in injuring enemy production were already generally recognized in the First World War. Then, however, the technological means of affecting the civilian productive processes directly were but in their infancy. The belligerents had to resort to indirect means, such as blockades and submarine warfare. They attempted to interfere directly with civilian life through air attacks and long-range bombardment only sporadically and with indifferent results.

The Second World War has made the latter methods of direct interference the most effective instrument for the destruction of a nation's productive capacity and ability to resist. The interest in the mass destruction of civilian life and property coincided with the ability to carry such mass destruction through, and this combination has been too strong for the moral convictions of the modern world to resist. Voicing the moral convictions of the first decades of the century, Secretary of State Cordell Hull declared on June 11, 1938, with reference to the bombardment of Canton by Japan, that the administration disapproved of the sale of aircraft and aircraft armaments to countries that had engaged in the bombing of civilian populations. In his speech of December 2, 1939, President Roosevelt declared a similar moral embargo against the Soviet Union in view of its military operations against Finnish civilians. Only a few years later all belligerents engaged in practices of this kind on a scale dwarfing those which American statesmen had condemned on moral grounds. Warsaw and Rotterdam, London and Coventry, Cologne and Nuremberg, Hiroshima and Nagasaki are stepping stones, not only in the development of the modern technology of war, but also in the development of the modern morality of warfare. The Indochina War for all practical purposes obliterated the distinction between combatants and the civilian population.

The national interest in the destruction of enemy productivity and his will to resist, as created by the character of modern war, and the opportunity the modern technology of warfare presents of satisfying that interest, have had a deteriorating effect upon international morality. This deterioration is further accentuated by the emotional involvement of the great masses of the warring populations in modern war. As the religious wars of the sixteenth and seventeenth centuries were followed by the dynastic wars of the later seventeenth and eighteenth centuries, and as the latter yielded to the national wars of the nineteenth and the early twentieth centuries, so war in our time tends to revert to the religious type by becoming ideological in character. The citizen of a modern warring nation, in contrast to his ancestors of the eighteenth and nineteenth centuries, does not fight for the glory of his prince or the unity and greatness of his nation, but he "crusades" for an "ideal," a set of "principles," a "way of life," for which he claims a monopoly of truth and virtue. In consequence, he fights to the death or to "unconditional surrender" all those who adhere to another, a false and evil, "ideal" and "way of life." Since it is this "ideal" and "way of life" that he fights in whatever persons they manifest themselves, the distinctions between fighting and disabled soldiers, combatants and civilians—if they are not eliminated altogether—are subordinated to the one distinction that really matters: the distinction between the representatives of the right and the wrong philosophy and way of life. The moral duty to spare the wounded, the sick, the surrendering and unarmed enemy, and to respect him as a human being who was an enemy only by virtue of being found on the other side of the fence, is superseded by the moral duty to punish and to wipe off the face of the earth the professors and practitioners of evil.

These tendencies destructive of moral limitations have been powerfully strengthened by the impersonal nature of modern war. Throughout history until the First World War, soldiers met face to face in combat. These deadly encounters were not devoid of a human element: men looked each other in the eye, trying to kill and avoid being killed. These encounters had room for human emotions, virtues, and vices, demonstrated and perceived by men. After Achilles has fatally wounded Lykaos, Homer has him bend over the doomed adversary and say "Die, friend."

Modern war is in large measure push-button war, anonymously fought by people who have never seen their enemy alive or dead and who will never know whom they have killed. Nor will the victims ever see the face of the enemy. The only connection between the enemies is the machinery with which they try to kill each other. Such a technologically dehumanized war is bound to be morally dehumanized as well. For the operator of the machinery, the experience of target practice is hardly different from that of a real attack, and an attack upon a military installation is for him indistinguishable from that upon a civilian target. As a pilot who flew bombing missions in Vietnam put it: "It's like being trained to fix TV's, like being a technician." Thus the technology of modern war drastically weakens, if it does not destroy altogether, the ability to make those factual distinctions without which it is impossible to discriminate between moral and immoral acts of war.

Under the impact of this fundamental change in the conception of warfare, not only were the moral limitations upon killing in war, to which we have referred above, extensively violated during the Second World War, but belligerents have tended to justify on moral grounds the refusal to take prisoners, the killing of prisoners, and the indiscriminate killing of members of the armed forces and of civilians, and thus to assuage their moral scruples, if not to shake them off altogether. Thus, while the moral limitations upon killing in times of peace remain intact, the moral limitations upon killing in war have proved to be largely ineffective. What is by and large more important for the purposes of this discussion, they have shown a tendency under the impact of a fundamentally altered conception of war to weaken and disappear altogether as rules of conduct.

Nearly a century ago, in an era of general optimism, a great scholar clearly foresaw the possibility of this development and analyzed its elements. John Westlake, Whewell Professor of International Law at the University of Cambridge, wrote in 1894:

> It is almost a truism to say that the mitigation of war must depend on the parties to it feeling that they belong to a larger whole than their respective tribes or states, a whole in which the enemy too is comprised, so that duties arising out of that larger citizenship are owed even to him. This sentiment has never been wholly wanting in Europe since the commencement of historical times, but there have been great variations in the nature and extent of the whole to which the wider attachment was felt. . . . In our own time there is a cosmopolitan sentiment, a belief in a commonwealth of mankind similar to that of the Stoics, but stronger because the soil has been prepared by Christianity, and by the mutual respect which great states tolerably equal in power and similar in civilization cannot help feeling for one another. . . . There have been periods during which the level has fallen, and one such period it belongs to our subject to notice. The wars of religion which followed the Reformation were among the most terrible in which the beast in man ever broke loose, and yet they occurred in an age of comparative enlightenment. Zeal for a cause, however worthy the cause may be, is one of the strongest and most dangerous irritants to which human passion is subject; and the tie of Protestant to Protestant and of Catholic to Catholic, cutting across the state tie instead of embracing it unweakened in a more comprehensive one, enfeebled the ordinary checks to passion when they were most wanted. Such a degradation of war would tend to recur if socialism attained to the consistency and power of a militant creed, and met the present idea of the state on the field of battle. It is possible that we might then see in war a license equal to that which anarchism shows us in peace![8]

UNIVERSAL MORALITY VS. NATIONALISTIC UNIVERSALISM

The deterioration of international morality which has occurred in recent years with regard to the protection of life is only a special instance of a general and, for the purposes of this discussion, much more far-reaching dissolution of an ethical system that in the past imposed its restraints upon the day-by-day operations of foreign policy but does so no longer. Two factors have brought about this dissolution: the substitution of democratic for aristocratic responsibility in foreign affairs and the substitution of nationalistic standards of action for universal ones.

Personal Ethics of the Aristocratic International

In the seventeenth and eighteenth centuries, and to a lessening degree up to the First World War, international morality was the concern of a personal

---

[8]*Chapters on the Principles of International Law* (Cambridge: Cambridge University Press, 1894), pp. 267 ff.

sovereign—that is, a certain individual prince and his successors—and of a relatively small, cohesive, and homogeneous group of aristocratic rulers. The prince and the aristocratic rulers of a particular nation were in constant, intimate contact with the princes and aristocratic rulers of other nations. They were joined together by family ties, a common language (French), common cultural values, a common style of life, and common moral convictions about what a gentleman was and was not allowed to do in his relations with another gentleman, whether of his own or of a foreign nation. The princes competing for power considered themselves to be competitors in a game whose rules were accepted by all the other competitors. The members of their diplomatic and military services looked upon themselves as employees who served their employer either by virtue of the accident of birth or because of the promise of pay, influence, and glory.

In 1862, Bismarck, who had been posted in Russia, declined an offer from the Czar to serve in the Russian diplomatic service. What is important and significant for the purposes of our discussion is not that Bismarck declined the offer—many such offers had certainly been declined before and perhaps even a few have been since—but that he did so "courteously," and that even his report, written more than thirty years after the event, showed no trace of moral indignation. Only a century ago the offer to an ambassador, who had just been appointed prime minister, to transfer his loyalties from one country to another was considered by the recipient as a sort of business proposition that did not at all insinuate the violation of moral standards.

Let us imagine that a similar offer had been made in our time by a Russian Prime Minister to the American Ambassador or by the American President to any diplomat accredited in Washington, and visualize the private embarrassment of the individual concerned and the public indignation following the incident, and we have the measure of the profundity of the change that has transformed the ethics of foreign policy in recent times. Today such an offer would be regarded as an invitation to treason; that is, the violation of the most fundamental of all moral obligations in international affairs—loyalty to one's own country. When it was made and even when it was reported, shortly before the close of the nineteenth century, it was a proposition to be accepted or rejected on its merits without any lack of moral propriety attaching to it.

The moral standards of conduct with which the international aristocracy complied were of necessity of a supranational character. They applied not to all Prussians, Austrians, or Frenchmen, but to all men who by virtue of their birth and education were able to comprehend them and to act in accordance with them. It was in the concept and the rules of natural law that this cosmopolitan society found the source of its precepts of morality. The individual members of this society, therefore, felt themselves to be personally responsible for compliance with those moral rules of conduct; for it was to them as rational human beings, as individuals, that this moral code was addressed. When it was suggested to Louis XV that he counterfeit the bills of the Bank of England, the King rejected such a proposition, which "could be considered here only with all the indignation and all the horror which it deserves." When a similar proposition was made in 1792 with respect to the French currency in order to save Louis XVI, the Austrian Emperor Francis II declared that "such an infamous project is not to be accepted."

This sense of a highly personal moral obligation to be met by those in charge of foreign policy with regard to their colleagues in other countries explains the emphasis with which the writers of the seventeenth and eighteenth centuries counseled the monarch to safeguard his "honor" and his "reputation" as his most precious possessions. Any action Louis XV undertook on the international scene was his personal act in which his personal sense of moral obligation revealed itself and in which, therefore, his personal honor was engaged. A violation of his moral obligations, as they were recognized by his fellow monarchs for themselves, would set in motion not only his conscience but also the spontaneous reactions of the supranational aristocratic society, which would make him pay for the violation of its mores with a loss of prestige; that is, a loss of power.

Destruction of International Morality

When in the course of the nineteenth century democratic selection and responsibility of government officials replaced government by the aristocracy, the structure of international society and, with it, of international morality underwent a fundamental change. Until virtually the end of the nineteenth century, aristocratic rulers were responsible for the conduct of foreign affairs in most countries. In the new age their place has been taken by officials elected or appointed regardless of class distinctions. These officials are legally and morally responsible for their official acts, not to a monarch (that is, a specific individual), but to a collectivity (that is, a parliamentary majority, or the people as a whole). An important shift in public opinion may easily call for a change in the personnel conducting foreign policy. They will be replaced by another group of individuals taken from whatever group of the population prevails at the moment.

Government officials are no longer exclusively recruited from the aristocratic groups, but from virtually the whole population within which members of the "establishment" occupy a privileged position. This has, of course, been the tradition in the United States, yet it is unprecedented in such countries as Great Britain and the Soviet Union. Mr. Bevin, former General Secretary of the Transport and General Workers Union, became in 1945 British Secretary of State for Foreign Affairs. Mr. Molotov, a former professional revolutionary, was for many years responsible for Russian foreign policy.

In such countries as Great Britain, France, or Italy, where the government needs the support of a majority of parliament for its continuation in office, any change in the parliamentary majority necessitates a change in the composition of the government. Even in such a country as the United States, where not Congress, but only general elections can put an administration into office or remove it, the turnover of the policymakers in the State Department can be considerable. Within eighteen months, from July 1945 to January 1947, the United States had three secretaries of state. Of all the policymaking officials of the State Department—that is, the undersecretary and assistant secretaries—who held office in October 1945, none was still in office two years later. In the Reagan administration, a tendency which began in the Carter administration resulted in political appointments being made across the board in the Department of State down to the level of deputy assistant secretary positions. The fluctuation of the policymakers in international affairs and their responsibility to an amorphous collective entity has far-reaching consequences for the effectiveness, even for the very existence, of an international moral order.

This transformation within the individual nations changed international morality as a system of moral restraints from a reality into a mere figure of speech. When we say that George III of England was subject to certain moral restraints in his dealings with Louis XVI of France or Catherine the Great of Russia, we are referring to something real, something that can be identified with the conscience and the actions of certain specific individuals. When we say that the British Commonwealth of Nations, or even Great Britain alone, has moral obligations toward the United States or France, we are making use of a fiction. By virtue of this fiction international law deals with nations as though they were individual persons, but nothing in the sphere of moral obligations corresponds to this legal concept. Whatever the conscience of the monarch as the constitutional head of the British Commonwealth and of Great Britain demands of the conduct of the foreign affairs of Great Britain and of the Commonwealth is irrelevant for the actual conduct of those affairs; for the monarch is not responsible for those affairs and has no actual influence upon them. What of the Prime Ministers and the Secretaries of State for Foreign Affairs of Great Britain and of the Dominions? They are but members of the cabinet, which as a collective body determines foreign policy, as any other policy, by majority decision. The cabinet as a whole is politically responsible to the majority party, whose political preferences it is supposed to translate into political action. It is legally responsible to Parliament, of which it is, constitutionally speaking, only a committee. Parliament, however, is responsible to the electorate, from which it has received the mandate to govern and from which its individual members hope to receive another mandate at the next general election.

The individual members of the electorate, finally, may have no moral convictions of a supranational character at all which determine their actions on election day and in between, or, if they have such convictions, they will be most heterogeneous in content. In other words, there will be those who act according to the moral maxim: "Right or wrong—my country." There will be those who apply to their own actions with regard to international affairs as well as to the actions of the government the standard of Christian ethics. There will be those who apply the standard of the United Nations or of world government or of humanitarian ethics. The fluctuating members of the policymaking group or of the permanent bureaucracy of the Foreign Office may or may not reflect these and similar divisions of opinion. In any case, the reference to a moral rule of conduct requires an individual conscience from which it emanates, and there is no individual conscience from which what we call the international morality of Great Britain or of any other nation could emanate.

An individual statesman may follow the dictates of his own conscience in his conduct of foreign policy. If he does, it is to him as an individual that these moral convictions are attributed, not to the nation to which he belongs and in whose name he may even actually speak. Thus, when Lord Morley and John Burns felt that the participation of Great Britain in the First World War was incompatible with their moral convictions, they resigned from the British cabinet. This was their personal act and those were their personal convictions. When at the same moment the German Chancellor admitted as head of the German government the illegality and immorality of the violation of Belgium's neutrality, justified only by a state of necessity, he spoke for himself only. The voice of his conscience could not be and was not identified with the conscience of the collectivity called Germany. The moral principles that guided Laval as Minister of Foreign Affairs and Prime Minister of the pro-German Vichy regime during the Second World War were his, not those of France, and nobody pretended that the latter was the case.

Moral rules operate within the consciences of individual men. Government by clearly identifiable men, who can be held personally accountable for their acts, is therefore the precondition for the existence of an effective system of international ethics. Where responsibility for government is widely distributed among a great number of individuals with different conceptions as to what is morally required in international affairs, or with no such conceptions at all, international morality as an effective system of restraints upon international policy becomes impossible. It is for this reason that Dean Roscoe Pound could say as far back as 1923: "It might be maintained plausibly, that a moral . . . order among states, was nearer attainment in the middle of the eighteenth century than it is today."[9]

Destruction of International Society

While the democratic selection and responsibility of government officials destroyed international morality as an effective system of restraints, nationalism destroyed the international society itself within which that morality had operated. The French Revolution of 1789 marks the beginning of the new epoch of

---

[9]"Philosophical Theory and International Law," *Bibliotheca Visseriana*, Vo. I (Leyden, 1923), p. 74.

history which witnesses the gradual decline of the cosmopolitan aristocratic society and of the restraining influence of its morality upon foreign policy. Professor G. P. Gooch wrote:

> While patriotism is as old as the instinct of human association, nationalism as an articulate creed issued from the volcanic fires of the French Revolution. The tide of battle turned at Valmy; and on the evening after the skirmish Goethe . . . replied to a request for his opinion in the historic words, "From to-day begins a new era, and you will be able to say that you were present at its birth."[10]

Victory of Nationalism over Internationalism

The vitality of a moral system is put to its crucial test when its control of the consciences and actions of men is challenged by another system of morality. Thus the relative strength of the ethics of humility and self-denial of the Sermon on the Mount and of the ethics of self-advancement and power of modern Western society is determined by the extent to which either system of morality is able to mold the actions or at least the consciences of men in accordance with its precepts. Every human being, in so far as he is responsive to ethical appeals at all, is from time to time confronted with such a conflict of conscience, which tests the relative strength of conflicting moral commands. A similar test must determine the respective strength, with regard to the conduct of foreign policy, of supranational ethics and the ethics of nationalism. To supranational ethics, composed of Christian, cosmopolitan, and humanitarian elements, the diplomatic language of the time pays its tribute, and many individual writers postulate it. But the ethics of nationalism have been on the ascendancy throughout the world for the last century and a half.

It is indeed true that, even before that ascendancy of the ethics of nationalism, national ethics, as formulated, for instance, in the philosophy of reason of state of the seventeenth and eighteenth centuries, has in most conflict situations proved itself to be superior to universal moral rules of conduct. This is obvious from a consideration of the most elemental and also the most important conflict situation of this kind, the one between the universal ethical precept, "Thou shalt not kill," and the command of a particular national ethics, "Thou shalt kill under certain conditions the enemies of thy country." The individual to whom these two moral rules of conduct are addressed is confronted with a conflict between his allegiance to humanity as a whole, manifesting itself in the respect for human life as such, irrespective of nationality or any other particular characteristic, and his loyalty to a particular nation whose interests he is called upon to promote at the price of the lives of the members of another nation. In the words of Pascal:

> Why do you kill me? What! do you not live on the other side of the water? If you lived on this side, my friend, I should be an assassin, and it would be unjust to slay

---

[10]*Studies in Diplomacy and Statecraft* (London, New York, Toronto: Longmans, Green and Company, 1942), pp. 300, 301.

you in this manner. But since you live on the other side, I am a hero, and it is just.
. . . Three degrees of latitude reverse all jurisprudence; a meridian decides the
truth. . . . A strange justice that is bounded by a river! Truth on this side of the
Pyrenées, error on the other side.[11]

Most individuals today and during all of modern history have resolved this
conflict between supranational and national ethics in favor of loyalty to the
nation. In this respect, however, three factors distinguish the present age from
previous ones.

First, there is the enormously increased ability of the nation state to exert
moral compulsion upon its members. This ability is the result partly of the
almost divine prestige the nation enjoys in our time, partly of the control over
the instruments molding public opinion which economic and technological
developments have put at the disposal of the state.

Second, there is the extent to which loyalty to the nation requires the
individual to disregard universal moral rules of conduct. The modern technology of war has given the individual opportunities for mass destruction unknown
to previous ages. Today a nation may ask one single individual to destroy the
lives of hundreds of thousands of people by firing one missile with a nuclear
warhead. The compliance with a demand of such enormous consequences
demonstrates the weakness of supranational ethics more impressively than do
the limited violations of universal moral standards of conduct which were
committed in pre-atomic times.

Finally, there is today, in consequence of the two other factors, much less
chance for the individual to be loyal to supranational ethics when they are in
conflict with the moral demands of the nation. The individual, faced with the
enormity of the deeds he is asked to commit in the name of the nation, and with
the overwhelming weight of moral pressure which the nation exerts upon him,
would require extraordinary moral strength to resist those demands. The magnitude of the infractions of universal ethics committed on behalf of the nation,
and of the moral compulsion exerted in favor of them, affects the qualitative
relationship of the two systems of ethics. It puts in bold relief the desperate
weakness of universal ethics in its conflict with the morality of the nation and
decides the conflict in favor of the nation before it has really started.

Transformation of Nationalism

It is at this point that the impotence of universal ethics becomes an important
factor in bringing about a significant and far-reaching change in the relations
between supranational and national systems of morality. It is one of the factors
that lead to the identification of both. The individual comes to realize that the
flouting of universal standards of morality is not the handiwork of a few wicked
men, but the inevitable outgrowth of the conditions under which nations exist

---

[11]*Pensées*, translated by W. F. Trotter, Modern Library (New York: Random House, Inc.,
1941), Section V. (Reprinted by permission of the publisher.)

and pursue their aims. He experiences in his own conscience the feebleness of universal standards and the preponderance of national morality as forces motivating the actions of men on the international scene, and his conscience does not cease to be ill at ease.

On the one hand, the continuous discomfort of a perpetually uneasy conscience is too much for him to bear; on the other, he is too strongly attached to the concept of universal ethics to give it up altogether. Two possibilities to resolve that conflict are open to him. He can sacrifice the moral demands of his nation for the sake of universal ethics. It is indeed the starkness of the contemporary conflict that has driven a minority to make that sacrifice by refusing to support certain foreign policies of their respective nations in the name of a higher universal morality. The majority, however, in order to overcome that conflict identifies the morality of a particular nation with the commands of supranational ethics. It pours, as it were, the contents of a particular national morality into the now almost empty bottle of universal ethics. So each nation comes to know again a universal morality—that is, its own national morality—which is taken to be the one that all the other nations ought to accept as their own. The universality of an ethics to which all nations adhere is replaced by the particularity of national ethics which claims the right to, and aspires toward, universal recognition. There are then potentially as many ethical codes claiming universality as there are politically dynamic nations.

Nations no longer oppose each other, as they did from the Treaty of Westphalia to the Napoleonic Wars, and then again from the end of the latter to the First World War, within a framework of shared beliefs and common values, which imposes effective limitations upon the ends and means of their struggle for power. They oppose each other now as the standard-bearers of ethical systems, each of them of national origin and each of them claiming and aspiring to provide a supranational framework of moral standards which all the other nations ought to accept and within which their foreign policies ought to operate. The moral code of one nation flings the challenge of its universal claim with Messianic fervor into the face of another, which reciprocates in kind. Compromise, the virtue of the old diplomacy, becomes the treason of the new; for the mutual accommodation of conflicting claims, possible or legitimate within a common framework of moral standards, amounts to surrender when the moral standards themselves are the stakes of the conflict. Thus the stage is set for a contest among nations whose stakes are no longer their relative positions within a political and moral system accepted by all, but the ability to impose upon the other contestants a new universal political and moral system recreated in the image of the victorious nation's political and moral convictions.

The first inkling of this development from one genuinely universal system to a multiplicity of particular moral systems claiming, and competing for, universality can be detected in the contest between Napoleon and the nations allied against him. On both sides the contest was fought in the name of particular principles claiming universal validity: here the principles of the French Revolution, there the principle of legitimacy. But with the defeat of Napoleon and the failure of the Holy Alliance to uphold its principles in competition with the rising movement of nationalism, this attempt at erecting a particular code of ethics into a universal one came to an end and thus remained a mere historic interlude.

The present period of history in which generally and, as it seems, permanently universal moral rules of conduct are replaced by particular ones claiming universality was ushered in by Woodrow Wilson's war "to make the world safe for democracy." It is not by accident and it has deep significance that those who shared Wilson's philosophy thought of that war as a "crusade" for democracy. The First World War, as seen from Wilson's perspective, has indeed this in common with the Crusades of the Middle Ages—it was waged for the purpose of making one moral system, held by one group, prevail in the rest of the world. In the words of Robert C. Binkley:

> The World War not only brought to the top statesmen who were philosophers; it also brought the professional philosophers down from their intellectual pedestals. In every country these men used their high talents to give to the "issues" of the war a cosmic significance. They proved that the iniquities of the adversary had been present all along as implications of a national philosophy and culture, and that the triumph of their own party was necessary in the ethical scheme of the universe. Immediately upon the outbreak of hostilities, Bergson discovered that the war was a conflict between "life" and "matter," with the Entente Powers ranged on the side of life and the Central Powers defending matter. Scheler proclaimed that English philosophy and character were alike manifestations of cant; Santayana wrote of "egotism in German philosophy"; and the gentle Josiah Royce, himself deeply in the debt of Hegel, reached the conclusion that "Germany is the willful and deliberate enemy of the human race; it is open to any man to be a pro-German who shares this enmity." The philosophers were making a Great Schism out of a mere political conflict. Then, as if to make a permanent record of the prostitution of the philosophic art, the victorious governments issued to each soldier in their armies a bronze medal with the inscription, "Great War for Civilization."[12]

A few months after the democratic crusade had gotten underway, in October 1917, the foundations were laid in Russia for another moral and political structure that on its part, while accepted only by a fraction of humanity, was claimed to provide the common roof under which all humankind would eventually live together in justice and in peace. While, in the twenties, this latter claim was supported by insufficient power and, hence, was little more than a theoretical postulate, democratic universalism retired from the scene of active politics and isolationism took its place. It was only in the theoretical challenge that the priests of the new Marxian universalism flung in the face of the democratic world and in the moral, political, and economic ostracism with which the latter met the challenge that the conflict between the two universalism made itself felt at that time in the field of international politics.

---

[12]*Selected Papers of Robert C. Binkley*, edited by Max H. Fish (Cambridge: Harvard University Press, 1948), p. 328.

In the thirties the philosophy of National Socialism, grown in the soil of a particular nation, was proclaimed as the new moral code that would replace the vicious creed of bolshevism and the decadent morality of democracy and would impose itself upon mankind. The Second World War, viewed in the light of our present discussion, tested in the form of an armed conflict the validity of this claim to universality, and National Socialism lost the test. Yet, in the minds of many on the side of the United Nations, the principles of the Atlantic Charter and of the Yalta Agreement made the Second World War also a contest for universal democracy, and democracy, too, lost the test. Since the end of the Second World War the two remaining moral and political systems claiming universal validity, democracy and Communism, have entered into active competition for the dominion of the world, and that is the situation in which we find ourselves today.

It would be the most dangerous of illusions to overlook or even to belittle the depth of the difference that exists between this situation and the condition of the modern state system from the end of the religious wars to the entrance of the United States into the First World War. One needs only to pick at random any conflict which occurred in that latter period, with the exception of the Napoleonic Wars, and compare it with the conflicts which have torn the world apart in the last three decades in order to realize the importance of that difference.

Let us compare with the international issues of our time the issues that brought France and the Hapsburgs into almost continual conflict from the beginning of the sixteenth to the middle of the eighteenth century, or that pitted Great Britain and Prussia against France in the eighteenth century. These issues were territorial aggrandizement and dynastic competition. What was then at stake was an increase or decrease of glory, wealth, and power. Neither the Austrian nor the British nor the French nor the Prussian "way of life"—that is, their system of beliefs and ethical convictions—was at stake. This is exactly what is at stake today. In the seventeenth and eighteenth centuries, none of the contestants on the international scene aspired to impose its own particular system of ethics, provided it had one, upon the others. The very possibility of such an aspiration never occurred to them, since they were aware only of one universal moral code to which they all gave unquestioning allegiance.

That common "system of arts, and laws, and manners," "the same level of politeness and cultivation," and the "sense of honour and justice," which Gibbon had detected in "the general manners of the times," which for Fénelon, Rousseau, and Vattel were a lived and living reality and whose political results Arnold Toynbee has noted,[13] have today in the main become a historic reminiscence, lingering on in learned treaties, utopian tracts, and diplomatic documents, but no longer capable of moving men to action. Only shreds and fragments survive of this system of supranational ethics which exerts its restraining

---

[13]Arnold Toynbee, *A Study of History* (London: Oxford University Press, 1939).

influence upon international politics, as we have seen, only in isolated instances, such as killing in peacetime and preventive war. As for the influence of that system of supranational ethics upon the conscience of the actors on the international scene, it is rather like the feeble rays, barely visible above the horizon of consciousness, of a sun that has already set. Since the First World War, with ever-increasing intensity and generality, each of the contestants in the international arena claims in its "way of life" to possess the whole truth of morality and politics, which the others may reject only at their peril. With fierce exclusiveness, all contestants equate their national conceptions of morality with what all mankind must and will ultimately accept and live by. In this, the ethics of international politics reverts to the politics and morality of tribalism, of the Crusades, and of the religious wars.[14]

However much the content and objectives of today's ethics of nationalistic universalism may differ from those of primitive tribes or of the Thirty Years' War, they do not differ in the function they fulfill for international politics, and in the moral climate they create. The morality of the particular group, far from limiting the struggle for power on the international scene, gives the struggle a ferocity and intensity not known to other ages. For the claim to universality which inspires the moral code of one particular group is incompatible with the identical claim of another group; the world has room for only one, and the other must yield or be destroyed. Thus, carrying their idols before them, the nationalistic masses of our time meet in the international arena, each group convinced that it executes the mandate of history, that it does for humanity what it seems to do for itself, and that it fulfills a sacred mission ordained by Providence, however defined. Little do they know that they meet under an empty sky from which the gods have departed.

Human Rights and International Morality

We have seen that the conduct of foreign policy is not an enterprise devoid of moral significance; it is always subject to judgment, by the actor, those acted upon, and those who merely witness. To conclude from the omnipresence of the

---

[14]To what extent the profession of universalistic principles of morality can go hand in hand with utter depravity in action is clearly demonstrated in the case of Timur, the Mongol would-be conqueror of the world, who in the fourteenth century conquered and destroyed southern Asia and Asia Minor. After having killed hundreds of thousands of people—on December 12, 1398, he massacred one hundred thousand Hindu prisoners before Delhi—for the glory of God and of Mohammedanism, he said to a representative of conquered Aleppo: "I am not a man of blood; and God is my witness that in all my wars I have never been the aggressor, and that my enemies have always been the authors of their own calamity."

Gibbon, who reports this statement, adds: "During this peaceful conversation the streets of Aleppo streamed with blood, and re-echoed with the cries of mothers and children, with the shrieks of violated virgins. The rich plunder that was abandoned to his soldiers might stimulate their avarice; but their cruelty was enforced by the peremptory command of producing an adequate number of heads, which, according to his custom, were curiously piled in columns and pyramids. . . ." *The Decline and Fall of the Roman Empire* (Modern Library Edition), Vol. II, p. 1243.

moral element in foreign policy that a country has a mission to apply its own moral principles to the rest of humanity or to certain segments of humanity is something quite different. For there is an enormous gap between the judgment we apply to ourselves and our own actions, and the universal application of our own standards of action to others. Take so elemental and obvious a principle of action as respect for human life and the refusal to take human life except under the most extraordinary, exculpating circumstances. There are obviously civilizations and even groups within western civilization that have a much less strict conception of the sanctity of human life, that give much less heed to spending the lives of others than we would under similar circumstances.

So there exists of necessity a certain relativism in the relation between moral principles and foreign policy; one cannot overlook this if one wants to do justice to the principles of morality in international politics. The relativism is twofold. It is a relativism in time: certain principles are applicable in one period of history and not applicable in another. It is also a relativism in terms of culture—of contemporaneous culture—in that certain principles are obeyed by some nations, some political civilizations, but are not obeyed by others.

In recent years the relationship of foreign policy and international morality has often been discussed under the rubric of human rights. The problem at the heart of this issue is the extent to which it is both morally just and intellectually tenable to apply liberal democratic principles to states that, for a number of reasons, are impervious to them. It is obvious that the attempt to impose so-called human rights upon others or to punish them for not observing human rights assumes that human rights are of universal validity—that, in other words, all nations or all peoples living in different nations would respect human rights if they knew they existed and that in any event they are as inalienable for all men as the Declaration of Independence declares them to be for Americans.

It is unnecessary to enter into a discussion of the theological or strictly philosophic nature of human rights here. It suffices to say that whatever one's conception of their theological or philosophical nature, human rights as perceived by individuals are inevitably filtered through historic and social circumstances leading to different results in different times and under different circumstances. One need only look at the unique character of the American polity and at the very special, nowhere-else-to-be-found characteristics of human rights protection within the confines of the United States. There is, after all, an almost complete lack of respect for human rights in many nations, or even in most nations: consider that only a relatively few countries in Africa possess a pluralist political system; all others are authoritarian in character. Such reflection helps us realize how daring—or how ignorant if you will, which can also be daring—it is to try to impose upon the rest of the world our own respect for human rights, or in particular to punish other nations for not showing respect for those rights. What we see here is an abstract principle we happen to hold dear, which we happen to a considerable extent to have put into practice, presented to the rest of mankind not for imitation but for mandatory acceptance.

It is quite wrong to assume that this has long been the American tradition. It has not been the American tradition at all. John Quincy Adams argued that it was not for the United States to impose its own principles of government upon the rest of mankind, but, rather, to attract the rest of mankind through the example of the United States. Indeed this has been the principle the United States has usually followed. The American Revolution, to quote Thomas Paine, "was not made for America alone, but for mankind"; nevertheless, American policy has been that those universal principles the United States had put into practice were not to be exported by fire and sword, but presented to the rest of the world through successful example. This has been the great difference between the early conception of America and its relations to the rest of the world, on the one hand, and what might be called the Wilsonian conception, on the other.

Woodrow Wilson wanted to make the world safe for democracy: he wanted to transform the world through the will of the United States. The Founding Fathers wanted to present an example of what man can do to the nations of the world, calling upon them to go and do likewise. So there is a fundamental difference, both philosophic and political, between contemporary agitation in favor of human rights as a universal principle and the longer-lived American tradition in this matter.

Two other objections can be made to the Wilsonian conception. One is the impossibility of enforcing the universal application of human rights. We can tell the Soviet Union—and we should from time to time—that its treatment of minorities is incompatible with our conception of human rights. But once we have said this we will find that there is very little more we can do to change matters. History has shown that the Soviet Union may yield under certain conditions to private pressure. There are examples where private pressure—for example, the shaming of high officials in the Soviet Union—has had an obvious result. But it is inconceivable on general grounds that such pressure should be effective when exerted publicly. More particularly, in view of the nature of the Soviet Union's government—which uses every sign of external pressure to justify repression at home—American agitation for human rights has no chance of being effective. So there is a considerable confusion in our theory and practice of human rights, especially *vis-à-vis* other nations.

There is a second weakness of the Wilsonian approach. The United States is a great power with manifold interests throughout the world—of which human rights is only one—and not the most important one at that. Thus the United States cannot consistently follow the path of the defense of human rights without maneuvering itself into a Quixotic position. This is obvious in our different treatment of South Korea, China, and the Soviet Union. The United States dares to criticize and affront the Soviet Union because relations, in spite of periods of détente, are not particularly friendly. The United States has an interest in continuing the normalization of relations with mainland China, and for this reason seeks not to hurt Chinese feelings: little was heard in the Carter or Reagan administrations about China's human rights record. South Korea is an ally of the United States; it has achieved considerable military importance for American policymakers, so American policy will do nothing to harm its relations with that state.

In other words, the defense of human rights cannot be consistently applied in foreign policy because it can and must come in conflict with other interests that may be more important in a particular instance. To say that the defense of human rights must be woven into the fabric of American foreign policy is merely to conceal the necessary inconsistencies of any such effort.

Thus there are two basic hindrances to a foreign policy integrally committed to the defense of human rights. On the one hand, consistency in such defense is impossible, since it is not the prime business of a state, interacting as it must with other states, to defend human rights. On the other hand, it is not feasible to pursue human rights without taking into consideration other aspects of relations with other nations, which may be more important than those connected with human rights.

A further aspect of the role of human rights in foreign policy concerns the notion of responsibility for the human rights violations of others. The Cambodian genocide carried out by the Khmer Rouge in the late 1970s and early 1980s raised this question in a particularly acute fashion. The chain of events that culminated in the destruction of Cambodian society started with the American extension of the Vietnam War into Cambodia through the massive bombing of Cambodian territory. It was the policy of the Cambodian ruler, Prince Sihanouk, to keep Cambodia out of the armed conflict between the United States and North Vietnam. It was United States policy to involve Cambodia in active military operations in order to facilitate victory in the Vietnam War. There existed a causal nexus between American policy with regard to Cambodia and the catastrophe which befell that country. In other words, if the United States had not made Cambodia an active participant in the Vietnam War, Cambodia would, in all likelihood, have been spared catastrophe. This is not to say that the United States bore a direct moral responsibility for what happened in Cambodia but rather to demonstrate the continuous moral responsibility statesmen bear for the unforeseen and unforeseeable consequences of their actions. It would be quite another matter to assume that because of this causal nexus the United States had a moral obligation to prevent what happened in Cambodia or to alleviate the sufferings of the Cambodian people. Rather, as we have seen, moral as well as legal obligations are subject to the qualification which is expressed in the principle of Roman law that nobody is obligated beyond his capacity (*ultra vires nemo obligatur*). Thus, even if the United States were held morally responsible for what happened in Cambodia, it could not be held responsible to carry out any particular policy implementing that moral obligation. Even if the United States resolved to act, it would be unable to do so without disproportionate risks and losses.

The "Hawk" faction held that Cambodia would never have suffered such misery and destruction had the United States maintained its resolve to "stay the course" and win the war in Southeast Asia. But aside from the impossibility of foreseeing all the consequences of the loss of the Vietnam War, to forestall all possible consequences of the loss by winning it at whatever price would have violated the basic principle of foreign and military policy: that the risks taken and losses incurred in a particular action must be proportionate to the chances for the success of that action.

In this consideration of the relations of foreign policy and morality we are in the presence not of a peculiar, extraordinary situation but of a particular manifestation of the general human condition. We are all moral beings to some degree, simply because we are human. We all try to a greater or lesser extent to realize the moral principles with which we identify. Again and again we find ourselves faced with contradictions and difficulties. Perhaps the best we can do is to act upon what Abraham Lincoln proposed as the basis of political morality.

He warned against the exaggeration of moral virtue we claim for ourselves, and outlined the limits within which man can act morally and at the same time have a chance for success. Lincoln's statement was made during the Civil War and was a reply to a petition by a delegation of Presbyterian ministers who asked him to emancipate all slaves forthwith:

> In great contests each party claims to act in accordance with the will of God. Both *may* be, and one *must* be wrong. God can not be *for,* and *against* the same thing at the same time. . . .
>
> I am approached with the most opposite opinions and advice, and that by religious men, who are equally certain that they represent the Divine will. I am sure that either the one or the other class is mistaken in that belief, and perhaps in some respects both. I hope it will not be irreverent for me to say that if it is probable that God would reveal his will to others, on a point so connected with my duty, it might be supposed that he would reveal it directly to me; for, unless I am more deceived in myself than I often am, it is my earnest desire to know the will of Providence in this matter. *And if I can learn what it is I will do it!* These are not, however, the days of miracles, and I suppose it will be granted that I am not to expect a direct revelation. I must study the plain physical facts of the case, ascertain what is possible and learn what appears to be wise and right.[15]

---

[15] *The Collected Works of Abraham Lincoln,* edited by Roy P. Basler (New Brunswick, N.J.: Rutgers University Press), Vol. V, pp. 403 f., 419 f.

PART SIX

Limitations of National Power: International Law

16

The Main Problems of International Law

THE GENERAL NATURE OF INTERNATIONAL LAW

The same warning against extremes with which we started the discussion of international morality and of world public opinion must apply also to the discussion of international law. An increasing number of writers express the opinion that there is no such thing as international law. A diminishing number of observers hold that international law, if duly codified and extended to regulate the political relations of states, could becomes through its own inner force, if not a substitute for, at least a restraining influence upon, the struggle for power on the international scene. As J. L. Brierly put it:

> Too many people assume, generally without having given any serious thought to its character or its history, that international law is and always has been a sham. Others seem to think that it is a force with inherent strength of its own, and that if only we had the sense to set the lawyers to work to draft a comprehensive code for the nations, we might live together in peace and all would be well with the world. Whether the cynic or the sciolist is the less helpful is hard to say, but both of them make the same mistake. They both assume that international law is a subject on which anyone can form his opinions intuitively, without taking the trouble, as one has to do with other subjects, to inquire into the relevant facts.[1]

The modern system of international law is the result of the great political transformation that marked the transition from the Middle Ages to the modern period of history. It can be summed up as the transformation of the feudal system into the territorial state. The main characteristic of the latter, distinguishing it from its predecessor, was the assumption by the government of the supreme authority within the territory of the state. The monarch no longer

---

[1]J. L. Brierly, *The Outlook for International Law* (Oxford: The Clarendon Press, 1944), pp. 1, 2. (Reprinted by permission of the publisher.)

shared authority with the feudal lords within the state territory of which he had been in a large measure the nominal rather than the actual head. Nor did he share it with the Church, which throughout the Middle Ages had claimed in certain respects supreme authority within Christendom. When this transformation had been consummated in the sixteenth century, the political world consisted of a number of states that within their respective territories were, legally speaking, completely independent of each other, recognizing no secular authority above themselves. In one word, they were sovereign.

If there was to be at least a certain measure of peace and order in the relations among such entities endowed with supreme authority within their territories and having continuous contact with each other, it was inevitable that certain rules of law should govern these relations. That is to say, there must be certain rules of conduct defined beforehand, whose violation would normally call forth certain sanctions, also defined beforehand as to their nature and the conditions and mode of their application. States must, for instance, know where the frontiers of their territory are on land and on sea. They must know under what conditions they can acquire a valid title to territory either owned by no one at all (as in the case of discovery), or by another state (as in the case of cession or annexation). They must know what authority they have over citizens of other states living on their territory and over their citizens living abroad. When a merchant vessel flying the flag of State A enters a port of State B, what are the rights of State B with regard to that vessel? And what if the vessel is a warship? What are the rights of diplomatic representatives accredited to a foreign government, and what are the rights of the head of the state on foreign soil? What is a state allowed and obligated to do in times of war with respect to combatants, civilians, prisoners, neutrals, on sea and on land? Under what conditions is a treaty between two or more states binding, and under what conditions does it lose its binding force? And if a treaty or another rule of international law is claimed to have been violated, who has the right to ascertain the violation and who has the right to take what kind of enforcement measures and under what conditions? These and many other issues of a similar nature rise of necessity from the relations among sovereign states, and if anarchy and violence are not to be the order of the day, legal rules must determine the mutual rights and obligations in such situations.

A core of rules of international law laying down the rights and duties of states in relation to each other developed in the fifteenth and sixteenth centuries. These rules of international law were securely established in 1648, when the Treaty of Westphalia brought the religious wars to an end and made the territorial state the cornerstone of the modern state system. Hugo Grotius's *On the Law of War and Peace,* published in 1625, is the classic codification of that early system of international law. On its foundation, the eighteenth and, more particularly, the nineteenth and twentieth centuries built an imposing edifice, consisting of thousands of treaties, hundreds of decisions of international tribunals, and innumerable decisions of domestic courts. These treaties and decisions regulate, often in minute detail, the relations between nations arising from the multiplicity and variety of international contacts, which are the result of modern communications, international exchange of goods and services, and the great number of international organizations in which most nations have co-operated for the furtherance of their common interests. Such organizations include the International Red Cross, the International Court of Justice, Specialized Agencies of the United Nations, such as the International Labor Organization (ILO), the World Health Organization (WHO), the United Nations Economic, Scientific and Cultural Organization (UNESCO), the Universal Postal Union, the International Monetary Fund, and many others.

It is also worth mentioning, in view of a widespread misconception in this respect, that during the four hundred years of its existence international law has in most instances been scrupulously observed. When one of its rules was violated, it was, however, not always enforced and, when action to enforce it was actually taken, it was not always effective. Yet to deny that international law exists at all as a system of binding legal rules flies in the face of all the evidence. This misconception as to the existence of international law is at least in part the result of the disproportionate attention that public opinion has paid in recent times to a small fraction of international law, while neglecting the main body of it. Public opinion has been concerned mainly with such spectacular instruments of international law as the Briand-Kellogg Pact, the Covenant of the League of Nations, and the Charter of the United Nations. These instruments are indeed of doubtful efficacy (that is, they are frequently violated), and sometimes even of doubtful validity (that is, they are often not enforced in case of violation). They are, however, not typical of the traditional rules of international law concerning, for instance, the limits of territorial jurisdiction, the rights of vessels in foreign waters, and the status of diplomatic representatives.

To recognize that international law exists, however, is not tantamount to asserting that it is as effective a legal system as the national legal systems are and that, more particularly, it is effective in regulating and restraining the struggle for power on the international scene. International law is a primitive type of law resembling the kind of law that prevails in certain preliterate societies, such as the Australian aborigines and the Yurok of northern California.[2] It is a primitive type of law primarily because it is almost completely decentralized law.

The decentralized nature of international law is the inevitable result of the decentralized structure of international society. Domestic law can be imposed by the group that holds the monopoly of organized force; that is, the officials of the state. It is an essential characteristic of international society, composed of sovereign states, which by definition are the supreme legal authorities within their respective territories, that no such central law-giving and law-enforcing authority can exist there. International law owes its existence and operation to

---

[2]See A. R. Radcliffe-Brown, "Primitive Law," *Encyclopedia of the Social Sciences,* Vol. IX, pp. 203–4; for literature, see p. 262.

two factors, both decentralized in character: identical or complementary interests of individual states and the distribution of power among them. Where there is neither community of interest nor balance of power, there is no international law. Whereas domestic law may originate in, and be enforced by, the arbitrary will of the agencies of the state, international law is overwhelmingly the result of objective social forces.

That the balance of power is such a social force was recognized by one of the foremost modern teachers of international law. L. Oppenheim calls the balance of power "an indispensable condition of the very existence of International Law."[3] "Six morals," he states,

> can be said to be deduced from the history of the development of the Law of Nations:
> 1) The first and principal moral is that a Law of Nations can exist only if there be an equilibrium, a balance of power, between the members of the Family of Nations. If the Powers cannot keep one another in check, no rules of law will have any force, since an overpowerful State will naturally try to act according to discretion and disobey the law. As there is not and never can be a central political authority above the Sovereign States that could enforce the rules of the Law of Nations, a balance of power must prevent any member of the Family of Nations from becoming omnipotent.[4]

The balance of power operates as a decentralizing force only in the form of a general deterrent against violations of international law and in the exceptional cases when a violation of international law calls for a law-enforcement action. On the other hand, identical and complementary interests as decentralizing agents are continuously at work; they are the very lifeblood of international law. They exert their decentralizing influence upon three basic functions that any legal system must fulfill: legislation, adjudication, and enforcement.

THE LEGISLATIVE FUNCTION IN INTERNATIONAL LAW

Its Decentralized Character

In our contemporary domestic societies, the most important rules of law are created by legislators and courts; that is to say, by centralized agencies that create law either for all members of the national community, as do Congress and the Supreme Court of the United States, or for certain regional groups, as do state legislatures, city councils, and regional and local courts. In the interna-

---

[3]L. Oppenheim, *International Law*, 2nd ed. (London: Longmans, Green and Company, 1912) Vol, 1, p. 193. It is interesting to note that this and the following reference to the balance of power were eliminated by the editor from the later editions.

[4]Ibid., p. 80.

tional sphere there are but two forces creating law: necessity and mutual consent. International law contains a small number of rules concerning, for instance, the limits of national sovereignty, the interpretation of its own rules, and the like, which are binding upon individual states regardless of their consent; for without these rules there could be no legal order at all or at least no legal order regulating a multiple-state system. Aside from this small number of rules of what one might call common or necessary international law, the main bulk of rules of international law owe their existence to the mutual consent of the individual subjects of international law themselves—the individual nations. Each nation is bound only by those rules of international law to which it has consented.

The main instrumentality by which international law is created is the international treaty. An international treaty creates international law only for those nations which are a party to it. A treaty concluded among the American nations binds only them and no other nation. A treaty concluded between the Soviet Union and Iran has usually no legal effect for any third nation. Hence, the conditions under which the legislative function operates in the field of international law are similar to what would exist on the domestic scene if the legislative function within the United States were to be performed by the individual citizens themselves in the form of private contracts, instead of by legislatures and courts operating under the rule of *stare decisis;* that is, bound by precedents. Instead of a municipal law regulating sewage disposal or zoning in a certain municipality, these issues would be taken care of by a number of private agreements concluded among the residents of the different streets. The municipality, then, would have as many regulations as there are streets. The inevitable result of such a system of legislation would be, on the one hand, lack of legal regulation altogether whenever the unanimous consent of all those concerned was not forthcoming. On the other hand, there would be uncertainty about what the law actually was in a particular case, and there would be contradictions among the different sets of rules regulating the same situations with regard to different individuals. That is the situation which exists in international law, mitigated only by the relatively small number—about 160 sovereign nations—of subjects that might create international law by concluding treaties among themselves.

From this decentralized character of the legislative function two consequences follow for international law. On the other hand, many matters bearing upon international relations, such as immigration and many aspects of economic policies, are not regulated by international law. The interests of the different nations in these matters are so divergent that they are unable to agree upon legal rules. On the other hand, in those matters with regard to which agreement was possible, insecurity and confusion frequently reign. If one wants to know which rules of international law the United States considers to be binding upon itself, one must consult all the treaties ever concluded by the United States, after determining which are still in force at the moment of investigation. Then one must examine the decisions of international tribunals in cases to which the United States has been a party, and the decisions of American courts applying rules of international law. Finally, one must study the diplomatic documents in which the representatives of the United States in international negotiations have acknowledged certain rules of international law as binding upon the conduct of the United States in international affairs. The sum total of all these rules is what Charles C. Hyde has called *International Law Chiefly as Interpreted and Applied by the United States.*[5]

By a similarly tedious process, the rules of international law recognized by other nations have also been compiled. In order to know the sum total of the rules of international law binding in a particular period of history throughout the world, it would be theoretically necessary to make similar compilations with regard to all nations of the world. If such a task were actually undertaken, its results would show considerable divergencies with regard to general principles as well as particular rules. World-wide compilations in limited fields of international law illustrate this lack of agreement. Many writers refer to continental law in contrast to Anglo-American international law, to the international law of the Americas, and to the Russian conception of international law.[6]

To take as a specific example the breadth of the maritime belt—that is, the question as to how far into the sea the territorial jurisdiction of the adjacent state extends—the rules of international law recognized by different nations in this field differ sharply. While a number of nations adhere to the principle of the three-mile limit, Finland and Norway—over the objections of other states—claim a breadth of four miles for the maritime belt. Italy, Spain, Yugoslavia, India, Mexico, Iceland, Indonesia, the Soviet Union, Egypt, France, and Poland, for another instance, claim twelve miles. Albania claims fifteen, Ecuador two hundred miles. Other nations, such as Germany, Belgium and Great Britain, claim only three miles; but Britain claims a so-called contiguous zone beyond the territorial waters proper. Other nations, while rejecting the claim of these nations to a contiguous zone, recognize that under certain circumstances a nation has the right to extend its jurisdiction beyond the three-mile limit and to submit the merchant vessels of foreign nations to some measure of control. Part II, Section 2, Article 3 of the Law of the Sea Treaty of 1982 calls for a twelve-mile limit by states ratifying the treaty unless otherwise provided, but the question remains whether states with differing jurisdictional limits will ratify this provision and whether those who ratify it will at some point renounce such provisions.

This lack of precision, resulting from the confusing multitude of unilateral claims, permeates to a greater or lesser degree most branches of the law of nations, by virtue of the decentralized character of the legislative function.

---

[5] 2 vols. (Boston: Little, Brown, and Company, 1946).

[6] On these different conceptions of international law and the literature concerning them, cf. L. Oppenheim and H. Lauterpacht, *International Law*, 8th ed. (London: Longmans, Green and Company, 1955), Vol. I, pp. 48 ff.

Governments, however, are always anxious to shake off the restraining influence that international law might have upon their foreign policies, to use international law instead for the promotion of their national interests, and to evade legal obligations that might be harmful to them. They have used the imprecision of international law as a ready-made tool for furthering their ends. They have done so by advancing unsupported legal claims and by misinterpreting the meaning of generally recognized rules of international law. Thus the lack of precision inherent in the decentralized nature of international law is breeding ever more lack of precision, and the debilitating vice that was present at its birth continues to sap its strength.

Only those branches of international law, generally of a technical or humanitarian nature, which have been codified in general agreements, escape in a certain measure this weakness.[7] For a codification of international law is in its legal effects the equivalent of a genuine piece of international legislation in that it binds all or virtually all subjects of international law. It is only the requirement of the consent of all those who are to be bound by it—in contrast to the majority rule required by the democratic process of legislation—that sets codification of international law apart from genuine legislation.

Interpretation and Binding Force

The need to substitute the unanimous consent of all subjects of international law for genuine international legislation gives rise to yet another type of complication peculiar to international law. This is the problem of ascertaining the meaning of the provisions of international treaties, of the rights they confer, of the obligations they impose. In the domestic sphere, this problem is solved by the legislative bodies themselves, which generally try to make the legal rules they enact as precise as possible; by the courts, which are continually engaged in the task of interpreting the laws by applying them to concrete cases; and by the executive and administrative agencies, which issue orders performing the same function. International legal documents, such as the Charter of the United Nations, as well as many others of a purely technical character, are vague and ambiguous, not by accident or, like the American Constitution, for particular and exceptional reasons, but regularly and of necessity. For such documents, in order to obtain the approval of all subjects of the law, necessary for their acquiring legal force, must take cognizance of all the divergent national interests that will or might be affected by the rules to be enacted. In order to find a common basis on which all those different national interests can meet in harmony, rules of international law embodied in general treaties must often be vague and ambiguous, allowing all the signatories to read the recognition of their own national interests into the legal

---

[7]Examples are the codifications in the field of communications, such as the General Postal Convention of 1874, the Convention on International Civil Aviation of 1944, and many others, as well as the general international agreements referred to on pages 228 ff., which seek the humanization of warfare.

text agreed upon. If this should happen in the domestic sphere, as it has actually happened to a considerable extent with regard to the Constitution of the United States, some authoritative decision—whether of the Supreme Court as in the United States, or of Parliament as in Great Britain—would give concrete meaning to the vague and ambiguous provisions of the law.

In the international field, it is the subjects of the law themselves that not only legislate for themselves but are also the supreme authority for interpreting and giving concrete meaning to their own legislative enactments. They will naturally interpret and apply the provisions of international law in the light of their particular and divergent conceptions of the national interest. They will naturally marshal them to the support of their particular international policies and will thus destroy whatever restraining power, applicable to all, these rules of international law, despite their vagueness and ambiguity, might have possessed. Mr. Jean Ray well analyzed this situation when he said with regard to the Covenant of the League of Nations: "But the danger is obvious. If the members of the League as individuals have ultimate authority in matters of interpretation, divergent interpretations, all equally authoritative, are going to perpetuate themselves; and when an ambiguous text is being invoked in a conflict between two nations, there will be an impasse."[8] This has happened time and again in the history of the League of Nations, and the history of the United Nations has given us a number of instances of a similar nature.[9]

There is, finally, another difficulty that contributes to the weakness of international law from the legislative point of view, and that is the uncertainty as to whether a certain international treaty, duly signed and ratified, contains actually, in whole or in part, valid rules of international law binding upon the signatories. Such a question could hardly arise with regard to a piece of domestic legislation in the United States. For a federal law has either been passed by Congress and signed by the President in conformity with the constitutional requirements or it has not, and it has either been invalidated by the Supreme Court or it has not. There may be uncertainty as to its constitutionality or interpretation until the Supreme Court has spoken with final authority, but not as to its very existence as a valid rule of law. It is this uncertainty as to the existence of certain fundamental rules, duly signed and ratified by virtually all members of the international community, that shakes the very foundation of international law.

---

[8]*Commentaire du Pacte de la Société des Nations* (Paris: Sirey, 1930), p. 44.

[9]In order to remedy this situation, the General Assembly of the United Nations passed in its Second Session, on November 14, 1947, a resolution declaring it to be of paramount importance that the interpretation of the Charter and of the constitutions of the specialized agencies be based on recognized principles of international law. The resolution called specifically upon the agencies of the United Nations to seek advisory opinions from the International Court of Justice on points of law which have arisen in the course of their activities (*United Nations Documents*, A/459). Upon the request of the General Assembly, the Court has rendered a number of advisory opinions concerning the interpretation of the Charter and other international treaties.

Let us consider the most spectacular example of this type of international law, the Briand-Kellogg Pact of 1928, in which virtually all nations agreed "to renounce war as an instrument of national policy in their relations with one another." Has this agreement been from the beginning a rule of international law binding upon all signatories, or is it merely a statement of moral principle without legal effect? Has the international law of the Nuremberg trials, according to which the preparation for, and the waging of, aggressive war is an international crime, applied the already existing law of the Briand-Kellogg Pact, or has it created international law that did not exist before?[10] And has it done the one or the other only for the specific cases decided in Nuremberg, or for any similar cases that might occur in the future? Different schools of thought have answered these questions differently, and this is not the place to settle the controversy. What is important to note in the context of this discussion is the weakness of a legal system that is incapable of giving a precise answer to so fundamental a question as to whether it forbids collective acts of violence for certain purposes. Thus there is today no way of stating with any degree of authority whether any nation that went to war after 1929 in pursuance of its national policies has violated a rule of international law and is liable before international law for its violation; or whether only those individuals responsible for preparing and starting the Second World War are liable in this way; or whether all nations and individuals that will prepare for, and wage, aggressive war in the future will thus be liable.

What about the legal validity of the Convention with Respect to the Laws and Customs of War on Land of 1899 and 1907, and its binding force upon its signatories in the Second World War and in a future war? This convention, which was fairly well observed during the First World War and whose violations were then pointed out regularly, was, as we have seen, violated regularly and on a mass scale by all belligerents during the Second World War. Have these violations, unprotested and unpunished, put an end to the binding force of this convention, or has the convention survived the Second World War as a legal instrument that can be invoked, enforced, and made the standard of action in a future war? And what about similar questions with respect to the rules of maritime warfare which were also generally violated in the Second World War with hardly an attempt at enforcement being made? The Axis sank enemy ships indiscriminately and without warning, as did the Allies, and both sides bombed civilians, justifying these violations of the rules of war with military necessity. If rules of international law are consistently violated and the violations are accepted as a matter of course by all subjects of the law—if, therefore, the legal rules are treated by those who ought to enforce them as though they did not exist—the question arises: Do they still exist as binding legal rules? No precise answer can be given to these questions at the moment.

---

[10]Cf. Hans J. Morgenthau, Erich Hula, Moorhouse F. X. Millar, in *America*, Vol. 76, No. 10 (December 7, 1946), pp. 266–8.

International Courts

Since no legal system can be effective in limiting the activities of its subjects without compulsory jurisdiction over their disputes, the two other fundamental problems of adjudication—the organization of the judicial agencies and the effects of their decisions—are of subordinate importance. The establishment of the Permanent Court of International Justice and of its successor, the International Court of Justice, marks an important step, perhaps the most important of all, toward the centralization of functions in the field of international law. Up to the establishment of the Permanent Court in 1920, judicial organization in the international sphere was completely decentralized. That is to say, whenever two states agreed upon the judicial settlement of a specific dispute, they also agreed upon a particular person, such as the Pope, a prince, a famous international lawyer, or a group of persons to function as a tribunal for the decision of this particular case. With the settlement of this dispute, the judicial function of this tribunal was automatically at an end. The judicial settlement of another dispute required the establishment of another tribunal. The Tribunal of Geneva which in 1871 decided the Alabama case illustrates this situation.

The Hague Conventions for the Pacific Settlement of International Disputes in 1899 and 1907 tried to overcome this decentralization of the judicial organization by creating the so-called Permanent Court of Arbitration. The latter consists only of a panel of some 120 judges appointed by the different signatories to the convention. From this panel the parties to a specific dispute can select the members of a tribunal to be constituted for the adjudication of this specific dispute. It might, therefore, well be said that this institution is neither permanent nor a court. The so-called Court does not exist as a body; as such it does not fulfill judicial or any other functions. It is actually nothing more than a list of individuals "of recognized competence in questions of International Law, enjoying the highest moral reputation."[11] It facilitates the selection of judges for one of the special tribunals to be organized for the adjudication of a specific dispute. The so-called Permanent Court of Arbitration has never decided a case; only individual members of the panel have. It perpetuates the decentralization of judicial organization in the international field, while at the same time recognizing in the pretense of its name the need for a centralized judicial authority.

The main stumbling block for the establishment of a really permanent international court was the composition of the court. Nations were as anxious to preserve their freedom of action with respect to the selection of judges for each specific case as they were anxious to preserve their freedom of action with regard to the submission of each specific dispute to adjudication. More particularly, nations were reluctant to allow a dispute to be decided by an international tribunal of which neither one of their nationals nor a representative of their

---

[11]Article 44 of the Convention.

point of view was a member. No permanent international court with jurisdiction over more than a limited number of nations could meet the letter of such a requirement; for the number of nations subject to the jurisdiction of a world court would of necessity exceed the number of judges. The small nations, especially, feared that under these conditions most of them would be permanently deprived of representation in such a court, which might thus easily become an instrument of the great powers.

The Statute of the Permanent Court of International Justice and of its successor has solved this problem. The Court is composed of fifteen members, no two of whom may be nationals of the same state (Article 3). On the other hand, "The electors shall bear in mind . . . that in the body as a whole the representation of the main forms of civilization and of the principal legal systems of the world should be assured" (Article 19). The members of the Court are nominated and elected through a number of ingenious devices designed to insure high professional standards as well as compliance with the requirement of Article 19 of the Statute. The nominations are made by the members of the Permanent Court of Arbitration, organized into national groups, or by national groups appointed by their respective governments (Articles 4, 5, 6). The election is by absolute majority of the votes of the General Assembly and the Security Council of the United Nations, each body voting independently of the other (Articles 8–12). Article 31 of the Statute makes the additional concession of providing for special national judges who may be chosen by parties whose nationality is not represented among the members of the Court.

This Court, a truly centralized judicial agency, fulfills through its very existence two important functions for the international community. On the one hand, the Court, through being established in permanence and regardless of any dispute awaiting adjudication, is always available to nations that want to settle their differences by means of adjudication. Whatever else may stand in the way of a judicial settlement of their disputes, the problems of establishing a tribunal, selecting its members, providing for its procedure and substantive law have been solved for them once and for all by the Statute of the Court. The difficulties to which these problems, to be solved anew for each individual case of adjudication, may have given rise before 1920 no longer stand in the way of effective administration of international justice.

The International Court of Justice, whose members are elected for a period of nine years and may be re-elected, provides for continuity in the performance of its judicial task. This quality is necessarily absent in a tribunal convened for the settlement of a specific dispute and terminating its existence with the rendering of the judgment. A court whose membership is bound to remain approximately identical for many years—the judges being elected for nine-year terms—cannot fail to develop a tradition of its own which it transmits to its successive members and upon the continuance of which the prospective parties can rely. This element of calculability and stability which is thus introduced into the operations of an international tribunal is in sharp contrast to the haphazard proceedings typical of the arbitration courts before the First World War.

The Effect of Judicial Decisions

This stability and calculability are the psychological result of a permanent organization rather than the legal effect of the judicial operations of the Court. Indeed, concerning the legal effect of the judicial decisions of the Court, the Statute pays tribute to the principle of decentralization by providing in Article 59 that "the decision of the Court has no binding force except between the parties and in respect of that particular case." Although the social fact of the continuing operation of the same persons within one organization is conducive to the development of uniformity and of a tradition in the jurisprudence of the Court, the latter is under no legal duty, as the Anglo-American courts are, to follow the rule of *stare decisis* and to justify its decisions in the light of precedent. Nevertheless, because of the social pressure for uniformity discussed above, the jurisprudence of the Court during the first three decades of its existence would hardly have been different if the Court actually had been bound by the rule of *stare decisis.* Nevertheless, the Court was and remains free to disregard its previous decisions should it so choose. Situations may arise where a court bound by the rule of *stare decisis* would hesitate to disregard its previous decisions, while the International Court of Justice might not.

This element of uncertainty within the jurisprudence of the International Court of Justice itself is, however, small in comparison with the one that, by virtue of Article 59 of the Statute, affects the relations between the jurisprudence of the Court and the many and heterogeneous other judicial agencies operating in the international field. The strength of the national systems of adjudication as a means of putting effective restraints upon the actions of the individual citizens derives in large part from the hierarchical nature of that system. Whatever act the individual citizen may perform, a court stands ready to say whether or not the act meets the requirements of the law. When these courts have spoken, a higher court can be appealed to in order to approve or disapprove the decision of the lower court. And, finally, a supreme court will state with ultimate authority the law in the case. Since all these courts operate under the rule of *stare decisis,* their decisions are logically consistent with each other not only within the same court but also within the whole system of courts. The hierarchical character of their relations guarantees the uniformity of the decisions throughout the system.[12] The combina-

---

[12]This is true only ideally; it suffers exceptions in the actual operation of the domestic judicial systems. In the federal judicial system, for example, logical consistency of the decisions of the different federal courts is assured only in so far as the Supreme Court has and takes jurisdiction as the highest court of appeals. Where, either by law or because the Supreme Court refuses to hear an appeal, the several Circuit Courts of Appeals decide similar cases without recourse to a higher tribunal, the legal rules applied by them to similar cases may, and frequently do, differ

tion of hierarchical organization and of the rule of *stare decisis*, then, produces one system of jurisprudence throughout the judicial system, one body of coherent law ever ready to go into action at the request of whoever claims the protection of the law.

Nothing in the international sphere even remotely resembles this situation. The International Court of Justice is the one court that has potentially world-wide jurisdiction. But the multitude of other courts, created by special treaties for particular parties, for special types of disputes, or for specific single cases, have no legal connection at all either with each other or with the International Court of Justice. The International Court of Justice is in no sense a supreme court of the world which may decide, with final authority, appeals from the decisions of other international tribunals. It is but one international court among many others, outstanding through the permanency of its organization, the potential reach of its jurisdiction, and the generally high legal quality of its decisions. Yet in no sense is it hierarchically superimposed upon the other international courts. The decisions of the International Court of Justice may, by virtue of their professional excellence, put their imprint upon the decisions of other international courts. But, since they are not bound by the rule of *stare decisis*, other international courts are no more under the legal obligation to make their decisions consistent with the decisions of the International Court of Justice than they are to make their own decisions consistent with each other. Here again, decentralization is the earmark of the judicial function.

THE ENFORCEMENT OF INTERNATIONAL LAW

Its Decentralized Character

What for the legislative and judicial functions required elaborate proof is clear for all to see in the case of the executive function: its complete and unqualified decentralization. International law does not even provide for agencies and instrumentalities for the purpose of its enforcement apart from the agencies and instrumentalities of the national governments. Brierly describes the situation thus:

> The international system has no central organ for the enforcement of international legal rights as such, and the creation of any such general scheme of sanctions is for the present a very distant prospect. . . . This absence of an executive power means that each state remains free . . . to take such action as it thinks fit to enforce its own rights. This does not mean that international law has no sanction, if that word is used in its proper sense of means for securing the observance of the law; but it is true that the sanctions which it possesses are not systematic or centrally directed,

---

from each other. To this extent, then, there exists within the federal judicial system an exceptional situation that is rather normal in the realm of international adjudication.

and that accordingly they are precarious in their operation. This lack of system is obviously unsatisfactory, particularly to those states which are less able than others to assert their own rights effectively.[13]

In the same sense in which the individual nation is its own legislator and the creator of its own tribunal and of their jurisdiction, it is also its own sheriff and policeman. When individual A violates the rights of individual B within the national community, the law-enforcement agencies of this state will intervene and protect B against A and compel A to give B satisfaction according to the law. Nothing of the kind exists in the international sphere. If State A violates the rights of State B, no enforcement agency will come to the support of B. B has the right to help itself if it can; that is to say, if it is strong enough in comparison with A to meet the infringement of its rights with enforcement actions of its own. Only under very exceptional and narrow conditions, in the forms of self-help and self-defense, does domestic law give the victim of a violation of the law the right to take the law into his own hands and enforce it against the violator. What is a narrowly circumscribed exception in domestic law is the principle of law enforcement in international law. According to this principle, the victim, and nobody but the victim, of a violation of the law has the *right* to enforce the law against the violator. Nobody at all has the *obligation* to enforce it.

There can be no more primitive and no weaker system of law enforcement than this; for it delivers the enforcement of the law to the vicissitudes of the distribution of power between the violator of the law and the victim of the violation. It makes it easy for the strong both to violate the law and to enforce it, and consequently puts the rights of the weak in jeopardy. A great power can violate the rights of a small nation without having to fear effective sanctions on the latter's part. It can afford to proceed against the small nation with measures of enforcement under the pretext of a violation of its rights, regardless of whether the alleged infraction of international law has actually occurred or whether its seriousness justifies the severity of the measures taken.

The small nation must look for the protection of its rights to the assistance of powerful friends; only thus can it hope to oppose with a chance of success an attempt to violate its rights. Whether such assistance will be forthcoming is a matter not of international law but of the national interest as conceived by the individual nations, which must decide whether or not to come to the support of the weak member of the international community. In other words, whether or not an attempt will be made to enforce international law and whether or not the attempt will be successful do not depend primarily upon legal considerations and the disinterested operation of law-enforcing mechanisms. Both attempt and success depend upon political considerations and the actual distribution of power in a particular case. The protection of

---

[13]*The Law of Nations*, pp. 92, 93. (Reprinted by permission of The Clarendon Press, Oxford.)

the rights of a weak nation that is threatened by a strong one is then determined by the balance of power as it operates in that particular situation. Thus the rights of Belgium were safeguarded in 1914 against their violation by Germany, for it so happened that the protection of those rights seemed to be required by the national interests of powerful neighbors. Similarly, when in 1950 South Korea was attacked by North Korea, their concern with the maintenance of the balance of power in the Far East and of territorial stability throughout Asia prompted the United States and some of its allies, such as France and Great Britain, to come to the aid of South Korea. On the other hand, the rights of Colombia, when the United States supported the revolution in 1903 which led to the establishment of the Republic of Panama, and the rights of Finland, when attacked by the Soviet Union in 1939, were violated either with impunity or, as in the case of Finland, without the intervention of effective sanctions. There was no balance of power which could have protected these nations.

It must be pointed out, however, that the actual situation is much less dismal than the foregoing analysis might suggest. The great majority of the rules of international law are generally observed by all nations without actual compulsion, for it is generally in the interest of all nations concerned to honor their obligations under international law. A nation will hesitate to infringe upon the rights of foreign diplomats residing in its capital; for it has an interest, identical with the interests of all other nations, in the universal observance of the rules of international law which extend their protection to its own diplomatic representatives in foreign capitals as well as the foreign diplomats in its own capital. A nation will likewise be reluctant to disregard its obligations under a commercial treaty, since the benefits that it expects from the execution of the treaty by the other contracting parties are complementary to those anticipated by the latter. It may thus stand to lose more than it would gain by not fulfilling its part of the bargain. This is particularly so in the long run, since a nation that has the reputation of reneging on its commercial obligations will find it hard to conclude commercial treaties beneficial to itself.

Most rules of international law formulate in legal terms such identical or complementary interests. It is for this reason that they generally enforce themselves, as it were, and that there is generally no need for a specific enforcement action. In most cases in which such rules of international law are actually violated despite the underlying community of interests, satisfaction is given to the wronged party either voluntarily or in consequence of adjudication. And it is worthy of note that of the thousands of such judicial decisions which have been rendered in the last century and a half, voluntary execution was refused by the losing party in fewer than ten cases.

Thus the great majority of rules of international law are generally unaffected by the weakness of its system of enforcement, for voluntary compliance prevents the problem of enforcement from arising altogether. The problem of enforcement becomes acute, however, in that minority of important and generally spectacular cases, particularly important in the context of our discussion, in which compliance with international law and its enforcement have a direct bearing upon the relative power of the nations concerned. In those cases, as we have seen, considerations of power rather than of law determine compliance and enforcement.

PART SEVEN

International
Politics in the
Contemporary
World

17

The New Moral Force of Nationalistic Universalism

NATIONALISM, OLD AND NEW

We should now be able to answer the question we asked when we pointed to the intellectual and moral tradition of the Western world as the force that through the instrumentality of the balance of power kept the modern state system together from the end of the religious wars to the First World War. What is left of this heritage today? we asked then. What kind of consensus unites the nations of the world in the period following the Second World War?

The answer can only be that the moral limitations upon the struggle for power on the international scene are weaker today than they have been at any time in the history of the modern state system. The one international society of the seventeenth and eighteenth centuries has been replaced by a number of national societies that provide for their members the highest measure of social integration. In consequence, the international morality that in past centuries kept the aspirations for power of the individual nations within certain bounds has, except for certain fragmentary restraints, given way to the morality of individual nations. This morality not only does not recognize any moral obligations above and apart from it, but even claims universal recognition from all the world. World public opinion is but an ideological shadow without even that substance of common valuations and reactions which in other times at least the international aristocracy shared. The main bulk of the rules of international law owes its existence to the sovereignty of the individual nations. To surround that sovereignty with legal safeguards is one of the main tasks of the rules of international law. Far from restraining the aspirations for power of individual nations, they see to it that the power position of individual nations is not adversely affected by whatever legal obligations they take upon themselves in their relations with other nations. What national morality is in the field of ethics, what national public opinion is in the domain of the mores, sovereignty is for international law. Sovereignty refers in legal terms to the nation as the recipient of the individual's ultimate secular loyalties, as the mightiest social force, as the supreme authority giving and enforcing laws for the individual citizen.

The supranational forces, such as universal religions, humanitarianism, cosmopolitanism, and all the other personal ties, institutions, and organizations that bind individuals together across national boundaries, are infinitely weaker today than the forces that unite peoples within a particular national boundary and separate them from the rest of humanity. This weakening of the supranational forces, which must be strong in order to impose effective restraints upon the foreign policies of nations, is but the negative by-product of the great positive force that shapes the political face of our age—nationalism. Nationalism, identified as it is with the foreign policies of individual nations, cannot restrain these policies; it is itself in need of restraint. Not only has it fatally weakened, if not destroyed, the restraints that have come down to us from previous ages, it has also supplied the power aspirations of individual nations with a good conscience and a Messianic fervor. It has inspired them with a thirst and a strength for universal dominion of which the nationalism of the nineteenth century knew nothing.

The nationalism of the late twentieth century is essentially different from what traditionally goes by that name and what culminated in the national movements and the nation state of the nineteenth century. Traditional nationalism sought to free the nation from alien domination and give it a state of its own. This goal was considered to be a rightful one not for one nation only, but for all nations. Once a nation had united its members in one state, national aspirations were satisfied, and there was room for as many nationalisms as there were nations that wanted to establish or preserve a state of their own.

The international conflicts in which the nationalism of the nineteenth century was involved were, therefore, essentially of two kinds: the conflicts between a nationality and an alien master—the Balkan nations and Turkey, the Slav nations of the Danube basin and the Austro-Hungarian monarchy, the Poles and Russia—and the conflicts between different nationalities over the delimitation of their respective spheres of dominion, such as the struggle between the Germans, on the one hand, and the Poles and the French, on the other. International conflicts in the nineteenth century grew out of either different interpretations of the national principle or the refusal to accept it at all. It was hoped as late as the aftermath of the First World War that, once the aspirations of all nations for nation states of their own were fulfilled, a society of satisfied nations would find in the legal and moral principles of national self-determination the means for its own preservation.

To call by the same name what inspired the oppressed and competing nationalities of the nineteenth century and what drives the superpowers of the late twentieth century into deadly combat is to obscure the fundamental change that separates our age from the preceding one. The nationalism of today, which is really a nationalistic universalism, has only one thing in common with the nationalism of the nineteenth century—the nation as the ultimate point of reference for political loyalties and actions. But here the similarity ends. For the nationalism of the nineteenth century the nation is the ultimate goal of political action, the endpoint of the political development beyond which there are other nationalisms with similar and equally justifiable goals. For the nationalistic universalism of the late twentieth century the nation is but the starting-point of a universal mission whose ultimate goal reaches to the confines of the political world. While nationalism wants one nation in one state and nothing else, the nationalistic universalism of our age claims for one nation and one state the right to impose its own valuations and standards of action upon all the other nations.

This evil would not necessarily be mitigated, but might be aggravated, by the fusion of a number of nations into a supranational union. The nations of Western Europe, for instance, are too weak to make themselves singly the effective spearheads of the new nationalistic universalism. The time has passed when the French or the Germans could dream of making the world over in their own image. Yet if the nations of Western Europe were able to unite and form a new political and military unit of considerable potentialities, they would then have acquired the power basis for a new crusading spirit, common to all of Western Europe, to compete with the nationalistic universalism of other nations. That the traditional nation state is obsolescent in view of the technological and military conditions of the contemporary world is obvious. Yet, while trying to replace it with a larger unit, better attuned to these conditions, it is well to take care that it not be replaced simply by a more efficient vehicle for the crusading nationalism of our age.

It is one of the characteristics of nationalistic universalism, stemming from its universalistic character and aspirations, that, although it is connected with a nation, it is not connected with any particular one. The Soviet Union has indeed been the vehicle on which Communism has tried to transform the world. But who can say that in this respect China or some other nation will not tomorrow take the place of the Soviet Union, at least in Asia? The nationalism of the nineteenth century grew indeed from the peculiar character and aspirations of a particular nation and could not be divorced from it without losing its meaning and functions. The nationalistic universalism of our age is different in these respects. It is a secular religion, universal in its interpretation of the nature and destiny of man and in its Messianic promise of salvation for all mankind. A particular nation will bear its torch at any particular time, but in principle any nation can. Thus the claims to universal dominion in the name of the new crusading nationalism may shift from nation to nation according to the conditions of spirit and power.

PART EIGHT

The Problem of Peace: Peace through Limitation

18

Disarmament

THE PROBLEM OF PEACE IN OUR TIME

Two world wars within a generation and the potentialities of nuclear warfare have made the establishment of international order and the preservation of international peace the paramount concern of Western civilization. War has always been abhorred as a scourge. As the rise of the territorial state transformed the Holy Roman Empire from the actual political organization of Christendom into an empty shell and a legal fiction, writers and statesmen reflected more and more on substitutes for the lost political unity of the Western World. Erasmus in the sixteenth century, Sully, Éméric Crucé, Hugo Grotius, and William Penn in the seventeenth, and the Abbé de Saint-Pierre, Rousseau, Bentham, and Kant in the eighteenth were the great intellectual forerunners of the practical attempts undertaken in the nineteenth and twentieth centuries to solve the problems of international order and peace.

Of these attempts, the Holy Alliance, the Hague Peace Conferences of 1899 and 1907, the League of Nations, and the United Nations are the outstanding examples. These organizations and conferences, together with other less spectacular endeavors to shape a peaceful world, were made possible by four factors—spiritual, moral, intellectual, and political—which started to converge at the beginning of the nineteenth century and culminated in the theory and practice of international affairs prevalent in the period between the two world wars.

Since the time of the Stoics and the early Christians, there has been alive in Western civilization a feeling for the moral unity of mankind which strives to find a political organization commensurate with it. The Roman Empire was such a political organization of universal scope. After its downfall, the Roman Empire remained throughout the ages a symbolic reminder of the unity of the Western World, and the ultimate goal and standard which inspired Charlemagne no less than Napoleon and determined the policies of the Holy Roman Empire until the beginning of the religious wars. It is not by accident that the dissolution of the Holy Roman Empire in 1806 coincided with Napoleon's attempt to revive it and antedates by little less than a decade the beginning of that period of modern history which has made the restoration of international order one of its major objectives.

The moral root of these attempts to establish a stable and peaceful international order is to be found in the increase in the humaneness and civilized character of human relations which the last centuries have witnessed in the Western world. The philosophy of the Enlightenment and the political theory of liberalism postulated respect for human life and the promotion of human welfare. The great political and social reforms of the nineteenth and twentieth centuries drew their inspiration from these postulates. To extend the reign of law, peace, and order to the international sphere was then the great humanitarian task that the modern age had to solve.

The intellectual factor promoting this development is connected with the rise of the commercial classes first to social and then to political importance. With them rose to prominence the commercial and scientific spirit which dreaded war and international anarchy as irrational disturbances of the calculable operations of the market. "A war in the midst of different trading nations," the French philosopher Diderot noticed, "is a fire disadvantageous to all. It is a process which threatens the fortune of a great merchant and makes his debtors turn pale."[1] According to Kant, "the commercial spirit cannot coexist with war."[2] Thus, toward the end of the eighteenth century, it had become the conviction of many that war was obsolete or in any case an atavism that a concerted rational effort of humanity could banish from the earth with relative ease.

It was, however, the cataclysm of the Napoleonic Wars that demonstrated the need for supplementing with practical measures the theoretical quest for the solution of the problem of international order and peace. The importance of the Napoleonic Wars in this respect is twofold. They destroyed the balance of power and threatened temporarily to replace it with a universal empire. While this factor passed with the definitive defeat of Napoleon in 1815, the other element has threatened the stability of the modern state system for a century and a half and has not yet spent its force. This other element is nationalism. The idea of nationalism, evoked by the French Revolution and carried by the Napoleonic conquests through Europe, challenged the principle of dynastic legitimacy, which had been the organizing principle of the modern state system and was still the foundation of the peace settlements of 1815.

The convergence of these four experiences at the beginning of the nineteenth century and their dynamic release into the political arena through the shock of the Napoleonic Wars provided the intellectual and moral energy that has sustained for nearly two centuries the search for alternatives to war and international anarchy. This search, in so far as it has left the realm of mere

---

[1] "Fragments politiques," (*Euvres complètes*, Vol. IV (Paris: Garnier Frères, 1875), p. 42.
[2] *Perpetual Peace* (New York: The Macmillan Company, 1917), p. 157.

ideas, hopes, and admonitions and has materialized in actual measures and institutions of an international character (it is with the latter that we are here alone concerned), has been carried on through three different media: (1) limitation of the destructive and anarchical tendencies of international politics, (2) transformation of international politics by eliminating its destructive and anarchical tendencies altogether, and (3) accommodation of divergent interests by depriving the destructive and anarchical tendencies of international politics of their rational objectives.

Of the attempts to achieve peace through limitation, the most persistent has been that of disarmament.

HISTORY OF DISARMAMENT

Disarmament is the reduction or elimination of certain or all armaments for the purpose of ending the armaments race. It is believed that, by doing away with one of the typical manifestations of the struggle for power on the international scene, one can do away with the typical effects of that struggle: international anarchy and war.

Four basic distinctions must be kept in mind: Between disarmament and arms control, between general and local disarmament, between quantitative and qualitative disarmament, and between conventional and nuclear disarmament. While disarmament is the reduction or elimination of armaments, arms control is concerned with regulating the armaments race for the purpose of creating a measure of military stability. When we speak of general disarmament, we refer to a kind of disarmament in which all the nations concerned participate. Examples are the Washington Treaty for the Limitation of Naval Armaments of 1922, signed by all major naval powers, and the World Disarmament Conference of 1932, at which practically all members of the community of nations were represented. We speak of local disarmament when only a limited number of nations are involved. The Rush-Bagot Agreement of 1817 between the United States and Canada is an example of this type. Quantitative disarmament aims at an over-all reduction of armaments of most or all types. This was the goal of most nations represented at the World Disarmament Conference of 1932. Qualitative disarmament envisages the reduction or abolition of only certain special types of armaments, such as the aggressive weapons Great Britain tried to have outlawed by the World Disarmament Conference of 1932, or nuclear weapons, the abolition and control of which were discussed by the Atomic Energy Commission of the United Nations and were the object of the so-called SALT Agreements (Strategic Arms Limitation Treaty) and START (Strategic Arms Reduction Talks) between the United States and the Soviet Union. The distinction between nuclear and conventional weapons bears upon the political and military preconditions for arms control and disarmament.

ARMS CONTROL IN THE NUCLEAR AGE

Why has arms control, the effort to strengthen international peace by increasing military stability, been only moderately successful in the nuclear field and failed altogether with regard to conventional arms? As concerns the latter, the reasons for failure are identical with those for the failure of disarmament. The quantity and disposition of conventional weapons have a direct bearing upon the distribution of military power. Since the nations concerned compete for military advantage, an agreement on the control of conventional weapons would signify the end of competition. The termination of military competition, however, depends upon the settlement of the outstanding political issues.

The control of nuclear weapons is made possible in theory at least by the ability of major nuclear powers to reach that optimum of assured destruction beyond which it is irrational to go. This measure can be defined as the availability of the number of nuclear warheads and invulnerable delivery systems necessary to destroy the military installations and industrial and population centers of a prospective enemy. A nation which possesses this capability has realized its maximum military potential both in terms of deterrence and of the actual waging of nuclear war. The acquisition of additional warheads and delivery vehicles is wasteful because it adds nothing to the military power of the nation concerned. Consequently, the conventional conceptions of military superiority and inferiority here become within certain limits meaningless. A nation which is capable of inflicting unacceptable damage on its prospective enemy ten times over under the worst of circumstances gains nothing militarily by increasing its already abundant nuclear capability, and its prospective enemy, capable of inflicting unacceptable damage upon the other nation "only" six times over is not militarily inferior to the latter and gains no additional military power by increasing its nuclear capability. Once the two nations have reached this optimum of assured destruction, they are equal in usable nuclear capabilities: within certain limits quantitative differences do not affect that qualitative equilibrium. These limits would be left behind if one nation gained so great an advantage that it would be capable of destroying the retaliatory capability of the other nation in a first strike.

Mindful that disparity must remain within these limits, the United States and the Soviet Union have a common interest in stabilizing the nuclear arms race by regulating it. They can do so in three different ways. First, they can limit the production of nuclear weapons and delivery vehicles by unilateral action, based upon their own judgment of what is enough in terms of deterrence and actual nuclear war. The United States has done this by cutting back or discontinuing the production of certain types of missiles and airplanes, and it can be assumed that the Soviet Union has done the same.

Second, nations can control their armaments by tacit agreement, one side's action or omission being predicated upon the other side's example, and vice versa. On that basis, the United States and the Soviet Union refrained from testing nuclear weapons in the atmosphere from 1958 to 1961; in 1964 they announced a cutback in the manufacture of fissionable materials.

Third, nations can control their armaments by formal agreement. The partial test ban treaty, concluded in 1963 by Great Britain, the Soviet Union, and the United States, is a case in point. It prohibits the testing of nuclear devices above ground and under water but permits the continuation of underground tests. It thereby stabilizes the technology of nuclear weapons insofar as their development depends upon atmospheric or underwater tests. The Interim Agreement on Offensive Missiles (SALT I) draws from the unique nature of nuclear weapons the most far-reaching consequences for arms control thus far. It roughly stabilizes the quantity of nuclear weapons, but allows for their qualitative improvement. More particularly, by providing for moderate increases in the number of submarines and submarine-based missiles, it takes account of the technological shift away from land-based missiles, which have become vulnerable to quantitatively and qualitatively improved offensive missiles.

Arms control can also take the form of excluding certain types or all kinds of weapons from certain geographical regions or groups of nations. The Antarctic Treaty of 1961, the Outer Space Treaty of 1967, the Latin American Nuclear Free Zone Treaty of 1967, the Nonproliferation Treaty of 1970, the Seabed Treaty of 1971, and The Convention on the Prohibition of the Development, Production, and Stockpiling of Bacteriological (Biological) and Toxic Weapons of 1972 all fall into this category. It must, however, be pointed out that most of these treaties do nothing more than ratify through legal stipulations what the nations concerned would have been unwilling or unable to do anyhow. With continuing poor relations between countries such as the United States and the Soviet Union and Iraq and Iran, progress in certain areas appeared threatened by reversals.

The nuclear debate has raised a number of seemingly vital issues, including the military balance of power between the United States and the Soviet Union at present and in the future, the potentialities of certain weapons systems, and the possibility of verifying Soviet compliance with arms treaties. Yet the debate has also brought to the fore an element that the various camps share and that in the long run is likely to prove more important for the future of the United States than all the scenarios, details, and technicalities upon which our attention has been focused so far: the *obsolescence* of our modes of thought and action with regard to nuclear weapons. What Einstein said half a century ago is still true today: "The unleashed power of the atom has changed everything except our way of thinking." In other words, the unleashed atom presents us with problems of unprecedented novelty, requiring for their solution modes of thought and action of similar novelty. However, many parties on both sides continue to think and act largely as though the atomic revolution of 1945 had not occurred.

The availability of nuclear weapons has fundamentally altered the traditional relationship between political aims and physical violence. Down to 1945

a great power, such as the United States, had a rational choice between violence and non-violence in achieving its ends vis-à-vis other nations. If it wanted
a certain result badly enough, and could not achieve it by peaceful means, it
might well resort to violence, provided a calculus of risk and advantage favored
such a resort. Such a calculus *a priori* counsels against the use of nuclear
weapons since their very destructiveness, in both the short- and long-terms,
eliminates all possible advantage. The use of nuclear weapons, even initially on
a limited scale, is an unmitigated disaster, which in the end can only lead to the
destruction of both sides.

Thus even our conventional use of language, dealing with nuclear phenomena in terms of "weapons" and "war," shows a certain atavistic inade-
quacy. For terms such as "weapons" and "war" imply a rational relationship
between those concepts and certain human objectives. A "weapon" traditionally serves a certain rational purpose, and "war" is traditionally undertaken for
such a rational purpose; both are absent in the nuclear relations between two
nuclear powers. Thus use of conventional language, when dealing with nuclear
weapons and nuclear war, conceals the new reality for whose novelty appropriate words have not been found.

Use of conventional words for novel phenomena not only tends to hide the
truth; it also suggests that the truth is to be found in the conventional meaning
of conventional words. Since these words have over long stretches of history
accumulated a network of associations, assumptions, and conclusions, the un-
critical application of such words to nuclear phenomena precludes adequate
understanding and successful action. Thus it is fatal to the cause of nuclear arms
control and disarmament to deal with nuclear weapons and nuclear war as
though they were but a quantitative extension of conventional weapons and
war. In truth, they are different in kind because they are instruments of total
destruction, spatially and temporally; therefore they are incapable of performing the functions that history has taught us to assign to weapons and war.

In recognition of irrationality, the superpowers have tried to control the
nuclear arms race, such control issuing ultimately—it is hoped—in nuclear
disarmament. In the process they have shown alarmingly the extent to which
they are in practice oblivious to the distinction between conventional and
nuclear arms control and disarmament. They have bargained and haggled for
years over issues which might be relevant for conventional weapons but which
are, in most cases, irrelevant to the nuclear field. What does it mean, for
instance, that certain Russian missiles are allowed to carry only a specified
number of independently targetable warheads? What would happen if they
were to carry more, either by mutual consent or in violation of the treaty? As
long as the number of warheads does not affect the principle of mutually
assured destruction, the quality and quantity of the mutual means of destruction are irrelevant. To use a conventional metaphor: as long as my enemy has
one gun with which to kill me it is irrelevant for our mutual relations that he
has also the finest collection of guns in town. To repeat, *the strategic nuclear
balance between the United States and the Soviet Union, which must indeed*

be maintained, rests upon the mutual ability of utter destruction, which, in turn, rests not upon equality of numbers and performance but exclusively upon the ability to destroy the enemy regardless of the quality and quantity of nuclear weapons he may have.

Comparable military strength is but one concept among many, hallowed by tradition, that have been rendered obsolete by the nuclear revolution. Defense, limited war, victory, alliances, verification, and the distinction between combatants and noncombatants are other familiar concepts similarly invalidated by the availability of nuclear weapons. What is disquieting and ominous is the reluctance of most of those who do our thinking in these matters to desist from applying obsolete modes of thought and action to the novel conditions of the times. The confused and confusing debate on SALT II and the halting and unsuccessful character of subsequent negotiations are prime examples of the operation of a cultural lag, one which leads us to attempt to solve issues of the nuclear age with the modes of thought and action of a bygone age.

In a fundamental way, this cultural lag has dominated the theory and practice of nuclear weapons since 1945. The history of nuclear military doctrine and practice is the story of a succession of futile attempts to assimilate nuclear weapons to the traditional purposes of the nation state. For more than three decades—from the so-called "clean" H-bomb to the counterforce strategy—we have tried to make it appear that nuclear weapons are just conventional weapons writ large, to be manipulated in a conventional way.

The heart of that debate is the issue of strategic superiority between the United States and the Soviet Union. Both sides in the debate recognize in the abstract the irrelevance of the concept when applied to nuclear weapons. Henry Kissinger gave vent to that irrelevance when, during a press conference in July 1974, he declared: "What in the name of God is strategic superiority? What is the significance of it . . . at these levels of numbers? What do you do with it?" Yet in his statement to the Senate Foreign Relations Committee on July 31, 1979, he voiced for whatever reasons his regret at having intimated in 1974 that strategic superiority had become a meaningless concept:

> My statement reflected fatigue and exasperation, not analysis. If both sides maintain the balance, then indeed the race becomes futile and SALT has its place in strengthening stability. But if we opt out of the race unilaterally, we will probably be faced eventually with a younger group of Soviet leaders who will figure out what can be done with strategic superiority.

It hardly needs to be pointed out that this is a less than convincing argument in favor of strategic superiority.

Kissinger and others have admitted the meaninglessness of the concept of superiority in the conventional military sense while endeavoring to give it a new political meaning. Once a nation has attained the nuclear optimum in terms of assured destruction, so the argument runs, additional nuclear weapons can add significantly to its political power, if what counts in the power calculus is not only the actual power available, but the perception, by other nations, of the power available. That is to say, if the Soviet Union possesses more war-heads than the United States, it does not thereby become militarily more powerful than the United States, but it increases its political power vis-à-vis the United States because people perceive it—falsely—to have become more powerful militarily.

The argument, left at this point, is incomplete: it lacks a qualification centered on the people who are doing the perceiving. To be frank, the argument assumes those doing the perceiving are ignorant. For only ignorant people, unaware of the distinction between conventional and nuclear weapons, will attribute significance—military or political—to the possession of nuclear weapons in excess of the military optimum.

The defenders of the intellectual status quo have also advanced a political and military argument that is a typical example of obsolete thinking. The strategy of mutual assured destruction, so the argument runs, limits drastically the options of the President of the United States. The government of the United States is faced with two equally unacceptable choices: the slaughter of tens of millions of civilians or, if it is repelled by this barbarous alternative, appeasement. Nuclear arms beyond the optimum for assured destruction make it possible to wage limited nuclear war, that is, a kind of atomic warfare that leaves in its wake "merely" the kind of limited destruction with which modern conventional war has acquainted us.

This search for a way of dealing with nuclear weapons in a conventional manner has been, in different guises, a *leitmotif* of nuclear strategy since 1945. An enumeration of the different attempts at a new strategy, which would allow us to use nuclear weapons without the universal, uncontrolled destructive effects which, in theory, we correctly associate with nuclear weapons is instructive. Take the so-called clean H-bomb, which made its appearance at the beginning of the 1950s—that is, an H-bomb that would not have the devastating, indiscriminate effects which even the kiloton bombs dropped on Hiroshima and Nagasaki had. It was a bomb which would have little or no fallout and whose effects would be those of a gigantic conventional bomb. In the words of a former Chief of Staff of the American Air Force, General Curtis LeMay, the nuclear bomb is "just another bomb." The U.S. Atomic Energy Commission made short shrift of this idea in *The Effects of Nuclear Weapons*, published in 1962. The commission said that there is no such thing as a clean H-bomb, and that all H-bombs are more or less "unclean"—even though the distribution of blast, fire, and radiation may be different in different designs of the bomb. The idea that it is possible to devise an H-bomb which is not essentially different from a conventional bomb is utterly mistaken.

Consider, as another example, the conception of "graduated deterrence." This is a method of waging nuclear war which does not escalate almost immediately into all-out war. Instead—in a rational, almost predetermined way similar to a chess game—one side makes a move by, say, "taking out" one city, and the other side makes another move, "taking out" a city of its opponent. Thus each side, in a perfectly detached, rational way, inflicts a certain degree of damage upon the other. This idea has gained wide acceptance in certain so-called think tanks, where playing games with survival issues is highly developed. An argument can be made in favor of reviewing the hypothetical possibilities that exist. However, in practical terms, it is inconceivable that living human beings, with the ideological conceptions and values which the policymakers in the Soviet Union, the United States, and China possess, would look at, say, the destruction of Chicago by the Soviet Union or at the destruction of Minsk by the United States with the same detachment with which chess players look at the exchange of pawns. They would quickly arrive at a point where—quite aside from the aroused emotions which make calculation difficult—one side or the other would feel that in any rational simulation of a chess game one side would take advantage of the other. The equivalence theoretically assumed between Minsk and Chicago would not be self-evident to the players of the game under such circumstances. The Soviet Union will inevitably find that Minsk is more important than Chicago—and the United States will find that Chicago is more important than Minsk. They will find that this type of graduated deterrence is really not deterrence at all, because it leads inevitably by its own dynamism to escalation and to an all-out strategic war, which it was the purpose of the enterprise to avoid in the first place. Once the United States has arrived at the conclusion that Chicago is more important than Minsk, it will take out two Soviet cities, which are regarded as the equivalent of another American city, whereupon the Soviet Union will take out two American cities, which are regarded as the equivalent of one Soviet city. Furthermore, we have to reckon with the passions of the people at large and those of the policymakers, for in such an undertaking, started in a rational way, enormous powers of passion come into play on both sides. The population of the United States will not look with equanimity at the successive, however rational, elimination or partial destruction of American cities and their inhabitants; neither will the people and the government of the Soviet Union. Once again, we have a force that almost inevitably will lead to escalation and to the various effects which the graduated deterrence was intended to avoid. Since we are confronted with the possibility of nuclear war, we want to make nuclear war as painless as possible, as limited as possible, one might even say, if so grotesque a juxtaposition is allowed, as humane as possible. On the other hand, the official military doctrine of the Soviet Union has never accepted those distinctions. Soviet doctrine assumes that a war, especially a European war, which starts as a conventional or limited nuclear war and whose stakes the belligerents regard as of prime importance, is bound to escalate into all-out nuclear war. Thus the idea of the fire break—the pause between either conventional war or limited nuclear war, on the one hand, and all-out nuclear war, on the other—is alien to the military doctrine of the Soviet Union.

The strategy of counterforce, first enunciated by Secretary of Defense Robert S. McNamara in 1962, was another example of a fundamental misunderstanding of nuclear war. It was an attempt to limit nuclear war, thus making it acceptable as an instrument of national policy. The counterforce strategy was simple; it assumed that a nuclear war could be waged and ought to be waged not against population and industrial centers, but against strictly military objectives. The revival of this doctrine in recent times rests on the same assumption, fortified by the increase in the sophistication of nuclear weapons. In 1962 one could well make the case that it was impossible, in view of the character of nuclear weapons, to distinguish in practice strictly between military and civilian objectives, that the indiscriminate and widespread destructiveness of nuclear weapons was so enormous that a nuclear weapon aimed at a military objective was bound to destroy, by virtue of the mere proximity of civilian objectives, the latter as well. That argument is still valid. If the Soviet Union tries to take out the missile sites near Phoenix and Cheyenne, to give only two examples, the Soviet missiles are not likely to be so accurate as to destroy the missile sites without any negative effect upon the adjacent population and industrial centers. Recent increases in accuracy may have improved the situation somewhat and there may be a grain more merit in the revival of the counterforce strategy than in its original formulation.

A more profound question about the counterforce strategy can be asked, however, namely the question as to its ultimate military purpose. In the case of the American version of the counterforce strategy, which has been the most familiar one, the United States will not initiate a nuclear war by a first strike. It will wait until the other side has initiated a nuclear war by a first strike; only then will it attack military targets, which the other side presents not merely in the form of missile sites but also of the missiles themselves. But the first strike would already have emptied of meaning the distinction between missile sites which still contain their missiles and other missile sites from which the missiles have already departed.

But let us suppose that this distinction can nevertheless be made, and that this exchange operates as intended. This of course presupposes that the enemy who started the war has not destroyed all one's own missile sites, and that one has a sufficient number of missiles left with which to destroy enemy missile sites which still contain missiles. Accept all of this and assume that the two belligerents knock out their land-based missiles reciprocally, what have they gained? They are in the same position that they were originally, except that now they have to rely exclusively upon the seaborne deterrent and perhaps upon the airborne deterrent. So one would have the same distribution of destructive power with the same deterrent effect one had at the beginning of the war with only the difference that the mechanics would have changed from land-based to sea-based missiles. Some authorities argue that land-based missiles are obsolete anyhow, and that they should be phased out through arms control negotiations between the United States and the Soviet Union. If this position is correct, then in the projected counterforce exchange we would simply have engaged in a mutual disarmament enterprise by knocking out each other's land-based missiles. We would then be in the same position as we were before—that is to say, there would be no victor and no vanquished.

This leads to another point—the basic distinction between victory and defeat in war—which is again a distinction that is deeply ingrained in consciousness because it has been derived from millennia of historical experience. Thus the military, in particular, have found it unacceptable both in Korea and Vietnam that a conventional war should not end in the clear-cut victory of that side whose cause is regarded to be just—which is of course one's own side. The same reluctance to give up the distinction between victory and defeat is apparent in thinking on nuclear war. The idea that a nuclear war should necessarily end in a stalemate or in the mutual destruction of the belligerents is unacceptable to those who have made it their profession to prepare for victorious wars. They are in the position of a businessman whose main purpose in life is to make a profit for his company; then he is suddenly faced with the assertion that the best he can hope for is to break even. He will never make a profit, never again pay a dividend: obviously such an idea goes against his nature. As far as nuclear war is concerned, however, this is the sort of situation we face, a situation utterly different from any in the past: war itself becomes a completely senseless, irrational enterprise. Even if one can keep it limited (counterforce strategy), it will simply end in the same kind of equilibrium with which it started, except the composition of forces making up the equilibrium will be different.

Or take the concept of defense. It has been axiomatic throughout history that any new weapon will sooner or later call forth a counterweapon, a defense against it. Let us assume that this axiom is borne out by historical experience. Yet the destructiveness of nuclear weapons is so enormous that it is inconceivable—in view of present technology, and in particular of costs which were blithely overlooked by some in the Reagan administration—that an effective defense against nuclear weapons can be devised. Thus the abolition, for all practical purposes, of antiballistic missiles (ABMs) by the two SALT negotiations was a recognition of objective facts of the nuclear age. Once we have a defense against nuclear weapons, we have removed the main deterrent against nuclear war. It is this reality which proposals for star war defenses overlooks. If mankind expects to survive a nuclear war, then to wage or not to wage nuclear war involves an approach similar to that of conventional war, a pragmatic calculation of expedience.

A tactical nuclear war strategy is another attempt to make possible a nuclear war which will not lead to the destruction of both sides, but which can lead to the victory of one side. The conception of tactical nuclear war—that is to say, of the battlefield use of nuclear weapons—faces a number of practical and theoretical difficulties. First, there is the impossibility of drawing an objective, generally recognized and recognizable line between tactics and strategy in general. Military schools of thought in all countries have debated this question without arriving at a definitive conclusion. The distinction is not so much in the objective situation on the battlefield as in the minds of the military planner or director of military operations. The fact that the Hiroshima and Nagasaki bombs today are classified as tactical nuclear weapons shows how far tactics can be stretched to cover what generally would be regarded as strategy. What might be intended by one side as a tactical maneuver may thus be interpreted by the other side as a strategic move, and the reply of the other side may be interpreted in either tactical or strategic terms by the first side. Since in such situations both sides are inclined to use a worst-case approach to the problems, that is, to assume the worst in terms of the intentions of the enemy, the distinction is bound to break down very quickly. While this is true of conventional as well as nuclear war, the problem is aggravated by the nature of the latter.

Instead of adapting our thinking to the phenomenon of nuclear weapons we have tried to adapt the proposed use of nuclear weapons to our conventional way of thinking. But as more than three decades of debate have shown, it cannot be done. Limited nuclear war with limited damage is conceivable only on the premise that the stakes of the war are equally limited. Yet it is difficult to imagine a rational resort to nuclear weapons on behalf of interests which are not of the first magnitude, justifying—initially or through escalation—unlimited nuclear commitment and potentially unlimited damage. This is the main reason why nuclear weapons have not been used since 1945. Their limited application is a contradiction in terms: nuclear weapons are instruments of uncontrollable and potentially unlimited destruction, coordinated to interests of the first rank. Thus Soviet military doctrine stipulates that nuclear war on behalf of limited interests, while possible in the initial stages of a nuclear war, is likely to escalate into all-out nuclear war. If they are used on behalf of first-rank interests, such as in Europe, they will be used as instruments of total war.

The conventional modes of thought which have dominated the nuclear debate thus far are not accidental. They are the symptoms of a pervasive unwillingness to part with conventions hallowed by all of history and of a determination to apply to nuclear weapons the modes of thought and action appropriate to bygone eras. The issue of nuclear arms control is a literally vital issue, not only for the superpowers, not only for their allies, but for all of humanity. For with proliferation now underway in earnest, there is little doubt that a nuclear arms race—no longer limited to two superpowers with cautious governments that are mortally afraid of each other—but spreading over the whole globe, is bound, sooner or later, to lead to an unspeakable catastrophe. For history shows, if history shows anything, that all nations have been governed at times by fools and knaves, and even a combination of both. That was bad enough before nuclear weapons existed. But imagine a fool or knave or a combination of both in the possession of nuclear weapons, and nuclear war becomes unavoidable. So it is the almost inevitable danger of actual nuclear war, inherent in the dynamism of a generalized unlimited nuclear arms race, which makes nuclear arms control and in the end nuclear disarmament a question of life or death for all mankind.

Yet what is theoretically required is particularly difficult to obtain. The control of nuclear weapons is made possible by the ability of major nuclear powers to reach that optimum of assured destruction beyond which it is irrational to go. But in practice it is predicated upon the stability of nuclear technology; for it is only on that assumption that the nations concerned can afford to desist from competition. Thus the major nuclear powers could agree upon the cessation of atmospheric and underwater tests since for the time being no technological progress can be expected from testing in these media. Yet they continue to test underground and in outer space, and to engage in research and experimentation, searching for opportunities of improving existing weapons technologies and discovering new ones. Nuclear arms control, in view of its dependence upon technological stability, is likely to remain both limited and temporary. As long as with respect to conventional arms the political incentive to military competition persists and the basic distinction between conventional and nuclear weapons is not consistently recognized, disarmament is impossible and arms control at best precarious.

19

Security

The more thoughtful observers have realized that the solution for the problem of disarmament does not lie within disarmament itself. They have found it in security. Armaments are the result of certain psychological factors. So long as these factors persist, the resolution of nations to arm themselves will also persist, and that resolution will make disarmament impossible. The generally professed and most frequent actual motive for armaments is fear of attack; that is, a feeling of insecurity. Hence, it has been argued that what is needed is to make nations actually secure from attack by some new device and thus to give them a feeling of security. The motive force and the actual need for armaments would then disappear; for nations would find in that new device the security they had formerly sought in armaments. Since the end of the First World War, all politically active nations of the world have been, at one time or another, legally committed to two such devices: collective security and an international police force.

COLLECTIVE SECURITY

In a working system of collective security, the problem of security is no longer the concern of the individual nation, to be taken care of by armaments and other elements of national power. Security becomes the concern of all nations, which will take care collectively of the security of each of them as though their own security were at stake. If A threatens B's security, C, D, E, F, G, H, I, J, and K will take measures on behalf of B and against A as though A threatened them as well as B, and vice versa. One for all and all for one is the watchword of collective security. As Bismarck put it to the British Ambassador Lord Loftus on April 12, 1869, according to the latter's report to the British Foreign Secretary, the Earl of Clarendon, on April 17, 1869: "If you would only declare that whatever Power should wilfully break the Peace of Europe, would be looked upon by you as a common enemy—we will readily adhere to, and join you in that declaration—and such a course, if supported by other Powers, would be the surest guarantee for the Peace of Europe."

We have already pointed out that the logic of collective security is flawless, provided it can be made to work under the conditions prevailing on the international scene. For collective security to operate as a device for the prevention of war, three assumptions must be fulfilled: (1) the collective system must be able to muster at all times such overwhelming strength against any potential aggressor or coalition of aggressors that the latter would never dare to challenge the order defended by the collective system; (2) at least those nations whose combined strength would meet the requirement under (1) must have the same conception of security which they are supposed to defend; (3) those nations must be willing to subordinate their conflicting political interests to the common good defined in terms of the collective defense of all member states.

It is conceivable that all these assumptions may be realized in a particular situation. The odds, however, are strongly against such a possibility. There is nothing in past experience and in the general nature of international politics to suggest that such a situation is likely to occur. It is indeed true that, under present conditions of warfare no less than under those of the past, no single nation is strong enough to defy a combination of all the other nations with any chance for success. Yet it is extremely unlikely that in an actual situation only one single nation would be found in the position of the aggressor. Generally, more than one nation will actively oppose the order collective security tries to defend, and other nations will be in sympathy with that opposition.

The reason for this situation lies in the character of the order defended by collective security. That order is of necessity the status quo as it exists at a particular moment. Thus the collective security of the League of Nations sought the preservation of the territorial status quo as it existed when the League of Nations was established in 1919. But in 1919 a number of nations were already strongly opposed to that territorial status quo—the nations defeated in the First World War, as well as Italy, which felt itself despoiled of some of the promised fruits of victory. Other nations, such as the United States and the Soviet Union, were at best indifferent toward the status quo. For France and its allies, who were the main beneficiaries of the status quo of 1919 and most anxious to defend it by means of collective security, security meant the defense of the frontiers as they had been established by the peace treaties of 1919 and the perpetuation of their predominance on the continent of Europe. Security for the dissatisfied nations meant the exact opposite: the rectification of those frontiers and a general increase in their power relative to France and its allies.

This grouping of nations into those in favor of the status quo and those opposed to it is not at all peculiar to the period following the First World War. It is, as we know, the elemental pattern of international politics. As such, it recurs in all periods of history. Through the antagonism between status quo and imperialistic nations, it provides the dynamics of the historic process. This antagonism is resolved either in compromise or in war. Only on the assumption that the struggle for power as the moving force of international politics might subside or be superseded by a higher principle can collective security have a chance for success. Since, however, nothing in the reality of international affairs corresponds to that assumption, the attempt to freeze the particular status quo by means of collective security is in the long run doomed to failure. In the short run, collective security may succeed in safeguarding a particular status quo because of the temporary weakness of the opponents, as in the Persian Gulf war of 1991. Its failure to succeed in the long run is due to the absence of the third assumption upon which we have predicated the success of collective security. In the early 1980's, Britain and Argentina clashed over the Falkland Islands, Israel invaded Lebanon, and the United States sent troops into Grenada. Whatever resolutions the United Nations passed, neither it nor its members were able to turn back the states engaged in these actions.

In the light of historic experience and the actual nature of international politics, we must assume that conflicts of interest will continue on the international scene. No nation or combination of nations, however strong and devoted to international law, can afford to oppose by means of collective security all aggression at all times, regardless of by whom and against whom it may be committed. The United States and the United Nations came to the aid of South Korea when it was attacked in 1950 because they had the strength and interest to do so. Would they make themselves again the champions of collective security if tomorrow Indonesia should be the victim of aggression, or Chile, or Egypt? What would the United States and the United Nations do if two different aggressors should start marching at the same time? Would they oppose these two aggressors indiscriminately, without regard for the interests involved and the power available, and would they refuse to violate the principles of collective security and refrain from taking on only the one who was either more dangerous or easier to handle? And if tomorrow South Korea should turn the tables and commit an act of aggression against North Korea or China, would the United States and the United Nations then turn around and fight South Korea?

The Italo-Ethiopian War

After Italy's attack on Ethiopia, the League of Nations put into motion the mechanism of collective security provided for in Article 16 of the Covenant. It soon became apparent that none of the assumptions upon whose realization the success of collective security depends was present or could have been present under the actual conditions of world politics.

The United States, Germany, and Japan were not members of the League system of collective security and were, furthermore, divided in their sympathies. Germany had already openly embarked upon policies designed to overthrow the existing status quo in Europe. Japan was already well on its way to overthrow the status quo in the Far East. Both, therefore, could only look with favor on an undertaking that, by overthrowing the status quo in an out-of-the-way region, would weaken the position of Great Britain and France, who were vitally interested in the preservation of the status quo in Europe and the Far East. The United States, on the other hand, approved of the attempts to strengthen the defense of the status quo, while the temper of public opinion in the country prevented it from taking an active part in such attempts. The nations who were prepared to do everything they could for the success of the League experiment were either too weak to do much of consequence—such as the Scandinavian countries—or—as in the case of the Soviet Union—their ulterior motives were suspect. Furthermore, the Soviet Union was lacking in naval strength, indispensable under the circumstances, and had no access to the theater of decisive operations without the co-operation of the geographically intervening nations, which was not forthcoming.

Thus the case of collective security vs. Italy was in essence the case of Great Britain and France vs. Italy. This was a far cry from the ideal prerequisite of a concentration of overwhelming power which no prospective lawbreaker would dare to challenge. It is of course true that the combined strength of Great Britain and France would have sufficed to crush Italy. Yet Great Britain and France were not only members of the League system of collective security; they had other moral, legal, and political commitments. Nor were they engaged in defending the status quo against Italy alone. They were involved in a world-wide struggle for power, of which the conflict with Italy was only one—and not the most important—segment. While they were opposing Italy's attack upon the status quo, they could not overlook the progressing attack of Japan, nor could they be oblivious to the preparations for attack going on east of the Rhine. Nor, finally, were they able to divorce from their policies toward the Soviet Union their fear of Communism as a revolutionary movement threatening the domestic status quo. What Great Britain and France conceived as their national interests contradicted what collective security required them to do. More particularly, they were resolved and made their resolution known not to go so far in defense of Ethiopia as to risk war with Italy. In the already quoted words of Sir Winston Churchill: "First, the Prime Minister had declared that sanctions meant war; secondly, he was resolved that there must be no war; and thirdly, he decided upon sanctions. It was evidently impossible to comply with these three conditions."[1]

Unwilling to subordinate their national interests to the requirements of collective security, Great Britain and France were also unwilling to pursue their national interests without regard to collective security. This was the fatal error of British and French foreign policy. By pursuing either cause halfheartedly and without consistency, they failed in both. Not only did they not save the status quo in East Africa, but they also pushed Italy into the arms of Germany. They destroyed the collective system of the League of Nations as well as their own prestige as defenders of the status quo. Among the causes for the increasing boldness of the anti-status quo nations in the late thirties, culminating in a war of aggression, this loss of prestige holds a prominent place.

The debacle of collective security, as applied to the Italian aggression against Ethiopia, conveys two important lessons. It shows the contradiction between an ideally perfect scheme of reform and a political reality that lacks all the elements upon which the success of the scheme was predicated. It shows

---

[1] *London Evening Standard,* June 26, 1936.

also the fatal weakness of a foreign policy that is incapable of deciding whether to be guided by the national interest, however defined, or by a supranational principle embodying what is considered to be the common good of the community of nations.

The Korean War

The lessons that could have been learned from the theoretical analysis of collective security, and that were borne out by the experience of the Italo-Ethiopian War, were fully confirmed by the experience of the Korean War.

The attack of North Korea against South Korea on June 25, 1950, joined by China in November of the same year, was as clear-cut a case of aggression as one can imagine. In the absence of even the slightest doubt as to the legal merits of the case, collective security would have required that all members of the United Nations come to the aid of South Korea, the victim of aggression. In view of the nature and the military consequences of the aggression, this aid, to be effective, could only have taken the form of the dispatch of armed forces to the battlefront. Yet of the sixty members of the United Nations, only sixteen sent armed forces of any kind, and of these only the United States, Canada, Great Britain, and Turkey can be said to have contributed more than token forces. South Korea, the country immediately concerned, and the United States provided about ninety percent of the armed forces that fought in Korea. In the course of the war, one great power, China, joined the aggressor as an active participant in the aggression itself. Other members of the United Nations with military capabilities, such as Argentina, Brazil, Czechoslovakia, India, Mexico, Poland, remained on the side lines, taking no active part in the military operations on either side. Thus the reality of collective security, as applied in the Korean War, corresponds exactly to the pattern outlined above. Given the conditions of contemporary world politics, it could not have been otherwise.

In order to understand the different attitudes taken by different nations with regard to the Korean War, it is neither sufficient nor necessary to consult the legal texts concerning the obligations imposed upon the member states by a system of collective security. It is, however, sufficient and indeed indispensable to consult their interests and the power available to them in support of those interests.

As was shown above,[2] the very existence of Korea as an autonomous state has been for more than two thousand years a function of the balance of power in the Far East, either in terms of the supremacy of one power that controlled and protected Korea or in terms of rival imperialisms meeting on the Korean peninsula and establishing there a very unstable equilibrium for generally short duration. The controlling and protecting power was traditionally China, challenged from time to time with varying success by Japan. Toward the end of the nineteenth century, Russia replaced China as the competitor of Japan for the

---

[2]See page 196.

control of Korea. At the end of the Second World War, with China and Japan too weak to perform their historic function with regard to Korea, the United States and the Soviet Union took over that function, the United States, as it were, taking the place of Japan and the Soviet Union that of China. Neither the United States nor the Soviet Union could allow the other power to control all of Korea. As seen from the vantage point of Japan, whose protection is a vital interest of the United States, Korea in the hands of a potentially hostile power is like a drawn dagger and so it is as seen from the vantage point of Russia and, more particularly, China. Thus the division of Korea into an American and Russian zone at the end of the Second World War was the expression both of the interests of the two nations concerned and of the power available to them, since at that time neither was in a position to risk a major conflict over the control of all of Korea.

This issue of the control of all of Korea was reopened when South Korea was attacked by North Korea, supported by the Soviet Union. The all-out support of the United States for South Korea was justified by its interest in the security of Japan and the over-all stability of the Far East. It was that latter interest that justified the substantial support of Canada and Great Britain. The token contributions of other nations, such as Australia, Belgium, Colombia, France, Luxembourg, and Turkey, can be explained either by the same interest or by their special dependence upon the good will of the United States. And the failure of most nations to contribute anything derives from lack of interest or lack of power, or from both.

But even this support, slight when compared with the total military strength of the members of the United Nations, would have been ample for the repulsion of the North Korean aggression, short of a major war. In other words, collective security could have operated successfully even under the less than ideal conditions that prevailed before the intervention of China. That intervention transformed completely the character of the Korean War. Before it, the war could still be called a collective security war or a police action by virtue of the preponderant military force opposing the aggressor. With that intervention the conflict took on the character of a traditional war in which the approximately equal forces of two coalitions oppose each other. Short of a general conflagration, there was no possibility for either side to defeat the other, as South Korea would have been able to defeat North Korea with the assistance of the United Nations forces. From the moment a great power joined the aggressor, only a collective security effort commensurate with the magnitude of the aggression—that is, all-out war against a great power—could have defeated the aggressors. In short, collective security, conceived as an instrument for the protection of the status quo by peaceful means, defeats its avowed purpose and becomes an instrument of all-out war if the aggressor is a great power.

The Korean War did not put collective security to the full test of this paradox, for the interests of the great powers involved in it limited the war to the Korean peninsula. China intervened against the United Nations advance into North Korea for the same reasons that had led to the intervention of the

United States against the North Korean advance into South Korea: the fear of a united Korea in potentially hostile hands. Collective security would have required not only the momentary repulsion of aggression, but also the establishment of security for the future, an objective to be achieved only by the defeat of China in an all-out war. Similarly, the restoration of traditional Chinese control over the Korean peninsula would have required the defeat of the United States in an all-out war. Neither the United States nor China was willing to take upon itself the burden and risks demanded by such an enterprise. Thus both nations were satisfied with a temporary continuation of the division, however precarious and unstable, of Korea into two spheres of influence, reflecting the balance of power in the Far East.

In this respect, as in the others discussed before, the dilemmas and contradictions to which the Korean War, considered as a collective security action, has given rise stem from the contradictions inherent in the very idea of collective security when it is put into practice under the political conditions of the contemporary world.

AN INTERNATIONAL POLICE FORCE

The idea of an international police force goes a step beyond collective security in that the application of collective force against an actual or prospective lawbreaker no longer lies within the control of the individual nations. The international police would operate under the command of an international agency, which would decide when and how to employ it. No such police force has ever operated as a permanent international organization. The members of the United Nations are, however, obligated by Articles 42 ff. of the Charter to create such a force in the form of a United Nations Armed Force. No substantial progress has yet been made in executing that obligation.

The hopes for the preservation of peace which have been connected with an international police force since the end of the First World War are derived from an analogy with the peace-preserving functions the police performs in domestic societies. This analogy is, however, misleading on three grounds.

Domestic societies are composed of millions of members of which at any one time normally only a very small fraction is engaged in violating the law. The spread of power among members of domestic societies is extreme, since there are very powerful and very weak members; yet the combined power of law-abiding citizens will normally be far superior to any combination of even the most powerful lawbreakers. The police as the organized agency of the law-abiding majority does not need to exceed relatively small proportions in order to be able to cope with any foreseeable threat to law and order.

In these three respects the international situation is significantly different. International society is composed of a relatively small number of members, amounting to more than 160 sovereign states. Among these there are giants, like the United States and the Soviet Union, and pygmies, such as Luxembourg and Nicaragua. What is more important, the power of any one of the giants constitutes a very considerable fraction of the total power of the community of nations. A giant in combination with one or two second-rate nations or a few small ones may easily exceed the strength of all the other nations combined. In view of such a formidable potential opposition, a police force of truly gigantic dimensions would obviously be needed if it should be able to squelch an infringement of law and order without transforming every police action into full-scale war. This would still be true, only on a proportionately smaller scale, if general disarmament should reduce drastically the armed forces of the individual nations. For the international police would still have to constitute a counterweight of overwhelming superiority to the military spirit and training, the industrial capacity, strategic advantages—in short, the power potential of the great powers—which in case of conflict could easily be transformed into actual military strength.

On the assumption, then—which is indeed merely hypothetical—that nations would be willing to surrender the instruments for the protection and furtherance of their own interests to an international police force, how is such an international police force to be composed? The nature of international society as it actually is allows no satisfactory answer to that question.

In domestic societies the police force is naturally composed of members who are fully identified with the existing law and order. But let us assume that among them there are some opposed to the existing law and order, and that their number is proportionate to the segment of the total population opposed to it; the number of the disaffected would be so small as to be virtually negligible and unable to affect the striking power of the police. An international police force would necessarily have to be composed of a proportionate or equal number of citizens of the different nations. These nations, however, as we have seen, are virtually always divided into defenders and opponents of the existing status quo; that is, of the existing law and order. Their citizens as members of the international police force could not but share the national preferences in this respect. Would they be expected to fight against their own nations in defense of a status quo to which they, as members of their nations, must be opposed? Given the relative strength of national and international loyalties in the contemporary world, in case of conflict the national loyalties could not but attract the respective members of the international police force like so many magnets, thus dissolving the international police force before it could ever meet a challenge to the existing law and order.

These general considerations, applying to international society as a whole and more particularly to its most powerful members, are of course not invalidated by the exceptional possibility for an international police force to prevent strictly circumscribed local breaches of the law, provided all the nations directly concerned have an interest in that prevention. The classic example of this possibility is the United Nations Emergency Force established after the Suez invasion of 1956 to protect the frontiers between Egypt and Israel around the Gaza Strip and to enforce the demilitarization of the Straits of Tiran. The example of UNEF is also illustrative of the limitations created by the opposing states when one recalls the immediate compliance with Egypt's request to withdraw the force in 1967.

To judge the prospects for an internatioinal peace force by the coalition assembled in the Gulf would be premature. A relatively small number of nations supplied most of the troops. The problem of an international police force, to be solved at all, must be solved within the framework of a world society that commands the ultimate secular loyalty of its individual members and has developed a conception of justice by which the individual nations composing it are willing to test the legitimacy of their individual claims.[3]

---

[3]Cf. in greater detail, Hans J. Morgenthau, "The Political Conditions for an International Police Force," *International Organization,* Vol. XVII, No. 2 (Spring 1963), pp. 393 ff; and "The Impartiality of the International Police," in Salo Engel and B. A. Métall, *Law, State, and International Legal Order: Essays in Honor of Hans Kelsen* (Knoxville: The University of Tennessee Press, 1964), pp. 209 ff.

20

International Government

The remedies for international anarchy and war which have been discussed thus far are all specific remedies. They attack a particular problem in which the lack of international order and the tendency toward war are manifest, and they endeavor to solve the general problem of international order and peace through a solution of the particular problem. International government owes its existence to the recognition that peace and order are the products, not of a specific device meeting a particular problem, but of the common bond that unites an integrated society under a common authority and a common conception of justice. How to found such an authority in a society of sovereign states and to create such a conception of justice is, then, the task any attempt at international government must try to solve.

Each of the three world wars of the last two centuries was followed by an attempt to establish an international government. The total failure to keep international order and peace called forth an over-all effort to make international order and peace secure. The Holy Alliance followed the Napoleonic Wars; the League of Nations, the First World War; the United Nations, the Second World War. With regard to each of these attempts at international government, three questions must be asked: (1) Where is the authority to govern vested, or who is to govern? (2) By what principle of justice is the government to be guided, or what is the conception of the common good to be realized by the government? (3) To what extent has the government been able to maintain order and peace?

THE HOLY ALLIANCE

History

The international government commonly called the Holy Alliance was based upon three treaties: the Treaty of Chaumont of March 9, 1814, the Quadruple

Alliance signed at Paris on November 20, 1815, and the Treaty of the Holy Alliance of September 26, 1815. In the Treaty of Chaumont, Austria, Great Britain, Prussia, and Russia concluded an alliance for twenty years, for the purposes of preventing the Napoleonic dynasty from returning to France and of guaranteeing the territorial settlement to be made at the end of the war against Napoleon. The Quadruple Alliance reaffirmed the provisions of the Treaty of Chaumont and in its Article VI laid down the principles of what is known as "congressional government" or "diplomacy by conference."[1]

In contrast with the Quadruple Alliance—which presented, as it were, the constitutional law of the international government of the Holy Alliance—the Treaty of the Holy Alliance itself, from which the international government received its name, contained no principles of government at all. It proclaimed the adherence of all rulers to the principles of Christianity, with God as the actual sovereign of the world. It is replete with phrases such as "reciprocal service," "unalterable good will," "mutual affection," "Christian charity," "indissoluble fraternity." Originally signed by the rulers of Austria, Prussia, and Russia, the Holy Alliance was adhered to by all European rulers, with the exception of the Pope and the Sultan.[2] Obviously inspired by Czar Alexander I of Russia, it reaffirmed the moral unity of Europe. That reaffirmation of a moral consensus among the nations is the main function the Treaty of the Holy Alliance actually fulfilled.

The Treaty of the Holy Alliance was of no significance for the actual operations of the international government that bore its name. Its principles were invoked from time to time by the Czar, affirmed in words and rejected in action by the other powers. Castlereagh, British Foreign Minister at the time of its conclusion, called it "a piece of sublime mysticism and nonsense," and the Austrian Chancellor Metternich made vulgar jokes at its expense. Yet it served as moral justification for the principles of justice that the three original signatories of the Treaty propounded and for the policies by which they endeavored to realize these principles. Thus the Treaty of the Holy Alliance also fulfilled an ideological function and became the symbol of this whole era of international relations.

In 1818, the four signatories of the Quadruple Alliance admitted France as a fifth member to take part in all further meetings to be held by virtue of Article VI of that treaty. In a circular signed in 1820 at the Congress of Troppau, Austria, Prussia, and Russia pledged themselves never to recognize the right of

---

[1]Article VI reads as follows: "To assure and facilitate the execution of the present Treaty, and to consolidate the intimate relations which to-day unite the 4 Sovereigns for the good of the world, the High Contracting Parties have agreed to renew, at fixed periods, whether under the immediate auspices of the Sovereigns, or by their respective Ministers, reunions devoted to the great common interests and to the examination of the measures which, at any of these periods, shall be judged most salutary for the repose and prosperity of the peoples, and for the maintenance of the peace of the State."

[2]The British monarch, for constitutional reasons, could not formally adhere; the Prime Minister acceded informally.

any people to circumscribe the power of their king. This compact is known as the Neo-Holy Alliance. Castlereagh, in two dispatches of the same year, refused to have any part in policies whose purpose was to interfere by force in the internal affairs of other countries. His successor, George Canning, maintained this principle at the Congress of Verona in 1822, the last of the congresses Great Britain attended.

When the news of the failure of the Congress of Verona reached him, Canning, in a letter to the British diplomat Bagot of January 3, 1823, hailed the end of international government by congresses and the beginning of a new era, as far as Great Britain was concerned, by invoking the religious principle of the Holy Alliance with a vengeance: "Every nation for itself, and God for us all!" International government by conference as a going concern did not survive the British defection. After two more abortive attempts—one with reference to the Spanish colonies, the other concerning Greece and Turkey—it came to an end in 1825.

The system of an over-all international government instituted by Article VI of the Quadruple Alliance of November 20, 1815, did not last even a decade. The lifetime of the system of ambassadorial conferences for the settlement of special problems was even shorter. It, too, was established by the Treaties of 1815 and consisted of three agencies: the ambassadors to France of Austria, Great Britain, Prussia, and Russia, dealing mainly with the problems raised by the peace treaties with France, yet acting in a general way as the paramount executive organ of the Quadruple Alliance; the ambassadors of the great powers meeting in London to organize the abolition of the slave trade; and the ambassadorial conference at Frankfort for the discussion of German problems. All these agencies had disappeared by 1818.

GOVERNMENT BY THE GREAT POWERS

The international government of the Holy Alliance was government by the great powers. The Austrian statesman and writer Friedrich Gentz described its general character thus:

> The system which has been established in Europe since 1814 and 1815 is a phenomenon unheard-of in the history of the world. The principle of equilibrium or, to put it better, of counterweights formed by particular alliances, a principle which has governed and too often also troubled and covered Europe with blood for three centuries, has been superseded by a principle of a general union, uniting the sum total of states in a federation under the direction of the major powers. . . . The second-, third-, and fourth-rate states submit in silence and without any previous stipulation to the decisions jointly taken by the preponderant powers; and Europe seems to form finally a great political family, united under the auspices of an areopagus of its own creation.[3]

[3]Friedrich Gentz, *Dépêches Inédites du Chevalier de Gentz aux Hospodors de Valachie* (Paris: E. Plon, 1876), Vol. 1, p. 354. The English translation has been supplied by the author.

The distinction between great and small powers as a political fact pointing to the extreme differences in power among nations is of course one of the elemental experiences of international politics. As an institution of international politics and organization, carrying differences in legal status, it sprang from the brain of Castlereagh and became the very foundation of the scheme adopted in 1815. It is true that the protocol of the Congress of Aix-la-Chapelle of November 15, 1818, providing for future meetings of the five great powers, also stipulated "that in the case of these meetings having for their object affairs specially connected with the interests of the other States of Europe, they shall only take place in pursuance of a formal invitation on the part of such of those States as the said affairs may concern, and under the express reservation of their right of direct participation therein, either directly or by their Plenipotentiaries." Yet this stipulation remained without appreciable influence upon the policies of the Holy and, more particularly, of the Neo-Holy Alliance.

Dual Meaning of the Status Quo

To the question as to what principle of justice guided the Holy Alliance, the answer seems to be clear: the maintenance of peace on the basis of the status quo. This principle was never more clearly stated than in the declaration of the five great powers signed at Aix-la-Chapelle on November 15, 1818: "The object of this Union is as simple as it is great and salutary. It does not tend to any new political combination—to any change in the Relations sanctioned by existing Treaties. Calm and consistent in its proceedings, it has no other object than the maintenance of Peace, and the guarantee of those transactions on which the Peace was founded and consolidated."

This answer, however, becomes highly ambiguous if one raises the further question as to what was meant by the status quo. What Great Britain meant from the very beginning was not at all what Russia meant, and the conception of the status quo which guided the policies of the Neo-Holy Alliance was diametrically opposed to the conception behind the policies of Castlereagh and Canning. The status quo that Great Britain tried to preserve through the instrumentality of the Holy Alliance was strictly limited to the political situation that existed at the end of the Napoleonic Wars with regard to France. To the British statesmen, the mortal peril into which Napoleon had put the British Isles was identical with the threat to the European balance of power which had emanated from the Napoleonic Empire. Great Britain was willing to support an international government whose purpose was to forestall the rise of a new conqueror from French soil and to that end to enforce the peace settlement of 1815 against France. The British conception of the status quo was limited to the territorial settlement of 1815 and the exclusion of a member of the Napoleonic family from the French throne. In this respect there was no difference between the foreign policies of Castlereagh and Canning.

The conception of the status quo which determined the policies of Russia from the outset, and those of Austria, Prussia, and France from the end of the second decade of the nineteenth century, was unlimited territorially and as to subject matter. According to that conception, formulated in more uncompromising terms than the actual political conditions permitted to realize, it was the purpose of the international government of the Holy Alliance to maintain everywhere in the world the territorial status quo of 1815 and the constitutional status quo of the absolute monarchy. The instrument of the realization of the latter purpose was bound to be intervention into the internal affairs of all nations where the institution of the absolute monarchy seemed to be in danger.

The inevitable by-product of such intervention was an increase in the power of the intervening nations. The more widespread national and liberal movements became, the greater was the chance for the intervening nation or group of nations to increase their strength and expand and thus disturb the balance of power again. The main beneficiary of such a development was bound to be Russia. At this point Great Britain and Russia parted company.

Great Britain had not, for almost a quarter of a century, fought the Napoleonic Empire, nourished by the dynamism of the French Revolution, to exchange it for a Russian Empire, inspired by the religious mysticism of universal brotherhood and of absolute government. In the measure that the spread of national and liberal movements gave the Neo-Holy Alliance an opportunity to test its principles of general intervention, Great Britain held aloof from it and opposed its policies. When in 1818 Russia proposed to send an allied army to aid Spain in the war against its American colonies, Great Britain prevented the execution of the plan. Yet, when in 1820 revolutions broke out in Naples, Piedmont, and Portugal, Austria, in the name of the Neo-Holy Alliance, restored the absolute monarchies of Naples and Piedmont to their thrones by force of arms. In 1820, a revolution broke out in Spain. Against the constitutional regime installed by it, France intervened by force of arms in 1823, acting on its own behalf, but with the moral support of Austria, Prussia, and Russia.

Peace, Order, and the National Interest

These actions of the Holy Alliance reveal two facts. One is the absence of a serious threat of war in any of these situations. The disparity of power between the intervening state and the object of intervention—the revolutionary group that had to contend not only with its own antirevolutionary compatriots but also with a foreign army—was such as to give the intervention the character of a punitive expedition rather than of a war.

The other fact is the determination of the policies of all nations by their national interests, however much the language of diplomacy of the period made concessions to the mystical predilections of the Russian Czar. This is most obvious in the actions of Great Britain. Neither Castlereagh nor Canning—who was particularly frank and eloquent in this respect—took pains to hide the fact that he was guided by the traditional interests of Great Britain, limited only by the general interest in peace and security. Both the Austrian intervention in Italy and the French intervention in Spain were dictated by traditional national interests. This connection is demonstrated by the very fact that the policy of interventions on the part of Austria and France in the affairs of their neighbors to the south survived the Holy Alliance by almost half a century.

More important still in view of our discussion is the victory the particular national interests gained over the general principles of the Holy Alliance whenever both came into conflict. This happened twice, in 1820 and in 1822. In both cases Russia proposed a collective intervention on the part of all the members of the Alliance and to that end offered to send a large Russian army into Central and Western Europe. That Great Britain would have opposed such a proposal is obvious from what has already been said of the British return to its traditional balance-of-power policy. That Great Britain should have been joined in this opposition by Austria, the other pillar of the Neo-Holy Alliance, demonstrates the ideological character of the principles of the Holy Alliance. These principles were invoked when they seemed to be able to give moral justification to policies dictated by the national interest. They were discarded when nothing was to be gained for the national interest by invoking them.

The attitude of the powers when in 1821 the Greeks revolted against the Turks is instructive in this respect. This is also the only situation arising during the era of the Holy Alliance which contained the germs of a general war and which in the century following it led time and again to the actual outbreak of war. The principles of the Neo-Holy Alliance allowed of only one attitude to be taken vis-à-vis a national revolt against a legitimate government: the legitimate government must be given active support. Yet this was not the answer the national interest of the most affected power demanded.

Russia had been the traditional protector of the subjects of the Ottoman Empire who were of the Orthodox Christian faith. The possession of Constantinople was a centuries-old dream of the rulers of Moscow. Thus, when the Greek revolt broke out, the Russian Czar was inclined, in complete disregard of the principles of the Neo-Holy Alliance, to declare war against Turkey. Austria and Great Britain, on the other hand, could only see with misgivings, felt before and for almost a century afterward, the extension of Russian power in the Balkans and Russia's advance toward the Mediterranean. Thus Castlereagh, the opponent of the Neo-Holy Alliance, and the Austrian Chancellor Metternich, its ardent supporter, joined hands in order to dissuade Russia from taking active steps in support of the Greek insurgents. That they made successful use of the principles of the Neo-Holy Alliance against their author is an ironic comment on the difficulties facing a foreign policy based upon abstract principles rather than upon a clear recognition of the national interest. As Castlereagh wisely put it: It is difficult enough in international affairs to hold the balance "between conflicting nations," it is still more difficult to hold the balance "between conflicting principles."

When, finally, in 1826 the danger of war between Russia and Turkey became acute, it was not the defunct Holy Alliance that averted it, but Canning's audacious move of entering into an agreement with Russia for the purpose of forcing Turkey to make concessions to the Greeks, without Russia's gaining immediate advantages from such internal reforms. After Canning's death, the event occurred that Canning had been successful in preventing: in 1828 Russia alone declared war on Turkey, thus having the latter at its mercy. The outbreak of this war may have been partly due to the decline of British statesmanship after Canning's death. It certainly was not at all due to the absence of the international government of the Holy Alliance.

The Holy Alliance, then, was a short-lived experiment that contributed nothing to the maintenance of international peace. As an international government imposing its rule upon its sphere of domination, it was successful for hardly more than half a decade. At the very hour of its ascendancy, in 1818, Friedrich Gentz, one of its architects and its outstanding philosopher, put his finger on its congenital weakness:

> The strongest objection to the present system is the obvious difficulty to maintain for long the combination of heterogeneous elements of which it is composed. The most divergent interests, the most antagonistic tendencies, the most contradictory predictions, views, and secret thoughts are for the moment encompassed and submerged in the common action of a league which resembles much more a coalition, created for an extraordinary purpose, than a genuine alliance based upon distinct and permanent interests. Unique circumstances were needed to bring about such a league; it would be against human nature and the nature of things for it to take for any length of time the place of that opposition and strife to which the diversity of situations, interests, and opinions always leads a number of independent nations, each of necessity with its own particular character and plan of action.[4]

Two congenital infirmities made the early demise of the Holy Alliance inevitable. One was the diametrical opposition between the two main members of the Alliance as to what the defense of the status quo—upon which they had all agreed as the guiding principle of justice in the abstract—meant in concrete political terms. That meaning was determined by the national interests of the individual members. If those interests happened to coincide, the Alliance could act in unison as one collective body. If those interests diverged, as they were bound to do from time to time and as they did permanently in the case of Great Britain and Russia, the Alliance ceased to operate.

The other infirmity from which the Holy Alliance suffered was the contrast between the principle of justice upon which the governments of Russia, Prussia, and Austria agreed as a guide to concrete political action, and the conception of justice adhered to by the majority of the individuals living under the rule of the Holy Alliance. The conflict between the principles of legitimate government and the principles of liberalism and nationalism made the operation of an international government inspired by the former dependent upon the continuous use of armed force in order to protect and restore absolute monarchies and their possessions throughout the world.

It is a matter for conjecture how long an international government could have performed such a task had all its members shared the convictions and the zeal of Alexander I of Russia. The Holy Alliance could not prevail against the

---

[4]Ibid., p. 355.

opposition of some of its members and of the peoples subject to its rule. In the era of Castlereagh, that dual opposition moved without contact on parallel lines, Castlereagh abstaining from active cooperation with the policies of the Neo-Holy Alliance. It was Canning's great innovation, favored by the increasing strength of the national and liberal movements and later perfected by his successor Palmerston, to use those movements in support of British purposes; that is, as weights in the scales of the balance of power. With that innovation, Canning ushered in the British policy toward the continent of Europe which was to remain dominant throughout the nineteenth century.

The international government of the Holy Alliance lacked any kind of permanent organization and consisted, aside from the ephemeral ambassadorial committees mentioned above, of nothing but a number of international congresses for the purpose of settling current international affairs. Nevertheless, the Holy Alliance was an international government in the true sense of the term. An incomplete list of the issues on the agenda of the Congress of Aix-la-Chapelle will illustrate the range of its governmental activities: the claims of the German mediatized princes against the abuses of their new sovereigns, the petition of the Elector of Hesse to exchange his title for that of king, the request by Napoleon's mother for the release of her son, the grievances of the people of Monaco against their prince, the claims of Bavaria and the House of Hochberg to the succession in Baden, a dispute between the Duke of Oldenburg and Count Bentinck about the lordship of Knupenhaussen, the situation of the Jews in Prussia and Austria, the rank of diplomatic representatives, the suppression of the slave trade and of the Barbary pirates, and the question of the Spanish colonies.

The Concert of Europe

In comparison with these widespread governmental activities of the Holy Alliance, the subsequent century was retrogressive. The spectacle of a government of great powers sitting in judgment over the affairs of the world did not reappear until in 1919 the Council of the League of Nations re-enacted the role that the Holy Alliance had played. Yet the era between the Holy Alliance and the League of Nations was not devoid of *ad hoc* attempts at settling international problems through the concerted action of the great powers. After the demise of the Holy Alliance, the great powers continued to assume responsibility for the settlement of political issues that without such settlement might have led to war. That responsibility was realized in a number of conferences dealing with problems endangering the peace, such as the Belgian question at the beginning of the 1830s, the Eastern question at the beginning of the 1850s and again in 1878, and the problems of Africa at the beginning of the twentieth century. It was to that responsibility of the great powers for the peace of the world, operating through *ad hoc* conferences and generally known as the Concert of Europe, that Sir Edward Grey appealed in vain on the eve of the First World War.

The Concert of Europe differed from a genuine international government in two respects. On the one hand, it was not institutionalized. There was no agreement among the great powers to meet regularly or to meet at all. The great powers met whenever the international situation seemed to demand concerted action. On the other hand, the Concert of Europe was no longer animated, as has already been noted,[5] by a strong moral consensus that could have neutralized conflicts and supplied standards for common judgments and actions. The cleavage between nationalism and legitimacy which the French Revolution had opened remained open throughout the nineteenth century. It might at times narrow or widen, but it did not close. Only at the end of the First World War did the national principle triumph, carrying to their doom the monarchies of Central and Eastern Europe.

Yet, despite the lack of a strong moral consensus, of an institutionalized government by conferences, let alone of an organized one, the Concert of Europe was most successful in preserving general peace during the ninety years of its existence. The only major international war the world experienced during that period, the Crimean War of 1854–56, was due to a series of accidents. Had any one of these accidents failed to materialize, the war might well have been avoided. The Concert of Europe had already agreed upon the formula for peace, but a delay of twenty-four hours in the transmission of the formula changed the picture.

What accounted for the success of the Concert of Europe in preventing general wars? Three factors must be mentioned. In that period of history the moral consensus of the European community lived on as a feeble echo, strengthened, however, by the humanitarian moral climate of the times. The political configuration favored expansion into politically empty spaces with accommodation of conflicting interests. Finally and most importantly, however, that period of history saw a succession of brilliant diplomatists and statesmen who knew how to make peace, how to preserve peace, and how to keep wars short and limited in scope. The lesson their work conveys to our age will be pondered later in this book.

THE LEAGUE OF NATIONS

With the end of the First World War, a new epoch began in the history of international government. The League of Nations showed in its functions a great deal of similarity with the Holy Alliance. In its organization, however, it constituted a radical departure from the experiment that had preceded it a century before.

Organization

The League of Nations, in contrast to the Holy Alliance, was a real organization with a legal personality, agents, and agencies of its own. Its political agencies

---

[5]See pages 244 ff.

were the Assembly, the Council, and the Permanent Secretariat. The Assembly was composed of representatives of all the member states. In the Assembly as well as in the Council each state had one vote, and unanimity of all members present was required for all political decisions, including those which concerned the prevention of war.[6] The main exceptions were Article 15, paragraph 10,[7] and the rule that in decisions concerning the settlement of international disputes the votes of the parties to the dispute were not to be counted.

The Council consisted of two types of members: permanent and nonpermanent. All great powers belonging at a particular time to the League were permanent members; e.g., originally France, Great Britain, Italy, and Japan, to which were later added Germany and the Soviet Union. The nonpermanent members numbered originally four. Their numbers were increased successively until in 1936 the Council comprised eleven nonpermanent members. Thus originally permanent and nonpermanent members were equal in numbers. From 1922 on, the nonpermanent members had an ever-increasing majority over the permanent ones. In 1939, after Germany, Italy, and Japan had resigned and the Soviet Union had been expelled, the Council comprised two permanent (France and Great Britain) and eleven nonpermanent members.

What is important in view of the distribution of power between great and small nations is not their numerical relationship but the permanent membership of the great powers in the Council. By virtue of this permanent membership, in conjunction with the rule of unanimity, the great powers could be sure that the Council could make no decisions without the consent of all of them. Furthermore, the distribution of voting strength in an international agency never tells the whole story. No great power will ever be alone in voting in favor of or against a certain measure if it does not want to be alone, nor need any group of great powers ever run the risk of being outvoted if it is anxious not to be in the minority on a particular question. Most small and medium powers depend economically, militarily, and politically upon the support of a great power. Such a nation will hardly cast its vote against a great power that has intimated that the smaller nation is expected to heed its advice. Thus every great power controlled a number of votes of the small and medium members of the League. On any important issue France could be certain of the votes of

---

[6]Cf. the emphasis the Permanent Court of International Justice placed upon the principles of unanimity in the Advisory Opinion concerning Article 3, paragraph 2, of the Treaty of Lausanne (Frontier between Turkey and Iraq): "In a body . . . whose mission is to deal with any matter 'within the sphere of action of the League or affecting the peace of the world,' observance of the rule of unanimity is naturally and even necessarily indicated. Only if the decisions of the Council have the support of the unanimous consent of the Powers composing it, will they possess the degree of authority which they must have: the very prestige of the League might be imperilled if it were admitted, in the absence of an express provision to that effect, that decisions on important questions could be taken by a majority. Moreover, it is hardly conceivable that resolutions on questions affecting the peace of the world could be adopted against the will of those amongst the Members of the Council who, although in a minority, would, by reason of their political position, have to bear the larger share of the responsibilities and consequences ensuing therefrom." (*P. C. I. J.* Series B, No. 12, p. 29.)

[7]For the text, see page 309, note 8.

Belgium, Czechoslovakia, Yugoslavia, Rumania, and—for more than a decade—Poland. Great Britain could count upon the votes of the dominions, the Scandinavian countries, and Portugal.

This controlling influence of the great powers, regardless of the legal structure of the organization, operated in the League of Nations side by side with the brilliant intellectual leadership of the representatives of a number of small and medium nations. These representatives exerted an influence upon the work of the League of Nations out of all proportion to, and irrespective of, the power of their particular countries. The scene of that leadership was primarily the Assembly. The Assembly of the League of Nations, in contrast to the General Assembly of the United Nations, had the authority to render binding decisions not only with regard to routine matters or questions of secondary importance, but also concerning political problems, such as peace-preserving measures.[8] To that extent the Assembly of the League of Nations played the role of a real parliament where leadership fell many times to the best qualified representative, regardless of the power and sometimes even of the interests of his country.

But that leadership stopped at the line where the vital interests of the great powers began. In the great crises of the League the leadership of the great powers asserted itself. When in a conflict of first-rate political importance, such as the Italo-Ethiopian War or the Spanish Civil War, the attitude of some of the small and great powers diverged, the policies of the great powers were bound to win. For the preponderance of the great powers on the international scene is a fact, as the preponderance of great economic organizations is a fact, in domestic society. No legal arrangement nor organizational device, short of destroying that preponderance of power itself, can undo the political consequences of that disparity of power. Thus in the League the small nations enjoyed a greater opportunity for influence and independent action than they ever did before or since in modern times. Yet the international government of the League of Nations, at least in the sphere of high politics, was a government of the great powers.

Dual Meaning of the Status Quo: France vs. Great Britain

What were the principles of justice which the international government of the League of Nations was to realize? That question has found a symbolic answer

---

[8]See Article 3, paragraph 3, of the Covenant: "The Assembly may deal at its meetings with any matter within the sphere of action of the League or affecting the peace of the world." See also Article 15, paragraphs 9, 10: "The Council may in any case under this Article refer the dispute to the Assembly. The dispute shall be so referred at the request of either party to the dispute provided that such request be made within fourteen days after the submission of the dispute to the Council.

"In any case referred to the Assembly, all the provisions of this Article and of Article 12 relating to the action and powers of the Council shall apply to the action and powers of the Assembly, provided that a report made by the Assembly, if concurred in by the Representatives of those members of the League represented on the Council and of a majority of the other members of the League, . . . shall have the same force as a report by the Council concurred in by all the Members thereof. . . ."

in the fact that the twenty-six articles of the Convenant of the League of Nations are identical with the first twenty-six articles of the peace treaties that settled the issues of the First World War. The intimate connection between the League of Nations and the status quo of 1919 was thus made obvious from the very outset. The provisions of the Covenant put that connection in explicit legal terms. The Preamble refers to "international law as the actual rule of conduct among governments" and to "a scrupulous respect for all treaty obligations." Article 10 makes the League of Nations the defender of the territorial status quo of 1919 by establishing the legal obligation of the members "to respect and preserve as against external aggression the territorial integrity and existing independence of all members of the League." All provisions of the subsequent articles concerning the settlement of disputes and its enforcement must be read in the light of this provision of Article 10. This provision lays down the standard by which the agencies of the League were to be guided in evaluating the claims and actions of nations and in devising methods to meet a threat to the peace.

It is true that the framers of the Covenant tried to relieve the League from the stigma of being completely identified with the status quo of 1919. To that end, they provided in Article 19 for peaceful change. We have already pointed to the intrinsic weakness of that provision, which remained a dead letter from the beginning. But aside from its intrinsic defects, Article 19 pales into insignificance if seen in its orphanlike isolation within the structure of the Covenant and if compared with the organic connection in which Article 10 stands to the peace treaties of 1919, on the one hand, and to the peace-preserving and law-enforcing provisions of Articles 11–16 of the Covenant, on the other. Article 19, then, was little more than a verbal concession to the undeniable fact of change. Its fundamental law no less than its origin, identical with the peace treaties of 1919, made it inevitable that the League as a working organization of international government should judge and act as the defender of the status quo.

Two principles were at the foundation of the status quo of 1919: the permanent inability of Germany to wage war, and the principle of national self-determination. Yet, from the very outset, the two nations mainly responsible for the policies of the League, Great Britain and France, interpreted these two principles in distinctly different ways and tried to shape the policies of the League according to these different interpretations. For France, Germany's permanent inability to wage war was synonymous with the permanent preponderance of France on the continent of Europe. For Great Britain, Germany's permanent inability to wage war was not incompatible with the comeback of Germany as a great power within controlled limits so that at least the semblance of a balance of power would again exist on the continent of Europe.

France looked to the League of Nations primarily as a kind of collective sheriff that would add its strength to the military might of France for the defense of the status quo of 1919. Great Britain considered the League of Nations primarily a kind of clearinghouse where the statesmen of the world would meet to discuss their common problems and seek agreement by way of compromise. Finally, France used the principle of national self-determination as a political weapon with which to strengthen its allies in Eastern Europe against Germany. Great Britain saw in it a principle capable of universal application, at least on the European continent, which one might well use to strengthen Germany at the expense of the allies of France.

At the bottom of these divergent interpretations of standards of justice and of political principles we find again the basic pattern of international politics. France subordinated all its policies as one of the leading members of the international government of the League of Nations to its overriding desire to maintain the status quo of 1919. This status quo was identical with France's hegemony on the European continent. Great Britain thought it could regain the controlling influence it had exerted over the affairs of Europe during the nineteenth century. To that end, it tried to restore the power configuration that had existed during that period: a balance of power on the European continent with Great Britain as its "holder." Thus its policies as the other leading member of the international government of the League were all directed toward undermining the status quo of 1919—within manageable limits which Great Britain thought it could determine at will. This goal of British foreign policy could only be attained by weakening France.

This conflict between the British and French conceptions and policies did not, however, wreck the League of Nations, as the conflict between Great Britain and Russia had the Holy Alliance. It rather led to a creeping paralysis in the political activities of the League and to its inability to take determined action against threats to international order and peace. It culminated in the triumph of the British over the French conception. The distribution of power between Great Britain and France was in the main responsible for this development.

The margin of French superiority started to shrink in the mid-twenties in proportion to the growth of German strength, first slowly and imperceptibly, and then—following Hitler's ascent to power—with ever-increasing speed. In 1919, France sought the separation of the left bank of the Rhine from Germany and treaties of alliance with Great Britain and the United States. France received neither. It was able to make only two additions to its own military strength which barely concealed its intrinsic weakness in comparison with the potentialities of German power. One addition was the alliances with Poland, Czechoslovakia, and Rumania, and the treaty of friendship with Yugoslavia. These allies, however, were at best medium states. Some, if not all of them, were militarily overrated and could not be relied upon to act always in unison. The other addition was the Locarno Treaties of 1925, putting the Franco-German frontier under the joint guarantee of Great Britain and Italy. Yet France was unable to obtain a similar guarantee for the German-Polish frontier, nor was it able to gain British support for an automatic system of collective security which would have closed certain loopholes left open by the Covenant of the League of Nations.[9]

---

[9]See pages 314–316.

Under such conditions of hegemonial power in the short run and incurable weakness in the long run, France started in the mid-twenties to follow the British lead in its policies within the League of Nations, at first hesitatingly, and in the thirties without alternative.[10] For by then, due to its own indecision and now apparent weakness, France was no longer able to seek on its own account the implementation of those provisions of the Covenant through which the League could have played the role of an international government for the maintenance of international order and the prevention of war. France by itself did not have the power to make the League play that role. Great Britain had no interest in making the League play it. For the performance of that role would have meant the perpetuation of unchallenged French supremacy on the European continent—a supremacy that Great Britain was resolved to bring to an end. Thus the British conceptions and policies put their imprint upon the governmental activities of the League of Nations.

Three Weaknesses of the League of Nations

This is not to say that the League of Nations did not exercise important governmental functions. The League of Nations governed two territories: the Saar Basin and the City of Danzig. It governed indirectly—according to the text of Article 22 of the Covenant—rather than in actuality the mandated territories.[11] Yet, when it came to the maintenance of international order and the preservation or restoration of peace, it governed only in the rare instances when either the interests of the great powers among its members were not affected or the common interests of the most influential among them seemed to require it.

The League of Nations did not act as an international government when

---

[10]This trend was interrupted only for a short while in 1934 when French Foreign Minister Barthou prepared the ground for a military alliance with the Soviet Union, which, however, none of his successors dared to implement. The foreign policy of Laval in that period, while strongly anti-British in intent and favoring an understanding with the Axis powers, was identical with that of Great Britain in undermining the status quo of 1919.

[11]Cf. the following provisions of Article 22: "To those colonies and territories which as a consequence of the late war have ceased to be under the sovereignty of the States which formerly governed them and which are inhabited by peoples not yet able to stand by themselves under the strenuous conditions of the modern world, there should be applied the principle that the well-being and development of such peoples form a sacred trust of civilisation and that securities for the performance of this trust should be embodied in this Covenant.

"The best method of giving practical effect to this principle is that the tutelage of such peoples should be entrusted to advanced nations who, by reason of their resources, their experience or their geographical position, can best undertake this responsibility, and who are willing to accept it, and that this tutelage should be exercised by them as Mandatories on behalf of the League. . . .

"In every case of mandate, the Mandatory shall render to the Council an annual report in reference to the territory committed to its charge.

"The degree of authority, control or administration to be exercised by the Mandatory shall, if not previously agreed upon by the Members of the League, be explicitly defined in each case by the Council.

"A permanent Commission shall be constituted to receive and examine the annual reports of the Mandatories and to advise the Council on all matters relating to the observance of the mandates."

in 1920 Poland seized Vilna, the old Lithuanian capital; for that violation of international law was committed by the strongest ally of France, and the intervention of the League was opposed by the Soviet Union. But in 1925, incipient war between Bulgaria and Greece was easily stopped by the President of the Council of the League, who sent a telegram to the parties demanding immediate cessation of hostilities. He was actively supported by France and Great Britain, who acted on this occasion in unison and used their influence in particular to deter Greece from offensive action.

The League of Nations refused to act when in 1923 Italy occupied the Greek island of Corfu. It did nothing even approaching the nature of enforcement action after Japan invaded Manchuria in 1931, and after it invaded China proper in 1937. The League did nothing to prevent or stop the Chaco War between Bolivia and Paraguay in 1932–35, except to recommend an arms embargo. From 1935 on, the League did nothing effective to maintain its authority within the territory of Danzig, and it did nothing in the face of the continuous violations of the Treaty of Versailles by Germany. What the League did in 1935–36 with respect to Italy's attack upon Ethiopia could not, as we have seen,[12] have been different had it been calculated to be ineffective. From 1936–39, the League did nothing to control the international effects of the Spanish Civil War. In December 1939, however, the League expelled the Soviet Union because of its attack against Finland. It was the last and—aside from the sanctions against Italy—the most drastic of the League's political actions.

The League of Nations prevented no major war, and it was ineffective in maintaining international order. The reasons for this failure, aside from the prevalence of the British conception over the French, are threefold: constitutional, structural, and political.

Constitutional Weakness

The Covenant of the League of Nations did not outlaw war as such. The members of the League were not allowed to go to war under certain conditions. By the same token, they were allowed to go to war in the absence of those conditions. Thus the Preamble to the Covenant stipulated "the acceptance of obligations[13] not to resort to war." Article 12 provided that the members should not "resort to war until three months after the award by the arbitrators. . . ." By virtue of Article 13, paragraph 4, the members agreed "that they will not resort to war against a member of the League which complies" with the judicial decision of a dispute. Finally, according to Article 15, paragraph 6, "If a report by the Council is unanimously agreed to by the members thereof other than the Representatives of one or more of the parties to the dispute, the Members of the League agree that they will not go to war with any party to the dispute which complies with the recommendations of the report."

Only the two latter provisions contain an outright prohibition to go to war.

---

[12]See pages 292–294.

[13]In contradistinction to "the obligation." The French text: *("certaines obligations")* is more emphatic on that score.

As Jean Ray put it: "We are convinced that this timidity of the authors of the Covenant has serious consequences and puts in jeopardy the new system which they tried to erect. As a matter of fact, since the contrary opinion was not clearly expressed, it remained tacitly admitted that war is a solution, the normal solution, of international conflicts. These obligations, as a matter of law, are presented only as exceptions; the implicit rule is the recourse to war."[14] Even if the members had lived up to the provisions of the Covenant, they would have found in the fundamental law of the League an instrument for the prevention of some wars and for the legalization of others.

Structural Weakness

This constitutional weakness, however, did not affect the actual operations of the League, for the League did not live up to its constitution. On the other hand, the structural weakness of the League had a direct bearing upon its failure to prevent the wars that occurred under its jurisdiction. That weakness consisted in the contrast between the distribution of power within it and the distribution of power in the world at large.

The structure of the League was predominantly European in a period when the main factors of international politics were no longer predominantly European. Both great powers that in turn dominated it, France and Great Britain, were European powers. The only non-European great power that was a member of the League was Japan. Of the two nations that in the twenties were already potentially the two most powerful nations on earth, the United States was never a member, and the Soviet Union only during the League's declining years, from 1934 to 1939.

It is, of course, true that of the thirty-one original members, only ten were European and of the thirteen nations that joined it later, only seven. But here again numbers do not tell the story. An international organization whose main purpose is the maintenance of international order and peace does not need to be universal in the sense that all nations of the world belong to it. It must, however, be universal in the sense that all powerful nations, which are most likely to disturb the peace of the world, are under its jurisdiction.

Article 17 of the Covenant, therefore, attempted to make the jurisdiction of the League universal regardless of membership. It gave the League authority in case of a dispute between two states, one or both of which were not members of the League, to invite the nonmembers "to accept the obligations of membership in the League for the purposes of such disputes, upon such conditions as the Council may deem just. . . . If a state so invited shall refuse to accept the obligations of membership and shall resort to war against a member of the League," the sanctions of Article 16 shall be applicable against such a state. "If both parties to the dispute . . . refuse to accept the obligations of membership . . . the Council may take such measures, and make recommendations as will prevent hostilities and will result in the settlement of the dispute."

---

[14]*Commentaire du Pacte de la Société des Nations* (Paris: Sirey, 1930), pp. 73–4.

This last paragraph of Article 17 endeavored to make the League of Nations a world government for the purpose of preserving peace. The feasibility of such a government must again depend upon the distribution of power between the members of the League acting in unison and those states over which the governmental functions are to be exercised. The League would have had no difficulty in making its will prevail over two small or medium states. Let us suppose, however, that a dispute had broken out between a member of the League, on the one hand, and the United States or the Soviet Union or both, on the other; or between the two latter powers any time between 1919 and 1934, when neither country was a member of the League. Under such circumstances, the attempt to impose the League's will upon the United States or the Soviet Union or both would have amounted to a world war between the members of the League and either one or two of the potentially most powerful nations on earth, with a number of nonmember nations either joining the latter or remaining neutral. The attempt to preserve peace on a universal scale would have led to war on a universal scale. Thus the membership of some great powers and the nonmembership of other great powers rendered the League powerless to preserve peace on a world-wide scale.

This lack of universality in the membership of the great powers also indicates the fundamental reason for the failure of British and French policies in the period between the two world wars. The policies of both countries were anachronistic. The policies of France might perhaps have succeeded in the age of Louis XIV. Then the main weights of the balance of power were located in Central and Western Europe, and such a preponderence as France gained in 1919 would have given it a real chance to establish its permanent hegemony over the continent. Yet after Russia had become one of the main factors in the balance of power, Napoleon had to learn that a hegemony over the European continent meant little, with the resources of Eastern Europe and of the better part of Asia either uncommitted or hostile. This lesson was heeded by the brilliant French diplomatists who in the two decades preceding the First World War founded French foreign policy upon close ties with Russia. Their successors in the period between the two world wars based their hopes upon a system of alliances with the balkanized countries of Eastern and Southeastern Europe, a poor substitute for the "grand alliance" with Russia. Obsessed with the fear of revolution, very much like the French aristocrats in the years after 1789, they were ready to commit national suicide rather than yield to the logic of a new international configuration.

British foreign policy in that period was as anachronistic as the French. Great Britain was intrinsically as weak with regard to the continent of Europe as France was with regard to Germany. The role that Russia played in relation to France was similar to the one the United States and, to a much lesser degree, Japan played in relation to Great Britain. A policy that was still successful in the age of Disraeli was doomed to failure in the age of Stanley Baldwin. Throughout the nineteenth century, Great Britain's back yard, as it were, had been secure; the British navy controlled the seas without challenge. In the thirties, other great naval powers had arisen, one of them potentially the most powerful nation on earth. Furthermore, the airplane brought the British Isles closer to the continent than ever before. Such conditions allowed British foreign policy but two alternatives. It could place its weight permanently in that scale of the European balance of power where British interests in the long run seemed to be most secure. Or it could make itself the spearhead of American policy in Europe.[15] What British policy could not do was to continue the policy of "splendid isolation." And this is what it did.

It will remain forever a moot question whether or not France and Great Britain had any real choice in the face of the policies actually pursued by the Soviet Union and the United States. It is, however, beyond doubt that an international government never had a chance whose leading members, either by choice or by necessity, followed policies so completely at odds with the actual distribution of power in the world.

Political Weakness

This would have been true even on the assumption that the League of Nations had been able to act as a unit in the face of a threatening war of major proportions. Actually this assumption was never realized. Divergent national interests pursued by the great powers prevailed over the principles of justice defined by the League of Nations in terms of the status quo. In 1921, immediately after the First World War, the four permanent members of the Council of the League were still able to act in unison with respect to relatively important political issues, such as the fortification of the Aaland Islands involving Finland and Sweden and the partition of Upper Silesia, which was a bone of contention between Germany and Poland. After these promising beginnings, it was not only the conflict between France and Great Britain that incapacitated the League for collective action on matters of major importance, but the separate and generally antagonistic policies of the great powers.

When Germany joined the League in 1925, it pursued a policy of undermining the status quo of Versailles, mainly using the principle of national self-determination as the dynamite with which to crack the foundations of the territorial status quo. This policy was at odds with the policies of France and its Eastern allies and was aimed, first surreptitiously and later openly, at the termination of their preponderance on the continent of Europe. In addition to the principle of national self-determination, Germany used the dual fear of bolshevist revolution and Russian imperialism, which obsessed the Western powers, as a weapon with which to strengthen its own position. While alternately offering itself as a bulwark against bolshevism and threatening to ally itself with the Soviet Union, Germany was able to wring concessions from the Western powers, to isolate Poland from France, and to paralyze the League.

Italy, on its part, pursued in the twenties a policy somewhat similar to the one pursued by Great Britain. Italy welcomed the comeback of Germany

---

[15]It is worthy of note that since the end of the Second World War Great Britain has pursued these two foreign policies simultaneously.

within certain limits as a means to weaken France and its Eastern allies, especially Yugoslavia. When in the thirties the impotence of the League had become obvious, Italy used Germany as Germany was using the Soviet Union, alternately as common menace and as a silent partner, and made an open bid against Great Britain and France for domination of the Mediterranean.

The Soviet Union was as isolated within the League as it had been without. Its potential strength as a nation and its sponsorship of world revolution made it a dual menace to the Western powers. It proved to be impossible for France, Great Britain, and the Soviet Union to unite for common action in any of the great crises from 1934 to 1939, with the exception of the sanctions against Italy. In all those crises the Western powers and the Soviet Union found themselves in opposite camps. Even when in 1939 Germany threatened both the Soviet Union and the Western powers with war, they were unable to agree upon common preventive action. Instead, each side tried to deflect the threatening stroke of lightning to the other side. It was only Hitler's folly in waging war against both at the same time that made them allies despite themselves.

Finally, Japan, smarting under the inferiority which the treaties of 1922 had imposed upon it, prepared for the moment when it could establish its own hegemony in the Far East. Japan could do so only by dislodging Great Britain and the United States from their positions in the Far East and by "closing the door" to China which, as a matter of traditional policy, Great Britain and the United States had insisted upon keeping open for all nations. Thus, when Japan took the first step toward establishing its Far Eastern empire by invading Manchuria in 1931, it could not help coming into conflict with France and Great Britain, the leading members of the League of Nations. It is not without ironic significance that Japan, in establishing its dominion, made use of the same principle of national self-determination which had carried France and Great Britain to dominance in the League. Now it was employed to rally the colored races of the Far East against the colonialism of the leaders of the League. Yet neither while Japan remained a member of the League nor after its resignation in 1932 did Great Britain feel strong enough to lead the League in effective collective action in order to stop Japan's attack against China.

The ability of the League of Nations to prevent war was predicated upon the unity of its members, and especially of the great powers. By virtue of the principle of unanimity, any member of the League, except parties to a dispute, could veto a decision by voting against a motion to take action. Given the antagonistic policies pursued by the leading members of the League, the very likelihood of a veto impeded even attempts at decisive collective action. Only an overriding principle of justice could have made such action possible. As we have seen, such principles of justice did exist in the abstract as collective defense of the status quo against the nations vanquished in the First World War and as national self-determination.

Confronted with a political situation demanding concrete action, these abstract principles transformed themselves into ideological justifications for the separate policies pursued by the individual nations. Thus these abstract principles of justice, far from providing common standards of judgment and guides for common action, actually strengthened international anarchy by strengthening the antagonistic policies of individual nations. The inability of the League of Nations to maintain international order and peace, then, was the inevitable result of the ascendancy that the ethics and policies of sovereign nations were able to maintain over the moral and political objectives of the international government of the League of Nations.

21

International Government: The United Nations

In order to understand the constitutional functions and actual operations of the United Nations, it is necessary to distinguish sharply between the constitutional provisions of the Charter and the manner in which the agencies of the United Nations, under the pressure of unforeseen political circumstances, have actually performed their functions under the Charter. The government of the United Nations, like the government of the United States, can be understood only by confronting the provisions of the constitution with the realities of political practice. Such a separate analysis of constitutional function and actual performance points up a series of significant transformations not only in the particular political functions performed by the agencies of the United Nations, but in the very character of the United Nations as an international organization.

THE UNITED NATIONS ACCORDING TO THE CHARTER

Government by Superpowers

In its constitutional organization the United Nations resembles the League of Nations. It, too, has three political agencies: the General Assembly composed of all members of the United Nations, the Security Council as the political executive of the organization, and the Secretariat. The distribution of functions between the General Assembly and the Security Council, however, differs distinctly from that between the Council and the Assembly of the League of Nations. The tendency toward government by the great powers, which was already unmistakable in the League of Nations, completely dominates the distribution of functions in the United Nations. This tendency manifests itself in three constitutional devices of the Charter: the inability of the General Assembly to make decisions in political matters, the limitation of the requirement of unanimity to the permanent members of the Security Council, and the right of parties to disputes to veto any enforcement measures against themselves.

The Assembly of the League of Nations was, as we have seen, a real international parliament, which could take action in political matters alone or in competition with the Council of the League. The General Assembly of the United Nations, according to Articles 10–14 of the Charter, has only the power to make recommendations in political matters either to the parties concerned or to the Security Council. With regard to the maintenance of international peace and security, it can debate, investigate, and recommend, but it cannot act. Even those modest functions are qualified by Article 12 of the Charter, which precludes the General Assembly from making even recommendations on matters that are on the agenda of the Security Council. Thus the concurrent jurisdiction of a deciding Council and a deciding Assembly, which was a distinguishing feature of the League of Nations, is replaced by the alternate jurisdiction of a deciding Security Council and a recommending General Assembly. When the Security Council concerns itself with a matter, the General Assembly may still debate, but it can no longer even recommend.

This device enables the Security Council to control indirectly the functions of the General Assembly in matters of political importance. By simply putting a matter on its agenda, the Security Council can transform the General Assembly into a debating society without even the right to express its collective opinion on the matter.

This limitation of the functions of the General Assembly has endowed the United Nations with a split personality. The General Assembly may with two-thirds majority recommend to the Security Council a solution of an international problem which the Security Council may disregard at its discretion. This discretion of the Security Council would be no serious matter if the General Assembly were an advisory body of limited membership and not the representative body of virtually all the nations of the world. As it is, the distribution of functions between the Security Council and the General Assembly is a constitutional monstrosity. The United Nations may speak with respect to the same issue with two voices—the General Assembly's and the Security Council's— and between these two voices there is no organic connection. Two-thirds or more of the total membership of the United Nations may recommend one thing, and nine of the fifteen members of the Security Council may disregard the recommendation and decide something else.

The vice of this constitutional arrangement does not lie in the predominance of the great powers, which we found to exist in the Holy Alliance and the League of Nations as well. The vice lies rather in the opportunity for the General Assembly to demonstrate its impotence. The Holy Alliance was frankly an international government of the great powers. The League of Nations was an international government of the great powers with the advice and consent of all member nations, each of which, by virtue of the principle of unanimity and save for Article 15, paragraph 10, of the Covenant, could stop the international government from acting. The United Nations is an international government of the great powers which resembles in its constitutional arrangements the Holy Alliance and in its pretense the League of Nations. It is the contrast between pretense and constitutional actuality, between the democratic expectations roused by the words of the Charter and the autocratic performance envisaged by the actual distribution of functions which characterizes the constitutional provisions of the United Nations.

The international government of the United Nations, then, is identical with the international government of the Security Council. The Security Council appears, as it were, as the Holy Alliance of our time. The predominance of the Security Council having thus been established, the Charter proceeds to establish the predominance of the great powers within the Security Council. For in actuality it is the five permanent members that are supposed to perform the governmental functions. We have seen that the principle of unanimity has been abrogated with respect to all decisions of the Security Council and has been replaced with regard to substantive decisions by the requirement of nine affirmative votes in which the votes of the five permanent members must be included. Given the preponderant influence of some of the five permanent members (China, France, Great Britain, the Soviet Union, the United States), their unanimous decision is expected to attract at least four more votes of other members of the Security Council.

The United Nations, then, is predicated upon the continuing unity of the permanent members of the Security Council. In the scheme of the Charter, these five members are, as it were, the nucleus of a world federation, a Holy Alliance within a Holy Alliance. By limiting the principle of unanimity to them, the Charter makes them the international government of the United Nations. It follows that with but one permanent member dissenting there can be no international government of the United Nations.

This great-power monopoly of governmental action is still further enhanced by Article 27, paragraph 3, according to which a party to a dispute is prevented from voting only with regard to the pacific settlement of disputes under Chapter VI of the Charter. In other words, the great-power veto applies to the enforcement measures under Chapter VII. When a great power is a party to a dispute, the Security Council can render a decision by virtue of Article 27, paragraph 3, regardless of the attitude of that great power. If the Security Council should try to enforce that decision, the dissent of any of the great powers, although a party to the dispute, would erect a legal barrier to enforcement action. In such a contingency the decision of the Security Council would remain a dead letter.

Actually, however, the international government of the United Nations is government of the great powers to a still greater degree than the foregoing analysis would indicate. Of the five permanent members of the Security Council only two, the United States and the Soviet Union, are really great powers. Great Britain and France are medium powers; China is only potentially a great power. Under present conditions of world politics, most members of the Security Council, the permanent members included, can be prevailed upon, if need be, to support the position taken by the United States, China, and the Soviet Union. The international government of the United Nations, stripped of its legal trimmings, then, is really the international government of the United States, China, and the Soviet Union acting in unison. At best—if they are united—they can govern the rest of the world for the purpose of maintaining order and of preventing war. At worst—if they are disunited—there will be no international government at all.

Ideally the United Nations is an instrument for governing the world through the combined power of the United States, China, and the Soviet Union. The Charter of the United Nations, however, does not envisage the possibility that the United Nations operate as an international government for the purpose of establishing or maintaining order in the relations among the United States, China, and the Soviet Union or of preventing war among them. The device of the veto excludes the purpose of subjecting the United States, China, and the Soviet Union to an international government against their will.

Undefined Principles of Justice

The standards of justice which shall guide the judgment and actions of the agencies of the United Nations are found in three places: in the Preamble, in Chapter 1 dealing with Purposes and Principles, and interspersed through the Charter. Yet, in contrast to the basic principles of the Holy Alliance and of the League of Nations, the principles of justice upon which the United Nations is founded are beset by two kinds of inner contradictions: one concerning the mode of actions to be performed by the United Nations, the other concerning the purposes for which the actions are to be performed.

The Preamble reaffirms "faith . . . in the equal rights . . . of nations large and small," and Article 2, paragraph 1, declares that "the Organization is based on the principle of sovereign equality of all its Members." That principle is strengthened by Article 2, paragraph 7, which exempts "matters which are essentially within the domestic jurisdiction of any state" from the jurisdiction of the United Nations, except in so far as enforcement measures under Chapter VII are concerned. Yet the whole structure of the United Nations, as laid out in the main body of the Charter, is based upon what one might call paradoxically the "sovereign inequality" of its members. We have already pointed to the fact that if the United Nations were to operate as provided for in its Charter, all its members who are not members of the Security Council would lose their sovereignty and would remain sovereign in name and form only. Thus the principle of sovereign equality proclaimed by the Charter in its introductory provisions is contradicted by the actual distribution of functions which the Charter itself provides.

The Preamble and Chapter I formulate five political purposes of action: (1) maintenance of international peace and security, (2) collective security, (3) prohibition of the use of force "against the territorial integrity or political independence of any state" and reservation of its use for "the common interest" as defined in the Charter, (4) maintenance of "justice and respect for the obligations arising from treaties and other sources of international law," and (5) national self-determination.

Of these five purposes, the first two are general and of an instrumental nature. They tell us that whatever the United Nations does it should do peacefully and according to the principle of collective security. The other three principles are specific and concrete. They tell us what the United Nations should or should not do in concrete situations. It should use force under certain conditions and not use it under others; it should act justly and in harmony with the rules of international law and with the principle of national self-determination.

It is significant that the Charter is most explicit in elaborating and implementing the first two purposes (cf. particularly Chapters VI and VII) and that it is virtually silent with regard to the remaining three. Article 11, paragraph 1, and Article 24, paragraph 2, refer the General Assembly and the Security Council in general terms to the Purposes and Principles as guides for their deliberations and actions. But the concrete meaning of such concepts as justice, respect for international law, and national self-determination is not self-evident, nor is it the same everywhere and at all times. In the abstract, most men may be able to agree upon a definition of those terms. It is the concrete political situation that gives these abstract terms a concrete meaning and enables them to guide the judgment and actions of men. Nowhere in the main body of the Charter is there a definition of, or reference to, a substantive principle of justice. Nor are there any other sources that would give unequivocal content to these abstractions.

THE UNITED NATIONS—POLITICAL REALITY

A shift in the distribution of voting strength resulted from the fact that the massive increase in the membership of the United Nations primarily benefited nations belonging to the so-called Afro-Asian bloc. The Afro-Asian bloc comprises more than one-third of the membership of the United Nations. Thus, if it were to vote in unison, it could either exercise a veto on any resolution adverse to its interests or else, by joining either the American or the Soviet bloc, become the core of a working two-thirds majority. In reality, however, the Afro-Asian bloc has but rarely voted as a unit; its vote has typically been split, with some members voting with the American, others with the Soviet bloc, and a very considerable number abstaining. Consequently, as concerns the ability of the United Nations to function politically through the General Assembly, the Afro-Asian bloc has thus far performed a negative function. By splintering its vote between them, it has strengthened the power of the American and Soviet blocs to oppose the will of a simple majority with the veto of more than one-third of the membership. As a result, the General Assembly has found it difficult to pass resolutions calling for substantive policies more specific than opposition to the remnants of colonialism and racial discrimination, invitations to warring parties to cease firing and negotiate a settlement, and authorizations to the Secretary General to investigate, observe, report, use his good offices, organize peace-keeping forces, and do what he deems necessary to restore peace and order. Thus the difficulty of two-thirds of the General Assembly to agree upon specific substantive policies resulted in the ascendancy of the Secretary General to the temporary eminence of chief executive officer of the United Nations.

The Charter intends the Secretary General to be "the chief administrative officer of the organization." He "may bring to the attention of the Security Council any matter which in his opinion may threaten the maintenance of international peace and security." And he "shall perform such other functions as are entrusted to him by (the) organs" of the United Nations. It is from this provision of the Charter that the new functions of the Secretary General as the apparent chief political agent of the United Nations derive.

The new functions are intimately related to the impotence of the General Assembly, as the responsibility for action which the General Assembly has taken on is intimately related to the impotence of the Security Council. And one can go one step further and say that the responsibility for the settlement of political issues with which the United Nations as a whole had been burdened is a by-product of the inability of the nations directly concerned, especially the great powers, to settle outstanding political issues among themselves. So they charge the United Nations with finding a settlement. The members of the General Assembly, taking the place of the paralyzed Security Council, are no more able to agree on a settlement collectively than they were when acting as individual nations. So they charged the Secretary General with finding a solution.

Thus the Secretary General became a kind of Prime Minister of the United Nations. By virtue of delegations of power, generally vague, by the Security Council or the General Assembly, his office took over political functions which the Security Council and the General Assembly themselves should have performed but were unable to. This transformation of the office owes much to the initiative and skill of Dag Hammarskjöld, who was Secretary General from 1953 to 1961. He transformed the United Nations, to use his own words, into "a dynamic instrument of governments." He set out, to quote him again, "to create a new executive responsibility somewhere . . ." and "to help fill any vacuum that may appear in the systems which the Charter and traditional diplomacy provide for the safeguarding of peace and security." Hammarskjöld even went beyond interpreting broadly the mandate he had received from the General Assembly or the Security Council and acted at times without any mandate at all and in the face of the explicit opposition of a member of the United Nations. Thus he established in 1959 a United Nations presence in Laos even though the Soviet Union had declared beforehand that it was opposed to his visit and specifically to his leaving a United Nations representative behind. Thus he decided in 1958 to enlarge the United Nations observer corps in Lebanon even though the Soviet Union had already vetoed an American proposal to enlarge it as well as a Japanese proposal that he should be given a free hand.

This enlargement of the Secretary General's office into something approaching a supranational political agency was bound not only to evoke the opposition of particular nations to particular measures taken by the Secretary General but also to pose in acute form the inner contradiction which has paralyzed all political international organizations: the contradiction between national sovereignty and the effectiveness of an international organization. The Soviet Union consistently defended national sovereignty against encroachments by international treaties and organizations and it consistently opposed the stewardship of Hammarskjöld and his predecessor, Trygve Lie, as the embodiment of the supranational aspirations of the United Nations. When Charles DeGaulle came to power in 1958, the Soviet Union was joined by France. The Soviet Union tried to destroy the power of the Secretary General through the so-called troika proposal which would have replaced a single Secretary General with three officials of equal power acting in unison, one each representing the uncommitted nations, the Soviet, and the Western blocs. Had this proposal succeeded, the office of the Secretary General would have been subjected to the veto and would have been paralyzed by it as the veto has paralyzed the Security Council. When it failed, both the Soviet Union, France, and the nations supporting them found another instrument to halt and reverse the supranational trend of the United Nations. They found it in the issue of financial support for the peace-keeping measures recommended by the General Assembly.

The defenders of national sovereignty and opponents of a strong United Nations won a definitive victory when in 1965 the General Assembly decided to forgo the enforcement of Article 19 of the Charter and to accept the principle of voluntary contributions to peace-keeping measures of the United Nations. This victory amounted to a veritable counterrevolution against the United Nations as it had developed by virtue of the extra-constitutional developments outlined above. This decision nullified these extra-constitutional developments of almost two decades. It returned the United Nations to the original intentions of the Charter.

That meant in practice that the Security Council became again the chief executive organ, still threatened with paralysis by the veto and by the expansion of its membership from eleven to fifteen, that the General Assembly was reduced essentially to a debating society debilitated by the massive influx of mini-states whose collective voting strength is out of proportion to their actual power, and that the Secretary General was stripped of the executive power which the General Assembly had bestowed upon him. Only the future can tell whether there exist now sufficient communities of interest among the permanent members of the Security Council to allow it to operate according to the intentions of the Charter and whether there exists now among the members of the General Assembly a sufficient awareness of their interest in a strong United Nations to restore to the General Assembly the power it once possessed. The Gulf experience is no definitive answer.

The decline of the powers of the Secretary General is the result not only of the opposition from within the United Nations to which we have referred, but also of the congenital weakness of his office. Parties to a political conflict can be induced by outsiders to agree on a peaceful settlement by four methods, employed alternately or simultaneously: they can be threatened with disadvantages expected to outweigh the advantages to be gained from continuing the conflict; they can be promised advantages greater than those to be expected from seeing the conflict through to a successful conclusion; they can be persuaded by rational arguments pointing to the advantages and disadvantages to be expected and to the intentions and capabilities of the other side and of interested third parties; they can be helped in taking the last small step toward the consummation of a settlement already achieved in substance through the elaboration of a face-saving and technically satisfactory formula. Of these four devices, the first two tower in importance over the two others, which perform essentially subsidiary functions. It is the measure of the weakness of the Secretary General's position as a political agent that he is almost completely deprived of the two most potent instruments of conciliation, threat and promise, and limited to the use of rational persuasion and formulation of agreements already substantially attained.

The weakness of the General Assembly, as presently composed, then, is reflected in the weakness of the Secretary General. Both can talk, explain, and formulate, but neither can at present put a hand on that lever of threats and promises which is the very soul of political action. The temporary eminence of the Secretary General was but a function of his personality and of the General Assembly's embarrassment at being called upon to act without being able to. When Secretary General Kurt Waldheim sought to free the hostages in Iran, he was met first by hostility from their captors and thereafter by criticism from Americans for his failure. And a call to action addressed to the General Assembly is in turn but the great powers' cry of despair at being unable to settle among themselves issues which, as long as they remain unsettled, carry within themselves the threat of war. Thus the actions of the Secretary General, like the resolutions of the General Assembly, are not so much harbingers of recovery, let alone a cure for the disease, as symptoms of its intractability. Yet they can also have the effect of sedatives for jangled nerves and of medication which prevents existing wounds from opening still wider. This is indeed the contribution which the United Nations is at present able to make to the peaceful settlement of international disputes.

The General Assembly is, at any rate for the time being, in the position in which the Security Council found itself from the very beginning: it is unable to act for the reason that the majority required by the Charter is lacking. Yet, while the Security Council was paralyzed from the outset by the foreseeable and almost automatic use of the veto by the Soviet Union, the paralysis of the General Assembly has been the result of a dynamic process which can be broken down into three phases: disintegration of the two-thirds majority led by the United States, the vain attempt by the two superpowers to fashion a two-thirds majority in support of their respective policies, and the attempt by the two superpowers to minimize the voting support of the other side, an action which U.N. Ambassador Jeane Kirkpatrick in the Reagan administration described as primarily one of forestalling action by others. This continual search for votes, or at least abstentions, has become one of the main preoccupations of the great powers in the General Assembly. Out of it, a new diplomatic procedure has developed, the significance of which is twofold. It forces the great powers to defer, at least in the formulation of their policies, to the preferences of the small member nations and thereby blunts the sharp edges of international conflict. It provides the nations concerned with an opportunity to shift the apparent responsibility for unpleasant decisions to the United Nations and thereby acts as a face-saving and shock-absorbing device. The exceptions have been the tenures of Ambassadors Kirkpatrick and Moynihan, both of whom chose to formulate and defend American policy in the United Nations in confrontational terms.

New Procedures

The powerful nation which needs for the successful execution of its policies the support of small nations can follow one of two courses of action. It can resort to the traditional method of diplomacy and bring its superior power directly to bear upon the weaker nations. In this way dependencies are established and alliances are formed. However, a powerful nation which tries to gain support for its policies through the United Nations General Assembly cannot rely upon its superior power alone. Superior power avails it nothing if it is unable to attract the number of votes sufficient for the purposes of its policy. Thus it must pursue a different course of action, which is determined by the procedures of the General Assembly. These procedures and the new United Nations diplomacy which has developed from them tend to diminish the distinction between great and small nations, since all of them have but one vote.

If a great power had only the task of fashioning an alliance with the techniques of traditional diplomacy, it would select the members of that alliance primarily in view of the power they could add to it. Yet the task of the new United Nations diplomacy is not so much to build an alliance with a maximum of political and military power as to form a majority with a maximum of voting strength. In the General Assembly, India's vote counts for as much as Iceland's and Qatar's is as valuable as Great Britain's. The most powerful member of an alliance can afford to disregard the preferences of small states whose power counts for nothing, making concessions only to those whose power counts. The most powerful member of a majority in the process of formation must heed the wishes of even the weakest nation whose vote is needed. For this reason, some U.N. Ambassadors of the United States, including Adlai Stevenson, Charles Yost, William Scranton, and Donald McHenry, are best remembered for their patient efforts in the corridors and cloak rooms seeking support for U.S. policies. Ambassador Thomas Pickering distinguished himself in 1990–91.

It stands to reason that the power of the big nation is still felt, as is the weakness of the small one; for the former speaks in the persuasive voice of power to which the latter can reply only in the whisper of weakness. Yet while power and weakness still count in the new United Nations diplomacy, they do not count for as much as they do in the traditional one. Here lies the important distinction between the techniques of traditional and United Nations diplomacy: the latter is compelled to persuade where the former could afford not to care. Thus a great power must present the issues to be voted on in terms acceptable to the members whose votes are needed. This necessity involves a dual transformation of the measure from what it would be were it to serve exclusively the purposes of the great power.

First of all, the measure must be presented in language reflecting the common interests of the prospective members of the two-thirds majority rather than the interests of a particular nation or more limited group of nations. This linguistic transformation may frequently amount to no more than the ideological justification and rationalization of national policies in terms of supranational ones. Yet the constant use of a certain terminology, not only for purposes of propaganda, but in the give and take of political transactions, may well exert a subtle influence upon the substance of the transactions themselves. For the language constantly used will create in the participants to the transaction expectations to which the transaction somehow must conform or from which, at the very least, it cannot completely deviate.

Thus a foreign policy with which a certain nation or limited group of nations is completely identified and for which the broad support of two-thirds of the General Assembly is sought may well undergo a subtle change if, for the purpose of gaining such broad support, it is constantly presented in supranational terms. Such a change would hardly ever go so far as to run counter to the objectives and methods envisaged by the original national policy. Yet it may well result in the blunting of the sharp edges of a national policy, its retreat from an advanced position, and its reformulation and adaptation in the light of the supranational principles embodied in the language of the resolution. The more experienced U.N. diplomats have gained recognition for their skill in drawing other nations to their side by trimming and adjusting their own policies to accord with those of an emerging majority of states.

The same result will be directly and almost inevitably achieved in the course of the negotiations by which a two-thirds majority in support of the resolution is formed. The divergence of interests, capabilities, and points of view among the members whose support is sought necessitates a search for a common denominator, which is bound to be below the maximum desired by the originator of the national policy. How far below that maximum the measure enacted by the General Assembly is going to be will depend in part upon the skill with which different nations make use of the new methods of United Nations diplomacy. In large measure, however, the distribution of material power between the nations seeking support for a policy and the nations whose support is sought will decide the extent to which the former must give way in order to gain that support. For the nations that can afford to do so will use their power as a lever through which to gain concessions and avoid making them. It is here that old and new diplomacy merge.

Yet the United Nations presents two great inducements for making concessions, at least in the formulation of policies: it is at present powerless to act, and it speaks with a voice which pretends and appears to be, and within certain limits actually is, different from that of the great powers. Thus nations in conflict with each other can afford to do vis-à-vis the United Nations what they think they cannot afford to do in their relations with each other—make concessions in the formulation, if not the substance, of their policies without fear of losing face. This is particularly so if the face-saving formula is proposed by a "neutral" nation or group of nations. For then the parties to the dispute appear to make concessions, not to each other, but to the majority of the General Assembly in whose name the "neutral" nation appears to speak. Conversely, the refusal to make concessions appears in the circumstances not so much as defense of one's own rightful position against the enemy, but rather as defiance of the "political voice of mankind itself." However intangible and imponderable these influences are which the General Assembly is able to bring to bear by virtue of its very existence as an operating agency, they do exist and are being taken into account by the nations concerned.

The Secretary General, as designer of the face-saving formula, personifies both the "neutral" nations and the "political voice of mankind" and partakes of the influences they exert in the General Assembly. However, he has at his disposal two more devices which enable him under favorable circumstances to mitigate international conflicts. One is a function of his office and the sole means of real pressure at his disposal. He can warn a reluctant party that he will bring the situation to the attention of the General Assembly as a threat to international peace and security, and in terms which place the blame where the Secretary General thinks it belongs. By doing this, he threatens to bring those influences into motion which enable the General Assembly to play the mediating and mitigating role to which we have referred.

The other instrument at the disposal of the Secretary General is a function of his personality and lies purely in the realm of persuasion. The late Mr. Hammarskjöld's tenure of office shows impressively how dependent the peace-promoting functions of the Secretary General are upon the intellectual and moral qualities of the holder of that office. Only a man of Hammarskjöld's personality could have tried to do what he did in this respect, and have achieved what he achieved.

In view of the magnitude of the unsettled issues, it is fair to say that what he achieved is little enough, and this judgment must be extended to the United Nations as a whole. But in view of the enormity of the consequences with which these unsettled issues threaten not only individual nations but civilization itself, it must also be said that the little that has been achieved by the United Nations is better than nothing.

PART NINE

The Problem of
Peace: Peace
through
Transformation

22

The World State

Our investigation of the problem of international peace has left us with two conclusions: no attempt to solve the problem of international peace by limiting the national aspirations for power has succeeded, and none could have succeeded under the conditions of the modern state system. What, then, accounts for the instability of peace and order in the relations among states, and what accounts for their relative stability within states? In other words, what factor making for peace and order exists within national societies which is lacking on the international scene? The answer seems obvious—it is the state itself.

National societies owe their peace and order to the existence of a state which, endowed with supreme power within the national territory, keeps peace and order. This was indeed the doctrine of Hobbes, who argued that without such a state national societies would resemble the international scene and the war "of every man against every man"[1] would be the universal condition of mankind. From this premise it was logically inevitable to conclude that peace and order among nations would be secure only within a world state comprising all the nations of the earth. Since the breakdown of the universal order of the Middle Ages, this conclusion has been advanced from time to time.[2]

The experience of two world wars within a quarter of a century and the prospects of a third one to be fought with nuclear weapons have imparted to the idea of a world state an unprecedented urgency. What is needed, so the argument runs, in order to save the world from self-destruction is not limitation of the exercise of national sovereignty through international obligations and institutions, but the transference of the sovereignties of individual nations to a world authority, which would be as sovereign over the individual nations as the individual nations are sovereign within their respective territories. Reforms within the international society have failed and were bound to fail. What is needed, then, is a radical transformation of the existing international society of sovereign nations into a supranational community of individuals.

The argument rests upon an analogy with national societies. It is, there-

---

[1] *Leviathan*, Chapter XIII.
[2] See the references on pages 283 ff.

fore, our first task to find out how peace and order are preserved in national societies.

CONDITIONS OF DOMESTIC PEACE

Peace among social groups within the nation reposes upon a dual foundation: the disinclination of the members of society to break the peace and their inability to break the peace if they should be so inclined. Individuals will be unable to break the peace if overwhelming power makes an attempt to break it a hopeless undertaking. They will be disinclined to break the peace under two conditions. On the one hand, they must feel loyalties to society as a whole which surpass their loyalties to any part of it. On the other hand, they must be able to expect from society at least an approximation of justice through a modicum of satisfaction for their demands. The presence of these three conditions— overwhelming force, suprasectional loyalties, expectation of justice—makes peace possible within nations. The absence of these conditions on the international scene evokes the danger of war.

What are the factors that make for the presence of these conditions? And what is the role the state plays in this respect? A closer consideration of the interplay of social forces that make for peace within the nation will help us to answer these questions.

Suprasectional Loyalties

National societies are composed of a multiplicity of social groups. Some of these are antagonistic to each other in the sense that their respective claims are mutually exclusive. That mutual exclusiveness of opposing claims is particularly obvious in the economic sphere, where one group may demand a share in the economic product which another group refuses to grant. This problem of the distribution of the economic product is only a spectacular instance of a ubiquitous social phenomenon. Political parties, religious denominations, racial groups, regions, and localities meet in similar contests. How are those conflicts being prevented from degenerating into violence?

First of all, citizen A, who as a member of economic group E1 opposes citizen B as a member of another economic group E2, is unable to identify himself completely with E1 and give it his undivided loyalties. He is unable to do so for three reasons.

A is not only a member of E1, but also of the religious group R, the political group P, and the ethnic and cultural group C. All these groups make demands on his allegiance; and if he wants to do justice to all of them, he cannot identify himself completely with any. While he acts as a member of E1, he cannot forget that he also has responsibilities to R. While he throws himself into the struggle for the objectives of P, he cannot help being mindful of what he owes to C. This pluralism of domestic groupings and conflicts, then, tends to impress upon the participants the relativity of their interests and loyalties and thus to mitigate the clashes of different groups. This pluralism brings about, as it were, an economy in the intensity of identification, which must be spread wide in order to give every group and conflict its share.

Furthermore, while A as a member of El opposes B as a member of E2, he might find himself in another respect on the same side of the fence with B, both being members of P. In other words, A and B are enemies in the economic sphere, yet they are friends in politics. They are opposed to each other economically, yet they are united politically. A and B are also members of religious, ethnic, and regional groups, and so forth, and both of them may have similar relations of conflict and association with any number of members of these groups. A, then, is not only at the same time identified with a plurality of different social groups, but he is also, as a member of these different groups, simultaneously the friend and foe of any number of his fellows, in so far as they belong to different groups of which he is either a member or an opponent.

This plural role of friend and opponent which A plays with regard to a number of his fellows imposes restraints upon him as both a friend and a foe. He cannot identify himself completely with his political friends who are also his economic opponents without the risk of losing the struggle for economic advantage. He cannot push the struggle for economic advantage to extremes without losing the political support he needs as a member of the political group. If A wants to be economic opponent and political friend at the same time, he must take care to be both within such limits that one does not get in the way of the other. Thus the overlapping of social roles played by different members of society tends to neutralize conflicts and to restrain them within such limits as to enable the members of society to play their different roles at the same time.

Finally, A and B are not only members of contending economic groups and have not only identical political affiliations, not to speak of all the other social groupings to which they belong, but by definition they are also members of the same national society. They partake of the same language, the same customs, the same historic recollections, the same fundamental social and political philosophy, the same national symbols. They read the same newspapers, listen to the same radio programs, observe the same holidays, and worship the same heroes. Above all, they compare their own nation with other nations and realize how much more they have in common with each other than with members of the other nations. More particularly, they are convinced that the national characteristics they have in common are superior in all important respects, especially those of morality, to the qualities of those who belong to a different nation. Thus A and B come to feel not only that they belong to the same national family, but also that because of that family relation they have something very precious in common, something that enhances their worth and makes them "better" men in every important respect in comparison with outsiders.

The self-respect of A and B, as well as the esteem in which they hold each other, is intimately connected with their membership in the same national community. Their intellectual convictions and moral valuations derive from that membership. How that membership gives vicarious satisfaction to their power drives has already been related in detail.[3] The loyalties with which they cling to the nation are more than the mere repayment of a debt of gratitude for benefits received. They are the very conditions of those benefits. It is only by being faithful to the nation, by adhering to it as to the fountainhead of all earthly goods, by identifying one's self with it that one will experience as one's own the security of belonging, the exultation of national pride, the triumphs of the Fatherland in the competition with other nations. Thus protection of the nation against destruction from without and disruption from within is the overriding concern of all citizens. Likewise, loyalty to the nation is a paramount commitment of all citizens. Nothing can be tolerated that might threaten the coherence of the nation. Interests, ideas, and loyalties which might not be compatible with the concern for the unity of the nation must yield to that concern.

This concern imposes an ever present limitation upon the kind of issues which will be allowed to separate A and B and places ever present restraints upon the methods by which A and B fight these issues out. Whatever the stakes of their conflicts, they will not raise the issue of national unity itself. Whatever methods A and B may employ in order to settle the conflict on their own terms, they will not resort to measures that might put the coherence of the nation itself in jeopardy. All conflicts within a nation are thus limited as to objectives pursued and means employed. They are, as it were, embedded within the densely woven fabric of the national community which keeps them within bounds. In conjunction with the pluralism and overlapping of sectional loyalties, it is the limiting and restraining influence of national loyalties that constitutes the first of the three factors that make for peace within the nation.

Expectation of Justice

How do national societies create the expectation on the part of hostile social groups that none of their claims will be completely ignored, but that all have a chance for at least partial satisfaction? How are all contending groups enabled to expect at least an approximation of justice from the national society to which they belong?

In national societies the problem of justice is posed on two levels. One is the level of general principles shared by society as a whole; the other is the level of specific claims advanced by particular groups. On the level of general principles no threat to the peace arises, for all are agreed upon the general principles by which the common good of society is defined. Principles such as democracy, social justice, equality, and freedom of speech do not give rise to conflicts endangering the peace of society so long as they remain in the realm of abstractions defining the ultimate goal of society's collective endeavors.

---

[3]See pages 117 ff.

These abstractions, however, become potent weapons in social conflicts when seized upon by social groups that advance their conflicting claims in the name of these principles. These claims confront society with its supreme challenge. Society may be able to disregard the claims of small and weak groups without endangering its peace. Its social cohesion and monopoly of organized violence are strong enough to keep the resentment and disaffection of such small and weak groups from turning openly against the social order. Yet society cannot afford to remain deaf to the claims for justice of large and potentially powerful groups without inviting the risk of revolution and civil war; that is, without endangering its peace and its very survival as an integrated whole.

It is here that the intricate mechanism of peaceful change comes into play, giving all groups a chance to submit their claims for justice to the arbitrament of public opinion, of elections, of parliamentary votes, of examination boards, and the like. These mechanisms guide the conflicting claims of social groups into peaceful channels by giving them a chance to make themselves heard and to compete with each other for recognition according to rules binding upon all. Under the conditions of these contests, no group can be sure to prevail in the long run, but all groups can rely upon the chance of taking at one time or another some forward steps toward the attainment of justice.

Overwhelming Power

The third factor in preserving peace within national societies is the overwhelming power with which society can nip in the bud all attempts at disturbing the peace. This overwhelming power manifests itself in two different ways: in the form of material force as a monopoly of organized violence, and in the form of irresistible social pressure.

The power that is at the disposal of society in the form of a monopoly of organized violence is set apart by two characteristics from any other form of violence, especially the one we encounter in the international sphere.

The organized violence of national societies is in some measure neutral with regard to the conflicting claims of social groups so long as they remain within the limits of the law and avail themselves of peaceful means. The liberal doctrine of the nineteenth century held that the organized violence of society was completely neutral, standing above the turmoil of conflicting interests, ready to enforce the law against whoever had violated it. Against that doctrine Marxism claims that the organized violence of society is nothing but the weapon with which the ruling class maintains its rule over the exploited masses. Actually, the compulsory organization of society cannot be completely neutral, for, as we have seen,[4] the legal order it enforces is not completely neutral and cannot help favoring the status quo to which it owes its existence. If challenged, the status quo can count upon the support of the compulsory organization of society.

---

[4]See pages 296 ff.

It is, however, the peculiar characteristic of the compulsory organization of society that it has a bias in favor of the status quo, but in large measure not a bias in favor of any particular status quo. The compulsory organization of American society has defended the status quo of 1800, of 1900, of 1932, and of 1940. The compulsory organization of British society has supported in succession the status quo of feudalism, capitalism, and socialism. Yet it may be that a particular status quo is offensive to the fundamental moral convictions and the vital interests of a considerable portion of the population and that a considerable fraction of the enforcement agents sympathize with their uncompromising opposition to the status quo. In such a case, the legal order embodying the status quo will not be enforced. In the United States, the constitutional background of the Civil War and the fate of prohibition illustrate that case.

The other characteristic peculiar to the compulsory organization of national societies is the scarcity of its collective action. As a rule, the compulsory organization of national societies maintains peace and order only against individual lawbreakers. It is a rare exception for it to oppose as a collective force another collectivity that threatens to disturb the peace. The use of force in labor disputes is the outstanding example of this kind. Normally, the very existence, in the hands of society, of a monopoly of organized violence, ready to intervene in case of need, deters collective disturbances of domestic peace. The very fact of its existence makes it unnecessary for the compulsory organization of society to act.

Aside from this factor and probably surpassing it in importance is the enormous unorganized pressure society exerts upon its members to keep the peace. A group, in order to be able to escape that pressure, would have to erect within the very framework of the national society a social structure of its own, more integrated, more compelling, and commanding higher loyalties than the national society in whose midst it dwells. In our times, the intensity of nationalism, its transformation into the political religion of nationalistic universalism, the ubiquity of the modern mass media of communications, and their control by a small and relatively homogeneous group have multiplied and magnified the social pressures that in national societies tend to keep dissenting groups within the bounds of law and peace.

The Role of the State

What is the contribution of the state to the maintenance of domestic peace? "State" is but another name for the compulsory organization of society—for the legal order that determines the conditions under which society may employ its monopoly of organized violence for the preservation of order and peace. When we have spoken in the preceding pages of the compulsory organization and of the legal order of society we have really spoken of the state. Its functions for the maintenance of domestic peace are threefold: (1) The state provides the legal continuity of the national society. It thus enables the individual to experience the nation as a continuum in time and space, as a personality in whose name men act, who demands and receives services and bestows benefits, to whom one can feel personal loyalties that are felt toward few other social groups except the family and the church. (2) The state provides most of the institutionalized agencies and processes of social change. (3) The state provides the agencies for the enforcement of its laws.

It remains for us to determine how important the state's contribution to domestic peace is. The answer to this question is twofold. The state's contribution to domestic peace is indispensable, but it is not in itself sufficient. Without the state's contribution there can be no domestic peace, but with nothing but the state's contribution there can be no domestic peace either.

That there can be no domestic peace without the state is already implicit in what we have said about the problems of power, of the balance of power, and of sovereignty. Hostile social groups will use whatever means are at their disposal for the purpose of gaining the objectives they consider vital to themselves. If such social groups control the means of physical violence, as sovereign states do in their mutual relations, they will use them in two different ways. They will either exert pressure upon their opponents by displaying what they consider to be their superiority, or they will employ them for the destruction of the opponent's means of physical violence. In either alternative the purpose of physical violence is the breaking of the opponent's will to resist the demands of the other side.

The history of national societies shows that no political, religious, economic, or regional group has been able to withstand for long the temptation to advance its claims by violent means if it thought it could do so without too great a risk. However strongly the other social factors might have supported the cause of peace, their effectiveness did not long survive the promise of a speedy and definitive victory which violence holds out to its possessor. Thus national societies have disintegrated and have split into a number of smaller units, either temporarily or permanently, whenever the state was incapable of maintaining its monopoly of organized violence and of using effectively whatever means of violence it retained for the purpose of maintaining peace and securing its own survival.

Since whoever is able to use violence will use it if the stakes seem to justify its use, a social agency is needed strong enough to prevent that use. Society might find substitutes for the legal unity the state conveys to it in time and space and for the agencies for social change through which the state regulates the dynamics of the social processes. Society has no substitute for the power of the Leviathan whose very presence, towering above contending groups, keeps their conflicts within peaceful bounds.

The state is indispensable for the maintenance of domestic peace; such is the true message of Hobbes's philosophy. Yet the state by itself cannot maintain domestic peace; such is the great omission of Hobbes's philosophy. That the power of the state is essential, but not sufficient, to keep the peace of national societies is demonstrated by the historic experience of civil wars. If there had been only few of them over a long period of history, they might be disregarded as exceptions to the rule. However, of a total of two hundred and seventy-eight wars fought between 1480 and 1941, seventy-eight—28 per cent of the total— were civil wars. In the period from 1840 to 1941, the ratio between civil and international wars was, with eighteen of the former and sixty of the latter, approximately one to three. For the period between 1800 and 1941, the figures are twenty-eight civil and eighty-five international wars, the ratio being almost exactly one to three.[5] Concerning the costliness of civil wars, Quincy Wright observes: "Civil wars such as the French Huguenot wars of the sixteenth century, the British War of the Roses of the fifteenth century and the Civil War of the seventeenth century, the Thirty Years' War from the standpoint of Germany, the Peninsula War from the standpoint of Spain, the American Civil War, and the Chinese Taiping Rebellion were costly both in lives and in economic losses far in excess of contemporary international wars."[6]

The frequency and destructiveness of civil wars demonstrate that the existence of the state does not assure the preservation of domestic peace. The reason lies in the nature of the state itself. The state is not the artificial creation of a constitutional convention, conceived in the image of some abstract principles of government and superimposed upon whatever society might exist. On the contrary, the state is part of the society from which it has sprung, and prospers and decays as society prospers and decays. The state, far from being a thing apart from society, is created by society.

The peace of a society whose intergroup conflicts are no longer limited, restrained, and neutralized by overriding loyalties, whose processes of social change no longer sustain the expectation of justice in all the major groups, and whose unorganized forces of compulsion are no longer sufficient to impose conformity upon these groups—the peace of such a society cannot be saved by the state, however strong. The forces of destruction arising within society in the form of class, racial, religious, regional, or purely political struggles will erupt in revolutions, coups d'état, and civil wars. The state does not stand apart from these conflagrations as a fire department stands apart from fires, ready to extinguish them when they break out. The state is inevitably involved in these conflagrations in a dual sense. On the one hand, the state is the prime target of revolution, against which it must defend itself through the use of force. On the other hand, the dissensions that disrupt society also split its compulsory organization, the state. The state, then, will either cease to operate as one body, its discordant parts will join the warring groups in society at large, and the unity of the state will dissolve in civil war, or else—and this is more likely in our time in view of the monopoly of effective power which modern technology gives to the state—the issues that divide the people will be fought out not by the people at large, but through internecine struggles within the organization of the state in the form of coups d'état, conspiracies, and purges.

---

[5]Quincy Wright, *A Study of War* (Chicago: University of Chicago Press, 1942), Vol. I, p. 651.
[6]Ibid., p. 247.

The Triple Test of Popular Support

This triple test devised for specific forms of government may well be applied to the world state. Are the peoples of the world willing to accept world government, or are they at least not so unwilling as to erect an insurmountable obstacle to its establishment? Would they be willing and able to do what is necessary to keep world government standing? Would they be willing and able to do or refrain from doing what world government requires of them so that it may fulfill its purposes? The answers to these questions are implicit in what has been said above in connection with the problems of nationalism, nationalistic universalism, international morality, and world public opinion. The answers are also implicit in what has been said about the conditions for the maintenance of domestic peace. The answers are bound to be in the negative.

No society exists coextensive with the presumed range of a world state. What exists is an international society of sovereign nations. There does not exist a supranational society that comprises all individual members of all nations and, hence, is identical with humanity politically organized. The most extensive society in which most men live and act in our times is the national society. The nation is, as we have seen, the recipient of man's highest secular loyalties. Beyond it there are other nations, but no community for which man would be willing to act regardless of what he understands the interests of his own nation to be. Men are willing to give food, clothing, and money to the needy regardless of nationality. But they prefer to keep the needy where they are rather than to allow them to go where they please and thus become useful citizens again. For, while international relief is regarded as compatible with the national interest, freedom of immigration is not. Under the present moral conditions of mankind, few men would act on behalf of a world government if the interests of their own nation, as they understand them, required a different course of action. On the contrary, the overwhelming majority would put what they regard as the welfare of their own nation above everything else, the interests of a world state included. In other words, the peoples of the world are not willing to accept world government, and their overriding loyalty to the nation erects an insurmountable obstacle to its establishment.

Nor are the peoples of the world willing and able to do what is necessary to keep world government standing. For they are not prepared to perform that revaluation of all values, that unprecedented moral and political revolution, which would force the nation from its throne and put the political organization of humanity on it. They are willing and able to sacrifice and die so that national governments may be kept standing.

The odds are so much in favor of the nation that men who might be willing and able to sacrifice and die that the world state be kept standing do not even have the opportunity to do so in the world as it is constituted today. The man who would want to oppose the interests and policy of his own nation for the sake of humanity and its state would by that act of opposition (weakening his own nation) strengthen the nation with which his own government might be engaged in deadly combat. At best he might make himself the martyr of his convictions by inviting the punishment that the nation metes out to traitors. Nothing shows more strikingly the absence of the social and moral preconditions for anything resembling a world state than the moral paradox that a man who would want to act as a citizen of the world would by the conditions of the world be forced to act as partisan of another nation and as traitor to his own. For above one's own nation there is nothing political on behalf of which a man could act. There are only other nations besides one's own.

We shall not dwell upon the problem of how the different peoples of the world shall be represented in legislative agencies for social change. Numerical representation would obviously be unacceptable to the white races, since it would put the world under the domination of the colored ones. Any type of representation that in violation of the majority principle would tend to stabilize white supremacy in the world would meet with the opposition of the colored races, who would thus be held in a permanent state of inferiority. Nor shall we dwell upon the obvious impossibility of putting such legislative agencies in operation, even if it were possible to establish them. A parliament representing peoples of such different moral convictions, political interests, and abilities for self-government as the Americans, the Chinese, the Indians, and the Russians would hardly be able to create out of these differences an operating whole. None of its constituent groups would willingly submit to the majority vote of a legislative assembly thus constituted. The threat and the actuality of civil war would hang over such institutions, which would have to substitute compulsion for the lacking moral and political consensus.

Let us consider two concrete issues with regard to which the claims of different nations traditionally collide: immigration and trade. A world state, like any other federal state, could not leave the regulation of interstate migration and interstate trade to the discretion of its component parts. It would itself have to regulate these issues. Even if the authority of the world state in these two respects were strictly circumscribed by the world constitution, is there any chance that the American people would be prepared to give a world government powers to open the borders of the United States for the annual immigration of, say, 100,000 Russians, 250,000 Chinese, and 200,000 Indians? Would the American people allow the import of any quantity of foreign agricultural products which might compete with domestic ones on equal terms? Is there any likelihood that the Russians would allow cheap consumer goods to be imported which might upset their planned economy and undermine confidence in their political system as well? If these questions must be answered in the negative, as obviously they must, how is a world state expected to govern at all? How is a world state expected to be able to resolve peacefully the tensions between nations which threaten the peace of the world?

There is no shirking the conclusion that international peace cannot be permanent without a world state, and that a world state cannot be established under the present moral, social, and political conditions of the world. In the light of what has been said thus far in this book, there is also no shirking the further conclusion that in no period of modern history was civilization more in need of permanent peace and, hence, of a world state, and that in no period of modern history were the moral, social, and political conditions of the world less favorable for the establishment of a world state. There is, finally, no shirking the conclusion that, as there can be no state without a society willing and able to support it, there can be no world state without a world community willing and able to support it.

TWO FALSE SOLUTIONS

How, then, can a world state be created? Two solutions have been offered: world conquest and the examples of Switzerland and of the creation of the United States by the Constitutional Convention of 1787.

World Conquest

All historic political structures that have come close to being world states have had one thing in common: One powerful state created them by conquering the other members of what was then the known political world. Most of these world states have another thing in common: They hardly ever survived the lifetime of the founders.

In Western civilization, the sole exception to that rule is the Roman Empire. This world state owed its unique longevity to two unusual transformations. The Roman conquerors transformed the conquered into Romans either by receiving them into the dominant civilization as Roman citizens or by uprooting them from their native civilizations and making them into slaves. Yet in the process of conquest, especially of the Hellenistic world, the Roman conqueror transformed himself by remaking his own civilization in the image of the civilizations of the conquered. Through this dual process of amalgamation, Rome created a new moral and political community coextensive with its conquests and capable of lending stability to the new state. To these two transformations must be added the further circumstance that after the conquest of the Mediterranean world the Roman Empire expanded into politically empty spaces, settled by barbarians whose loosely organized civilizations disintegrated under the impact of the superior and attractive civilization of the conqueror.

Most of the other world states disintegrated as soon as conquest had built them. For, beneath the political and military superstructure erected by force, the national societies lived on, each with its separate moral values and political interests and each trying to shake off the conqueror's yoke. These world states were not the natural outgrowth of a world community coextensive with them, but a creation of force artificially superimposed upon a multiplicity of unwilling national societies. It is of course true that, for instance, Napoleon's would-be world state was destroyed by the untapped reserves of Great Britain and Russia. Yet, when in 1812 that empire for the first time showed its military weakness by failing in a major task of expansion, the national societies of which it was composed reasserted themselves and joined Great Britain and Russia in putting an end to it.

Conquests on a smaller scale, which are unable to unite the conquering and conquered populations in a new community, face the smaller risk of revolt and irredentist separatism. The relations between Ireland and Great Britain and between the nations of Eastern Europe and Russia are cases in point. If the conqueror can muster overwhelming strength, no danger to the peace may arise from the conflict of two national societies living within the same state. If, however, the strength of the conquered people is not out of all proportion to the conqueror's, a potential state of civil war between the conqueror and the conquered will sap the strength of the state, even though under the modern conditions of warfare it may not endanger its existence.

Such are the likely consequences of limited conquests that are unable to create a new community coextensive with themselves. It follows that a world state created by conquest and lacking the support of a world community has a chance to maintain peace within its borders only if it can create and maintain complete discipline and loyalty among the millions of soldiers and policemen needed to enforce its rule over an unwilling humanity. Such a world state would be a totalitarian monster resting on feet of clay, the very thought of which startles the imagination.

The Examples of Switzerland and the United States

What the world state is expected to bring about, Switzerland seems to have already achieved—the creation of a new federal state out of a number of sovereign nations with language, culture, history, loyalties, and policies of their own. Switzerland has been able to unite twenty-two sovereign states, speaking four different languages, in one political organization. Why should the 150-odd nations of the world not be able to do the same? Let them adopt a federal constitution as the Swiss have done, let them act toward each other as the Swiss states do, and the problem of the world state will be solved. The argument seems to be persuasive and is considered frequently in popular discussions. It dissolves, however, when confronted with the facts of Swiss history.

First of all, the unified Swiss state dates from 1848. Before then the Swiss states formed a confederation that resembled more a successful League of Nations or United Nations than a single state. That confederation grew from a number of permanent alliances concluded among the so-called Forest Cantons and some of the City Cantons in the course of the fourteenth century. These alliances were the result of certain identical and complementary interests that drew these states together in defense against common dangers. Why did these alliances survive the special occasions from which they arose and even harden into the close ties of a confederation with common agencies of government? The answer to that question will provide the explanation to the phenomenon of Switzerland.

(1) The thirteen members of the original Confederation, occupying a contiguous territory, were united in a common opposition to the German Empire and the Hapsburgs, of whom they had all been subjects, from whom they had liberated themselves in common efforts, and who remained the common enemies of the liberties of all of them. (2) The famous victories of the Swiss armies over the knights in the fourteenth and fifteenth centuries had a dual effect. They established for centuries the reputation of the Swiss as the most redoubtable soldiers in Europe, and they proved the virtual immunity from foreign attack of the mountain valleys which were the core of the original Confederation. (3) Compared with these military risks which an attack upon the Swiss entailed, the attractions of victory were small. In view of the poverty of these valleys in natural resources, these attractions were exclusively strategic; that is, the control of some of the Alpine passes joining Italy with the North of Europe. Yet for four centuries, with the one significant exception of the Napoleonic Wars, the great rival powers adjacent to Switzerland found it more advantageous to have the Swiss defend the Alpine passes against all warring nations than to try to capture them from the Swiss. It is, however, significant that the balance of power exerted this protective influence only as long as the rivalry among Switzerland's powerful neighbors lasted. The Napoleonic victories in Italy at once destroyed that protection, and from 1798 on Switzerland was the hapless prey of contending armies. It is also worth remembering that while Austria, Germany, and Italy were joined in the Triple Alliance, the Italian general staff proposed six times to the German general staff to march through Switzerland in a joint campaign against France.

Thus it was not merely an act of will expressing itself in a constitutional arrangement, but a number of peculiar and, in their combination, unique circumstances that made it possible for Switzerland to be born and survive. While these circumstances allowed Switzerland to survive in the midst of powerful neighbors, they did not permit it to maintain peace among its component states. Within the span of little more than 300 years, the Swiss states fought among themselves numerous minor wars and five religious wars involving all or virtually all of them, the last as late as 1847. A great number of revolutions and coups d'état round out the picture of civil strife.

What light, then, does the history of Switzerland shed upon the problem of the world state? We can subscribe to Rappard's conclusions that Switzerland as a confederation had limited national security only "by virtue of special circumstances alien to this regime itself. . . . In so far as the Swiss experience of five centuries of collective security can suggest a lesson to the present generation, this lesson is clearly negative. It confirms at the same time the observations drawn from the most recent past and the teachings of simple common sense. As long as the security of the international society depends only upon the free cooperation of fully sovereign states, it remains necessarily frag-ile."[7] Thus the Swiss experience confirms our own conclusions concerning the fragility of peace by limitation, while it emphasizes both the need and difficulty of establishing a state above the national states.

The example of the way in which the United States was created is often cited as proof of the feasibility of creating a world state here and now by way of a constitutional convention. Actually, the example of the United States proves only the dependence upon a pre-existing moral and political community of any state that can be expected to endure.

When the Constitutional Convention met in 1787, the thirteen states were sovereign in name rather than in political actuality. They did not constitute thirteen separate sovereignties about to merge into a single one. After they had declared their independence from Britain in 1776, sovereignty remained in suspense. By establishing the United States, they exchanged one sovereignty— that of the British Crown—for another. And they exchanged one common loyalty for another common loyalty. All the while they retained the same language, the same culture, the same national heritage, the same moral convic-tions, the same political interests that had just been tested in a revolutionary war fought in unison under a single command. The thirteen colonies formed a moral and political community under the British Crown, they tested it and became fully aware of it in their common struggle against Britain, and they retained that community after they had won their independence. As John Jay put it in No. II of *The Federalist:*

> . . . Providence has been pleased to give this one connected country to one united people; a people descended from the same ancestors, speaking the same language, professing the same religion, attached to the same principles of government, very similar in their manners and customs, and who, by their joint counsels, arms and efforts, fighting side by side throughout a long and bloody war, have nobly estab-lished their general liberty and independence. . . .
>
> Similar sentiments have hitherto prevailed among all orders and denomina-tions of men among us. To all general purposes, we have uniformly been one people. Each individual citizen everywhere enjoying the same national rights, privileges, and protection. As a nation, we have made peace and war: as a nation, we have vanquished our common enemies: as a nation, we have formed alliances and made treaties, and entered into various compacts and conventions with foreign states.

What the Convention of Philadelphia did was to replace one constitu-tion, one sovereignty, one state with another one, both resting upon the same preexisting community. The Convention did not create one state where before there had been thirteen separate ones. Far from proving that a state can be created by agreement on the text of a constitution, the creation of the

---

[7]William E. Rappard, *Cinq Siècles de Sécurité Collective (1291–1798)* (Paris: Librairie du Recueil Sirey, 1945), p. 594.

United States proves the truth of the two propositions advanced earlier: Wars can occur within states as well as among states, and the United States was founded upon a moral and political community the Constitution did not create but found already in existence. The community of the American people antedated the American state, as a world community must antedate a world state.

23

The World Community

This last conclusion—that a world community must antedate a world state—has given birth to two efforts to create a world community: the United Nations Educational, Scientific and Cultural Organization, known as Unesco, and the other specialized agencies of the United Nations.[1]

THE CULTURAL APPROACH: UNESCO

According to Article 1 of the Constitution of Unesco:

The purpose of the Organization is to contribute to peace and security by promoting collaboration among the nations through education, science and culture in order to further universal respect for justice, for the rule of law and for the human rights and fundamental freedoms which are affirmed for the peoples of the world, without distinction of race, sex, language or religion, by the Charter of the United Nations.

To realize this purpose the Organization will:

(a) collaborate in the work of advancing the mutual knowledge and understanding of peoples, through all means of mass communication and to that end recommend such international agreements as may be necessary to promote the free flow of ideas by word and image;

(b) give fresh impulse to popular education and to the spread of culture;

by collaborating with Members, at their request, in the development of educational activities;

by instituting collaboration among the nations to advance the ideal of equality of educational opportunity without regard to race, sex or any distinctions, economic or social;

---

[1]See, in connection with this chapter, what has been said above in Chapter 7 about world public opinion.

by suggesting educational methods best suited to prepare the children of the world for the responsibilities of freedom;

(c) maintain, increase and diffuse knowledge;

by assuring the conservation and protection of the world's inheritance of books, works of art and monuments of history and science, and recommending to the nations concerned the necessary international conventions;

by encouraging cooperation among the nations in all branches of intellectual activity, including the international exchange of persons active in the fields of education, science and culture and the exchange of publications, objects of artistic and scientific interest and other materials of information;

by initiating methods of international cooperation calculated to give the people of all countries access to the printed and published materials produced by any of them.

In order to evaluate the contribution Unesco is able to make for the preservation of international peace, three distinctions must be made: (1) We are here not concerned with the contribution Unesco is able to make to the dissemination and improvement of culture and education as ends in themselves. (2) We are here not concerned with the contribution Unesco is able to make to the preservation of international peace through the very fact of international co-operation; this aspect of the problem will be dealt with in the last section of this chapter. (3) We are here concerned only with the question of what Unesco can do for the preservation of international peace by promoting international understanding, education, and general cultural activities.

What the Carnegie Endowment for International Peace declared in its appraisal of Unesco's program for 1948, "Above all else its individual items were not always clearly and obviously related to the safeguarding of peace and security,"[2] is true of all activities of Unesco, however meritorious they may be intrinsically. This defect is not an accidental quality of certain programs undertaken by Unesco, which only need to be revised and tightened in order to fulfill their peace-preserving function. On the contrary, the defect is congenital, growing from the very philosophy that is at the foundation of the agency and permeates all its activities. Thus, summing up on November 17, 1952, the discussions of the General Conference of Unesco, Mr. Jaime Torres Bodet, its outgoing Director-General, warned "that the greatest danger Unesco has to guard against is dissipation of its efforts."

The philosophy of Unesco assumes that education (especially when it aims at international understanding), cultural exchange, and, in general, all activities that tend to increase contacts among members of different nations and make them understand each other contribute necessarily to the creation of an international community and the maintenance of peace. Implicit in this assumption is the supposition that nations are nationalistic and go to war with each other because they do not know each other well enough and because they operate on different levels of education and culture. Both assumptions are erroneous.

---

[2]*International Conciliation*, No. 438, February 1948, p. 77.

Cultural Development and Peace

There are primitive peoples, completely lacking in institutionalized education, who are generally peace-loving and receptive to the influence of foreign cultures to the point of suicide. There are other peoples, highly educated and steeped in classical culture, such as the Germans, who throughout most of their history have been nationalistic and warlike. The Athenians under Pericles and the Italians of the Renaissance created cultures not equaled in the history of Western civilization, and both were at least as nationalistic and warlike in that period of their history as at any time before or after.

Furthermore, in the history of some nations, such as the British and the French, periods of nationalistic exclusiveness and warlike policies alternate with cosmopolitan and peaceful ones, and no correlation exists between these changes and the development of education and culture. The Chinese people have a tradition of respect for learning superior to that of any other people, and they can look back upon a history of cultural attainments longer than any other and at least as creative. These high qualities of education and culture have made the Chinese look with contempt on the profession of the soldier as well as upon all other nations, which at the beginning of the nineteenth century were still regarded as barbarian vassals of the Chinese emperor. Yet all this has not made the Chinese people less nationalistic and more peaceful. Russian education in our time has reached a higher level of achievement than ever before, especially in the fields of literacy and technical education. Its excellence has had no influence upon the receptiveness of the Russian people to foreign ideas or upon the foreign policies of the Russian government.

These examples, taken at random, show that the quantity and quality of education and culture as such is obviously irrelevant to the issue of a world community. That issue hinges, not upon knowledge and the creation and appreciation of cultural values, but upon a moral and political transformation of unprecedented dimensions.

Cultural Unity and Peace

What has been said of education and culture as such holds true also of educational and cultural activities aiming at the interchange of the products of different national cultures. The existence of a multitude of interpersonal relations transcending national boundaries is no answer to our problem. More particularly, the existence of intellectual and esthetic ties across national boundaries proves nothing in favor of a world community. A world community with political potentialities is a community of moral standards and political action, not of intellect and sentiments. That an intellectual elite in the United States enjoys Russian music and literature and that Shakespeare has not been banned from the Russian stage has no relevance at all for the problem with which we are concerned. This sharing of the same intellectual and esthetic experiences by members of different nations does not create a society, for it does not create morally and politically relevant actions on the part of the members of different nations with respect to each other which they would not have undertaken had they not shared in those experiences.

It should be remembered that on a much higher plane than the intellectual and esthetic, and with the objective of clearly defined action, the nations of the West, Russia included, have shared the same experiences for more than a thousand years. They have prayed to the same God, have held the same fundamental religious beliefs, have been bound by the same moral laws, and have had the same ritual symbols in common. That community of religious experiences, much more intimately related to the whole personality of the individual and to his actions than anything that supranational intellectual and esthetic experiences have to offer, has been able to create an international community of sorts, but not an international community sufficiently integrated to make a world state possible. How, then, can we expect that the melodies of Tchaikovsky, the profundities of Dostoevski, the insights of *The Federalist*, and the imagery of *Moby Dick*, which might be shared by all Americans and Russians alike, could create not only a fleeting community of feeling, but a community of moral valuations and political actions shunting aside old loyalties and establishing new ones?

History has given an unmistakable answer to that question. Cultural unity, much closer than anything Unesco can plan and achieve, has coexisted with war in all periods of history. We are not speaking here of civil wars, which by definition are fought by members of the same national culture. The wars among the Greek city states, the European wars of the Middle Ages, the Italian wars of the Renaissance, the religious wars of the sixteenth and seventeenth centuries, even the wars of the eighteenth century in so far as the elite was concerned, were fought within the framework of a homogeneous culture. These cultures had all essentials in common: language, religion, education, literature, art. Yet these cultures did not create a community, coextensive with themselves, that could have kept disruptive tendencies in check and channeled them into peaceful outlets. How, then, can one expect that such a community will be created through interchange among cultures, so diverse in all the respects in which those historic ones were homogeneous?

International Understanding and Peace

It is in the third purpose of Unesco, international understanding, that the basic fallacy of Unesco's conception of international affairs comes to the fore. International conflicts, it is believed, are the result of an intellectual deficiency, of ignorance and lack of judgment as to the qualities of other peoples. If Americans could only come to understand the Russians, and vice versa, they would realize how much they are alike, how much they have in common, and how little they have to fight about. The argument is fallacious on two counts.

Individual experience, which anybody can duplicate at will, shows that increased friendship is not necessarily a concomitant of increased understanding. There are, of course, numerous instances in which A has misunderstood the character and the motives of B and in which clarification of the facts will remove the source of conflict. Such is not the case when A and B are engaged in a conflict in which their vital interests are at stake. A does not fight B for economic advantage because he misunderstands the intentions of B; it is rather because he understands them only too well. Many an American GI went to France full of sentimental friendship for the French people whom he did not know. His friendly feelings did not survive the shock of understanding. The similar experiences of many friendly visitors to Russia are too typical to need elaboration.

Among those who from the beginning were most firmly opposed to the foreign objectives of the National Socialist regime, even at the risk of war, were some who had a profound understanding of German culture. It was exactly that understanding that made them implacable enemies of the National Socialist regime. Similarly, the students of Russian history and culture, those who really understand Russia and the Russians, have as a rule been equally unaffected by the pro- and anti-Russian hysteria. They have known the traditional objectives of Russian expansionism as well as the traditional methods of Russian diplomacy. If their understanding had had an influence upon the conduct of foreign affairs in the Western democracies, that conduct would certainly have been more intelligent and successful than it actually was. Whether or not such understanding would have made for better relations with the Soviet Union is an open question. An intelligent and successful foreign policy depends upon the Americans' and the Russians' understanding what both nations are and want. Peace between the United States and the Soviet Union depends in the last analysis upon whether what one of them is and wants is compatible with what the other one is and wants.

This observation points up the other fallacy in Unesco's conception of international affairs. The conception that international conflicts can be eliminated through international understanding rests on the implicit assumption that the issues of international conflicts, born as they are of misunderstandings, are but imaginary and that actually no issue worth fighting about stands between nation and nation. Nothing could be farther from the truth. All the great wars that decided the course of history and changed the political face of the earth were fought for real stakes, not for imaginary ones. The issue in those great convulsions was invariably: Who shall rule and who shall be ruled? Who shall be free and who slave?

Was misunderstanding at the root of the issue between the Greeks and the Persians, between the Athenians and the Macedonians, between the Jews and the Romans, between emperor and pope, between the English and the French in the late Middle Ages, between the Turks and the Austrians, between Napoleon and Europe, between Hitler and the world? Was misunderstanding of the other side's culture, character, and intentions the issue, so that those wars were fought over no real issue at all? Or could it not rather be maintained that in many of these conflicts it was exactly the misunderstanding of the would-be conqueror's culture, character, and intentions that preserved peace for a while, whereas the understanding of these factors made war inevitable? So long as the Athenians refused to heed the warnings of Demosthenes, the threat of war remained remote. It was only when, too late for their salvation, they understood the nature of the Macedonian Empire and of its policies that war became inevitable. That correlation between understanding and the inevitability of conflict is one of the melancholy lessons history conveys to posterity: The more thoroughly one understands the other side's position, character, and intentions, the more inevitable the conflict often appears to be.

Irrespective of its great intrinsic merits, the program of Unesco is irrelevant to the problem of world community because its diagnosis of the bars to world community so completely misses the point. The problem of world community is a moral and political and not an intellectual and esthetic one. The world community is a community of moral judgments and political actions, not of intellectual endowments and esthetic appreciation. Let us suppose that American and Russian education and culture could be brought to the same level of excellence or completely amalgamated, and that Russians would take to Mark Twain as Americans would take to Gogol. If that were the case, the problem of who shall control the Middle East would still stand between the United States and the Soviet Union, as it does today. So long as men continue to judge and act in accordance with national rather than supranational standards and loyalties, the world community remains a postulate that still awaits its realization.

THE FUNCTIONAL APPROACH

The Specialized Agencies of the United Nations

How is such a transformation of standards and loyalties to be brought about? The specialized agencies of the United Nations have pointed a way. They are autonomous organizations, owing their existence to particular agreements among a number of states whose identity differs from agency to agency. They have their own constitutions, their own budgets, their own policymaking and administrative bodies, and each agency has a membership of its own. The names of some of these agencies are indicative of the functions they fulfill: International Labor Organization, Food and Agriculture Organization, International Bank for Reconstruction and Development, International Monetary Fund, International Telecommunication Union, Universal Postal Union, International Civil Aviation Organization, Unesco, World Health Organization.

Chapters IX and X of the Charter of the United Nations provide for organizational and functional relations between the specialized agencies and the United Nations. The Charter stresses to a degree unknown in the history of international organization the responsibility of the United Nations for the rights and the well-being of the individual regardless of national affiliation. It has created in the Economic and Social Council a special organ for the discharge of that responsibility. The Economic and Social Council has the authority to conclude agreements—and has done so in a number of instances—with the specialized agencies, "defining the terms on which the agency concerned shall be brought into relationship with the United Nations."[3] The United Nations may "make recommendations for the coordination of the policies and activities of the specialized agencies."[4] The Economic and Social Council may take steps to receive regular and special reports from the specialized agencies and may perform services at the request of members of the United Nations and of specialized agencies.[5]

What is the philosophy underlying the social and economic activities the specialized agencies are undertaking with the co-operation of the United Nations? What is the relevance of that philosophy for the problem of the international community? This question has been answered with great brilliance and persuasiveness by Professor Mitrany.

> If the evil of conflict and war springs from the division of the world into detached and competing political units, will it be exorcised simply by changing or reducing the lines of division? Any political reorganization into separate units must, sooner or later, produce the same effects; any international system that is to usher in a new world must produce the opposite effect of subduing political division. As far as one can see, there are only two ways of achieving that end. One would be through a world state which would wipe out political divisions forcibly; the other is the way discussed in these pages, which would rather overlay political divisions with a spreading web of international activities and agencies, in which and through which the interests and life of all the nations would be gradually integrated. That is the fundamental change to which any effective international system must aspire and contribute: to make international government co-extensive with international activities. . . . It must care as much as possible for common needs that are evident, while presuming as little as possible upon a social unity which is still only latent and unrecognized. . . . [In that way] The community itself will acquire a living body not through a written act of faith but through active organic development. . . . That trend is to organize government along the lines of specific ends and needs, and according to the condition of their time and place, in lieu of the traditional organization on the basis of a set constitutional division of jurisdiction of rights and powers. . . . The functional approach . . . would help the growth of such positive and constructive common work, of common habits and interests, making frontier lines meaningless by overlaying them with a natural growth of common activities and common administrative agencies.[6]

This is indeed the way in which communities grow and in which governments grow out of communities. We have already noted that sovereignty was

---

[3]Article 63, paragraph 1.
[4]Article 58; cf. also Articles 62, 63, paragraph 2.
[5]Articles 64, 66, paragraph 2.
[6]David Mitrany, *A Working Peace System* (4th ed.; London: National Peace Council, 1946), pp. 14, 15, 18, 28, 34, 35. (Reprinted by permission of the author.)

a fact before it was a theory, and that the American people formed a community before they created a state. How, then, can a community be created where none exists?

According to Professor Mitrany, an international community must grow from the satisfaction of common needs shared by members of different nations. The specialized agencies of the United Nations, serving peoples all over the world regardless of national boundaries, could create by the very fact of their existence and performance a community of interests, valuations, and actions. Ultimately, if such international agencies were numerous enough and served the most important wants of most peoples of the earth, the loyalties to these institutions and to the international community of which they would be the agencies would supersede the loyalties to the separate national societies and their institutions. For proof that such a development is feasible under present world conditions, Professor Mitrany relies in the main upon the experiences which the Allies had during the Second World War with functional international agencies, such as the Anglo-American Raw Materials Board and the Middle East Supply Centre. These examples put in sharp focus the problem raised by the functional approach.

In war, the loyalties to the common cause and the common interest in victory over the common enemy overrode separate national loyalties and made possible the successful operation of international functional agencies of major importance. In peace, what the nation has to offer the individual seems to outweigh by far the benefits to be derived from the international functional agencies, although it is ever more widely recognized that the citizens of different nations have certain interests in common, such as physical survival through avoidance of nuclear war and non-proliferation of nuclear weapons, protection of the natural environment, and economic well-being through the control of international trade, the monetary system, and global corporations, which can be satisfied only a supranational basis. More particularly, the conflicts of power which separate nations and the insecurity they create make identification with the nation the overriding concern of most members of all nations. The nation offers the individual protection, vicarious gratification of power drives, and immediate satisfaction of material needs. With few sporadic exceptions, such as the assistance of the World Health Organization in combating an epidemic, the specialized agencies of the United Nations offer hopes and satisfactions far removed from the direct experiences of ordinary people and which may make themselves felt only through the intermediary of a number of national agencies, so that its international origins are hard to trace. When mailing a letter to a foreign country, who would think of giving thanks to the Universal Postal Union for the contribution that international agency is making to the operation?

Thus the contributions international functional agencies make to the well-being of members of all nations fade into the background. What stands before the eyes of all are the immense political conflicts that divide the great nations of the earth and threaten the well-being of the loser, if not his very existence. This is not primarily a matter of false emphasis born of ignorance. It is rather

The Specialized Agencies and IAEA	The United Nations
International Atomic Energy Agency (IAEA)	United Nations Truce Supervision Organization in Palestine (UNTSO)
International Labour Organisation (ILO)	United Nations Military Observer Group in India and Pakistan (UNMOGIP)
Food and Agriculture Organization of the United Nations (FAO)	United Nations Peace-Keeping Force in Cyprus (UNFICYP)
United Nations Educational, Scientific and Cultural Organization (UNESCO)	Main Committees
World Health Organization (WHO)	Standing and Procedural Committees
International Monetary Fund (IMF)	Other Subsidiary Organs of General Assembly
International Development Association (IDA)	United Nations Relief and Works Agency for Palestine Refugees in the Near East (UNRWA)
International Bank for Reconstruction and Development (IBRD)	United Nations Conference on Trade and Development (UNCTAD)
International Finance Corporation (IFC)	Trade and Development Board
International Civil Aviation Organization (ICAO)	United Nations Development Programme (UNDP)
Universal Postal Union (UPU)	United Nations Capital Development Fund
International Telecommunication Union (ITU)	United Nations Industrial Development Organization (UNIDO)
World Meteorological Organization (WMO)	United Nations Institute for Training and Research (UNITAR)
Inter-Governmental Maritime Consultative Organization (IMCO)	United Nations Children's Fund (UNICEF)
General Agreement on Tariffs and Trade (GATT)	United Nations High Commissioner for Refugees (UNHCR)
	Joint United Nations -FAO World Food Programme

The United Nations System

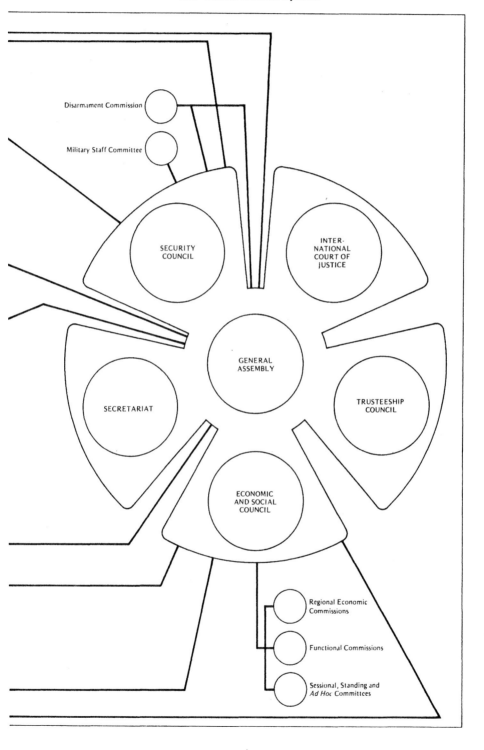

the recognition of the undeniable fact that, from a functional point of view, what the national government does or does not do is much more important for the satisfaction of individual wants than what an international functional agency does or does not do. More important than anything else is the ability of the national government to defend its territory and citizens against foreign aggression and within its territory to maintain peace and keep in operation the processes of social change. The neglect with which the public treats international functional agencies is but the exaggerated reflection of the minor role these agencies play for the solution of important international issues.

PART TEN

The Problem of Peace: Peace through Accommodation

24

Diplomacy

We have seen that international peace cannot be preserved through the limitation of national sovereignty, and we found the reasons for this failure in the very nature of the relations among nations. We concluded that international peace through the transformation of the present society of sovereign nations into a world state is unattainable under the moral, social, and political conditions prevailing in the world in our time. If the world state is unattainable in our world, yet indispensable for the survival of that world, it is necessary to create the conditions under which it will not be impossible from the outset to establish a world state. As the prime requisite for the creation of such conditions, we suggested the mitigation and minimization of those political conflicts which in our time pit the two superpowers against each other and evoke the specter of a cataclysmic war. This method of establishing the preconditions for permanent peace we call peace through accommodation. Its instrument is diplomacy.

FOUR TASKS OF DIPLOMACY

We have already had occasion to emphasize the paramount importance of diplomacy as an element of national power. The importance of diplomacy for the preservation of international peace is but a particular aspect of that general function. For a diplomacy that ends in war has failed in its primary objective: the promotion of the national interest by peaceful means. This has always been so and is particularly so in view of the destructive potentialities of total war.

Taken in its widest meaning, comprising the whole range of foreign policy, the task of diplomacy is fourfold: (1) Diplomacy must determine its objectives in the light of the power actually and potentially available for the pursuit of these objectives. (2) Diplomacy must assess the objectives of other nations and the power actually and potentially available for the pursuit of these objectives. (3) Diplomacy must determine to what extent these different objectives are compatible with each other. (4) Diplomacy must employ the means suited to the

361

pursuit of its objectives. Failure in any one of these tasks may jeopardize the success of foreign policy and with it the peace of the world.

A nation that sets itself goals which it has not the power to attain may have to face the risk of war on two counts. Such a nation is likely to dissipate its strength and not to be strong enough at all points of friction to deter a hostile nation from challenging it beyond endurance. The failure of its foreign policy may force the nation to retrace its steps and to redefine its objectives in view of its actual strength. Yet it is more likely that, under the pressure of an inflamed public opinion, such a nation will go forward on the road toward an unattainable goal, strain all its resources to achieve it, and finally, confounding the national interest with that goal, seek in war the solution to a problem that cannot be solved by peaceful means.

A nation will also invite war if its diplomacy wrongly assesses the objectives of other nations and the power at their disposal. We have already pointed to the error of mistaking a policy of the status quo for a policy of imperialism, and vice versa, and of confounding one kind of imperialism with another.[1] A nation that mistakes a policy of imperialism for a policy of the status quo will be unprepared to meet the threat to its own existence which the other nation's policy entails. Its weakness will invite attack and may make war inevitable. A nation that mistakes a policy of the status quo for a policy of imperialism will evoke through its disproportionate reaction the very danger of war which it is trying to avoid. For as A mistakes B's policy for imperialism, so B might mistake A's defensive reaction for imperialism. Thus both nations, each intent upon forestalling imaginary aggression from the other side, will rush to arms. Similarly, the confusion of one type of imperialism with another may call for disproportionate reaction and thus evoke the risk of war.

As for the assessment of the power of other nations, either to overrate or to underrate it may be equally fatal to the cause of peace. By overrating the power of B, A may prefer to yield to B's demands until, finally, A is forced to fight for its very existence under the most unfavorable conditions. By underrating the power of B, A may become overconfident in its assumed superiority. A may advance demands and impose conditions upon B which the latter is supposedly too weak to resist. Not suspecting B's actual power of resistance, A may be faced with the alternative of either retreating and conceding defeat or of advancing and risking war.

A nation that seeks to pursue an intelligent and peaceful foreign policy cannot cease comparing its own objectives and the objectives of other nations in the light of their compatibility. If they are compatible, no problem arises. If they are not compatible, nation A must determine whether its objectives are so vital to itself that they must be pursued despite that incompatibility with the objectives of B. If it is found that A's vital interests can be safeguarded without the attainment of these objectives, they ought to be abandoned. On the other hand, if A finds that these objectives are essential for its vital interests, A must

---

[1]See pages 77 ff., 106 ff.

then ask itself whether B's objectives, incompatible with its own, are essential for B's vital interests. If the answer seems to be in the negative, A must try to induce B to abandon its objectives, offering B equivalents not vital to A. In other words, through diplomatic bargaining, the give and take of compromise, a way must be sought by which the interests of A and B can be reconciled.

Finally, if the incompatible objectives of A and B should prove to be vital to either side, a way might still be sought in which the vital interests of A and B might be redefined, reconciled, and their objectives thus made compatible with each other. Here, however—even provided that both sides pursue intelligent and peaceful policies—A and B are moving dangerously close to the brink of war.

It is the final task of an intelligent diplomacy, intent upon preserving peace, to choose the appropriate means for pursuing its objectives. The means at the disposal of diplomacy are three: persuasion, compromise, and threat of force. No diplomacy relying only upon the threat of force can claim to be both intelligent and peaceful. No diplomacy that would stake everything on persuasion and compromise deserves to be called intelligent. Rarely, if ever, in the conduct of the foreign policy of a great power is there justification for using only one method to the exclusion of the others. Generally, the diplomatic representative of a great power, in order to be able to serve both the interests of his country and the interests of peace, must at the same time use persuasion, hold out the advantages of a compromise, and impress the other side with the military strength of his country.

The art of diplomacy consists in putting the right emphasis at any particular moment on each of these three means at its disposal. A diplomacy that has successfully discharged its other functions may well fail in advancing the national interest and preserving peace if it stresses persuasion when the give and take of compromise is primarily required by the circumstances of the case. A diplomacy that puts most of its eggs in the basket of compromise when the military might of the nation should be predominantly displayed, or stresses military might when the political situation calls for persuasion and compromise, will likewise fail.

INSTRUMENTS OF DIPLOMACY

These four tasks of diplomacy are the basic elements of which foreign policy consists everywhere and at all times. One might say that the chieftain of a primitive tribe maintaining political relations with a neighboring tribe will have to perform these four functions in order to be successful and preserve peace. The need for the performance of these functions is as old and as widespread as international politics itself. Only the performance of these functions by organized agencies is of relatively recent origin.

The organized instruments of diplomacy are two: the foreign offices in the capitals of the respective nations and the diplomatic representatives sent by the foreign offices to the capitals of foreign nations. The foreign office is the policy-forming agency, the brains of foreign policy where the impressions from the outside world are gathered and evaluated, where foreign policy is formulated, and where the impulses emanate which the diplomatic representatives transform into actual foreign policy. While the foreign office is the brains of foreign policy, the diplomatic representatives are its eyes, ear, and mouth, its fingertips, and, as it were, its itinerant incarnations. The diplomat fulfills three basic functions for his government—symbolic, legal, and political.

Symbolic Representation

The diplomat is first of all the symbolic representative of his country. As such, he must continuously perform symbolic functions and expose himself to symbolic functions on the part of other diplomats and of the foreign government to which he is accredited. These functions serve to test, on the one hand, the prestige in which his nation is held abroad and, on the other, the prestige with which his own nation regards the country to whose government he is accredited. The American ambassador in London will, for instance, represent the President of the United States at the official functions to which he is invited and at those which he gives himself, such as state dinners, receptions, and the like. He extends and receives congratulations and condolences upon occasions joyful or sad for the nations concerned. He performs the symbolic functions of the diplomatic ceremonial.[2]

As a significant example of the symbolic function of diplomacy, mention has been made of the lavish entertainment most diplomatic missions feel constrained to offer to the members of the government to which they are accredited, to their fellow diplomats, and to the high society of the capital where they reside. This custom, which has been the object of much adverse comment in democratic countries, is not primarily the expression of a love for luxury on the part of the individual diplomats, but fulfills a special function in the scheme of diplomatic representation.

While entertaining, the diplomat does not act for himself as an individual, but as the symbolic representative of his country. It is the Soviet ambassador as such who invites guests to a reception in commemoration of the October Revolution of 1917. Through him (his identity is irrelevant for this symbolic purpose), it is the Soviet Union that entertains, celebrates, and tries to impress its guests—as well as those who pointedly have not been invited—with its wealth and generosity. It is not by accident that in the thirties, after the Soviet Union had regained an important, yet suspect position in the society of nations, the parties given by the Soviet embassies throughout the world were famed for their lavishness and for the quantity and quality of food and drink. The purpose of this extravagance was not to show the bourgeois inhabitants of the Western world how well off the Russian people were. The purpose was rather to com-

---

[2]See pages 87 ff.

pensate for the political inferiority from which the Soviet Union had just barely escaped and into which it feared it might sink again. By instructing its diplomatic representatives to act in matters of entertainment as the equals, if not the betters, of their colleagues in foreign capitals, the Soviet Union—not unlike an upstart who has just crashed society—endeavored to demonstrate symbolically that it was at least as good a nation as any other.

Legal Representation

The diplomat also acts as the legal representative of his government. He is the legal agent of his government in the same sense in which a domestic corporation with its seat in Wilmington, Delaware, is represented by legal agents in other states and cities. These agents act in the name of that legal fiction which we call a corporation, make declarations binding upon it, sign contracts obligating it, and act within the limits of the corporate charter as though they were the corporation. Similarly, the American ambassador in London performs in the name of the government of the United States the legal functions that the Constitution, the laws of the United States, and the orders of the government allow him to perform. He may be authorized to sign a treaty or to transmit and receive ratification documents by which a treaty already signed is brought into force. He gives legal protection to American citizens abroad. He may represent the United States at an international conference or in the agencies of the United Nations and cast his vote in the name, and according to the instructions, of his government.

Political Representation

The diplomat, together with the foreign office, shapes the foreign policy of his country. This is by far his most important function. As the foreign office is the nerve center of foreign policy, so are the diplomatic representatives its outlying fibers maintaining the two-way traffic between the center and the outside world.

Upon the diplomats' shoulders lie the main burden of discharging at least one of the four tasks of diplomacy discussed above: They must assess the objectives of other nations and the power actually and potentially available for the pursuit of these objectives. To that end, they must inform themselves of the plans of the government to which they are accredited, through direct interrogation of government officials and political leaders, through canvassing the press and other mouthpieces of public opinion. Furthermore, they must evaluate the potential influence upon government policies of opposing trends within the government, political parties, and public opinion.

A foreign diplomat in Washington must keep his government informed about the present and probable future attitude of the different branches of the United States government with regard to current problems of international affairs. He must appraise the importance for the development of foreign policy of different personalities in the government and the political parties. What stands are different presidential candidates likely to take, in the event of their election, on the pending issues of foreign policy? What is the influence of a certain columnist or commentator upon official policy and public opinion, and how representative of official thinking and of the trends in public opinion are his views? Such are some of the questions the diplomat must try to answer. Upon the reliability of his reports and the soundness of his judgment the success or failure of the foreign policy of his government and its ability to preserve peace may well depend.

When it comes to evaluating the actual and potential power of a nation, the diplomatic mission takes on the aspects of a high-class and *sub rosa* spy organization. High-ranking members of the armed services are delegated to the different diplomatic missions where, as military, naval, and air attachés, they are responsible for accumulating, by whatever means are available, information about actual and planned armaments, new weapons, the military potential, military organization, and the war plans of the countries concerned. Their services are supplemented by the commercial attachés, who collect information about economic trends, industrial developments, and the location of industries, especially with regard to their bearing upon military preparedness. In this and many other respects too numerous to mention, the accuracy and soundness of the reports a government receives from its diplomatic missions abroad are indispensable for the soundness of its own decisions.

In this function of gathering information, especially secret information upon which the foreign policies of one's own nation could be founded, lies the root of modern diplomacy. In the Middle Ages it was taken for granted that the special envoy of a prince traveling in a foreign country was a spy. When in the course of the fifteenth century the small Italian states started to make use of permanent diplomatic representatives in their relations with stronger states, they did so primarily for the purpose of receiving timely information of aggressive intentions on the part of the latter. Even when in the sixteenth century permanent diplomatic missions had become general, diplomats were widely regarded as a nuisance and a liability for the receiving state. At the beginning of the seventeenth century Hugo Grotius, the founder of modern international law, went so far as to advocate their abolition.

Diplomatic representatives are not merely the eyes and the ears that report the events of the outside world to the nerve center of foreign policy as the raw material for its decisions. Diplomatic representatives are also the mouth and the hands through which the impulses emanating from the nerve center are transformed into words and actions. They must make the people among whom they live, and especially the mouthpieces of their public opinion and their political leaders, understand and, if possible, approve the foreign policy they represent. For this task of "selling" a foreign policy, the personal appeal of the diplomat and his understanding of the psychology of the foreign people are essential prerequisites.

In the performance of the peace-preserving functions of persuasion, negotiations, and threat of force, the diplomatic representative plays an out-standing part. His foreign office can give him instructions concerning the objec-tives pursued and the means to be employed. Yet for the execution of these instructions it must rely upon the judgment and the skill of the diplomatic representative himself. The foreign office can tell its representative to use persuasion or to threaten force or to avail himself of both tactics simultaneously, but must leave to the representative's discretion how and when to make use of those techniques. How persuasive an argument will be, what advantages a negotiated agreement will yield, what impression the threat of force will make, how effectively emphasis is placed upon one or the other of these techniques— all this lies in the hands of the diplomat, who has it in his power to bungle a good, and avoid the worst consequences of a bad, foreign policy. We have mentioned the spectacular contributions great diplomatists have made to the power of their nations.[3] Their contributions to the cause of peace are no less important.

THE DECLINE OF DIPLOMACY

Today diplomacy no longer performs the role, often spectacular and brilliant and always important, that it performed from the end of the Thirty Years' War to the beginning of the First World War. The decline of diplomacy set in with the end of the First World War. In the twenties, a few outstanding diplomatists were still able to make important contributions to the foreign policies of their countries. In the decade preceding the Second World War, the part diplomats took in shaping foreign policy became even smaller, and the decline of diplo-macy as a technique of conducting foreign affairs became more and more patent. Since the end of the Second World War, diplomacy has lost its vitality, and its functions have withered away to such an extent as is without precedent in the history of the modern state system. Five factors account for that decline.

Development of Communications

The most obvious of these factors is the development of modern communica-tions. Diplomacy owes its rise in part to the absence of speedy communications in a period when the governments of the new territorial states maintained continuous political relations with each other. Diplomacy owes its decline in part to the development of speedy and regular communications in the form of the satellite, the airplane, the radio, the telegraph, the teletype, the long-distance telephone.

When at any time before the First World War the governments of the United States and of Great Britain wanted to enter into negotiations, it was indispensable for them to have permanent representatives, endowed with a

---

[3]See pages 159 ff.

great deal of discretion, in London and Washington to carry on the negotiations. These permanent representatives were necessary because the facilities for transmitting rapidly and continuously detailed messages were cumbersome, and, more particularly, because the time consumed by travel made personal consultations impossible without disrupting the negotiations. Today an official of the State Department needs only to converse over the transatlantic telephone with his counterpart in the British Foreign Office or with the American ambassador in London, or to board a transatlantic plane in the evening to start negotiations in London the next morning. Whenever direct consultations with his government become necessary, a day is all he needs to cross and recross the Atlantic, inform his government of the latest developments, and receive its instructions.

Only seventy-five years ago, it would have been unthinkable for the Secretary of State to absent himself from Washington for weeks in order to participate in an international conference or visit foreign capitals. Now, when he is absent from the capital he remains in continuous contact with the State Department through telephone and radio, and an overnight trip will bring him back to Washington on a moment's notice. Thus as a rule important negotiations are carried on, not by diplomatic representatives, but by special delegates who may be the foreign ministers themselves or high officials of the foreign offices or technical experts. The modern technology of communications has made "shuttle diplomacy" possible.

Depreciation of Diplomacy

These technological developments are, however, not solely responsible for the discard into which the traditional methods of diplomacy have fallen. To the technological ability to part with the services of diplomacy must be added the conviction that those services ought to be parted with because they not only contribute nothing to the cause of peace, but actually endanger it. This conviction grew in the same soil that nourished the conception of power politics as an accident of history to be eliminated at will.[4]

That conviction and this conception both recognize the intimate relation between power politics and the functions of diplomacy, and in this they are right. The emergence of diplomacy as an institution coincides with the rise of the nation state and, hence, with the appearance of international relations in the modern sense. The contemporary emergence of diplomacy and the modern state system is, however, more than a mere coincidence. If there is to be intercourse at all among sovereign nations with the goal of creating and maintaining at least a modicum of order and peace in international affairs, that intercourse must be carried on by permanent agents. The opposition to, and depreciation of, diplomacy is then but a peculiar manifestation of hostility to the modern state system and the kind of international politics it has produced.

It is indeed true that the diplomat has been held morally in low esteem

---

[4]See pages 37 ff.

throughout modern history, and not only by those who thought that there was an easy way of eliminating the struggle for power from the international scene. The diplomat's reputation for deviousness and dishonesty is as old as diplomacy itself. Well known is the definition of a diplomat, attributed to Sir Henry Wotton, an English ambassador at the beginning of the seventeenth century, as "an honest man sent abroad to lie for his country." When Metternich was informed of the death of the Russian ambassador at the Congress of Vienna, he is reported to have exclaimed: "Ah, is that true? What may have been his motive?"

The modern version of that depreciation of diplomacy attaches special importance to one particular aspect of the diplomatic technique—its secrecy. During and after the First World War, wide currency was given to the opinion that the secret machinations of diplomats shared a great deal, if not the major portion, of responsibility for that war, that the secrecy of diplomatic negotiations was an atavistic and dangerous residue from the aristocratic past, and that international negotiations carried on and concluded under the watchful eyes of a peaceloving public opinion could not but further the cause of peace.

Woodrow Wilson was the most eloquent spokesman of this new philosophy of international affairs. The Preamble to and the first of his Fourteen Points are the classic statement of the new philosophy. The Preamble to the Fourteen Points states:

> It will be our wish and purpose that the processes of peace, when they are begun, shall be absolutely open, and that they shall involve and permit henceforth no secret understandings of any kind. The day of conquest and aggrandizement is gone by; so is also the day of secret covenants entered into in the interest of particular governments, and likely at some unlooked-for moment to upset the peace of the world. It is this happy fact, now clear to the view of every public man whose thoughts do not still linger in an age that is dead and gone, which makes it possible for every nation whose purposes are consistent with justice and the peace of the world to avow, now or at any other time, the objects it has in view. The first point reads: "Open covenants of peace, openly arrived at, after which there shall be no private international understandings of any kind, but diplomacy shall proceed always frankly and in the public view."[5]

Diplomacy by Parliamentary Procedures

It was in deference to this new philosophy that after the First World War the statesmen of the world began to depart from the established pattern of diplomacy. They created in the League of Nations and later in the United Nations a new type of diplomatic intercourse: diplomacy by parliamentary procedure. International problems requiring solution are put on the agenda of the deliberative bodies of these organizations. The delegates of the different governments discuss the merits of the problem in public debate. A vote taken in accordance with the constitution of the organization disposes of the matter.

---

[5]*Selected Addresses and Public Papers of Woodrow Wilson*, edited by Albert Bushnell Hart (New York: Boni and Liveright, Inc., 1918), pp. 247–8.

This method has been employed before by special conferences, such as the Hague Peace Conferences of 1899 and 1907. As an over-all method of dealing with international problems, it was employed for the first time by the League of Nations. Its use by that organization was, however, apparent rather than real. The public discussions of the Council and the Assembly of the League were as a rule carefully rehearsed, especially when political matters were under consideration. A solution to which all could agree was generally sought and often found by the traditional means of secret negotiations, preceding the public meetings. The latter, then, simply gave the delegates of the nations concerned an opportunity of restating their positions for public consumption and of ratifying, in compliance with the provisions of the Covenant, the agreement secretly reached.

The United Nations, on the contrary, has taken seriously the parliamentary methods of transacting the business of diplomacy. It has developed the new methods of United Nations diplomacy, whose purpose it is to recreate for every issue coming to a vote in the General Assembly the two-thirds majority required by the Charter. Generally speaking, the aim of the new diplomacy of the United Nations is not the settlement of an issue dividing the members, but the line-up of a two-thirds majority to outvote the other side. It is a vote at which its processes aim and in which they culminate.

The trend toward public parliamentary procedures instead of traditional diplomatic negotiations, of which the operations of the General Assembly of the United Nations are typical, has also affected the postwar international conferences which by composition, issues, and objectives most closely resemble the diplomatic gatherings of the nineteenth and early twentieth centuries. The Paris Peace Conference of 1946, attended by twenty-one nations, operated in the full light of publicity and duplicated in its procedures the pattern established by the deliberative agencies of the United Nations. The Foreign Ministers' Conferences, composed of the foreign ministers of France, Great Britain, the Soviet Union, and the United States, which tried to dispose of the legacy of the Second World War, have debated and voted either in full public view or behind the transparent screen of semisecrecy which allowed the public to follow the main phases of the debate as reported by the different delegations to the correspondents of the press.

However, the ease of communications, the condemnation of secret diplomacy, and the new parliamentary diplomacy cannot fully account for this over-all disintegration of diplomacy. Two additional factors must share responsibility for the decline: the peculiarly untraditional approach of the two superpowers to the issues of international politics, and the very nature of world politics in the second half of the twentieth century.

The Superpowers: Newcomers to Diplomacy

In its formative years the United States benefited from the services of an unusually brilliant diplomacy. From the Jacksonian era on, the eminent qualities of American diplomacy disappeared as the need for them seemed to disappear. When the need for an active American foreign policy became manifest in the late 1930s there was nothing to build on but a mediocre foreign service, the condemnation of power politics and of secret diplomacy transformed into moral indignation at "aggressor nations," and the tradition of the big stick, which had worked so well in the Western Hemisphere. Thus it was the improvisations of Franklin D. Roosevelt alone, guided at times by an intuitive grasp of the international realities, that kept American foreign policy in tune with American interests.

In that decisive period neither the Secretary of State nor the permanent staff of the State Department nor the diplomatic representatives abroad exerted more than a subordinate influence upon the conduct of American foreign policy. When Roosevelt, who for twelve years had almost single-handedly made American foreign policy, left the scene, there was no man or group of men capable of creating and operating that intricate and subtle machinery by which traditional diplomacy had given peaceful protection and furtherance to the national interest. Nor could that small group of able and devoted public servants who knew what foreign policy was all about rely upon the public understanding of, and popular support for, the rational and intricate processes of foreign policy, without which foreign policy in a democracy cannot be successfully conducted.

For quite different reasons the Soviet Union has found it difficult to develop adequate instruments for diplomatic intercourse. The Bolshevist Revolution of 1917 destroyed the Russian diplomatic service, which could look back upon a long tradition and had a number of brilliant achievements to its credit. The few old-school diplomats who were retained in office after the Revolution and the new diplomats of talent who rose from the ranks of the revolutionaries had little opportunity to prove themselves. The hostility between the Soviet Union and most other nations and the resulting isolation of the Soviet Union prevented the conduct of normal diplomatic relations.

Furthermore, the Russian diplomat was the emissary of a totalitarian government that punished failure, or even too much discretion in interpreting official orders, at least with loss of office. In consequence, postrevolutionary Russian diplomats have traditionally—and more than ever since the conclusion of the Second World War—conceived of their task as the transmission of the proposals of their governments, which other governments might accept or reject as they see fit. Counterproposals and other new elements in the negotiations call for new instruments from the foreign office. The content of these new instruments is again submitted to the other governments, which may take it or leave it, and so forth, until the patience of one or the other or of all parties is exhausted. Such a procedure destroys all the virtues of diplomatic negotiations, such as quick adaptation to new situations, clever use of a psychological opening, retreat and advance as the situation may require, persuasion, the *quid pro quo* of bargaining, and the like. Diplomatic intercourse, as practiced by the new Russian diplomacy, resembles nothing so much as a series of military orders relayed from the high command—the foreign office—to the field commanders—the diplomatic representatives—who in turn communicate the terms of agreement to the enemy.

A diplomat whose main concern must be to retain the approval of his superiors is usually only too eager to report what the latter would like to hear, regardless of whether the report is true. This tendency to bend the truth to the wishes of the foreign office and to paint the facts in favorable colors is found in all diplomatic services; for compliance enhances security in office and increases the chance for advancement.

25

The Future of Diplomacy

HOW CAN DIPLOMACY BE REVIVED?

The revival of diplomacy requires the elimination of the factors, or at least of some of their consequences, responsible for the decline of the traditional diplomatic practices. Priority in this respect belongs to the depreciation of diplomacy and its corollary: diplomacy by parliamentary procedures. In so far as that depreciation is only the result of the depreciation of power politics, what we have said about the latter should suffice for the former.[1] Diplomacy, however morally unattractive its business may seem to many, is nothing but a symptom of the struggle for power among sovereign nations, which try to maintain orderly and peaceful relations among themselves. If there were a way of banning the struggle for power from the international scene, diplomacy would disappear of itself. If order and anarchy, peace and war, were matters of no concern to the nations of the world, they could dispense with diplomacy, prepare for war, and hope for the best. If nations who are sovereign, who are supreme within their territories with no superior above them, want to preserve peace and order in their relations, they must try to persuade, negotiate, and exert pressure upon each other. That is to say, they must engage in, cultivate, and rely upon diplomatic procedures.

The new parliamentary diplomacy is no substitute for these procedures. On the contrary, it tends to aggravate rather than mitigate international conflicts and leaves the prospect for peace dimmed rather than brightened. Three essential qualities of the new diplomacy are responsible for these unfortunate results: its publicity, its major votes, and its fragmentation of international issues.

---

[1]See pages 37 ff.

The Vice of Publicity

Much of the confusion attending discussion of the problem of secret diplomacy results from the failure to distinguish between two separate aspects of the problem: between "open covenants" and "covenants openly arrived at," between publicity for the results of diplomatic negotiations and publicity for the diplomatic negotiations themselves. Disclosure of the results of diplomatic negotiations is required by the principles of democracy, for without it there can be no democratic control of foreign policy. Yet publicity for the negotiations themselves is not required by democracy and runs counter to the requirements of common sense. It takes only common sense derived from daily experience to realize that it is impossible to negotiate in public on anything in which parties other than the negotiators are interested. This impossibility derives from the very nature of negotiation and from the social context in which negotiations generally operate.

It is a common characteristic of negotiations that they are started by each side with maximum demands, which are whittled down in a process of persuasion, bargaining, and pressures until both sides meet on a level below the one from which they started. The saving grace of negotiations is the result that satisfies the demands of either side, at least up to a point, and tends to strengthen amity between the parties by demonstrating in the act of agreement the existence of identical or complementary interests binding them together. On the other hand, the process leading up to the result reveals the parties in roles in which they would rather not be remembered by their fellows. There are more edifying spectacles than the bluffing, blustering, haggling, and deceiving, the real weakness and pretended strength, which go with horse-trading and the drive for a bargain. To publicize such negotiations is tantamount to destroying, or at least impairing, the bargaining position of the parties in any further negotiations in which they might be engaged with other parties.

Not only will their bargaining positions suffer. Their social status, their prestige, and their power will face irreparable damage if publicity attends these negotiations, uncovering their weakness and unmasking their pretenses. Competitors for the gains the negotiators seek will take advantage of what the public negotiations have revealed to them. They will do so not only in further negotiations with the parties, but also in their over-all calculations, plans, and dispositions, which take into account the qualities and potentialities of all participants in the competition.

It is for these reasons that in a free market no seller will carry on public negotiations with a buyer; no landlord with a tenant; no institution of higher learning with its staff. No candidate for office will negotiate in public with his backers; no public official with his colleagues; no politician with his fellow politicians. How, then, are we to expect that nations are able and willing to do what no private individual would think of doing?

The disadvantage to which nations would be put by the publicity of their negotiations is further increased by the fact that the audience witnessing the spectacle of public international negotiations comprises not only a limited number of interested parties, but the whole world. More particularly, the governments concerned negotiate under the watchful eyes of their own peoples and, especially when they are democratically elected, in full view of the oposition. No government that wants to stay in power or simply retain the respect of its people can afford to give up publicly part of what it had declared at the outset to be just and necessary, to retreat from a position initially held, to concede at least the partial justice of the other side's claims. Heroes, not horsetraders, are the idols of public opinion. Public opinion, while dreading war, demands that its diplomats act as heroes who do not yield in the face of the enemy, even at the risk of war, and condemns as weaklings and traitors those who yield, albeit only halfway, for the sake of peace.

Furthermore, traditional diplomacy used to transact the business of state in a language and with manners well fitted for its purpose. The aim of diplomacy then was to promote the national interest with moderation and leave the door open for compromise in the form of a negotiated settlement. Measured words and formalized phrases, used in those transactions, committed the speaker to nothing or to just as much as he was willing to make good. These phrases and formalities are empty of, or in any case vague in, meaning and hence are susceptible to all kinds of interpretations in support of whatever policy or settlement seems to be advantageous in the end. They are also polite and, hence, make it easy for those who use them to get along with each other, however grave the issues may be that separate nations. In sum, they are the perfect instrument of the subtle, cautious, moderate, conciliatory negotiator.

Public diplomacy and its advocates can have nothing but contempt for such an instrument, which, so they think, belongs to a bygone age of aristocratic snobbery and moral indifference. Crusaders for the right—and that is what public diplomats are supposed to be—do not speak like that. Seated on a stage with the world as their audience, the public diplomats speak to the world rather than to each other. Their aim is not to persuade each other that they could find common ground for agreement, but to persuade the world and especially their own nations that they are right and the other side is wrong and that they are and always will remain staunch defenders of the right.

No man who has taken such a stand before the attentive eyes and ears of the world can in full public view agree to a compromise without looking like a fool and a knave. He must take himself at his public word and must stand unyielding "on principle," the favored phrase of public diplomacy, rather than on negotiation and compromise. He must defend the position initially taken, and so must the other side. Neither side being able to retreat or advance, a "phony war" of positions ensues. Both sides oppose each other inflexibly, each side knowing that the other will not and cannot move. To offer the public some semblance of activity, they fire into the air the empty shells of words, which explode noisily and, as everybody knows, are aimed at nothing. It is only in mutual vituperation that the minds of the delegates meet. When the delegates finally part, embittered and frustrated, they reach, however indignantly, an agreement of sorts at last on one point: the other side has engaged in propaganda. It so happens that on this point both sides are right.

This degeneration of diplomatic intercourse into a propaganda match is, then, the inevitable concomitant of the publicity of the new diplomacy. Not only is a publicly conducted diplomacy unable to reach agreement or even to negotiate for the purpose of reaching agreement, but each public meeting leaves international matters in a worse state than before. For each propaganda match strengthens the conviction of the different delegates and of their nations that they are absolutely right and that the other side is absolutely wrong and that the gap separating them is too deep and wide to be bridged by the traditional methods of diplomacy. There is much wisdom in the plea which the Secretary General of the United Nations made in his report of 1956, elaborated in the report of 1959, to "give greater emphasis to the United Nations as an instrument for negotiation of settlements, as distinct from the mere debate of issues."

The Vice of Majority Decision

The evil wrought by the public conduct of diplomacy is compounded by the attempt to decide issues by majority vote. In the General Assembly of the United Nations, this method has developed into the pattern of at least two-thirds of the members trying to vote down the rest. That this method of conducting the business of diplomacy has made no direct contribution to the peaceful settlement of a single outstanding issue is obvious from the results. For instance, the Soviet bloc was voted down time and again on the Korean issue. Yet the voting in the General Assembly was relevant for the settlement of the Korean issue only in so far as it demonstrated the voting strength, and thereby enhanced the political strength, of the Western bloc and enabled the nations supporting the United Nations action in Korea to act in unison vis-à-vis the Soviet bloc. Beyond that indirect contribution in terms of increasing the strength of one side, the voting contributed nothing to the settlement of the Korean issue. That issue was settled on the battlefield and in diplomatic negotiations between East and West, not in the chamber of the General Assembly. The reason why the outvoting of an opponent in a deliberative international body is a useless and may even be a mischievous undertaking, aside from its occasional use for strengthening a particular group, is to be found in the very nature of international society in contrast to national societies.

When the Congress of the United States votes down a minority, it actually decides the issue for the time being. It is able to do so for four reasons, all of which are absent on the international scene.

1. The parliamentary majority vote is an integral part of a whole system of devices for peaceful change, each being able to operate in supplementation or support of, or as a corrective upon, the others, and all limited and coordinated by the Constitution. The minority and the majority in Congress make up an integrated society. Aside from deliberative bodies deciding by majority

vote, the national society has created a series of devices, such as the presidential veto and judicial review, by which the majority vote can be overridden and the minority can be protected against unconstitutional use and arbitrary misuse of the majority vote. Behind a majority decision as well as behind the defeated minority stands the whole moral and political power of the national community, ready to enforce a decision of the majority and to protect the minority against injustice and abuse.

2. The instrumentalities of peaceful change which operate within the national community give the minority a chance to become a majority sometime in the future. That chance is inherent in the device of periodical elections and in the dynamics of the social process, which produce ever-new alignments and distributions of power. These dynamics also see to it that a minority in a deliberative assembly is never a minority in all the respects important to it. A group may be a religious minority, outvoted in issues of this kind, but may be part of the economic majority determining economic legislation, and so forth.

3. The numerical relation between minority and majority is at least an approximation to the actual distribution of power and interests within the whole population. When the House of Representatives votes a motion down— say, 270 to 60—it is generally safe to assume that only a relatively small minority of the American people is identified with the defeated measure.

4. While in Congress each vote cast counts for one, it is of course true, politically speaking, that all votes are not of equal weight. The negative vote of a powerful committee chairman, industrialist, farmer, or labor leader with respect to a piece of legislation affecting the interests of his respective group may well have a bearing upon the political, economic, or social consequences that the majority intended the piece of legislation to have. Yet even the most powerful single vote in Congress represents but a small fraction of the total power of the American people.

None of these four factors that make possible the contribution of the majority vote to domestic peaceful change operates on the international scene.

1. The majority vote is the sole device for compulsory peaceful change within the framework of the United Nations. There is no constitution, no presidential veto, no compulsory judicial review, no bill of rights, imposing substantive and procedural restraints upon the majority and protecting the minority against injustice and abuse. Nor is there a community imposing moral restraints upon majority and minority alike and able to enforce the decision of the majority against a recalcitrant minority. The majority can outvote the minority as often as its wants to and on any issue it chooses, and the minority can protect itself with the veto and its power against any majority decision it wants to annul.

2. A minority in the United Nations is likely, especially under present political conditions, to be a permanent one. For the same reason, its minority status is bound to extend to certain questions of major importance. The two-bloc system, modified by the independent position of China and the Third World Nations, that dominates contemporary world politics leads to permanent

alignments on either side of the divide. The tension between the two blocs transforms the majority of issues into political ones. When such issues come to a vote, the adherents of the two blocs are likely to split along the line separating the blocs.

3. The numerical relation between a minority and a two-thirds majority in the General Assembly obviously does not of necessity correspond to the actual distribution of power and interests among the members of the United Nations, nor does the vote of the most powerful members of the General Assembly represent a relatively small fraction of the total power of the community of nations. An overwhelming majority composed of all the small nations of Africa, Asia, Europe, and Latin America means little in terms of power as compared with the one vote of the United States or the Soviet Union.

To outvote habitually a powerful minority in a deliberative international agency, while it may have been a potent weapon in the Cold War, does not contribute to the preservation of peace. For the minority cannot accept the decision of the majority and the majority cannot enforce its decision short of war. At best, parliamentary procedures transferred to the international scene leave things as they are; they leave problems unsolved and issues unsettled. At worst, however, these procedures poison the international climate and aggravate the conflicts that carry the seeds of war. They provide a majority with an opportunity to humiliate the minority in public and as often as it wishes. In the form of the veto, the corollary of the majority vote in a society of sovereign nations, these procedures provide the minority with a weapon with which to obstruct the will of the majority and to prevent the international agency from functioning at all. Neither the majority nor the minority needs to use self-restraint or be aware of its responsibility to the international organization or to humanity, since what either side votes for or against cannot, as such, influence the course of events. For one group of sovereign nations to vote down habitually another group of sovereign nations is, then, to engage in a puerile game that can accomplish nothing for the peaceful settlement of international conflicts, but may well carry mankind further down the road to war.

The Vice of Fragmentation

The decision by majority vote implies the third of the vices that stand in the way of a revival of the traditional diplomatic practices: the fragmentation of international issues. By its very nature, the majority vote is concerned with an isolated case. The facts of life to be dealt with by the majority decision are artificially separated from the facts that precede, accompany, and follow them, and are transformed into a legal "case" or a political "issue" to be disposed of as such by the majority decision. In the domestic field, this procedure is not necessarily harmful. Here the majority decision of a deliberative body operates within the context of an intricate system of devices for peaceful change, supplementing, supporting, or checking each other, as the case may be, but in any case attuned to each other in a certain measure and thus giving the individual decisions coherence with each other and with the whole social system.

On the international scene, no such system of integrating factors exists. Consequently, it is particularly inadequate here to take up one "case" or "issue" after the other and to try to dispose of them by a succession of majority votes. A case or issue, such as the Middle East or Berlin, is always a particular phase and manifestation of a much larger situation. Such a case or issue is rooted in the historic past and extends its ramifications beyond its particular locale and into the future. Our discussion of the relations between disputes and tensions has given us an indication of the intimate relations that exist between the surface phenomena of international conflicts and those large and undefined problems which are buried deep under the surface of the daily occurrences of international life. To deal with cases and issues as they arise, and to try to dispose of them according to international law or political expediency, is to deal with surface phenomena and leave the underlying problems unconsidered and unsolved. The League of Nations fell victim to that vice, and the United Nations has been heedless of the League's experience.

For instance, there is no doubt that the League of Nations was right, according to international law, in expelling the Soviet Union in 1939 because of its attack upon Finland. But the political and military problems with which the Soviet Union confronted the world neither began with its attack on Finland nor ended there; it was unwise for the League to pretend that such was the case and to decide the issue on that pretense. History has proved the unwisdom of that pretense, for only Sweden's refusal to allow British and French troops to pass through Swedish territory in order to come to the aid of Finland saved Great Britain and France from being at war with Germany and the Soviet Union at the same time. Whenever the League of Nations endeavored to deal with political situations presented as legal issues, it could deal with them only as isolated cases according to the applicable rules of international law, not as particular phases of an over-all political situation which required an over-all solution according to the rules of the political art. Hence, political problems were never solved, but only tossed about and finally shelved according to the rules of the legal game.

What was true of the League of Nations has proved to be true of the United Nations. In its approach to many of the issues brought before its political agencies, the United Nations has remained faithful to the tradition established by the League of Nations. These cases have provided opportunities for exercise in parliamentary procedure and just that chicanery for which traditional diplomacy has so often been reproached, but only on rare occasions has even an attempt been made to face the political issues of which these situations are the surface manifestations.

The special political conferences of the postwar period have repeated the pattern of fragmentation established by the League of Nations and the United Nations. They have dealt, for instance, with Korea, German unification, or disarmament. None of these conferences has faced the problem of which all these issues are particular phases and manifestations and upon whose solution the settlement of these issues depends: the problem of the over-all relations between the United States and the Soviet Union. Since they were unwilling to come to grips with the fundamental problem of international politics, they were unable to settle any of the particular issues on which they concentrated their attention.

This failure of contemporary diplomacy even to see the problem upon whose solution the preservation of peace depends, let alone to try to solve it, is the inevitable result of the methods it has employed. A diplomacy that, instead of speaking in conciliatory terms to the other side, addresses the world for purposes of propaganda; that, instead of negotiating with compromise as its goal, strives for the cheap triumphs of futile majority decisions and of obstructive vetoes; that, instead of facing the primary problem, is satisfied with manipulating the secondary ones—such a diplomacy is a liability rather than an asset for the cause of peace.

These three essential vices of contemporary diplomacy are aggravated by the misuse of modern communications. The conquest of time and space by modern technology has inevitably reduced the importance of diplomatic representation. Yet it has by no means made necessary the confusion of function between the foreign office and diplomatic representation which is characteristic of contemporary diplomacy. A secretary of state or foreign minister is physically able to converse with any foreign capital within a few minutes' time by way of modern communications and to reach it in person within a few days at the most. Thus the tendency has grown for the men responsible for the conduct of foreign affairs to assume the role of roving ambassadors, hurrying from one conference to another, stopping in between conferences for a short while at the foreign office, and using their time there in preparation for the next meeting. The men who are supposed to be the brains of diplomacy, its nerve center, fulfill at best the functions of the nerve ends. In consequence, there is a void at the center. There is nobody who faces the over-all problem of international politics and sees all the particular issues as phases and manifestations of the whole. Instead, each specialist in the foreign office deals with the particular problems belonging to his specialty, and the fragmentation of the conduct of foreign affairs to which the techniques of contemporary diplomacy lend themselves is powerfully supported by the lack of over-all direction of foreign affairs.

THE PROMISE OF DIPLOMACY: ITS NINE RULES[2]

Diplomacy could revive if it would part with these vices, which in recent years have well-nigh destroyed its usefulness, and if it would restore the techniques which have controlled the mutual relations of nations since time immemorial. By doing so, diplomacy would realize only one of the preconditions for the preservation of peace. The contribution of a revived dipomacy to the cause of peace would depend upon the methods and purposes of its use. The discussion of these uses is the last task we have set ourselves in this book.

---

[2]We by no means intend to give here an exhaustive account of rules of diplomacy. We propose to discuss only those which seem to have a special bearing upon the contemporary situation.

Four Fundamental Rules

Diplomacy Must Be Divested of the Crusading Spirit
This is the first of the rules that diplomacy can neglect only at the risk of war. In the words of William Graham Sumner:

If you want war, nourish a doctrine. Doctrines are the most frightful tyrants to which men ever are subject, because doctrines get inside of a man's own reason and betray him against himself. Civilized men have done their fiercest fighting for doctrines. The reconquest of the Holy Sepulcher, "the balance of power," "no universal dominion," "trade follows the flag," "he who holds the land will hold the sea," "the throne and the altar," the revolution, the faith—these are the things for which men have given their lives. . . . Now when any doctrine arrives at that degree of authority, the name of it is a club which any demagogue may swing over you at any time and apropos of anything. In order to describe a doctrine, we must have recourse to theological language. A doctrine is an article of faith. It is something which you are bound to believe, not because you have some rational grounds for believing it is true, but because you belong to such and such a church or denomination. . . . A policy in a state we can understand; for instance, it was the policy of the United States at the end of the eighteenth century to get the free navigation of the Mississippi to its mouth, even at the expense of war with Spain. That policy had reason and justice in it; it was founded in our interests; it had positive form and definite scope. A doctrine is an abstract principle; it is necessarily absolute in its scope and abstruse in its terms; it is a metaphysical assertion. It is never true, because it is absolute and the affairs of men are all conditioned and relative. . . . Now to turn back to politics, just think what an abomination in statecraft an abstract doctrine must be. Any politician or editor can, at any moment, put a new extension on it. The people acquiesce in the doctrine and applaud it because they hear the politicians and editors repeat it, and the politicians and editors repeat it because they think it is popular. So it grows. . . . It may mean anything or nothing, at any moment, and no one knows how it will be. You accede to it now, within the vague limits of what you suppose it to be; therefore, you will have to accede to it tomorrow when the same name is made to cover something which you never have heard or thought of. If you allow a political catchword to go on and grow, you will awaken some day to find it standing over you, the arbiter of your destiny, against which you are powerless, as men are powerless against delusions. . . . What can be more contrary to sound statesmanship and common sense than to put forth an abstract assertion which has no definite relation to any interest of ours now at stake, but which has in it any number of possibilities of producing complications which we cannot foresee, but which are sure to be embarrassing when they arise![3]

At the very beginning of colonial history, this conflict between self-interest and the crusading spirit was clearly recognized and decided in favor of the former by John Winthrop, the first governor of Massachusetts. In the words of Professor Edmund S. Morgan:

Winthrop had many more occasions to notice how self-righteousness extinguished charity. It also blinded men to realities. He knew that New England depended on

---

[3]"War," *Essays of William Graham Sumner* (New Haven: Yale University Press, 1934), Vol. 1, pp. 169 ff.

the outside world in its new economy, and his heart was gladdened every time another ship splashed off the ways at Boston to carry New England codfish to markets where idolatrous Roman Catholics paid good money for them. He also knew, what a good foreign minister had to know, that righteousness endangered his community when it produced a blind and undiscriminating defiance to surrounding evils. Thus, when his colleagues refused to aid Rhode Island against the Indians, he remarked that it was an error in state policy, for though the Rhode Islanders were "desperately erroneous and in such distraction among themselves as portended their ruin, yet if the Indians should prevail against them, it would be a great advantage to the Indians, and danger to the whole country by the arms, etc., that would there be had, and by the loss of so many persons and so much cattle and other substance belonging to above 120 families. Or, if they should be forced to seek protection from the Dutch, who would be ready to accept them, it would be a great inconvenience to all the English to have so considerable a place in the power of strangers so potent as they are."[4]

The Wars of Religion have shown that the attempt to impose one's own religion as the only true one upon the rest of the world is as futile as it is costly. A century of almost unprecedented bloodshed, devastation, and barbarization was needed to convince the contestants that the two religions could live together in mutual toleration. After World War II, two political religions took the place of the two great Christian denominations of the sixteenth and seventeenth centuries. We asked, will the political religions of our time need the lesson of the Thirty Years' War, or will they rid themselves in time of the universalistic aspirations that inevitably issue in inconclusive war?

Upon the answer to that question depends the cause of peace. For only if it is answered in the affirmative can a moral consensus, emerging from shared convictions and common values, develop—a moral consensus within which a peace-preserving diplomacy will have a chance to grow. Only then will diplomacy have a chance to face the concrete political problems that require peaceful solution. If the objectives of foreign policy are not to be defined in terms of a world-embracing political religion, how are they to be defined? This is the fundamental problem to be solved once the crusading aspirations of nationalistic universalism have been discarded.

The Objectives of Foreign Policy Must Be Defined in Terms of the National Interest and Must Be Supported with Adequate Power

This is the second rule of a peace-preserving diplomacy. The national interest of a peace-loving nation can only be defined in terms of national security, and national security must be defined as integrity of the national territory and of its institutions.[5] National security, then, is the irreducible minimum that diplomacy must defend with adequate power without compromise. But diplomacy must ever be alive to the radical transformation that national security has undergone under the impact of the nuclear age. Until the

---

[4]Edmund S. Morgan, *The Puritan Dilemma: The Story of John Winthrop* (Boston: Little, Brown & Co., 1958), pp. 189, 190.

[5]For a more extensive discussion of the relevant problems, see Chapter 19.

advent of that age, a nation could use its diplomacy to purchase its security at the expense of another nation. Today, short of a radical change in the atomic balance of power in favor of a particular nation, diplomacy, in order to make one nation secure from nuclear destruction, must make them all secure. With the national interest defined in such restrictive and transcendent terms, diplomacy must observe the third of its rules.

Diplomacy Must Look at the Political Scene from the Point of View of Other Nations

"Nothing is so fatal to a nation as an extreme of self-partiality, and the total want of consideration of what others will naturally hope or fear."[6] What are the national interests of other nations in terms of national security, and are they compatible with one's own? The definition of the national interest in terms of national security is easier, and the interests of the two opposing nations are more likely to be compatible, in a bipolar system than in any other system of the balance of power. The bipolar system, as we have seen, is more unsafe from the point of view of peace than any other, when both blocs are in competitive contact throughout the world and the ambition of both is fired by the crusading zeal of a universal mission. ". . . Vicinity, or nearness of situation, constitutes nations' natural enemies."[7]

Yet once they have defined their national interests in terms of national security, they can draw back from their outlying positions, located close to, or within, the sphere of national security of the other side, and retreat into their respective spheres, each self-contained within its orbit. Those outlying positions add nothing to national security; they are but liabilities, positions that cannot be held in case of war. Each bloc will be the more secure the wider it makes the distance that separates both spheres of national security. Each side can draw a line far distant from each other, making it understood that to touch or even to approach it means war. What, then, about the interjacent spaces, stretching between the two lines of demarcation? Here the fourth rule of diplomacy applies.

Nations Must Be Willing to Compromise on All Issues That Are Not Vital to Them

All government, indeed every human benefit and enjoyment, every virtue and every prudent act, is founded on compromise and barter. We balance inconveniences; we give and take; we remit some rights, that we may enjoy others; and we choose rather to be happy citizens than subtle disputants. As we must give away some natural liberty, to enjoy civil advantages, so we must sacrifice some civil liberties, for the advantages to be derived from the communion and fellowship of a great empire. But, in all fair dealings, the thing bought must bear some proportion to the purchase paid. None will barter away the immediate jewel of his soul.[8]

---

[6]Edmund Burke, "Remarks on the Policy of the Allies with Respect to France" (1793), *Works*, Vol. IV (Boston: Little, Brown, and Company, 1889), p. 447.

[7]*The Federalist*, No. 6.

[8]Edmund Burke, "Speech on the Conciliation with America," loc. cit., Vol. II, p. 169.

Here diplomacy meets its most difficult task. For minds not beclouded by the crusading zeal of a political religion and capable of viewing the national interests of both sides with objectivity, the delimitation of these vital interests should not prove too difficult. Compromise on secondary issues is a different matter. Here the task is not to separate and define interests that by their very nature already tend toward separation and definition, but to keep in balance interests that touch each other at many points and may be intertwined beyond the possibility of separation. It is an immense task to allow the other side a certain influence in those interjacent spaces without allowing them to be absorbed into the orbit of the other side. It is hardly a less immense task to keep the other side's influence as small as possible in the regions close to one's own security zone without absorbing those regions into one's own orbit. For the performance of these tasks, no formula stands ready for automatic application. It is only through a continuous process of adaptation, supported both by firmness and self-restraint, that compromise on secondary issues can be made to work. It is, however, possible to indicate *a priori* what approaches will facilitate or hamper the success of policies of compromise.

First of all, it is worth noting to what extent the success of compromise—that is, compliance with the fourth rule—depends upon compliance with the other three rules, which in turn are similarly interdependent. As the compliance with the second rule depends upon the realization of the first, so the third rule must await its realization from compliance with the second. A nation can only take a rational view of its national interests after it has parted company with the crusading spirit of a political creed. A nation is able to consider the national interests of the other side with objectivity only after it has become secure in what it considers its own national interests. Compromise on any issue, however minor, is impossible so long as both sides are not secure in their national interests. Thus nations cannot hope to comply with the fourth rule if they are not willing to comply with the other three. Both morality and expediency require compliance with these four fundamental rules.

Compliance makes compromise possible, but it does not assure its success. To give compromise, made possible through compliance with the first three rules, a chance to succeed, five other rules must be observed.

Five Prerequisites of Compromise

Give Up the Shadow of Worthless Rights for the Substance of Real Advantage

A diplomacy that thinks in legalistic and propagandistic terms is particularly tempted to insist upon the letter of the law, as it interprets the law, and to lose sight of the consequences such insistence may have for its own nation and for humanity. Since there are rights to be defended, this kind of diplomacy thinks that the issue cannot be compromised. Yet the choice that confronts the diplomat is not between legality and illegality, but between political wisdom and political folly. "The question with me," said Edmund Burke, "is not whether you have a right to render your people miserable, but whether it is not your interest to make them happy. It is not what a lawyer tells me I *may* do, but what humanity, reason and justice tell me I ought to do."[9]

Never Put Yourself in a Position from Which You Cannot Retreat without Losing Face and from Which You Cannot Advance without Grave Risks
The violation of this rule often results from disregard for the preceding one. A diplomacy that confounds the shadow of legal right with the actuality of political advantage is likely to find itself in a position where it may have a legal right, but no political business, to be. In other words, a nation may identify itself with a position, which it may or may not have a right to hold, regardless of the political consequences. And again compromise becomes a difficult matter. A nation cannot retreat from that position without incurring a serious loss of prestige. It cannot advance from that position without exposing itself to political risks, perhaps even the risk of war. That heedless rush into untenable positions and, more particularly, the stubborn refusal to extricate oneself from them in time is the earmark of incompetent diplomacy. Its classic examples are the policy of Napoleon III on the eve of the Franco-Prussian War of 1870 and the policies of Austria and Germany on the eve of the First World War. Its outstanding contemporary example is the American involvement in Indochina. These examples also show how closely the risk of war is allied with the violation of this rule.

Never Allow a Weak Ally to Make Decisions for You
Strong nations that are oblivious to the preceding rules are particularly susceptible to violating this one. They lose their freedom of action by identifying their own national interests completely with those of the weak ally. Secure in the support of its powerful friend, the weak ally can choose the objectives and methods of its foreign policy to suit itself. The powerful nation then finds that it must support interests not its own and that it is unable to compromise on issues that are vital not to itself, but only to its ally.

The classic example of the violation of this rule is to be found in the way in which Turkey forced the hand of Great Britain and France on the eve of the Crimean War in 1853. The Concert of Europe had virtually agreed upon a compromise settling the conflict between Russia and Turkey, when Turkey, knowing that the Western powers would support it in a war with Russia, did its best to provoke that war and thus involved Great Britain and France in it against their will. Thus Turkey went far in deciding the issue of war and peace for Great Britain and France according to its own national interests. Great Britain and France had to accept that decision even though their national

---

[9]"Speech on Conciliation with the Colonies" (1775), *The Works of Edmund Burke* (Boston: Little, Brown, and Company, 1865), Vol. II, p. 140.

interests did not require war with Russia and they had almost succeeded in preventing its outbreak. They had surrendered their freedom of action to a weak ally, which used its control over their policies for its own purposes.

The Armed Forces Are the Instrument of Foreign Policy, Not Its Master

No successful and no peaceful foreign policy is possible without observance of this rule. No nation can pursue a policy of compromise with the military determining the ends and means of foreign policy. The armed forces are instruments of war; foreign policy is an instrument of peace. It is true that the ultimate objectives of the conduct of war and of the conduct of foreign policy are identical: both serve the national interest. Both however, differ fundamentally in their immediate objective, in the means they employ, and in the modes of thought they bring to bear upon their respective tasks.

The objective of war is simple and unconditional: to break the will of the enemy. Its methods are equally simple and unconditional: to bring the greatest amount of violence to bear upon the most vulnerable spot in the enemy's armor. Consequently, the military leader must think in absolute terms. He lives in the present and in the immediate future. The sole question before him is how to win victories as cheaply and quickly as possible and how to avoid defeat.

The objective of foreign policy is relative and conditional: to bend, not to break, the will of the other side as far as necessary in order to safeguard one's own vital interests without hurting those of the other side. The methods of foreign policy are relative and conditional: not to advance by destroying the obstacles in one's way, but to retreat before them, to circumvent them, to maneuver around them, to soften and dissolve them slowly by means of persuasion, negotiation, and pressure. In consequence, the mind of the diplomat is complicated and subtle. It sees the issue in hand as a moment in history, and beyond the victory of tomorrow it anticipates the incalculable possibilities of the future. In the words of Bolingbroke;

> Here let me only say, that the glory of taking towns, and winning battles, is to be measured by the utility that results from those victories. Victories, that bring honour to the arms, may bring shame to the councils, of a nation. To win a battle, to take a town, is the glory of a general, and of an army. . . . But the glory of a nation is to proportion the ends she proposes, to her interest and her strength; the means she employs to the ends she proposes, and the vigour she exerts to both.[10]

To surrender the conduct of foreign affairs to the military, then, is to destroy the possibility of compromise and thus surrender the cause of peace. The military mind knows how to operate between the absolutes of victory and defeat. It knows nothing of that patient, intricate, and subtle maneuvering of diplomacy, whose main purpose is to avoid the absolutes of victory and defeat and meet the other side on the middle ground of negotiated compromise. A

---

[10]*Bolingbroke's Defence of the Treaty of Utrecht* (Cambridge University Press: 1932), p. 95.

foreign policy conducted by military men according to the rules of the military art can only end in war, for "what we prepare for is what we shall get."[11]

For nations conscious of the potentialities of modern war, peace must be the goal of their foreign policies. Foreign policy must be conducted in such a way as to make the preservation of peace possible and not make the outbreak of war inevitable. In a society of sovereign nations, military force is a necessary instrument of foreign policy. Yet the instrument of foreign policy should not become the master of foreign policy. As war is fought in order to make peace possible, foreign policy should be conducted in order to make peace permanent. For the performance of both tasks, the subordination of the military under the civilian authorities which are constitutionally responsible for the conduct of foreign affairs is an indispensable prerequisite.

The Government Is the Leader of Public Opinion, Not Its Slave

Those responsible for the conduct of foreign policy will not be able to comply with the foregoing principles of diplomacy if they do not keep this principle constantly in mind. As has been pointed out above in greater detail,[12] the rational requirements of good foreign policy cannot from the outset count upon the support of a public opinion whose preferences are emotional rather than rational. This is bound to be particularly true of a foreign policy whose goal is compromise, and which, therefore, must concede some of the objectives of the other side and give up some of its own. Especially when foreign policy is conducted under conditions of democratic control and is inspired by the crusading zeal of a political religion, statesmen are always tempted to sacrifice the requirements of good foreign policy to the applause of the masses. On the other hand, the statesman who would defend the integrity of these requirements against even the slightest contamination with popular passion would seal his own doom as a political leader and, with it, the doom of his foreign policy, for he would lose the popular support which put and keeps him in power.

The statesman, then, is allowed neither to surrender to popular passions nor disregard them. He must strike a prudent balance between adapting himself to them and marshaling them to the support of his policies. In one word, he must lead. He must perform that highest feat of statesmanship: trimming his sails to the winds of popular passion while using them to carry the ship of state to the port of good foreign policy, on however roundabout and zigzag a course.

CONCLUSION

The road to international peace which we have outlined cannot compete in inspirational qualities with the simple and fascinating formulae that for a century and a half have fired the imagination of a war-weary world. There is

---

[11]William Graham Sumner, op. cit., p. 173.
[12]See pages 164 ff.

something spectacular in the radical simplicity of a formula that with one sweep seems to dispose of the problem of war once and for all. This has been the promise of such solutions as free trade, arbitration, disarmament, collective security, universal socialism, international government, and the world state. There is nothing spectacular, fascinating, or inspiring, at least for the people at large, in the business of diplomacy.

We have made the point, however, that these solutions, in so far as they deal with the real problem and not merely with some of its symptoms, presuppose the existence of an integrated international society, which actually does not exist. To bring into existence such an international society and keep it in being, the accommodating techniques of diplomacy are required. As the integration of domestic society and its peace develop from the unspectacular and almost unnoticed day-by-day operations of the techniques of accommodation and change, so the ultimate ideal of international life—that is, to transcend itself in a supranational society—must await its realization from the techniques of persuasion, negotiation, and pressure, which are the traditional instruments of diplomacy.

The reader who has followed us to this point may well ask: But has not diplomacy failed in preventing war in the past? To that legitimate question two answers can be given.

Diplomacy has failed many times, and it has succeeded many times, in its peace-preserving task. It has failed sometimes because nobody wanted it to succeed. We have seen how different in their objectives and methods the limited wars of the past have been from the total war of our time. When war was the normal activity of kings, the task of diplomacy was not to prevent it, but to bring it about at the most propitious moment.

On the other hand, when nations have used diplomacy for the purpose of preventing war, they have often succeeded. The outstanding example of a successful war-preventing diplomacy in modern times is the Congress of Berlin of 1878. By the peaceful means of an accommodating diplomacy, that Congress settled, or at least made susceptible of settlement, the issues that had separated Great Britain and Russia since the end of the Napoleonic Wars. During the better part of the nineteenth century, the conflict between Great Britain and Russia over the Balkans, the Dardanelles, and the Eastern Mediterranean hung like a suspended sword over the peace of the world. Yet, during the fifty years following the Crimean War, though hostilities between Great Britain and Russia threatened to break out time and again, they never actually did break out. The main credit for the preservation of peace must go to the techniques of an accommodating diplomacy which culminated in the Congress of Berlin. When British Prime Minister Disraeli returned from that Congress to London, he declared with pride that he was bringing home "peace . . . with honor." In fact, he had brought peace for later generations, too; for a century and a half there has been no war between Great Britain and Russia.

We have, however, recognized the precariousness of peace in a society of sovereign nations. The continuing success of diplomacy in preserving peace depends, as we have seen, upon extraordinary moral and intellectual qualities that all the leading participants must possess. A mistake in the evaluation of one of the elements of national power, made by one or the other of the leading statesmen, may spell the difference between peace and war. So may an accident spoiling a plan or a power calculation.[13]

Diplomacy is the best means of preserving peace which a society of sovereign nations has to offer, but, especially under the conditions of contemporary world politics and of contemporary war, it is not good enough. It is only when nations have surrendered to a higher authority the means of destruction which modern technology has put in their hands—when they have given up their sovereignty—that international peace can be made as secure as domestic peace. Diplomacy can make peace more secure than it is today, and the world state can make peace more secure than it would be if nations were to abide by the rules of diplomacy. Yet, as there can be no permanent peace without a world state, there can be no world state without the peace-preserving and community-building processes of diplomacy. For the world state to be more than a dim vision, the accommodating processes of diplomacy, mitigating and minimizing conflicts, must be revived. Whatever one's conception of the ultimate state of international affairs may be, in the recognition of that need and in the demand that it be met, all men of good will can join.

If authority were needed in support of the conception of international peace presented in these pages, it can be found in the counsel of a man who committed fewer errors in foreign policy than any of his contemporaries—Sir Winston Churchill. Viewing with concern the contemporary scene in his speech to the House of Commons of January 23, 1948, and asking himself, "Will there be war?" Mr. Churchill called for peace through accommodation—as he had done in almost fifty speeches since the outbreak of the Cold War—when he said:

> I will only venture now to say that there seems to me to be very real danger in going on drifting too long. I believe that the best chance of preventing a war is to bring matters to a head and come to a settlement with the Soviet Government before it is too late. This would imply that the Western democracies, who should, of course, seek unity among themselves at the earliest moment, would take the initiative in asking the Soviet for a settlement.
>
> It is idle to reason or argue with the Communists. It is, however, possible to deal with them on a fair, realistic basis, and, in my experience, they will keep their bargains as long as it is in their interest to do so, which might, in this grave matter, be a long time, once things are settled. . . .
>
> There are very grave dangers—that is all I am going to say today—in letting everything run on and pile up until something happens, and it passes, all of a sudden, out of your control.
>
> With all consideration of the facts, I believe it right to say today that the best chance of avoiding war is, in accord with the other Western democracies, to bring matters to a head with the Soviet Government, and, by formal diplomatic pro-

---

[13]See pages 174 ff.

cesses, with all their privacy and gravity, to arrive at a lasting settlement. There is certainly enough for the interests of all if such a settlement could be reached. Even this method, I must say, however, would not guarantee that war would not come. But I believe it would give the best chance of coming out of it alive.[14]

What Churchill proposed as an approach to the conflict between East and West applies equally to the possible conflicts of the future involving North and South. Months, if not years, of neglect of a growing Iraqi threat to the balance of power in the Middle East brought on the Gulf crisis of 1990–91. If diplomacy was used in the 1980s or before August of 1990, it was not used effectively. President Reagan was more candid than his successor when he declared, regarding the diplomacy of the period, "we goofed." The diplomacy Churchill prescribed and which presidents from Eisenhower to Reagan pursued in meetings at the summit with leaders such as Khrushchev and Gorbachev eventually bore fruit. Having learned to practice wise diplomacy in Soviet-American relations, it would be tragic for leaders of the west not to profit from the lessons it provides for foreign policy around the globe.

---

[14]*Parliamentary Debates (Hansard), House of Commons.* Vol. 446, No. 48, pp. 562–3.

Historical Glossary

Adams, John

> 1735–1826. Second President of the United States (1797–1801). Appointed one of the peace commissioners to France in 1777; one of the negotiators of the Treaty of Paris (1783) to end the American War of Independence; envoy to Great Britain (1785–88). As President, Adams prevented a war with France by a moderate, conciliatory policy.

Adams, John Quincy

> 1767–1848. Sixth President of the United States (1825–29). Minister to the Netherlands (1794–97) and to Prussia (1797–1801); U.S. Senator (1803–8); Minister to Russia (1809–14); helped draw up Treaty of Ghent (1814), ending the War of 1812; Minister to Great Britain (1815–17). As Secretary of State (1817–25) he played a large role in the enunciation of the Monroe Doctrine.

Alabama Claims

> United States claims against England resulting from damage inflicted during the Civil War upon Northern ships by the Confederate cruiser *Alabama*, which had been built and fitted out in England. The claims were finally settled in 1871 by an arbitration tribunal meeting in Geneva.

Alexander I

> Czar of Russia (1801–25). The failure of Napoleon's invasion left Alexander one of the most powerful rulers in Europe. Inspired by a strange combination of mysticism and reaction, he promoted the Holy Alliance.

Alexander the Great

> King of Macedon, 336–23 B.C. Through the military conquest of Thrace, Illyria, and Egypt, and the invasion of Persia and northern India, Alexander became virtual master of the Mediterranean center of civilization.

Angell, Norman

> 1874–1967. British pacifist. He became famous through his popular book, *The Great Illusion* (1910), which presented the thesis that wars did not pay and drew the inference that if nations would only realize this there would be no more wars.

Atlantic Charter

> Statement of general principles, signed by President Roosevelt and Prime Minister Churchill in August 1941, setting forth the national policies of the United States and Great Britain with respect to the postwar world; included principles of na-

tional self-determination, opposition to aggression, disarmament, and equal access to trade and raw materials.

Augustus

Adopted son and heir of Julius Caesar. First Roman Emperor (27 B.C.–A.D. 14); gained control of Italy, Africa, Sardinia, and Sicily; became sole ruler of the Roman world by defeating Anthony and Cleopatra at the battle of Actium (31 B.C.).

Austerlitz, Battle of

In 1805 at Austerlitz, in what is now Czechoslovakia, Napoleon I defeated the Russian and Austrian armies. Considered Napoleon's most brilliant victory, this battle marked the peak of Napoleon's fortunes.

Bacon, Francis (Viscount St. Albans)

1561–1626. English philosopher.

Baldwin, Stanley

1867–1947. British Conservative leader; Chancellor of the Exchequer, 1922–23; Prime Minister, 1923–24, 1924–29, 1935–37.

Barbarossa, Frederick

Epithet of Frederick I, Holy Roman Emperor and King of Germany, 1152–90.

Barrère, Camille E. P.

1851–1940. French Ambassador to Italy (1897–1924).

Barthou, Jean Louis

1862–1934. French statesman. As Foreign Minister (1934) he sought to strengthen France's relations with Russia, Great Britain, and the Little Entente.

Bay of Pigs

A part of the Cuban coastline where in 1961 a group of Cuban refugees staged an invasion under American auspices and failed.

Beard, Charles A.

1874–1948. American historian and political scientist.

Beneš, Eduard

1887–1948. Czechoslovakian statesman. As Foreign Minister (1918–35) and Premier (1921–22), he was largely responsible for the Little Entente and the Czech alliance with France. Elected President in 1935; went into exile after Munich Pact (1938); headed provisional government during Second World War; re-elected President in 1946; resigned shortly after Communist coup of 1948.

Bentham, Jeremy

1748–1832. English philosopher and jurist; founder of the utilitarian school.

Berlin, Congress of

1878. Called by the signatories of the Treaty of Paris (1856), which ended the Crimean War, to reconsider the terms of the Treaty of San Stefano, forced on the Ottoman Empire by Russia earlier in 1878.

Beveridge, Albert J.

1862–1927. U.S. Senator (1889–1911) and biographer of John Marshall. As a politician his fame rests upon his support of imperialism in international politics and the progressive movement in domestic politics.

Big Stick Policy

The characterization of a vigorous exercise of national power, derived from President Theodore Roosevelt's (1901–9) famous dictum: "Speak softly, but carry a big stick."

Bismarck, Otto von

1815–98. German statesman. Prussian Premier (1862–71) and German Chancellor (1871–90); he united Germany under Prussian leadership and made the German Empire one of the great powers.

Boer War

1899–1902. War between British and Dutch colonists (called Boers) in South Africa.

Bohlen, Charles E.

1904– . American diplomat. Ambassador to the Soviet Union (1953–57).

Bolingbroke, Henry St. John, 1st Viscount

1678–1751. English Tory statesman and writer.

Bose, Subhas Chandra

1897–1945. Indian nationalist, jailed by the British for his Axis sympathies during the Second World War. He escaped, fled to Germany, and headed Japanese-sponsored "provisional government of India."

Bourbons

Royal family, originally of France, with branches that ruled Spain, the Two Sicilies, and Parma; ruled France, except during the French Revolution and the Napoleonic era, from the end of the sixteenth century to 1848.

Boxer Rebellion

1900. Violent attacks on foreigners and Christians in China (especially Peking), perpetrated by an anti-foreign military organization known as the Boxers.

Briand-Kellogg Pact

A treaty, also called Pact of Paris, signed in 1928 by the United States and 43 other nations, pledging the signatories to renounce war as an instrument of national policy and to seek the settlement of international disputes by peaceful means only. Chiefly the work of United States Secretary of State Kellogg and French Foreign Minister Briand.

Bright, John

1811–89. Member of British parliament. Liberal champion of the middle-class reform movement in England.

Bryce, James

1838–1922. English historian, statesman, diplomat, and jurist. Chiefly known in the United States for his classic study of American society and politics, *The American Commonwealth* (1888) and his ambassadorship to the United States (1907–13).

Bukharin, Nikolai I.

1888–1938. Russian Communist; chief party theoretician after Lenin's death; member of Politburo; executed in 1938 purge.

Burke, Edmund

1729–97. British statesman and political philosopher of enlightened conservatism.

Burns, John

1858–1943. British socialist and member of Parliament (1892–1918).

Caesar, Julius

100–44 B.C. Roman statesman and general, who founded the Roman Empire.

Calhoun, John C.

1782–1850. American statesman and political philosopher. Defender of the interests of the Southern planter aristocracy and author of the constitutional theory of nullification. Secretary of War (1817–25); Vice-President (1825–29); Secretary of State (1844–45).

Cambon, Jules M.

1845–1935. French diplomat; brother of Pierre Paul Cambon. Ambassador to the United States during the Spanish-American War, to Spain (1902–7), and to Germany (1907–14).

Cambon, Pierre Paul

1843–1924. French diplomat; brother of Jules Cambon. As Ambassador to England (1898–1920) he helped to create the Entente Cordiale (1904) and the Anglo-Russian Agreement of 1907, and he encouraged England to enter the First World War.

Canning, George

1770–1827. British statesman; Prime Minister (1827); Foreign Secretary (1807–9, 1822–27).

Carthaginian Peace

The destruction of Carthage effected by Rome in 146 B.C. at the end of the Third Punic War, 149–46 B.C.

Castlereagh, Robert Steward, Marquess of Londonderry, Viscount

1769–1822. British Tory statesman. Secretary of War (1805, 1807–9); Foreign Secretary (1811–22).

Catherine the Great (Catherine II)

Czarina of Russia (1762–96). Expanded and strengthened the Russian Empire, chiefly at the expense of Turkey.

Cato (the Elder)

234–149 B.C. Roman statesman, implacable foe of Carthage; his influence helped to bring on the Third Punic War.

Cavour, Camillo B.

1810–61. Italian statesman, Premier of Sardinia (1852–59, 1860–61); achieved the political unification of Italy.

Chaco War

1932–35. War between Bolivia and Paraguay over possession of the Chaco territory.

Chamberlain, Joseph

1836–1914. British statesman. As Colonial Secretary (1895–1903) he advocated imperial expansion, consolidation, and reform.

Chamberlain, Neville

1869–1940. English statesman; son of Joseph Chamberlain. As Prime Minister (1937–40) he was the outstanding advocate of a policy of "appeasement" toward the Axis; forced to resign after British debacle in Norway (April 1940).

Charlemagne

Emperor of the West (800–814); King of the Franks (768–814).

Charles II

King of England, Scotland, Ireland (1660–85).

Charles V

Emperor of Holy Roman Empire (1519–58) and (as Charles I) King of Spain (1516–56).

Charles VIII

King of France (1483–98). Invaded Italy in 1494; forced to retreat by league comprising Ferdinand V of Spain, Emperor Maximilian I, Pope Alexander VI, and the rulers of Milan and Venice.

Chesterfield, Philip Dormer Stanhope, 4th Earl of

1694–1773. English statesman and author.

Churchill, Winston L. S.

1874–1965. British statesman and author. First Lord of the Admiralty (1911–15, 1939–40); held various cabinet posts before and after First World War; Prime Minister (1940–45, 1951–55).

Clausewitz, Karl von

1780–1831. Prussian general and writer on military strategy. His masterpiece, *On War*, has had an enormous influence on military strategy and tactics and the theory of war.

Clemenceau, Georges

1841–1929. French statesman, twice Premier (1906–9, 1917–19). Chief antagonist of Woodrow Wilson at the Paris Peace Conference (1919).

Cobden, Richard

1804–65. English statesman, leader in the liberal reform movement; especially concerned with the promotion of free trade.

Colombo Plan

A British Commonwealth plan, established in 1951, for co-operative economic development in South and Southeast Asia.

Corneille, Pierre

1606–84. French dramatist.

Council of Europe

International body created in 1949 by representatives of Great Britain, France, Belgium, the Netherlands, Luxembourg, Norway, Sweden, Denmark, Ireland, and Italy; joined by Greece and Turkey in 1950. The Council aims, through the work of its Committee of Ministers and Consultative Assembly, to achieve a European federation.

Covenant of the League of Nations

Constitution of the League of Nations.

Crimean War

1854–56. War in which France, Great Britain, and Turkey were allied against Russia. The Treaty of Paris (1856), ending the war, placed the Danubian principalities under the joint guaranty of the great powers, neutralized the Black Sea, and pledged the signatories to respect the independence and integrity of Turkey.

Cruce, Eméric

1590–1648. In *Le Nouveau Cynée* (1623), Crucé envisioned a council of ambassadors, representing all monarchs and sovereign republics, which would judge international disputes by majority vote and enforce its decisions.

Demosthenes

384–322 B.C. Greatest of Greek orators, he warned the Athenians in his *Philippics* (351, 344, 341 B.C.) about the threat of Philip II's Macedon, which conquered Greece in 338 B.C.

Descartes, René
1596–1650. French philosopher.

Diderot, Dénis
1713–84. French philosopher and man of letters.

Disraeli, Benjamin (Earl of Beaconsfield)
1804–81. British statesman and author; Prime Minister (1867–68, 1874–80). Revitalized the Tory Party with a twofold policy of imperialism and democratic reform.

Elizabeth I
Queen of England (1558–1603).

Erasmus, Desiderius
1469–1536. One of the great humanists of the Renaissance.

Eugene of Savoy
1663–1736. The greatest military leader of his time and a great statesman in the service of Austria.

European Defense Community
Abortive proposal agreed upon in 1952 by France, Germany, Italy, Belgium, the Netherlands, and Luxembourg, with the intention of creating a common defense force.

European Payments Union
Organization established in 1950 by members of the Organization for European Economic Cooperation (OEEC) in order to develop and liberalize inter-European exchanges. The Union, now replaced by the European Monetary Agreement, enabled members to balance their accounts with the other member states by utilizing any foreign currency to settle debit balances with any country.

Farewell Address
1796. President George Washington's advice to his countrymen upon retiring from office at the end of his second administration.

Fénelon, François
1651–1715. French theologian and author; Archbishop of Cambrai.

Fichte, Johann Gottlieb
1762–1814. German philosopher.

Foch, Ferdinand
1851–1929. Marshal of France; from March 1918 on, chief of the unified Allied command during the First World War.

Four Freedoms
In his message to Congress proposing Lend-Lease (January 6, 1941), President Franklin D. Roosevelt stated that four freedoms should prevail everywhere in the world—freedom of speech, freedom of worship, freedom from want, and freedom from fear.

Fourteen Points
President Woodrow Wilson's formulation of Allied war aims and of a general peace program, which he presented in an address to Congress, January 8, 1918.

Francis I
King of France (1515–47).

Francis II
Last Emperor of the Holy Roman Empire (1792–1806); first Emperor of Austria (as Francis I, 1804–35); King of Bohemia and Hungary (1792–1835).

Franklin, Benjamin

1706–90. American statesman, printer, scientist, and writer. One of the greatest diplomats of the American Revolution and the newborn nation; played a major role in gaining French recognition of the new republic (1778) and in negotiating peace with Great Britain in 1782.

Frederick II (Frederick the Great)

King of Prussia (1740–86). Through his brilliant military tactics, especially in the War of the Austrian Succession (1740–48) and the Seven Years' War (1756–63), he made Prussia the foremost military power in Europe.

Freeport, Sir Andrew

One of the characters invented by Richard Steele and Joseph Addison as mouth-pieces for their views on current affairs in the English daily *Spectator*, published in the early eighteenth century.

DeGaulle, Charles

1890–1970. French general and statesman. In the Second World War he opposed the Franco-German armistice in 1940, fled to England, and became leader of the Fighting French and of the French provisional government. In postwar France he was the leader of the nationalist-rightist party, R.P.F. *(Rassemblement du Peuple Français)*, and was elected in 1958 President of the Fifth Republic.

Genoa, Republic of

An Italian maritime power, which reached the peak of its strength in the 14th century. Annexed to France in 1805 and united with the Kingdom of Sardinia in 1815.

George III

King of Great Britain and Ireland (1760–1820).

George VI

King of Great Britain (1936–52).

Goethe, Johann Wolfgang von

1749–1832. German poet, dramatist, and novelist.

Gogol, Nicolai V.

1809–52. Russian novelist and playwright.

Good Neighbor Policy

A phrase that President Franklin D. Roosevelt chose to characterize his policy, begun under President Hoover's administration, of eschewing armed intervention in Latin America in favor of a program of friendly co-operation.

Grey, Edward Grey, 1st Viscount

1862–1933. British statesman. As Foreign Secretary (1905–16) he played a major role in the formation of the Triple Entente.

Grotius, Hugo

1583–1645. Dutch jurist and humanist, the "father" of international law. Wrote the first systematic text on international law *(De jure belli ac pacis)*.

Guicciardini, Francesco

1483–1540. Italian historian and diplomat. A follower of Machiavelli, Guicciardini is chiefly known for his history of the period of the Italian Wars (1492–1534).

Guizot, François

1787–1874. French historian and liberal statesman.

Gustavus Adolphus

1594–1632. King of Sweden; leader of the Protestants in the Thirty Years' War.

Hague Conventions

Treaties, signed by the United States and other major powers, resulting from the Hague Peace Conferences of 1899 and 1907. Provided for a so-called Permanent Court of Arbitration, defined the laws and usages of land warfare, rights and obligations of neutrals, etc.

Hamilton, Alexander

1757–1804. American statesman. Delegate to the Federal Constitutional Convention, where he was a strong proponent of a centralized government; with Madison and Jay, author of *Federalist Papers*. As Secretary of the Treasury and a leader of the Federalist party during Washington's administration, Hamilton exercised great influence over foreign, as well as fiscal, affairs.

Hannibal

247–182 B.C. Carthaginian general; invaded Italy by crossing the Alps in the Second Punic War (218–201 B.C.).

Hapsburg

Ruling house of Austria from 1282 to 1918; from it were chosen the Emperors of the Holy Roman Empire from 1438 to 1806.

Hegel, Georg Wilhelm Friedrich

1770–1831. German philosopher.

Henry II

King of France (1547–59); continued the struggle of his father, Francis I, against Emperor Charles V and Charles's son, Philip II of Spain.

Henry VIII

King of England (1509–47).

Hilferding, Rudolph

1877–1941. German socialist and economist; Finance Minister (1923, 1928–29).

Hobbes, Thomas

1588–1679. English philosopher.

Hobson, John A.

1858–1940. English economist.

Holy Roman Empire

962–1806. A Western European political entity claiming to be the successor to the Roman Empire, which was suspended in 476. Remained until the sixteenth century a European commonwealth, though European nations did not recognize its suzerainty. It lost virtually all political importance as a result of the Thirty Years' War (1618–48), and was dissolved in 1806.

Hull, Cordell

1871–1955. U.S. Secretary of State (1933–44).

International Bank for Reconstruction and Development

Autonomous institution affiliated with the United Nations. Its function is to make loans to member nations and foreign investors in order to facilitate productive investment, encourage foreign trade, and discharge international debts.

International Bureau of Weights and Measures

Intergovernmental organization established in 1875 to standardize weights and measures. Affiliated with the United Nations since 1949.

International Civil Aviation Organization

Affiliate of the United Nations, organized in 1947; designed to expand international air trade and make it safer and more economical.

International Danube Commission

Established by Treaty of Versailles (1919) to administer the internationalized section of the river; repudiated by Germany in 1936 and dissolved in 1940.

International Institute of Agriculture

Founded in 1905, with the object of collecting and disseminating knowledge relating to agriculture.

International Monetary Fund

Autonomous organization, affiliated since 1947 with the United Nations; co-operates closely with the International Bank for Reconstruction and Development; designed to facilitate international trade, reduce inequities in exchange, and stabilize currencies.

International Telecommunication Union

Designed to maintain and extend international co-operation for the improvement and rational use of all kinds of telecommunication. It was established in 1934 as an amalgamation of the International Telegraph Union, established in 1865, and the International Radiotelegraph Union, established in 1906.

International Telegraph Union

Established in 1865, this organization was the first important public international union. Became known as the Telecommunication Union in 1934; now a specialized agency of the United Nations.

James, William

1842–1910. American philosopher and psychologist.

Jay, John

1745–1829. President of the Continental Congress (1778); Minister Plenipotentiary to Spain on a mission to seek aid and recognition (1779); one of the commissioners to negotiate peace with Great Britain. Author, with Hamilton and Madison, of *Federalist* papers. Secretary of Foreign Affairs (1784–89); first Chief Justice of the Supreme Court (1789–95). Concluded (1794) Jay's Treaty with England, settling difficulties arising out of violations of the Treaty of Paris (1783).

Jefferson, Thomas

1743–1826. Third President of the United States (1801–9). Author of the Declaration of Independence; Governor of Virginia; served in Continental Congress; succeeded Franklin as Minister to France (1785); Secretary of State (1790–93).

John of Salisbury

c. 1115–80. English scholastic philosopher.

Kant, Immanuel

1724–1804. German philosopher.

Kautsky, Karl Johann

1854–1938. Leading German-Austrian theoretician of socialism.

Kennan, George F.

1904– . American diplomat and historian. Ambassador to the Soviet Union (1952).

Korean War

Began with the attack by North Korea on South Korea (June 1950) across the 38th parallel of latitude, the postwar dividing-line fixed by an agreement between

Russia and the United States. South Korea was joined by United Nations forces, under United States command, after the United Nations passed a resolution (June 25) charging a breach of peace and demanding cessation of hostilities and withdrawal of North Korean forces. North Korea was joined by Chinese Communists in November 1950 when United Nations forces approached the Manchurian border. In 1951 the battle lines were again stabilized at the 38th parallel. An armistice was concluded in July 1953.

Laval, Pierre

1883–1945. French politician; Premier (1931–32, 1935–36); virtual dictator of the Vichy government under Pétain (1942–45). After the Second World War he was executed for collaborating with the Germans.

Lenin, V. I.

1870–1924. Russian revolutionist and statesman; founder of Bolshevism, the Third International, and the Soviet Union.

Leopold I

King of Belgium (1831–65).

Leopold II

King of Belgium (1865–1909).

Little Entente

Treaties of alliance concluded in 1920 and 1921 among Czechoslovakia, Rumania, and Yugoslavia for the common defense of the status quo of 1919.

Lloyd George, David (1st Earl of Dwyfor)

1863–1945. British statesman and Prime Minister during World War I.

Locarno Treaties

1925. Included a treaty of mutual guaranty of the Franco-German and Belgo-German frontiers (signed by Germany, France, Belgium, and by Great Britain and Italy as guarantors), various arbitration treaties, and a Franco-Polish and Franco-Czechoslovakian treaty for mutual assistance in case of attack by Germany. Created a brief period of international good feeling known as the "spirit of Locarno."

Locke, John

1632–1704. English philosopher.

Long, Huey

1893–1935. Governor of Louisiana (1928–31); U.S. Senator (1931–35).

Louis XIV

King of France (1643–1715).

Louis XV

King of France (1715–74).

Louis XVI

King of France (1774–92).

Love, Alfred Henry

1830–1913. American pacifist.

Luxemburg, Rosa

1870–1919. German Marxist; founded Spartacus Party in the First World War and aided in its transformation into the German Communist Party.

Macedonian Empire

Reached peak of its power during the reign of Alexander the Great in the third century B.C.; defeated, divided, and annexed by Rome in the second and first centuries B.C.

Machiavelli, Niccolò

1469–1527. Italian political philosopher and statesman.

Madison, James

1751–1836. Author, with Hamilton and Jay, of *Federalist Papers;* Secretary of State (1801–8) under Jefferson, whom he succeeded as President (1809–17).

Maginot Line

System of fortifications along the eastern frontier of France; named for André Maginot, French Minister of War (1922–24, 1929–31), who began its construction. Considered impregnable, the whole line became useless when the Germans turned it by means of the breakthrough at Sedan, which initiated the invasion of France in 1940.

Mahan, Alfred Thayer

1840–1914. American historian, naval officer, and publicist; formulated a doctrine of sea power, which exerted great influence in the United States, Great Britain, Germany, Japan, and Russia.

Mahomet II

1429–81. Ottoman sultan (1451–81); completed conquest of Byzantine Empire; founder of Ottoman Empire.

Maria Theresa

Empress of Austria-Hungary (1740–80).

Marx, Karl

1818–83. German economist and social philosopher, who laid the theoretical foundation of modern socialism.

Mazarin, Jules

1602–61. French statesman; Cardinal of the Roman Catholic Church. Leading minister (1643–61) in the first period of Louis XIV's reign.

Mediatization

The act by which in the Holy Roman Empire the "immediate" relationship between a state and the Empire was transformed into a "mediate" one through the intercession of a superior state, who represented from then on the mediatized state in its relations with the Empire.

Metternich, Prince Klemens von

1773–1859. Austrian Foreign Minister (1809–21), Chancellor (1821–48); took a major part in shaping the diplomacy of Europe during the Napoleonic Wars, and was the leading statesman of Europe from 1815 to 1848.

Mill, John Stuart

1806–73. English philosopher and economist.

Minorities Treaties

Treaties, concluded after the First World War, binding most of the states of Central and Eastern Europe to protect minorities within their borders by assuring them liberty to practice their religions, speak their own languages, and educate their children in the minority cultures. The League of Nations was responsible for enforcing these stipulations.

Morley, John, Viscount Morley of Blackburn

1838–1923. English liberal statesman and man of letters.

Munich Settlement

September 1938. Marked the peak of the policy of "appeasement." England, represented by Neville Chamberlain, and France, represented by Édouard Daladier, surrendered to Hitler's demands and permitted Germany to occupy the Sudetenland in Czechoslovakia. Although France and Britain guaranteed the new boundaries, neither acted when Hitler took over all of Czechoslovakia in March 1939.

Napoleon I

1769–1821. Emperor of France (1804–15).

Napoleon III

1808–73. Emperor of France (1852–70); nephew of Napoleon I. As President of the Second Republic after the revolution of 1848 he made himself dictator and then Emperor; abdicated after defeat in the Franco-Prussian War (1870–71).

Napoleonic Wars

1796–1815. Wars waged by France, under Napoleon I's military and political leadership, against England, Austria, Prussia, Russia, and most of the other countries of Europe at various times and in various combinations. Ended with Napoleon's defeat at Waterloo.

National Socialists

Members of the National Socialist German Workers Party (abbreviated to the term "Nazis"), founded after the First World War and led by Hitler.

Nehru, Jawaharlal

1889–1964. A leader of the Indian independence movement; President of the Indian National Congress since 1929; Prime Minister of independent India, 1947–1964.

Nietzsche, Friedrich Wilhelm

1844–1900. German philosopher.

Nine Power Treaty

1922. The United States, Great Britain, Japan, and six other members of the Washington Conference bound themselves to respect the "sovereignty, the independence, and the territorial and administrative integrity of China," and to uphold the principle of the Open Door.

North, Frederick North, 7th Baron

1732–92. English Prime Minister (1770–82).

Nuremberg Trials

1945–47. Trials of Nazis for "war crimes" by an International Military Tribunal sitting in Nuremberg, Germany.

Nye Committee

Senate committee (1934–36), headed by Senator Gerald P. Nye (North Dakota), formed to investigate the activities of bankers and munitions manufacturers in the First World War. It concerned itself chiefly with proving that war profiteers had been responsible for American intervention. The popularity of this thesis was reflected in the neutrality legislation of 1935–37.

Open Door

United States policy toward China, originally promulgated by Secretary of State John Hay in 1899 in the form of identical notes to the great powers calling for the observation of equal commercial rights in China, and expanded by a similar note in 1900 upholding China's territorial integrity and political independence as well.

Paléologue, Maurice

1849–1944. French diplomat and writer; Ambassador to Russia (1914–17).

Palmerston, Henry John Temple, 3rd Viscount

1784–1865. British Foreign Secretary (1830–41); Prime Minister (1855–58).

Paris, Treaty of

1856. See *Crimean War*.

Peel, Sir Robert

1788–1850. British Home Secretary (1822–27); Prime Minister (1834–35, 1841–46).

Penn, William

1644–1718. English Quaker; founder of Pennsylvania. In his *Essay towards the Present and Future Peace of Europe* (1693), Penn put forth the idea of a league of nations whose disputes would be settled by an international court of arbitration.

Permanent Court of International Justice

Otherwise known as the World Court. Established in 1921, pursuant to the Covenant of the League of Nations; terminated in 1945 when its functions were transferred to the International Court of Justice provided by the Charter of the United Nations.

Peter the Great (Peter I)

Czar of Russia (1682–1725); founder of the modern Russian state.

Philip II

King of Spain, Naples, and Sicily (1556–98), and (as Philip I) King of Portugal (1580–98). Philip's foreign policy was directed toward preserving Spanish hegemony on the continent of Europe and securing the triumph of the Roman Church over heresy. Undertook disastrous expedition against England, which resulted in the defeat of the Spanish Armada in 1588.

Pitt (the Younger), William

1759–1806. English statesman; Prime Minister (1783–1801, 1804–6).

Potsdam Agreement

Result of a conference (1945) of the United States, the Soviet Union, and Great Britain at Potsdam, Germany. Transferred the chief authority in Germany to the American, Russian, British, and French occupation authorities and to a four-power Allied Control Council; laid down the terms of denazification, demilitarization, and democratization. Delivered, with the concurrence of China, a surrender ultimatum to Japan.

Proudhon, Pierre J.

1809–65. French social philosopher.

Punic Wars

Wars between Carthage (whose language was called "Punic"), which controlled Northwest Africa and the Western Mediterranean, and Rome. First Punic War, 264–241 B.C. Second Punic War, 218–201 B.C. Third Punic War, 149–146 B.C. Ended in the destruction of Carthage and the ascendance of Rome as the greatest power in the Western world.

Quisling

Traitor or fifth columnist. The term is derived from Vidkun Quisling, a Norwegian fascist leader who helped Germany prepare the conquest of Norway in 1940 and was later made Premier. Executed in 1945.

Racine, Jean

1639–99. French dramatist.

Radiotelegraph Union

Established in 1906; amalgamated with the International Telegraph Union to form the present International Telecommunication Union.

Reform Acts

Three bills (1832, 1867, 1884), which reformed the British electoral system and extended the franchise.

Regensburg, Diet of

A permanent congress of the envoys of the princes of the Holy Roman Empire (1663–1806).

Rhinebund

A league of German princes formed in 1806 under the leadership of Napoleon I.

Richelieu, Armand Jean du Plessis, Duc de

1585–1642. French statesman; controlled the government as minister (1624–42) of Louis XIII; Cardinal of the Roman Catholic Church.

Robespierre, Maximilien Marie Isidore

1758–94. As head of the Jacobins, an extremist republican group, he instigated the Reign of Terror during the French Revolution and became virtual dictator of France, before he himself was executed.

Rousseau, Jean Jacques

1712–78. French philosopher.

Rucellai, Bernardo

1449–1514. Italian historian and diplomat.

Russo-Finnish War

1939–40. Began with a Russian attack on Finland (November 30, 1939); ended one hundred days later with the collapse of Finnish resistance. In the peace treaty of March 12, 1940, Finland ceded to the U.S.S.R. the Karelian Isthmus, the city of Viipuri, a naval base, and territories totaling 16,173 square miles, with a population of 450,000.

Saint-Pierre, Charles I. C., Abbé de

1658–1743. French social philosopher. In his *Project of Perpetual Peace* (1713) he advocated an international court of arbitration, the renunciation of war, and a league of Christian states, bound together in a perpetual alliance for mutual security.

Salisbury, Robert Arthur Talbot Gascoyne-Cecil, 3rd Marquess of

1830–1903. British Foreign Secretary under Disraeli (1878–80); Prime Minister (1885, 1886–92, 1895–1902).

Salt

Strategic Arms Limitation Talks between the United States and the Soviet Union.

Seven Years' War

1756–63. World-wide war fought in Europe, North America, and India between France, Austria, Russia, Saxony, Sweden, and (after 1762) Spain on one side and Prussia, Great Britain, and Hanover on the other; originated in the colonial rivalry between France and England and the struggle for supremacy in Germany between Austria and Prussia.

Sombart, Werner

1863–1941. German economist and sociologist who started out as a Marxist, then turned sharply against Marxism, and ended up as a supporter of National Socialism.

Spanish Succession, War of the

See *Treaty of Utrecht.*

Spencer, Herbert

1820–1903. English philosopher.

Stare decisis

The doctrine of adhering to precedents in applying the same principle of law to similar situations.

Sternberg, Fritz

1895–1963. Marxist writer.

Stoics

Adherents of the philosophy of Stoicism, founded by Zeno at the beginning of the third century B.C.

Sully, Maximilien de Béthune

1560–1641. French statesman. His Grand Design was a plan for the federation of all Christian nations.

Sumner, William Graham

1840–1910. American sociologist and economist; professor of political and social science at Yale University.

Suzerainty

The political control of one state over another, which preserves all outward attributes of sovereignty.

Tacitus, Cornelius

c. 55–120. Roman historian.

Talleyrand, Charles Maurice de

1754–1838. French Foreign Minister (1797–9, 1800–7, 1814–15).

Teheran Conference

Meeting in 1943 of Roosevelt, Churchill, and Stalin at Teheran, Iran; reached agreement on scope and timing of the invasion of France and operations against Germany.

Thiers, Louis Adolphe

1797–1877. French statesman, journalist, and historian. Three times Premier; first President of the Third Republic (1871–73).

Third Republic of France

Lasted from France's defeat in the Franco-Prussian War (1871) to the formation of the Vichy government under the German occupation in 1940.

Thirty Years' War

1618–48. A general European war, fought mainly in Germany; essentially a war of petty German princes and foreign powers—France, Sweden, Denmark, England—against the Holy Roman Empire, as represented by the Hapsburgs in Austria, Germany, Italy, the Netherlands, and Spain, as well as a religious war of Protestants against Catholics.

Thucydides

c. 460–400 B.C. Athenian historian.

Titulescu, Nicholas

1883–1941. Rumanian statesman. As Foreign Minister (1927–36) he championed the French-sponsored policy of collective security and was one of the architects of the Little Entente with Czechoslovakia and Yugoslavia.

de Tocqueville, Alexis

1805–59. French statesman, political theorist, and historian. After a visit to the United States in 1831, he wrote *Democracy in America* (1835–40), a penetrating analysis of the nature of American democracy and of democracy in general.

Trajan

Roman Emperor (98–117).

Troppau, Congress of

1820. International conference called by Metternich, under the provisions of the Holy Alliance, to consider means of suppressing the liberal uprisings against the kings of Sicily and Spain.

Truman Doctrine

Outlined by President Truman in an address to Congress (March 1947) in support of the Greek-Turkish aid bill. The policy that came to be known as the Truman Doctrine calls, in effect, for the "containment" of Communism by giving aid to governments seeking to repel "totalitarian aggression."

United Nations Economic and Social Council

Constituent organ of the United Nations with the function of investigating international economic and social questions and reporting to the General Assembly and other United Nations organs for action.

United Nations Food and Agriculture Organization

Established in 1946, with the object of bettering the conditions of rural life, improving agricultural production and distribution, and raising the level of nutrition.

United Nations Trusteeship Council

Supervises control of non-self-governing territories according to the Charter of the United Nations; consists of members administering trust territories, and an equal number of other member nations (including always the permanent members of the Security Council).

Universal Postal Union

Established in 1875 with headquarters in Bern, Switzerland; became a specialized agency of the United Nations in 1947.

UNRRA

United Nations Relief and Rehabilitation Administration, founded in 1943 to give aid to countries ravaged by the war; discontinued European operations in 1947; dissolved in 1949.

Urban II

Pope (1088–99).

Utrecht, Treaty of

Concluded the War of the Spanish Succession (1701–4) after the defeat of France by England and Holland.

Vattel, Eméric de

1714–67. Swiss philosopher and jurist; leading authority on international law.

Venice, Republic of

One of the great maritime powers of the fifteenth and sixteenth centuries, whose ambassadors developed diplomacy into a great art. Venice united with the Kingdom of Italy in 1866.

Verona, Congress of

1822. Last conference under provisions of Quadruple Alliance; called to consider what to do about a revolution in Spain. The Congress decided, against the opposition of the English Foreign Secretary, Canning, to send a French army to suppress this uprising.

Versailles, Treaty of

The principal treaty terminating the First World War.

Victoria

Queen of England (1837–1901) and Empress of India (1876–1901).

Vienna, Congress of

1814–15. Peace conference following the Napoleonic Wars, at which the great powers—Austria, Russia, Prussia, Great Britain, and France—agreed upon territorial and political terms of settlement.

Voltaire

1694–1778. French philosopher and author.

Wagram, Battle of

At Wagram, Austria, in 1809, Napoleon I won one of his most brilliant victories. Six days later Austria was forced to conclude an armistice.

Weber, Max

1864–1920. Most influential German sociologist.

Weimar, Republic of

1919–33. The German state that was established under a democratic federal constitution passed by a constitutional assembly in the city of Weimar.

Wellington, Arthur Wellesley, 1st Duke of

1769–1852. British soldier and statesman. Commander of British and allied armies in the wars against Napoleon (1808–15); won his most famous victory at Waterloo (1815); Prime Minister (1828–30); Foreign Secretary (1834–35).

Westphalia, Treaty of

1648. General settlement terminating the Thirty Years' War; ended the power of the Holy Roman Empire, with France emerging as the dominant European power.

William II

1859–1941. German Emperor (1888–1918).

William III

1650–1702. King of England, Scotland, and Ireland (1689–1702).

William the Conqueror (William I)

    1027–87. King of England (1066–87).

Wilson, Woodrow

    1856–1924. Twenty-seventh President of the United States (1913–21).

Wolsey, Thomas

    1472–1530. English statesman and Cardinal of the Roman Catholic Church; Privy Councilor and Lord Chancellor of Henry VIII.

World Health Organization

    United Nations specialized agency, established in 1948. Its object is "the attainment by all peoples of the highest level of health."

Yalta (or Crimea) Agreement

    Result of a meeting (1945) of Roosevelt, Churchill, and Stalin at Yalta, Crimea, U.S.S.R.; complete text not disclosed until 1947. Set forth the terms for the occupation of Germany, pledged the establishment of a new Poland on a democratic basis, and bound the signatories to give joint assistance to countries liberated from Nazi domination, enabling them to establish, through "free elections," governments "responsive to the will of the people." Announced a formula for big-power voting in the United Nations, and committed the Soviet Union to enter the war against Japan in return for the restoration of certain territories lost in the Russo-Japanese War (1904–5), and joint Chinese-Soviet operation of the Chinese-Eastern railway.

Index